Using groups to help people

The International Library of Group Psychotherapy
and Group Process

General Editors

Dr Malcolm Pines
Institute of Group Analysis (London) and
the Tavistock Clinic, London

Dr Earl Hopper
Institute of Group Analysis (London)

The International Library of Group Psychotherapy and Group Process
is published in association with the Institute of Group Analysis
(London) and is devoted to the systematic study and exploration of
group psychotherapy

Using groups to help people

Dorothy Stock Whitaker
Professor of Social Work
University of York

Tavistock/Routledge
London and New York

First published in 1985
by Routledge & Kegan Paul Ltd

First published in paperback in 1987

Reprinted in 1989
by Routledge
11 New Fetter Lane, London EC4P 4EE
29 West 35th Street, New York, NY 10001

Set in Times 10 on 12pt
by Input Typesetting Ltd, London
and printed in Great Britain by
TJ Press (Padstow) Ltd, Padstow, Cornwall

Library of Congress Cataloging in Publication Data

Whitaker, Dorothy Stock, 1925-

Using groups to help people.
(International library of group psychotherapy and
group process)
Bibliography: p.
Includes index.
1. Group counseling.   2. Group psychotherapy.
I. Title.   II. Series.
BF637.C6W47   1985   158'.3   84-15895

British Library Cataloguing in Publication Data

0-415-04283-6

To Galvin

Contents

Preface

My greatest hope for this book is that it be of practical use. It is written for clinical psychologists, social workers, psychiatrists, youth workers, psychiatric nurses and others who plan and conduct small groups with the intention of benefiting those who participate in them. Persons who become members of helping groups are very diverse: they face different situations, display different needs and bring different personal resources to the group. They include the anxious or depressed, the chronically psychiatrically ill, the youthful offender, accident victims, persons facing some difficult life transition, etc., etc. Many such persons may benefit through a group of some kind, but no single form of group can be expected to be a suitable vehicle for helping all populations in all situations. The question of what kind of group, how planned and how conducted and for what kind of person, is the subject of this book.

Because this book has been written for those who plan and conduct groups it is written from the conductor's perspective: what decisions and tasks face the conductor? what are his or her purposes and hopes in undertaking work with groups? how can the conductor of a group best understand what he or she sees and hears while a group is in session and how can this be used as a basis for action? what *is* a group: what are its special characteristics, what opportunities does it offer as a medium for help and what are its risks and hazards?; how can the conductor of a group best monitor a group and judge its effectiveness?

To organize this book, it was necessary to devise a framework which could encompass a considerable diversity of patient and client populations, a wide range of work settings, and a range of professional backgrounds in the helpers. As a framework, I have chosen the decisions and tasks which are necessarily a part of planning and conducting any group (see table of contents). Regardless of patient or client population, regardless of setting, regardless of background in training or experience, anyone who sets out to conduct a helping group is faced with the same set of decisions and tasks. These have to do with planning a suitable group, conducting it, monitoring it as it goes along, paying appropriate attention to the wider setting in which it operates, and learning from the experience while it is going on and after it ends.

The first chapter thus sets out a series of decisions and tasks, distinguishing between those which, once made, stay made and those which must be made early but might have to be re-made in the light of new information which becomes available as the activity gets under way.

Attention to decisions and tasks can help one to be explicit and specific about what is really entailed in planning and conducting a group. It can also help one to avoid taking some decisions for granted, or losing sight of the necessity for making certain decisions. However, knowing *that* decisions must be made and tasks undertaken is not enough in itself, since one also needs guidance as to *which* decisions and courses of action, amongst many possible ones, are to be preferred. I consider that guidance can best be provided through defining a clear set of purposes and through understanding the special nature of the group as a medium for help.

'Purpose', by dictionary definition is '[that] for which anything is done or made; end, aim'; and 'purposive' is 'acting or performed with conscious purpose or design' (*Shorter Oxford Dictionary*). When planning and conducting a group one needs a clear sense of destination – of what one hopes to achieve – in order to judge whether one is at any moment on the right track and in order to recognize the destination when one is approaching it. In planning and conducting a group one therefore needs to think in terms of purposes: one's overall purpose in seeking to conduct a group, and those sub-purposes and instrumental purposes which, if pursued, can be expected to contribute to achieving the overall purpose.

By definition, the basic and overall purpose of whoever conducts a helping group is to benefit the members. To do this, it is necessary both to use situations arising in the group for the benefit of members and also to work so as to maintain the group as a positive medium for help (rather than as a neutral or even damaging environment). Two sub-purposes are thus identified. Further sub-purposes or instrumental purposes, more specific in character, are appropriate to particular decisions and tasks during successive stages in planning and conducting groups.

The idea of purpose thus permeates this book. It arises first and inevitably in the course of discussing decisions and tasks in chapter 1, and at the end of that chapter 1 set out overall purpose and instrumental purposes formally. These are then referred to in the course of subsequent chapters when the sequence of decisions and tasks are taken up in detail.

Since a group, and the experience which persons can have in a group, is the medium which one is using to achieve purposes, an understanding of that medium with its opportunities and hazards functions as a further guide to decision-making. One needs to be alert to what *can* happen, and with what consequences, in groups, including the experiences which can be generated for members, the positions they may seek to occupy or be pressed into occupying, the pair relationships they may establish, and the conductor's capacity to influence and utilize events. Chapter 2 is devoted to a consideration of the character of the group as a medium for help, and in subsequent chapters the interconnections between group, individual, and pairs-within-the-group are returned to when considering successive decisions and tasks: during planning, when one is trying to anticipate the impact of planning decisions on how the group can later operate, and during the actual life of the group, when one is trying to conduct oneself in ways which further one's overall purpose of benefiting members.

Once this groundwork is laid in chapters 1 and 2, which constitute Part I, successive chapters consider in detail a number of planning decisions (chapters 3 through 7, which comprise Part II); the actual conduct of a group through its formative, established and final stages, with attention to making sense of what one sees and hears during sessions and to one's own position in the group (chapters 8 through 14, which comprise Part III); and thence to what can be learned retrospectively by reviewing a group after it ends (chapter 15, comprising Part IV).

This book is meant to be highly practical, as I have said, and a practical person cannot do without theory. That is, a practical person, who wants to seize opportunities, avoid obstacles, and forestall or quickly retrieve errors, needs concepts and more elaborated frameworks for understanding what he sees and hears, predicting the likely consequences of particular courses of action, and perceiving the import of consequences once action has been taken. I have tried to be parsimonious in the introduction of theory, introducing particular concepts or more elaborated models when I consider them helpful in making sense of complex events and choosing amongst alternative actions. Thus, since assessing a population of prospective group members is a necessary basis for planning, I suggest a way of categorizing populations for this purpose and some concepts which can help one to specify useful next steps which if undertaken could be expected to benefit persons drawn from the population. Later, when considering the work setting within which a group is to be conducted, I introduce Lewin's force field analysis as a way of identifying aspects of the work setting if this seems required. Still later, as a basis for actually conducting a group, I consider the kind and level of understanding of individuals which one can usefully seek to develop for different kinds of groups. I introduce group focal conflict ideas early (toward the end of chapter 2) because I find that I think in these terms anyway and do not wish to make a mystery of it and because I find it a useful framework for understanding group-level phenomena in almost all kinds of groups. French's nuclear conflict/focal conflict model for understanding individuals is introduced later (chapter 8) because, together with group focal conflict theory, it can help one to understand interconnections between individual dynamics and group dynamics in some kinds of groups. I have tried to keep specialized terminology to a minimum, and bring it in when ordinary language would be too circumlocutory or fail to convey the meaning intended. Much of the book will, I hope, strike the reader as common sense, plainly expressed. Where technical language is introduced which is at first unfamiliar, I hope that through subsequent discussion and especially through illustrative material, that too will become common sense.

I have wanted this book to be useful to inexperienced and to experienced persons, to persons working alone and to persons with access to colleagues, to persons responsible not only for planning and conducting small groups but to those responsible for programmes in which a small group is one part, to practitioners and to teachers and supervisors.

To support this, I have included at the end of most chapters some suggested exercises intended to help persons to develop the understandings and skills to which the chapter is addressed. Selected reading lists are also included. These should not be taken to be a full and comprehensive reference to the literature but as suggestions for extending one's understanding of the issues taken up in the chapter by looking at cognate or contrasting points of view.

I had some problems with terminology. Persons in the helping professions get called by different names: group worker, therapist, leader, facilitator – and I wanted this book to speak to all of them. I have therefore often used 'worker or therapist' or some other combination of terms, but have often used the more general term 'conductor'. Similarly in order to avoid too many multiple references to 'patients, clients, residents, or other' I have mostly used the term 'member', although perhaps 'participant' would have done as well.

I also had trouble with pronouns. Since I am, these days, engaged in social work education with young persons mostly in their twenties, I am acutely aware of how offended young women can feel at constant references to 'he' and 'him'. However, I could not bring myself to mangle the English language with constant references to 'him or her', 'herself or himself', or worst of all, 's/he', so I have resorted to the male pronoun, which I am used to, and hope that those who are sensitive to this issue will understand that it is done for the sake of convenience.

Incidentally, I have tried to write in a kind of mid-Atlantic version of English, avoiding as far as I could either conspicuously British or conspicuously American turns of phrase. I could not always avoid this, not least because I am no longer always sure as to what is American English and what is English English.

Acknowledgments

To acknowledge properly those who have made direct or indirect contributions to this book or to the thinking included in it requires going back some considerable distance in time: to Herbert A. Thelen, under whose tutelage I first became intrigued by groups; to Roy M. Whitman and Thomas French, who participated in early struggles to conceptualize groups in focal conflict terms; and to my colleague, Morton A. Lieberman, with whom I co-conducted a number of groups, collaborated in extended research and co-authored the book, *Psychology through the Group Process*.

Over the years my exposure to small groups moved from T-groups to therapeutic groups conducted in in-patient and out-patient settings, and thence to more varied kinds of groups conducted in a wide range of settings on behalf of clients or patients very differently situated and with widely varying needs. For this widening of experience I am grateful to large numbers of social work students and practice teachers, for it has been through following students into a vastly varied range of practice settings that I have become more strikingly aware of the flexibility of the small group as a medium for help.

In the course of writing this book I have benefited from many discussions with my husband, Galvin Whitaker, who helped me to find a suitable structure for the book and whose clear thinking about the logic of purpose helped me to sort out the overall and instrumental purposes which the conductor of a group can usefully adopt. At certain points when I got stuck in finding a way to express a point or to develop some idea he helped by interviewing me and taking notes as I talked freely about the issue. His notes and our subsequent discussions based on them tended to clear the way. I am grateful to a large number of students who read parts of earlier drafts and helped me to see which bits needed further explication or stating in plain language, and in particular to Suzanne Peskett who read almost all of the semi-final draft and who offered a series of comments which contributed towards greater intelligibility.

I wish to thank Jackie Grossman, who was a tremendous help in tracking down references; Lily Dodds, Wendy Amos-Binks and Sue Medd, who typed early drafts; and Shirley Holliday and Janice Vanham, who typed the final manuscript.

Part I

A decision-making orientation to working with groups

Chapter 1
Necessary decisions and tasks when planning and conducting groups

Consider the following persons and situations:

Mothers of young mentally handicapped children bring their children to an out-patient facility for assessment. These mothers are in varying states of distress or composure with reference to their situation, and face diverse practical problems.

Among a group of children about to enter a large secondary school from a small, family-style primary school there are four or five whom their teachers think will find the transition particularly difficult.

A number of long-stay hospitalized psychiatric patients are no longer actively psychotic and are judged to be potentially capable of living in the community. However, they have lost or have never learned such ordinary skills of living as using public transportation, preparing a meal or shopping for their own needs.

A number of anxious or depressed persons approach an out-patient facility asking for psychotherapy. They are functioning adequately in the sense of holding down a job and living within a family, yet they are anxious or depressed, and dissatisfied with their lives.

Social workers become aware of a number of unemployed, physically handicapped but otherwise healthy young adults who are living with their families but who are socially isolated and rarely go out.

Nurses, doctors and medical social workers are concerned about accident victims who have suffered irreparable physical damage (amputation, severe scarring from burns). These patients are ready to be discharged from hospital, having achieved maximum hospital benefit, but the staff are aware that they will face many practical and personal problems upon discharge.

A number of young offenders, 15 to 17 years old, are living at home and are on probation orders. Their probation officers are aware that they are at risk of re-offending, and also know of other youngsters in the community who have not yet offended but who may be at risk of doing so.

Through hospital records five or six women have been identified who are suspected of physically harming their young children. They have been referred to a social work agency. The women do not see themselves as being in need of help.

A number of wives of medium-term prisoners are known by prison welfare officers to be experiencing emotional distress and material hardship.

In these examples and in many others which could be cited, each mother, each schoolchild, each long-stay patient, stands for a population of persons similarly placed. Each might possibly benefit from some form of small group experience, although it is clear that the same kind of group could not be expected to suit all of them.

A small group can be an effective medium for help if it is planned carefully with the situation and requirements of its prospective members firmly in mind and if it is conducted in a way which develops and preserves the group as a helping medium and makes use of the special opportunities arising for benefiting specific members. Such a group is likely to include from six or seven persons to twelve or fifteen or so persons. It should not be so small as to preclude the emergence of those group and interactional dynamics which contribute to its potential value as a helping medium, nor so large as to lose the potential for direct face-to-face interaction. Ordinarily one or several persons are attached to the group who have special responsibility for conducting it. The conductor of a group, depending on setting and professional training, may be called the therapist, group worker, leader, facilitator, etc. The members of the group, depending on setting, may be called clients, patients, residents, participants, etc. A small group is a flexible device and may be planned to rely on open discussion, topic-based discussion, activities, exercises or games, or on some combination of these.

Whatever the population one wishes to serve and whatever the setting, certain basic decisions have to be made and certain tasks undertaken if one is to design a suitable group and conduct it in ways likely to benefit those concerned. For example, if a therapist, worker or leader is to work with groups at all, he must decide how to assemble or otherwise identify a group with which to work. Anyone who intends to work with a group needs to think out ahead of time the benefits which he hopes to achieve on behalf of prospective members, since this provides guidelines for designing a suitable group and, later, assessing its effectiveness. Before starting with a group, a therapist or worker must decide on a place to meet; on the duration of sessions; on whether the group is to proceed through open discussion, topic-oriented discussion, or some form of activity-based interaction; on whether or not and if so how to involve prospective members in planning; and so on. Once the group begins to meet, the therapist or worker is faced with the continuing task of responding to events which arise: when to speak and when to be silent; what to say or do when something noteworthy happens and indeed how to decide when something is noteworthy and when it is not; what to do when faced with what feels like a problem or a crisis; what to do when one realizes one has made an error; what to do when the issue of termination comes up; and many more. Some decisions and tasks have to do with context: what to tell colleagues about the group and when to tell them; whether and if so how to involve one or more colleagues in the actual conduct of the group; what to do if the work setting proves uncongenial to conducting groups.

In the best of all possible worlds the person who expects to conduct the group will also engage in planning, right from the very first step, although he may and in most settings should consult others. By being involved in planning from the start, the prospective conductor of the group has the best opportunity to think his way into his task, to get clear in his mind what he is aiming for, and to visualize the kind of group experience likely to suit those with whom he intends to work. I am aware that things do not always work out this way and that in some settings a group may be planned by one set of persons and then 'handed' to someone else to conduct. This is unfortunate, and anyone likely to be in this position should fight hard to participate in the planning, or at least to review all planning decisions before a group actually begins to meet.

In this chapter I shall specify the decisions and tasks involved in planning and conducting a group, and order them so that one can see what needs to be decided and worked on early, what then, what depends on what, which decisions once made remain unchanged and can be taken as a datum for subsequent decisions, and which decisions once made need to be reviewed and sometimes re-made in the light of new or expanding information. The decisions and tasks to be discussed have to do with planning a group, conducting it, and evaluating it and its impact on its members and on others.

The terms 'decision' and 'task' imply deliberate and conscious intent. I recognize, of course, that not all action on the part of a therapist, leader or group worker has this character. Some decisions and actions are based on deliberate and explicit thinking in terms of some underlying rationale; some decisions are the consequence of accumulated practice wisdom and may be made on the basis of a well-internalized sense of 'this is the way to do it'; and some actions are altogether spontaneous, based on intuition or the pressures of some immediate situation. Particularly while a group is in session, many of a therapist's or group worker's interventions may be quite spontaneous in character. Whilst wishing to acknowledge the inevitability and often the great aptness of spontaneous decisions and actions, I also believe that if group therapists, group workers and leaders are aware of and give thought to the decisions and tasks involved in planning and conducting groups, then both planned and spontaneous decisions and actions are more likely to be useful, and errors more likely to be avoided.

Substantial investment in planning can make the difference between a group which is manageable and likely to be a rewarding and useful experience for all concerned and a group which is unlikely to benefit its members, and which may become dysfunctionally stressful or even doomed to failure. Sometimes planning is skimped because of a worker's or therapist's eagerness to get started with a group. This can lead to problems which otherwise could have been avoided. A first, basic planning decision is:

1 Deciding on the population with which one intends to work

Sometimes this decision is made for one by the nature of the work setting. More frequently the work setting limits the range or pool of persons with whom one can work but certain choices nevertheless remain open. Working within a psychiatric hospital, for example, means that the pool of potential group members consists of persons regarded as unable to manage outside an institutional setting. Yet within this pool of persons there is diversity. It is likely to include ordinarily well-functioning persons temporarily overwhelmed by acute anxiety or depression, persons in the midst of some florid and severe breakdown, long-stay 'institutionalized' patients, persons who have just been admitted and persons about to leave. Working in a day centre for homeless men in a large city means that one's population is already defined, yet again diversity is present. Some of the men may be well established in a homeless lifestyle, others recently emerged from an institution or prison, still others recently wrenched or expelled from a family. Therapists in private practice generally select from a pool of persons who arc functioning within the community but may be experiencing intolerable levels of anxiety, depression, isolation, uncertainty or dissatisfaction. Each pool of potential clients or patients – whether it be the homeless, the psychiatric in-patient, the offender, the handicapped, the addicted – is a defined population but within its own limits it is diverse.

One has to make choices within the limits of the population(s) available, and will be further influenced by the official objectives of one's organization (supposing that one is working within an agency or an institution), and by one's own interests and level of skills. One usually tries to avoid working within an organization unless one can accept its official aims, but even so, one might well be more interested in some aspects of an organization's work than in others, or have personal interests different from but nevertheless consistent with the organization's aims. One might, for example, have a special interest in certain sub-populations, or an interest in gaining experience with a particular mode of practice, or an interest in creating an opportunity to. learn from a more experienced colleague. Levels of skill and type of experience are also factors to take into account. If one is very inexperienced and unsure of one's skills as a conductor of a group it seems only sensible to work in the first instance with an 'easy' group – that is, a group whose members are well motivated, likely to be eager to take advantage of the opportunities for sharing and for ventilating which the group offers, and unlikely to be disruptive and difficult to manage. As in skiing, there is much to be said for starting on the beginner's slope. The skills and the confidence gained by doing so are likely to stand one in good stead when tackling subsequent, more inherently difficult work.

Once one is clear about the population with which one intends to work, a next step is:

2 Thinking out the benefits one hopes to procure for persons drawn from the population

One cannot make further decisions about how to work with persons drawn from some identified population unless one specifies what one hopes to achieve on behalf of those persons. If one does not think this out, one decision is as good as another. As in setting out on a journey, unless one has a destination in mind one has no guide for deciding on which direction to take.

In working out the benefits one hopes to procure it is useful to think in terms of 'current state' and 'preferred state'. Any population can be defined in terms of current state, although of course the current state will be quite different for different populations. Populations differ with respect to where the members of it are in their lives and what they are facing: chronic anxiety or depression, retirement, divorce, looking after a handicapped child, being about to be discharged from a psychiatric hospital, etc. Populations also differ with respect to personal resources and level of current functioning. For example, persons who are chronically depressed but nevertheless working acceptably at their jobs are functioning differently, with a different set of personal resources than, say, persons in the back wards of a psychiatric hospital. Yet for both these populations and for any other, there are things which members of the population can do and things which they can't, things they understand and things they don't understand, matters which are important to them and matters which are not.

To assist in conceptualizing the current state of a population I offer two concepts: *preoccupying concern* and *frontier*. These are discussed fully in chapter 3 where their application is illustrated, but to anticipate, 'preoccupying concern' refers to some issue, life event or responsibility which is so important to the persons concerned that their lives are dominated by preoccupations with it and worries about how they will face or manage it. 'Frontier' marks the boundary between the understandings, skills and personal resources which persons already have and those which they do not yet have. All populations can be characterized in terms of frontier and some can be further understood in terms of preoccupying concern.

Once one has described the current state of a population in terms of frontier and/or preoccupying concern, it is possible to go a step further and identify a preferred state for that population. Presumably, one regards the current state as unsatisfactory in some sense, or else one would not wish to undertake work with a population. There is bound to be something which one prefers on behalf of the population over that which already is the case. That preferred state can be defined in general terms as some movement beyond current frontiers and/or more satisfactory and satisfying ways of coping with preoccupying concerns. Just as the current state differs for different populations, so also does the preferred state. One might consider, for example, that it would be preferable for the long-stay hospitalized patient to acquire practical skills of everyday life, or that it would be preferable for the apparently competent but depressed or anxious person to cease engaging in self-defeating behaviours, or that it would be preferable for the parents of handicapped children to manage everyday life at less personal cost to themselves. In every case, the preferred state marks what one hopes to achieve through working with the persons concerned: the benefits one hopes to procure. Thinking through the benefits which one hopes to achieve is not only a necessary preliminary to making further planning decisions, but also establishes criteria against which one later can judge the effectiveness of one's helping effort.

Having decided on a population with which one intends to work and having specified the benefits one hopes to procure, one can take the further step of:

3 Deciding whether or not a group is likely to be a useful and efficient device for helping persons drawn from the population.

One cannot assume that a group experience of some kind will be good for everyone under all circumstances. Certainly, persons are unlikely to profit from a group if they are unable to listen to and interact with others, or at the very least derive some comfort from being in physical proximity with others. These can be regarded as minimal criteria for the use of groups. By these criteria, few populations are ruled out: perhaps only the floridly psychotic, the most severely mentally handicapped, those for whom physical proximity in itself is profoundly threatening, and those so beset by internal concerns that they have virtually tuned out the outside world. In the literature on group psychotherapy and group work further criteria are sometimes suggested, for example, a capacity to introspect and to empathize. I prefer not to apply such further criteria, for while it is true that persons who lack such capacities are unlikely to profit from certain kinds of groups they might well profit from others. I hope to show later that many, many different kinds of groups can be designed to suit quite diverse populations. For this reason I consider it inappropriate to apply more than minimal criteria.

It should be emphasized that at this stage in planning one is thinking about the suitability of groups for populations, which means for persons in general within a population. It could well be the case that a group experience can be seen as potentially useful for a population, defined generally, but that individuals exist within that population for whom a group is contra-indicated. Decisions about individuals come later in the sequence of decisions, at a point where a membership is being formed.

Even though a group experience is regarded as potentially useful, some other form of help might be seen as more promising or time-efficient. For example one might consider that aversion therapy or contract-based individual work is a more direct route toward procuring the benefits one has in mind for members of a population. Sometimes some other form of help may be regarded as a necessary preliminary to a group experience. For example one might decide that a course of chemotherapy should precede a group experience, on grounds that it is likely to place prospective group participants in a better position to benefit from a group.

Up to now the issues being addressed are: 'what population of persons should I work with?' 'what benefits do I hope to procure for persons drawn from the population?' 'by what route (group or other) can these benefits best be procured?' These refer to decisions and tasks which must be undertaken before investing one's time in thinking more specifically about groups. They lead up to a first critical choice-point: is a group to be used with this population of persons? If one's answer to this is 'No', then of course one plans some other form of help. If one's answer to this is 'Yes', then one can move on to the initial planning of a group experience for members of the population. One is faced next with working out a group structure which will best suit the population one intends to work with and deciding whether to conduct the group on one's own or to involve others.

4 Deciding whether to work alone or with one or more co-workers or co-therapists

I place this decision next in the sequence of decisions and tasks (although it can be made later and is sometimes made earlier) because it is at this point that one is ready to think more specifically about the shape and character of the group. From this point onwards it is useful for all those likely to be involved in the actual conduct of the group to participate in the planning, so that they can influence decisions and make use of the experience of planning to ready themselves for actual work with the group.

Some types of groups require more than one leader, as when a relatively large group of adolescents is likely to spend part of the time in sub-group activities. In other instances, whether one works alone or with a colleague is a matter of preference or of organizational policy. Sometimes this decision is made for one, either because a suitable co-worker is not available and one must therefore work alone or because the organization or institution has established the practice of co-leadership or even because someone in authority assigns one to a particular group with a particular co-leader.

There are potential advantages and potential disadvantages in working together with someone else in a group. Whether the one outweighs the other depends very much on the persons concerned and whether or not they can find ways to work in a complementary, congenial and mutually supportive way. If one can make this decision tentatively in the first instance it is advantageous to do so. Discussing further planning decisions with a prospective co-therapist or co-worker is a good basis for predicting likely compatibility. During joint planning each person has the opportunity to try to shape the kind of group in which he feels he can function effectively and comfortably. Views can be shared about how groups can and should operate and about preferred styles of participation. Prospective co-therapists or co-workers can move ahead with greater confidence if their discussions together reveal a likely compatibility and complementarity between them. On the other hand, if discussions reveal unresolvable conflicts, or thinking which is so divergent that it is unlikely that these particular two or three persons can work well together, it is not too late to re-make the decision.

5 Working out a basic structure and character for the group

By basic structure I mean the expected duration of the group in terms of number of sessions, whether it is to be time-limited or not, and the duration and frequency of sessions. By basic character I mean whether the group is to rely on open discussion, topic-orientated discussion, activities or exercises, or some combination of these.

A vast number of different types of groups can be planned: a time-limited group which is to meet for one-and-a-half hours per week and is to go on for, say, twenty sessions, and rely on open discussion; a group which is to meet daily for five days, two hours at a time, in which each session is pre-planned to include periods of exercises and games and periods of open discussion; a group which is to meet twice a week for an hour-and-a-quarter and engage in open discussion with an indefinite termination point; an activity-based group which is to meet once a week for two-and-a-half-hours with no planned termination point; and so on.

In calling attention to the fact that definite decisions are required concerning structure and basic character, I am emphasizing the versatility of groups and the fact that many different kinds of groups can be planned to meet varying circumstances and requirements. Thinking out the most suitable group structure for a population of persons is a fairly complex task which requires an understanding of the population, information about the range of groups which *can* be designed, and an appreciation of the demands which different structures make on group members and of the experiences which different structures are likely to generate. It also requires making choices between alternative structures which may on the face of it appear equally suitable.

Working out a suitable structure is an act of the imagination. One tries to imagine and visualize a group experience which one can reasonably expect will help prospective members to move from their current state to some more preferred state. The concepts of frontier and of preoccupying concern can be invoked. If the frontier for a population is judged to be that of lacking social skills, then a group experience which offers practice in social skills may prove useful. If a population of mothers of prelingually deaf children can be assumed to be preoccupied with their children's handicap and their efforts to come to terms and cope with it, then a group which offers an opportunity to share experiences, work on own feelings and/or provide mutual help can reasonably be expected to be useful. And so on. There are good fits and poor fits between a group design and particular populations. One needs a design which 'suits', which means a design which members of the population are likely to be able to use, which is likely to make sense to them, and which is likely to facilitate their moving from their current state to a more preferred state.

When one has decided whether to work alone or with one or two others and has thought out a basic structure, one has created, still in the imagination, a model for a group which one thinks will work for members of the population. Although many detailed planning decisions are still to be made, one has in mind a model for or mock-up of a group which is sufficiently well developed so that one can form a judgment as to the likely internal viability of the group. That is, one should be able to judge whether the group is likely to 'work', both for its members and for those who are to conduct it. If one considers the group viable, then of course one can proceed with further planning. If not, more work has to be done, on structure and/or on decisions about who is to conduct the group.

Internal viability is of course essential but a group also has to survive in its environment. A next task involves:

6 Assessing the costs and benefits the group is likely to generate for persons outside it and for the organization(s) of which it is a part, and deciding in the light of this whether or not to go ahead with one's plan

Few if any groups operate isolated and insulated from a wider environment. The operation of a group may impinge upon and

be affected in turn by colleagues, neighbours, one's own organization or co-operating organizations.

A group is not always a good fit with the wider system of which
it is or will be a part. Especially if it is a new venture within an
organization, conducting a group may upset established ways of
thinking about accountability, of allocating work, of using space.
While pursuing purposes attached to the group one could find
oneself interfering with other goals important to one's organization. Colleagues might or might not be supportive of one's efforts.
In some work settings a small group experience is part of a wider
plan which might include one-to-one psychotherapy or casework,
a programme of activities and outings, community or ward meetings, planning groups, and the like. Or, a group or a programme
designed for those whom one primarily hopes to benefit may exist
side by side with groups designed for others connected with the
primary beneficiaries (for example, relatives' groups or support
groups for staff). In residential settings, planned groups are
embedded in communal life where residents are in informal
contact in the course of ordinary daily activities. Under any of
these circumstances decisions about one feature of a programme
should not be made without considering the likely impact on
others, lest conducting one part of a programme interferes with
the effectiveness of the programme as a whole.

The point being made here is that the potential costs and
benefits of undertaking work with a group are not restricted to
those directly concerned but occur also for those in the environment on whom the activity of the group impinges. Considering
the group in its environment and assessing these further costs and
benefits forms the basis for a further critical judgment: Is the
group likely to be externally viable? That is, can the group survive
and flourish in its environment without interfering with it or damaging it in some unacceptable way? If the answer to this question is
'Yes' then one proceeds with planning, but if it is 'No', one is
faced with either modifying one's plan in a way designed to avert
negative consequences for the group or for the environment or
else abandoning one's plan. A further alternative is to defer
further work on a plan for a group until one has assessed the
group's wider environment and understands better the ways in
which the proposed group is likely to be an interference fit with
it. On the basis of such an assessment one might seek to influence
some aspects of the environment, for example, the attitudes of

colleagues, policies and practices of one's organization, or policies and practices of co-operating organizations.

Let us suppose that one has come to a point where a group seems potentially viable, both in itself and within its environment. It is now possible to move ahead into the detailed planning still required before the group can actually begin to meet. Decisions which can be made at about the same time have to do with all further necessary detailed planning for the group itself, with procedures for monitoring and assessing the group, and with finding support and consultation for oneself while conducting the group.

7 Making detailed planning decisions about the structure of the group and the policies one intends to follow

Detailed planning decisions have to do with venue, the arrangement of the room, the number of persons to be included in the group, the kind of contact or communication which it is desirable or necessary to maintain with colleagues not directly involved with the group, the ways if any in which the leader intends to involve members in planning, the records which should be kept, and the choice of games, exercises or activities, if these are to be used. In addition a leader might wish to think through the policies he would like to see established about attendance, tardiness, confidentiality, behaviour during sessions, and the like, and the rules he might make for the members of the group and for himself as conductor of the group.

Many of these detailed decisions are interrelated and interdependent. They should of course be consistent with the earlier decisions about the basic structure and character of the group. It is useful to think out these details before the group starts because one can then be utterly clear to the patients, clients or members about such matters as the structure within which one hopes the group will operate, the areas open to choice and negotiation, the rules which one is prepared to enforce and the sanctions one is prepared to apply, and the policies which if accepted are likely to facilitate the work of the group. A leader who has thought such matters out is less likely to be taken by surprise by unexpected demands. He will have worked out for himself where he is prepared to be yielding and where he feels that he must stick to certain rules and policies in order for the group to be a useful experience.

I do not mean to imply that one should never change one's mind about structure and policy after the group starts. One may well do so in response to new information not available at the planning stage. Nevertheless, if one takes these planning decisions as far as one can one has created a basis from which to work.

At about this same time one should put one's attention to:

8 Deciding by what means to monitor and assess the group effort

It is important to make decisions about monitoring and assessing before the group actually begins because it is usually necessary for procedures for collecting information and reviewing one's work to be set up in advance. It is no use deciding by the sixth or eighth session that it would have been interesting and useful to have a tape of each session, or that co-therapists could profitably have engaged in discussions after each session, or (more formally) that it would have been useful to have certain measures of the level of functioning of the members at the start of the group so that one can judge what changes may have occurred.

I take it for granted that some form of monitoring and assessing should go on. One can only acquire useful feedback about the consequences of one's efforts by monitoring the group as it goes along and by maintaining an attitude of assessment about the unfolding events of the group. By 'monitoring' I mean noticing what is happening for the group as a whole and for members in it, being aware of periods of productive work and periods of difficulty or stagnation, and being aware of one's own behaviour and its consequences. By the term 'maintaining an attitude of assessment' I mean continually setting what one sees happening against one's purposes and hopes for the group and for the persons in it so that one continually judges as one goes along whether the group is proceeding as one might wish and notes factors which are helping or hindering it. One of the main reasons for monitoring and maintaining an attitude of assessment is to be able to take action while the group is still going on, when action can still influence events.

One is likely also to wish to assess a group after it finishes.

Again, the intention is to influence action, but this time the action has to do with 'shall I make the same or different decisions next time?'

It will be clear that what I am talking about here is not necessarily the same thing as conducting formal research on the group. A group leader or others concerned may very well decide to conduct formal research and may have good reasons for doing so. However, if this is to be done it should be done in addition to ongoing monitoring and assessing, which is essential to the effective conduct of any group. Formal research is useful for some purposes but it is not necessary to the effective conduct of a group.

Somewhat related to the task of monitoring and assessing the group effort is:

9 Finding a means for supporting oneself in one's efforts with a group in order to carry stress and to improve one's own understandings and skills

Conducting a group – any group – is a difficult task and is bound to be stressful from time to time. Especially when a therapist or group worker feels confused or wonders whether he has responded to some situation as well as he might, he will profit from an opportunity to talk things over with interested others. It is satisfying, also, to be able to share moments of pleasure and triumph. If several persons are working with a group, they can do this for one another through post-session discussions. If one is working alone, then it pays to find a colleague who is willing to act as a listener, sounding-board and consultant. Such arrangements provide useful personal support for continuing with a difficult task and help one to learn from the experience while it is going on.

The actual device which one uses may be the same one being utilized for some aspects of the monitoring task – for example, post-session discussions with one's co-worker or co-therapist, or with a consultant. Where such is the case, the two tasks of monitoring the group and finding the necessary support for oneself can be undertaken at the same time.

At this point in planning quite a lot of preparatory work will have been done but potential group members have not been approached directly. No promises have been made and no expectations have been raised. The group therapist or worker is still in a position to decide 'yes, I will go ahead with it' or 'no, I won't'. The next decision in the sequence is an internal one. It is critical because once made it cannot be undone without some degree of harm to clients, patients or members:

10 Making an internal decision to commit oneself to working with a group and resolving to carry that group effort through. Alternatively, deciding not to make this commitment

Once one begins to work with a group one may sometimes find oneself bored, exasperated, worried, stressed or overwhelmed and wishing that one had never taken on the group. But one *has* undertaken it and has thereby assumed certain responsibilities. To withdraw from the group, bring it prematurely to a close or turn it over to someone else could have damaging consequences for the members and so should not be done lightly. If a group worker or therapist has reservations about undertaking the work and seeing it through then it is better to decide not to go forward with the effort before contact has been made with potential patients or clients. This critical decision can best be made on the basis of an awareness of the special characteristics of groups and of likely events arising in consequence of them, together with some degree of self-understanding as to personal preferences and tolerances.

It is not unusual for a therapist or group worker to make a commitment to go ahead with a group much earlier in the planning sequence. However an argument can be made that it is best to hold off on a definite and final commitment until planning has reached this stage. If, for example, one makes a firm internal commitment before this point, one has done so before considering all of the implications of going forward. One might then be tempted to go ahead regardless of possible negative consequences for one's organization or for the larger programme of which one's group effort is a part, or regardless of the unlikeliness of eliciting necessary support from colleagues, or regardless of probable costs to oneself in terms of the time and energy required for adequate monitoring of one's work. By this argument, committing oneself earlier could fail to take into account all of the likely consequences of undertaking the work. Deferring commitment until later could damage the persons whom one brings into the group.

Having decided (we shall assume) to go ahead, the therapist or worker is now in a position to make his first contact with potential group members. His next task has to do with:

11 Identifying persons who are to be members of the group and then deciding whether or not to engage in some form of preparatory work with them

It is obvious enough that a therapist or worker cannot begin to work with a group until actual named persons are specified as members of it. Different routes exist for identifying these actual named persons. Sometimes the membership of a group is defined by circumstances, for example when one considers that one must work with all the residents of a hostel or when one decides to undertake group work with the members of an existing adolescent gang. Sometimes one wishes to form a membership by open invitation to a potential population of participants. Sometimes one wishes to make decisions about selection and composition oneself. Sometimes one has the power to select and sometimes one does not.

Assuming that one has the power to select, a first decision is whether or not to exercise that power. Sometimes it is not appropriate to do so because one does not have the necessary information on which to base decisions about inclusion and exclusion. In some settings it will be colleagues, not oneself, who have information relevant to selection decisions, and then one must rely on them. Sometimes the prospective members themselves know best whether or not a particular group experience is likely to suit their needs, and then it is sensible to place the decision about whether or not to join a group in their hands.

Supposing that a group worker or therapist reserves to himself the power to select and compose a group, it is clear that such decisions cannot be based solely on one's understanding of the persons concerned, but always on one's understanding of a person in conjunction with an appreciation of group processes and of the experiences which a particular group structure is likely to generate.

Sometimes one is composing a group at the same time as one

is selecting for it. That is, one builds up the membership person by person. This affords the opportunity to consider as one goes along just what kind of composition one is building and whether it is likely to facilitate the work of the group. Predicting how a given combination of persons will work together and trying to form a membership which will 'work' rather than one which will not is a very inexact art. However, certain guidelines can be offered, for example, avoiding a majority of members who favour similar preferred personal defences, avoiding including a person highly likely to be disruptive of the efforts of others; and avoiding including someone whom one judges to be in a far more vulnerable state than all the others.

When those who are to be members of a group have been identified, should one take the further step of seeking to engage in preparatory work with prospective group members? There are some circumstances where preparation is not necessary, usually because potential members have had other opportunities available to them for becoming familiar with the kind of group they are being invited to join and have true choice as to whether or not to join it. Under other circumstances some preparatory experience is useful in order to help the person enter the group with relative ease rather than undue distress. One might, for example, invite a prospective group member to one or two preliminary interviews in order to provide an opportunity for him to air his expectations and worries and ask questions about the group, or one might provide a short-term group experience as preparation for a longer-term investment. With respect to preparation, doing nothing is as active a decision as is deciding on some specific form of preparation.

One more decision can be made before the group actually starts:

12 Deciding how to open the group

There are many ways to open a group. Amongst these are stating the purposes of the group as one sees them, laying down ground rules, laying down ground rules and declaring sanctions, describing a planned exercise, introducing the members to one another, or saying nothing.

Different openings are appropriate to different groups. If one has judged, for example, that a group, because of its membership and structure, is likely to be prone to chaos and disruptiveness then one might decide to start by declaring ground rules and sanctions or by telling members that there is a need for ground rules and inviting them to help think out what these should be. If one has judged that the members will profit from open discussion of their problems and feelings and are capable of such discussion, one might start with a minimal statement about purpose. If one has decided to make use of some activity or exercise, then opening comments are planned to steer the group into it. In general, whatever one does to open a group (including doing nothing) should be planned to support the structure one has in mind for the group.

At this point the group can be brought together and the series of sessions can begin. All concerned finally come together face-to-face. From this point onwards until the close of the group the leader, therapist or group worker is faced with a long and unrelenting series of choices about what to say and do, and what not to say and not to do moment by moment during the life of the group: during sessions, between sessions, to and in response to persons in the group, and to and in response to others on whom the group may impinge. The conductor of the group is faced with:

13 Responding actively or deciding not to respond to successive events in the group while it is in operation

One of the reasons that intervening in a group is a special skill is that whatever one says or does has a simultaneous although not necessarily similar impact on a number of persons at once and often also affects the course of the group as a whole. One never can address oneself to the group in general and expect not to have an impact on one or more particular persons in the group. One never can address oneself to an individual and assume that one is doing nothing further, since any comment addressed to one person will be heard by others and have some meaning for them.

In managing the complex task of conducting a group it is essential to carry on the internal work of noticing and trying to make sense of what is happening: noting what is happening for individuals, what is happening for the group as a whole, and what is happening inside oneself. Particularly, one should make a point of noticing the consequences of what one says and does in the group, since this constitutes feedback for oneself and can be used as a guide to subsequent action. If one keeps in touch with events as they unfold, one is in a better position to intervene in ways which help rather than hinder, and to discern errors and see ways to retrieve them.

Watching, listening and seeking to understand is a necessary basis for intervening but it is not sufficient in itself. One needs also to have a clear sense of what one is trying to achieve. One's overall purpose is to make use of the group to help the persons in it, and during the planning stage one has thought out the kinds of benefits one hopes to procure for the population from which group members are drawn. Now that the group is a reality, one is faced with deciding about what to do and how to act moment by moment, trying always to operate in a way which furthers one's overall purpose. I shall leave aside for the moment the issue of whether one 'decides' to respond or whether one simply responds. Most people who conduct groups find that their participation is a mix of planned and spontaneous interventions, and of semi-planned interventions in which a therapist or worker, on the basis of accumulated practice wisdom, sees an opportunity and grasps it without deliberating much about it.

The grandly stated purpose of 'helping' persons is too global to constitute a guide to action. *Ad hoc* purposes which spring to mind in response to specific situations may be useful but do not help one to identify initiatives which can be taken in a group, and may not take a wide enough timespan into account. At some middle level, between the overall purpose and a myriad of situation-specific purposes, one should be aiming at (1) maintaining the group as a positive medium for help, and (2) utilizing events which arise for the specific benefit of individuals.

A group is no use if it becomes non-viable, that is, if it dies an early death through numerous drop-outs, if it suffers fragmentation through frequent absences or if it limps along in a state of confusion about what it is meant to be all about. Even a group which appears viable in the sense that members come regularly and interact with one another is not viable as a helping medium if it goes along session by session in a flat, uninvolved manner or if it is so beset by conflict that work does not get done. One can best maintain a group as a positive medium for help, I believe, if one holds in mind the further, instrumental purposes of avoiding the irredeemable collapse of structure, seeking to maintain a general sense of safety such that members feel safe enough to stay in the group and to take personal risks, and working towards the establishment and maintenance of norms which support relatively uncensored, wide-ranging explorations and behaviours with respect to issues important to the members.

Much useful work will be accomplished by the members themselves, each on his or her own behalf and on behalf of one another, providing that the group can be maintained as a positive medium for help. However, more still can be accomplished if the therapist or worker is alert to special opportunities for benefiting particular members which arise in the course of the interaction. Such opportunities are likely to arise when resonances occur between themes which emerge for the group as a whole and concerns and preoccupations important to specific persons. Or, they may arise when two or three persons acquire special meanings for one another. At such times a therapist or worker can help by making room for the person(s) concerned to explore these resonances and special meanings and by facilitating their doing so if this is required.

Early in the life of a group the worker, therapist or leader will need to devote attention to:

14 Deciding whether or not the group can operate on the structure planned for it, and whether or not to re-negotiate or change that structure

All groups need to work within some structure which from the conductor's point of view suits the situation and requirements of those with whom he is working and which from the members' point of view makes sense and seems manageable. At the planning stage, the therapist or worker has planned a structure which seems right to him, and he will have opened the group in a way which reaffirms that structure and seeks to steer members towards using it. It is only when the group gets underway, however, that the structure is put to a real test, and one has an opportunity to see if and how it is working. The beginning of a group is a time during which members react to the structure put before them by the conductor and show through their behaviour whether it makes sense to them, and whether they are finding it easy or difficult, possible or impossible to use the structure. If events show that members are having difficulty with the structure then the leader is faced with trying to help the members make it work,or else with re-negotiating it or changing it. A group does not have to work to *the* structure planned for it in order to be viable, but it does have to work to *some* structure.

Deciding whether or not to change or re-negotiate a structure can be a difficult decision to make, as it is not infrequently the case that a group finds a structure difficult but in the end not impossible. Giving up on a potentially usable structure too soon is as much an error as persisting too long with an inappropriate structure. Making decisions in this area requires careful attention to the information and cues the group provides in response to attempts on the part of the leader to alleviate the fears, release or develop the capacities, or do whatever else is required to make possible a fair and thorough test of the usefulness of the structure. A leader needs to be open to the possibility that he has made an error in judgment in planning a particular structure, and to re-think the issue and sometimes remake the original decision.

At this point the therapist, worker or leader is asking the question: 'is the group, as planned, internally viable *in practice*?' If it is not, re-planning is required. An option not open to him at this point is cancelling the group, since a commitment to the members has already been made and should not be un-made.

In the course of a group's life, new information may come to the group worker or leader about the impact of the group on its environment and about the response of fellow workers to the group. A therapist or group worker may be faced with:

15 Deciding on what action to take if the operation of the group generates unforeseen problems with colleagues or with one's agency or institution

Decisions relating to the context in which the group is operating will have been made earlier, during the planning stage. However, at that point the group was a plan and not a reality. The reality may bring new information to colleagues, administrators and others on whom the group impinges as well as to the therapist or group worker. For example, the actual operation of the group may prove to interfere with other activities or goals of the agency or institution in ways not foreseen during the planning stage. Or, worries on the part of colleagues or line managers which could be handled or ignored when the group was still only a plan may emerge more powerfully and cause more concern when the group actually begins to operate. When the group has been in existence for a while it may well prove necessary to re-examine the relation of the group to its environment and take further action aimed at preserving the group but taking into account realities that could not be predicted before the group actually got underway.

Few groups go on forever, although some are planned to have a slowly evolving membership. For most groups, sooner or later the conductor of a group is faced with:

16 Deciding when and how to terminate a group

The *when* of terminating a group may have been decided much earlier if the group was planned in the first place to be time-limited. In groups without a planned closing date the issue of termination may come up when a number of persons declare themselves ready to leave the group. In the latter case one needs to consider whether as well as when to terminate. All groups, even very short-term ones, need a termination period as well as a termination date. When group members know that a group is soon to terminate, a phase begins which has a character of its own and presents a therapist or worker with special opportunities. In general terms, one wishes members to acknowledge and face the prospect of termination and to use the termination period gainfully.

Having completed a unit of group therapy or group work, or some project or programme, the conductor(s) concerned are in a position to turn their attention to:

17 Deciding about future work in the light of experience

At the close of any unit of work, one will have accumulated considerable experience. One will have gained information about how the group went, who benefited and who did not, whether or not initial plans made sense in the light of later events, and what helped and what hindered. One will have a more developed notion of the impact of the group on its wider environment, and of the wider environment on the group. Informal monitoring as the group went along, or formal evaluation (if undertaken) will have provided further information. In short, one will have information to hand about the internal and external viability of the group and its effectiveness. One often also learns a good deal about oneself: the situations one finds easy or difficult, the kinds of errors one is prone to make, a bit about the kinds of persons one seems able to help and enjoys working with, whether one prefers to conduct a group on one's own or with others, and so on.

This means that when thinking about future work, one is starting from a different base point than before. One has, one always hopes, gained something from the experience in the form of further understandings and more fully developed skills. One can bring these further understandings to bear on planning one's next helping effort.

The decisions discussed in this chapter and the relationships among them can be displayed diagrammatically as shown in Figure 1.1.

This diagram is a bare-bones representation of key decisions and tasks involved in planning and conducting groups. During the earlier discussion of these, reference has necessarily also been made to relevant information, to purposes and intentions, and sometimes also to concepts for organizing information.

Information pertinent to decision-making has to do with populations, with one's organization and its character and aims, with one's own interests and level of skills, with events occurring in a group while it is in operation, with specific persons who are members of the group, with events related to the group's operation occurring in its environment and with one's own feelings and behaviour as conductor of the group.

However well informed one may be, if one does not have purposes clearly in mind one has no guide for choosing one course of action rather than some other equally possible one. Purposes have been referred to throughout, sometimes explicitly, sometimes informally or even implicitly. Let us list them formally.

One's overall purpose must always be to make use of a group to help the persons in it. This can be stated more formally as: *to benefit the persons in a group through making as full use as possible of the potentials of the group as a medium for help*. A number of instrumental purposes and sub-purposes can then be identified which, if pursued, can each contribute to the achievement of this overall purpose.

During the actual life of a group I find it useful to hold in mind the following instrumental purposes:

1 to seek to conduct the group so as to maintain a general sense of safety at a level at which members feel safe enough to stay in the group and to take personal risks;
2 to seek to avoid the irredeemable collapse of structure;
3 to work toward the establishment and maintenance of norms in the group which support it as a positive medium for help;
4 to utilize events occurring in the group for the specific benefit of members;
5 to avoid doing harm: to members of the group, to oneself, or to the wider environment within which the group is operating; and
6 to discern and think out how to retrieve errors.

These instrumental purposes are directed toward maintaining the internal and external viability of the group and utilizing its positive potentials maximally for the benefit of members. One can best work toward achieving them if one pursues certain further purposes which direct one towards internal work during sessions and to think-work between sessions:

7 to arrange for consultation and support for oneself throughout the life of the group, preferably following each session;
8 to develop, refine and expand one's understanding of each person in the group;
9 to keep in touch with the dynamics of the group as a whole while it is in session and as it develops over time;
10 to keep in touch with one's own feelings and to note one's own behaviour and its consequences; and
11 to perceive connections between group and individual dynamics.

Much can be done during the planning stage to increase the likelihood of any given group proving useful to those who become members of it. In planning, one is trying to influence the probabilities in such a way that the group has a good chance rather than a poor chance of developing into a rich and fruitful environment

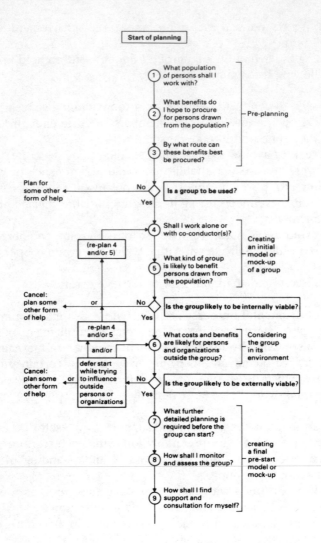

Figure 1.1

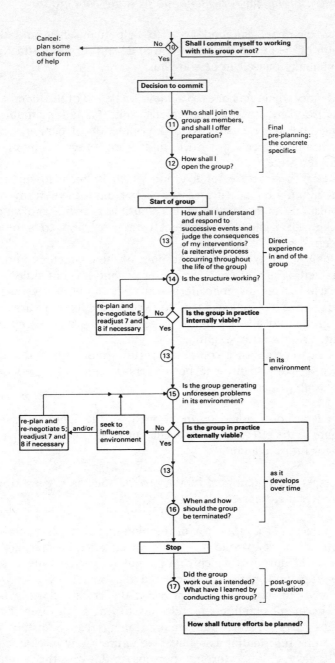

in which members can find ways to help themselves and the conductor of the group can help them to do so. Purposes attached to the planning phase can be stated as:

12 to identify what one hopes to achieve on behalf of the members of a group by assessing the current state (situation, requirements and likely capacities) of a population of persons with whom one expects to work and from this, specifying a preferred state;
13 to design a structure for a group which is likely to suit the population, i.e. a structure which persons drawn from the population can use, which seems plausible to them, and which is likely to facilitate movement from a current to a more preferred state;
14 in doing so, to take realistic account of the character of one's work setting and of one's own interests and level of skills;
15 to exclude from membership persons whom one judges could be damaged by being exposed to experiences likely to arise in the group and persons likely to be unmanageably disruptive of the group's efforts; and
16 to seek to establish a composition (both members and staff) which is likely to provide both support and challenge when the group comes into being.

One final purpose should be mentioned which, if pursued, can contribute to the effective use of a current group and also provide a basis for future planning:

17 to assess the functioning of the group, both as it goes along and after it closes.

As a conductor of a group (or in the planning stage, a would-be conductor of a group) one has access to information and has in mind a set of purposes which one intends to pursue. There is a gap between information as such and the pursuit of purposes which needs to be filled by conceptual devices for sorting out which bits of information are relevant to one's purposes, how information fits together and what meanings can plausibly be placed on it. Information can never be entirely raw in character since it is always filtered through persons, in this case the planner and conductor of a group. Not being a tape-recorder, the planner/conductor is bound to perceive events selectively and place meanings on them in the very act of observing events or of gathering information. The issue, then, is not *whether* to use concepts, models and theory to organize one's perceptions and understandings, since this is bound to happen in any case, but *which* concepts, models and theories can most usefully be invoked.

Certain concepts have already been brought into the discussion. For example, the concepts of 'frontier' and of 'preoccupying concern' were introduced as ways of conceptualizing the current state of a population. The concept of group norm, and the notion that some norms support the group as a medium for help while others work against it, was introduced as something to hold in mind while conducting a group. In the chapters which follow, concepts already introduced will be elaborated and further concepts, models and theory will be introduced at points when they seem useful in pointing to action.

Before proceeding to a more detailed consideration of the decisions and tasks which face persons who plan and conduct groups, a chapter is devoted to a discussion of the group as a potential medium for help. An understanding of the medium which one intends to utilize is basic to all else. The next chapter considers some special characteristics and features of a group, points to circumstances under which they can support or hinder the development and use of a group as a helping medium, and describes a model which can help one to see how features of a group interrelate and bear upon one another.

Chapter 2
The character of the group as a medium for help

Unless one understands the character of the helping medium which one is considering using one cannot even begin to make plans and decisions about who is likely to benefit from it and who not, how to plan the effort, and how to proceed while using it. This will be true of short-term one-to-one contract-based work, of behaviour modification, of psychoanalytically oriented individual psychotherapy, of interpersonal skills training, and of any other treatment or intervention approach which one can think of. A small face-to-face group, like any other medium for helping persons, has its special character, its advantages and limitations, its special opportunities and its potential hazards.

I shall approach the task of examining a group as a medium for help first by describing a number of special characteristics and features of groups, and their potential for facilitating or hindering the helping process, and then by putting forward a framework which can help one to see the relationships amongst these characteristics.

The special features and characteristics of groups to be discussed are: group moods and atmospheres, including emotional contagion; shared themes; norms and belief systems, including the possibility that some of these may take the form of collusive defences; the varying positions that individuals may hold with reference to norms and belief systems and the consequences for the individual of the stance he takes toward them; special pair and trio relationships in groups; the development of a group over time; degrees of cohesiveness and the consequences for members; varying positions of members with respect to power, centrality, and being liked or disliked; social comparison in groups; spectatorship; receiving and giving feedback; opportunities for trying out new behaviours; and the group as an environment in which collision and collusion may occur.

1 *Groups develop particular moods and atmospheres*. It is part of our ordinary use of language to make such comments as 'The group was feeling tense today', or 'The class was in a rebellious mood', or 'Apathy hung in the air'. It cannot literally be the case that a group has a mood since a group is not an organism capable of feeling. Yet such comments are in some sense correct in that there are times when particular moods or atmospheres develop in a group which are undeniably detectable and in some sense belong to the group as a whole. When one judges that a group is in a rebellious (depressed, apathetic, panicky, etc.) mood one does not necessarily mean that every single person present is experiencing the same mood but one does mean that enough persons are sharing in it and expressing it that it is reasonable to speak of it as a feature of the group as a whole. Group moods and atmospheres are expressed in what is said, how things are said, and how people behave. An apathetic mood is likely to be displayed by desultory conversation, monotonous tones, a slow pace, and a sense that participating is an effort. A tense atmosphere is likely to be demonstrated by tense body postures, wary expressions, and a kind of jerky pattern to the interaction. And so on.

Moods and atmospheres must emerge from within the membership of a group. There is, indeed, no other way in which they can emerge. Sometimes a particular atmosphere or mood is clearly triggered by some event which everyone knows about and which has a similar impact on most members of the group. A group which is meeting for the first time after a suicide has occurred on the ward, for example, can hardly fail to be influenced by this event. An atmosphere may be triggered by an event occurring within the group such as a person failing to turn up who has been very upset the time before, or someone bringing in a particularly distressing problem. At other times no obvious precipitating event can be identified: the atmosphere or mood seems to develop by accretion. One comment communicates a sense of tenseness, is picked up by someone else who comments in the same mode and as the discussion goes on that mode or mood becomes established in the group as a whole.

Atmospheres and moods have an impact on individuals in groups. Many people have had the experience of entering a group in which a tense atmosphere was already established and finding that they soon begin to feel tense themselves although they previously felt perfectly comfortable. This can occur with respect to a range of possible group atmospheres and moods. Thus, a person who has been feeling comfortable may come to feel unsafe in a particular group atmosphere; a person who came into the group in a neutral mood can come to feel depressed or fearful. The effect on the person can be beneficial or damaging depending on the meaning the affect has for him and the resources which he can bring to bear for dealing with it. If, for example, a person who ordinarily wards off depression by some defensive device becomes caught up in a general mood of depression, then he is experiencing a feeling which he ordinarily avoids. This carries both a hazard and an opportunity. If he feels overwhelmed by the feeling then he may experience unmanageable distress. If, on the other hand, he can muster the courage to accept and confront the feeling, or be helped to do so, then there is the possibility that he can face his depression and lose his fear of it. In the context of some prevailing mood it is often possible to help members explore how they experience the feeling involved, how they respond to it, what usually triggers it off, how easy or difficult they find it to tolerate, and the like.

Some atmospheres support the helping effort and some threaten to undermine it. The point was made in the preceding chapter that it is important that group members feel safe enough to stay in the group and take risks in it. A 'safe-enough' atmosphere facilitates the work of a group. Conversely, little of value can occur in an atmosphere so tense and risk-laden that all energy and attention is bent toward defending against being overwhelmed by anxiety.

Some group moods or atmospheres develop slowly over a period of time but others explode into existence abruptly and unexpectedly. When this occurs, one generally says that there is a contagion of affect in the group. One cannot see exactly how, not least because it happens so quickly, but quite suddenly the group is in a panic, or in a period of uncontrollable laughter, or into a period of wild and apparently uncontrollable behaviour. Periods of contagion are not essentially different in character from those moods and atmospheres which develop more slowly. However, it is more difficult to defend against being caught up in them simply because of the rapidity with which they develop. The potential for positive and negative consequences for persons in the group is much the same.

By what process does contagion come about in a group? Fritz Redl (1956) has suggested that when contagion occurs in a group there is an initiator and there are imitators. In order for contagion to occur, according to Redl, there must exist an acute conflict area within the imitators which involves strong impulses towards expressing some feeling and at the same time strong pressure from ego or superego forces to suppress the impulse. The impulse toward expressing the feeling is barely held in check by the pressures to contain it. Within the initiator there must be a similar strong urge toward the expression of an impulse but at the same time weak inhibiting forces. If this combination occurs then the initiator who expresses some strong affect makes it possible for others to express the same feeling without fear or guilt through a little understood process which Redl calls 'magical exculpation through the initiatory act'. As far as I know, no one knows just why it should be so, but it is generally recognized that he who casts the first stone is commonly held to be more guilty than those who follow with exactly the same behaviour. (The frequently heard childhood plaint, 'but he did it first', is well known to parents and teachers.) Another way of stating Redl's argument is to say that in order for feelings and behaviours to contage, the same impulse must be present in at least a latent form in all persons in a group but at least one of them must have a lower threshold for expressing it than the others. Under these conditions, that person functions as a trigger for the others, somehow giving permission for others to express the same feeling or behaviour.

2 *Shared themes can build up in groups*. A shared theme is an issue or a concern which comes to preoccupy a group and dominate the attention of the members for a period of time. A theme has affect attached to it but it also has content: a theme is about something. Not unusual group themes have to do with a sense of being bad, or a sense of being a victim of injustice, or a yearning for a quick, magical solution to one's problems. Many more examples could be cited. Shared themes build up through an associative process in the group. That is, in the course of interaction amongst members, each person who contributes something to a conversation or to an activity builds on what has gone before associatively.

A thread of some kind connects successive contributions such that a common theme begins to emerge. One person says something, the next picks up some aspect of that comment, the next elaborates on it, the next returns to a different element of the original contribution, the next ignores that element but returns to the one originally picked out of the first contribution, and so on. Within such an associative stream someone might say something which has no bearing at all on what has gone before. Such a comment could interrupt one theme and initiate another, but often it is ignored and other participants continue to build on the original theme. Over a relatively short period of time one begins to see that the members of a group are developing some particular concern or issue into a theme in which most share. Themes can become established through behavioural or through verbal means or, most often, through a combination of both.

The process of theme-building through an associative process can most easily be seen in relatively unstructured groups which have been designed to rely on open discussion or undirected activity – in other words in groups without a planned agenda. However, more highly structured groups, where members are directed into activities, exercises or pre-planned topics also display an associative process. Where a theme is 'given' to a group, for example, in the form of an assigned or suggested topic, it is the interaction of the members through an associative process which shapes its particular character. Within a highly structured team game, themes may emerge of 'it's not fair' or 'it's his fault'. In general, a group structure may restrict and channel the associative flow but it does not do away with it in that shared themes can be seen to emerge in and around and through the structure. The associative quality of conversations and activities is a general group phenomenon, not a special characteristic of helping groups. One need only recall conversations overheard on trains or in restaurants, or watch a group of children in a playground to find instances of theme-building in ordinary life.

In groups designed to help people, issues important to particular persons often can be explored within the context of a prevailing theme. Members both contribute to the building of a shared theme and experience its impact. The potential for benefit lies in the opportunity to explore issues of potential importance under conditions in which a number of people are involved and the shared character of the situation lends courage and support. One sometimes sees instances where an individual makes strenuous efforts to avert the emergence of some theme, presumably because he feels threatened by it. If a person fails in such efforts he may protect himself by some form of psychological insulation. The theme washes over him without affecting him. Often, however, an individual finds a theme manageable even though threatening because it *is* shared and because much mutual support for exploring it exists in the group. This then becomes one of the positive potentials of the group as a medium for help.

3 *Groups evolve norms and belief systems.* Although norms refer to behaviours and belief systems to thoughts and ideas, they have in common their shared character, their function in regulating the behaviour or attitudes of members, and the fact that persons who deviate from them are commonly put under pressures from others to conform.

All groups establish norms and belief systems. Some of these are brought by the members to the group and belong to the wider culture. No one questions them and they are established quickly, often remaining implicit. Norms about acceptable dress, taking turns in discussion and not unduly interrupting, arriving (more or less) on time, and the like, are familiar norms which belong to life outside the group and accompany persons into the group. Some norms and beliefs are specific to a particular collection of persons and take time to evolve. A group of hospitalized patients, for example, developed the shared belief that they were superior to persons outside the hospital because they had admitted that they had problems and recognized their need for help. Different groups establish different norms about the kinds of feelings it is permissible to express and how they shall be expressed. Is it acceptable, for example, to express anger directly, or through sarcasm, or through joking, or by some other means? Is it acceptable to acknowledge one's yearning to be looked after as if one were a much younger person? Shared beliefs can have to do with explanations as to how persons came to be psychiatrically ill or came to commit a crime, with assumptions about what can be expected of 'society', with assumptions about the route toward feeling better, and the like. Sometimes shared beliefs develop which are directed toward particular persons in the group. For example, one person might come to be regarded by all of the others as an expert, or a spoiled child, or as worse off than everyone else.

Norms are a necessary feature in groups. They serve an economic function in that they reduce the necessity continually to negotiate and renegotiate the rules on which the group will operate. They also function as safety-generators for the members. If everyone knows, for example, that in this group it is all right, or not all right, to express anger in particular ways, then members can steer their way through the group in such a way as to increase the likelihood that they will be acceptable to others. Persons in a small face-to-face group are not merely the passive recipients of norms but many if not all of the members will have been actively involved in creating them. For example, a norm that anger is to be expressed through joking behaviour can only evolve through the interaction of members (unless it is a culture-wide norm). Most likely such a norm fulfils a protective function in the group.

This latter point brings us to the recognition that norms and belief systems can constitute powerful collusive defences in a group. They can, for example, preclude facing certain kinds of feelings or experiences or support the members in avoiding dealing with a difficult person. Collusive defences function in a group to keep everyone comfortable but they also reduce or constrict the value of the group by restricting the areas in which exploration can occur. A potential source of conflict between group members and the therapist or group worker lies in the members' efforts to establish and maintain a collusive defence which the therapist or worker regards as restrictive or anti-therapeutic in character. Some collusive defences have a potential for damaging particular individuals within the group, as when one person occupies the role of scapegoat while others attack him, or when one person is prepared to confess unacceptable feelings to the group and to allow himself to be 'helped' by the others, thus exposing himself whilst at the same time protecting all others from the risks of self-exposure. Here, too, there is a potential for conflict between the group and the conductor, for the members may be well satisfied with this state of affairs while the therapist or worker is uneasy with it.

By no means are all norms or belief systems damaging or limiting. Some have the effect of opening up the boundaries of the group and making useful exploration possible. For example, the shared belief that 'we are all alike in having problems' supports a group as a positive medium for help since if everyone has problems no one need feel ashamed about talking about them. If a group establishes a norm that anger, or jealousy, or a wish to be nurtured and looked after is part of the general human condition, then again, boundaries for exploration become wider.

It sometimes happens in groups that a norm or belief is gradually gaining the support of most persons in the group but one person is unable to go along with it and either fails to conform or actively challenges it. Such a person can be said to be occupying a deviant position with respect to the norm or the likewise shared belief and is likely for a time at least to become a conspicuous and central person in the group in consequence of taking this position. Some years ago two colleagues and I conducted a study of three persons in three different groups who came to occupy a deviant position (Stock, Whitman and Lieberman, 1958). It was found that when it became apparent that a person was failing to accept a group norm, the first reaction on the part of the other members was to put pressure on him through persuasion and argument to conform to the norm or to accept the belief. However, rather than succumbing to these pressures, all three persons who were in a deviant position displayed remarkable and persistent resistance to quite strong and varied pressures from other members. In the end, it was the group which changed rather than the deviant member. The others, finding that their attempts to change the deviant member came to nothing, instead sought to understand, explain, and excuse his deviance, or else modified the norm in such a way that it now could encompass the behaviour of the deviant member. It will be seen that a challenge to an emerging norm or belief can in the end be a valuable thing both for the group as a whole and for the person who cannot accept the norm. For the group as a whole, the challenge requires the group to examine the norm or belief, to consider its necessity and function and often to shift towards a modified or new norm which may very well be more facilitating of the helping effort than the original one. For the member who challenges or cannot accept the norm, such an episode becomes a special opportunity for personal change.

Lest this sound contradictory, since I have already made the point that persons hold to their belief systems and preferred behaviours in the face of substantial pressure, I would underline the fact that during the period in which the norm is being explicitly examined and the person's inability to accept it is also under discussion, there is much opportunity for the individual to examine how it is that he is unable to accept something which others are able to accept. For example, in a group which has developed a shared view that sometimes experiencing anger towards parents is a common human feeling, members will press a person who cannot accept this norm at least to consider how it is that he cannot. Through such explorations a person who has been in a deviant position often moves from assuming that some particular way of behaving or of viewing himself or the world is given and unquestionable, to acknowledging that it is something which is *not* given, but needs to be examined and understood. The group dynamic has helped the person to move from an ego-syntonic to an ego-alien position.

To summarize, from the point of view of their impact on particular persons, norms and beliefs may be damaging in the direct sense of facing individuals with something they cannot tolerate or by placing them in a position where they are blamed or attacked. Norms and beliefs also can be non-therapeutic or anti-therapeutic in that they may prevent a group from exploring important areas and thus restrict a group's usefulness. On the other hand, norms and beliefs can function positively by helping persons to feel safe enough to explore anxiety-provoking issues or to try new behaviours. The *kinds* of norms and belief systems on which a group operates are of critical importance and can make the difference between a sterile or even destructive group and a useful one.

4 *Groups vary in cohesiveness and in the permeability of their boundaries.* A cohesive group is one in which the members experience a clear sense of belonging to the group, find the group appealing and attractive, and are quite clear as to who is and who is not a member of the group. In such groups the boundary of the group is clear and relatively impermeable. Not only are members and others quite clear about who belongs to the group and who does not, but leaving the group is a visible and noted act and entry into the group is likewise visible and noted. In contrast to this, a group marked by low cohesiveness has more permeable boundaries. It is less obvious both to the members and to others as to who belongs to the group and who does not; members are likely to take a more casual view of the group: the

group means less to them. It is easy to leave the group and leaving is an event of relatively little importance both to the person who leaves and for those who remain. Similarly it is a relatively easy and unmarked event for persons to come into the group. Absences and lateness are not only tolerated but hardly remarked on or noticed. Cohesiveness is not, of course, a fixed characteristic: a given group may vary in degree of cohesiveness in the course of its own life.

It will be apparent that the experience an individual has under conditions of cohesiveness or of non-cohesiveness is bound to be different. Pressures on members from the group as a whole will be different in that in a cohesive group there will be more pressure on persons to remain members, to conform to group norms and to accept shared beliefs than will be the case in a less cohesive group.

It is sometimes said that a group can become 'too cohesive'. This usually refers to a situation in which the continued existence of the group has become so important to the members that they avoid taking any risks that could damage the level of cohesiveness which they have achieved. If one's hopes for the group involve personal change or the development of new skills this degree of cohesiveness, whilst comfortable for the members, works against one's overall purpose in undertaking the work. Dysfunctional levels of high cohesiveness can be regarded as a form of collusive defence erected against some feared consequence of dissent or quarrelling. This is a further example of a way in which a dynamic of the group can have negative consequences for the members.

Is it also the case that cohesiveness can drop to such low levels that this too becomes dysfunctional? This depends on the nature of the patients or clients whom one is seeking to help, since conditions of low cohesiveness suit the needs of some populations but not of others. For some kinds of groups and some kinds of patients or clients one does not wish to encourage escape hatches from the group experience in the form of easily permeable bound-aries. One wishes a certain amount of pressure to be placed on persons to stick with the group and to face whatever events emerge within it. With other kinds of groups, however, a low degree of cohesiveness with permeable boundaries is a distinct advantage. This is particularly true when one is dealing with very vulnerable persons who need permission to protect themselves from the group from time to time through leaving it physically. Freedom to move in and out of the group is desirable and actually supports the helping process by holding in the group persons who otherwise might have to flee altogether.

5 *Groups develop and change their character over a period of time.* There is no doubt that a newly formed group has a character which is distinguishable from that same group once it is well established. It is also true that a group whose members know that it is soon to end is likely to display preoccupations and characteristics associated with termination. In most groups one can identify a formative phase, an established phase and a termination phase.

The formative phase of a group is marked by the members' efforts to find a place in the group which is comfortable and manageable, and to establish some working agreements as to what the group is all about and whether and how they can work together. In an established group, these issues have been worked on – not dealt with once and for all, but worked on – enough so that the survival of the group or of oneself in the group is no longer an issue. More energy can be put into exploring a range of issues and using the group for personal benefit. When a group approaches the end of its life preoccupations with loss and separation and with time running out are likely to flavour the group.

A question arises as to whether one can articulate phases in more elaborated or detailed ways. For example, can one predict the order in which themes, preoccupations and issues will emerge in a group? It has been my experience that one cannot make very precise predictions. Rather than moving from one issue to another in a predictable order, groups, at least those which rely on open discussion, seem to move in a kind of deepening spiral. One issue emerges into the foreground, is worked on for a while, then dropped, another takes its place, and so on. From time to time the members return to an early issue in a different way, usually taking it a bit further, before again leaving it for something else. Even when a series of themes or issues is imposed on a group through a series of set topics, I believe that the members of a group can move on a given topic at a given time only a certain distance and in their own way, and that it is therefore important to plan flexibly so that room is made for the subsequent re-examination of early topics.

Although one cannot predict precise order, one can predict with some confidence that certain basic human issues will preoccupy most groups at some time or other. These include such matters as the acceptability of the self; yearnings for closeness and nurturance; anger and its management; issues around power, control and autonomy; personal aspirations and the hopes, fears and despairs associated with them; envy; and personally held fears and guilts. In short, a range of basic human affects and issues is likely to emerge but the order and manner of their emergence is likely to depend on such infinitely variable factors as the composition of the group, the occurrence of fortuitous and unpredictable outside events and the leader's personality and style.

One can observe the three basic phases in groups of varying structure and duration. Any group is bound to engage in a formative stage during which the members test the structure which has been planned for the group and test whether they can work together within it. If the structure has been well planned to suit the population and if the composition of the group presents no great difficulties, then the testing process need not take long and the group can move into an established phase fairly quickly. Even a quite short-term group, if it is working well, can be seen to have a formative, an established and a termination phase. If the group is not working well it may be marked by an interminable and ineffectual formative stage which simply goes on until the group ends.

6 *Persons occupy different positions in groups with respect to power, centrality and being liked or disliked.* When a person first enters a group, he or she can be expected to seek a position in the group which is familiar and feels safe. Thus, some persons immediately seek a position of power and influence and make themselves and their views immediately known to the others. In such a position, they feel comfortable, safe and rewarded. Others seek a peripheral position and only feel comfortable if they are allowed to occupy it. If a person succeeds in establishing himself or herself in a preferred position then he or she is likely to feel reasonably safe. If not, not. Initially sought positions usually shift. As a person begins to feel safer within the group he or she is prepared to participate more flexibly and display more of his or her personal repertoire of behaviours in the group. Persons do sometimes get stuck in particular positions or roles in a group. They may insist on staying in their original position themselves,

but sometimes it is the other members who insist that they be and remain a particular kind of person in the group. It is usually the dynamics of the person in interaction with the dynamics of the group which accounts for the position(s) which a person occupies.

When persons shift around within a group – sometimes exercising power sometimes following, sometimes being active and central and sometimes being peripheral, sometimes going along with majority views and sometimes deviating, sometimes being liked and sometimes disliked – they are in a good position to gain because they are exposed to a wide range of situations and experiences. When on the other hand a person becomes fixed in a particular position in a group, then opportunities for self-understanding and for trying out new behaviours are limited.

7 *Individuals in groups sometimes find one or two other persons who are especially important to them because they are similar in some respect to significant persons in the individual's life or to significant aspects of the self.* Depending on its composition, a group can include persons who come to have some special significance or meaning for particular individuals. For example, an adolescent may find someone in the group who embodies his ego-ideal, or a young mother may find someone who acknowledges feelings which she senses exist in her but which she cannot bear to face, or a very psychiatrically ill man may find someone who voices his deepest fears through psychotic material, or a middle-aged woman may find a younger person who 'stands for' a rebellious son.

Projection may be involved in this process to a greater or lesser extent. Groups are composed of real people who display observable characteristics and behave in particular ways. These traits and behaviours sometimes resonate with the past experiences or current concerns of individual members. Mary finds in the group John, who really does resemble Mary's brother in some respect. Mary may, through projection, place more of her brother on to John than is really present, but there is something in John in the first place which forms a base for or assists this projection.

When special relationships form between pairs or trios of persons in a group, special opportunities arise for those concerned to confront their own feelings, explore an important relationship and experiment with ways of dealing with it, all through the medium of explorations and try-outs with surrogate persons in the here-and-now of the group.

8 *Social comparison can take place in a group.* In virtually any group individuals are likely to take note of their own position, opinions and feelings in relation to those of others. They will notice, for example, that things which make them angry do not make others angry; that feelings which they never dare to express are readily expressed by others; that assumptions which they make about themselves and the world are not necessarily or always a part of the assumptive world of others; that feelings or experiences which they consider peculiar to themselves are common to others. It is virtually impossible for such comparisons not to take place. They are likely to occur both for persons who participate actively and for persons who remain altogether silent.

Social comparison is one of the routes to personal benefit in groups. It can contribute to the reduction of feelings of social isolation, to an increase in self-acceptance, to a fuller acknowledgment and understanding of one's own feelings and situation, and to the establishment of new views about oneself and others. In theory, social comparison could have negative consequences, for example by confirming a sense of personal isolation ('No one is like me, really') or a low level of self-esteem ('No one is as unworthy as me'). This does not happen if a group has been able to get down to the fundamentals of human experience, for it is here that communalities exist. If communalities can be acknowledged about such basic human feelings as anger, yearnings for intimacy, etc., then differences can be acknowledged as to how one regards and expresses such basics.

9 *A group is an environment in which persons can observe what others do and say and then observe what happens next.* The fact that persons can not only participate actively in a group but watch others participate is a potential advantage which generates what are commonly called 'spectator effects'. It is not unusual that when a person is doing nothing more than watching and listening he notes events which have some particular meaning to him. For example, he might note that someone challenges the therapist or worker in an angry way. Perhaps he has always been afraid to challenge persons in authority for fear of the consequences of doing so, and therefore would never dream of challenging the

therapist or worker himself. Yet, he might well be sharing some of the angry or resentful feelings that leads someone else to behave in a challenging way. If this is the case, the individual who is not participating nevertheless observes challenging behaviour in the group and notes the consequences. He might note that just as he feared the challenger is punished in some way by the leader or group worker. More likely, however, he observes that no disaster follows upon such behaviours. The opportunity to observe this can generate useful internal learnings ('disaster doesn't occur for others and might not occur for me') and can be a step toward testing out new behaviours for himself. In this example occupying a spectator position allows for personal learnings which pave the way for more active participation and personal try-outs. Some persons in groups spend most (in extreme instances all) of their time in a spectator position. They may nevertheless gain substantially from their experience in the group.

Most therapists and group workers take the view that persons who participate actively are more likely to achieve benefit than those who remain in a spectator position. On the whole this opinion is justified, for the following reasons: a person who remains a spectator cannot influence the group in directions which are particularly relevant to his own concerns; social comparisons occur covertly and there is therefore no way for others to offer explicit support or commentary; the spectator is deprived of feedback; and, above all, he does not allow himself opportunities to test out personally the consequences of particular ways of behaving and of expressing himself. Thus many opportunities for personal gain are lost. Yet one should bear in mind that some persons who cannot bring themselves to participate actively can nevertheless benefit to a considerable extent.

10 *A group is an environment in which persons can receive feedback from others concerning their own behaviour or participation.*
By 'feedback' I mean responses from others – which may be verbal or non-verbal, direct or indirect – which follow on some behaviour or bit of participation on the part of any given person and which can be utilized by that person as information to be taken into account in guiding future action.

'Feedback' has become a jargon term and has become degraded in common use by professionals and others who work with groups and by many who participate in groups. In some groups one sees it taken to mean 'I will now tell you what your real motivation is', or 'This is what I really think of you', or 'You are doing/feeling this because . . . '. One sometimes sees very destructive statements justified on grounds that the perpetrator is 'offering feedback'. I am not using the term in any of these senses. Rather, consider that all behaviour, verbal and otherwise, has consequences. The consequence occurs in the form of a response: direct and explicit, indirect, or no discernible response. If I make a comment in a group, what happens next constitutes a form of feedback to me. It might or might not be explicitly intended as feedback by the persons responding. However, by listening to what is said or noting how persons act following my behaviour I learn something about its impact on others and how it is received. If, for example, I confess to feelings of jealousy in a group I might find that others are horror-stricken and rejecting or I might find that others also confess to having feelings of jealousy and are sympathetic. Either of these responses constitute feedback. More subtly, I might learn that under some circumstance my angry feelings are accepted by others and under other circumstances they are not. I might find that a statement that I regarded as warm and supportive was received by someone else as if it were patronizing. All of this constitutes information potentially useful to me, which I can use if I choose to, to re-examine my own feelings and intentions or to guide my future actions.

It will be clear that feedback in this form is available to people all of the time in ordinary life. In this sense a helping group is not different from ordinary experience. In helping groups of certain types, however, persons may be encouraged to note explicitly and take into account the feedback which is available to them. Group members may be encouraged to offer explicit verbal feedback which they might otherwise withhold. Because of the common misunderstandings about feedback, persons in groups sometimes need guidance as to what it is and what constitutes useful feedback. They may need to be told or shown that responses which are interpretations, explanations, disguised attacks or imputations of motives are rarely useful. When at the receiving end of such statements it is far too easy simply to deny or ignore the feedback even if it is 'correct'. It is far too easy to claim (and sometimes one is quite right) that such statements mainly reveal something about those expressing them and have little to do with the person to whom the 'feedback' is directed.

The most useful form of explicit feedback is that which follows the form 'when you said or did that, I felt . . .'. Such a response makes explicit the feelings or reactions stirred up by a particular behaviour or expression of feeling and avoids speculating about what might lie behind it. It is a form of feedback which is hard to evade because it is a statement of the feelings of the responder, who is, after all, in the best position to be aware of his own feelings and reactions. If he is being honest, he is providing straight information, not opinion or speculation.

Receiving feedback from others within the group is one of the advantages of the group as a context for help. Group members can gain information about the impact of their behaviour on others which is not ordinarily available to them. On the other hand, the notion of feedback can be carelessly defined, and destructive behaviours can be sanctioned by calling them 'feedback'. It is one of the responsibilities of the therapist or group worker to see to it that the forms of so-called feedback which are provided in the group are useful and not destructive in character

11 *A group is an environment in which new behaviours can be tried out.* In a group a person can, if he chooses and feels able to, try out new behaviours which are not a part of his established repertory. This is an important benefit-producing feature of all types of groups. In a group planned to effect personal therapeutic change, persons may dare to risk expressing feelings ordinarily concealed or behaving in ways ordinarily censored, and take the opportunity to observe the consequences of doing so, for themselves and for others. In groups designed to help persons face some transition, members can rehearse, in the group, new behaviours which they think their new circumstances will require of them. In groups designed to increase practical or interpersonal skills, the entire structure of the group and the way it is conducted are directed towards providing members with opportunities to practise new ways of behaving.

Trying out new behaviours and noting the consequences of doing so is an essential feature of what is commonly called 'the corrective emotional experience'. Persons typically come into a group with an already established repertory of interpersonal behaviours. There are usually certain behaviours (to which particular feelings are linked) which persons have ruled out for themselves because for one reason or another they do not regard it as safe or proper to express the behaviour or to acknowledge the associated feelings. It is fear of the consequences of acknowledging a feeling or expressing a behaviour which prevents acknowledgment or expression. Such fears may range all the way from mild fears of eliciting social disapproval to powerful unconsciously held fears of personal dissolution should some feeling be acknowledged to oneself, or intolerable abandonment or rejection should some behaviour be displayed or feeling be expressed to others. Under some conditions in a group, a person may feel safe enough to express certain feelings or behave in ways which he customarily avoids. Or the group, through processes of contagion and resonance, brings such feelings and behaviours to the surface. If this happens, if previously suppressed or censored feelings and behaviours do emerge, then an individual is in a position to note his or her own feelings and to receive explicit or implicit feedback from others. If the feedback received tells them that the consequences which they feared did not occur, this can constitute a corrective emotional experience. The individual 'corrects' long-held, often unconsciously maintained assumptions that disastrous or catastrophic consequences will inevitably follow from acknowledging certain feelings or expressing certain behaviours. If a person never puts his fears to the test, then he will remain constrained by them. If, on the other hand, a person can bring himself to try out some unaccustomed behaviour which from his point of view carries some risk, he will then find out for himself whether the consequences which he fears occur or not. Typically, the feared consequences do not occur, or if they do they are not so extreme as expected and/or are manageable. The person is then in a position to expand his repertory if he chooses to do so.

12 *In a group, members may collide and collude.* This final point is not a new one in that forms of collisions and collusions have been referred to in previous sections. It is, however, worth emphasizing because in some kinds of groups collisions and collusions are the material for personal change. The point has already been made that when persons enter groups they usually seek to establish a position for themselves which they find rewarding or at least comfortable and manageable. In attempting to do this they may find ready helpers in the person of other members and may seek to co-operate with them in order to establish positions of comfort. It is unlikely, however, that such helpers are fully or consistently

available. A certain amount of collision is likely to occur, in which efforts on the part of one person to establish a comfortable position cannot succeed because they interfere with similar (but differing) efforts on the part of others. If nothing but collision occurs, a person is unlikely to feel safe enough to stay in the group. If nothing but collusion occurs, new learnings and personal change will not happen. In a group, therefore one both expects and wishes for experiences of collision and collusion. A balance between these establishes the group as a manageable and potentially useful environment for the individual.

All of the special characteristics of groups referred to above can be expected to occur in most if not all groups. They are created by the members themselves through their interaction. None are in themselves beneficial or in themselves harmful. Rather, under some circumstances or in some forms they are likely to be beneficial; under other circumstances or in other forms, they are likely to be harmful.

This list of features and characteristics of groups is mixed in character. Some features have to do with the character of the group as a whole, some with how persons interact, some with the stance which persons take with respect to group phenomena, some with the possible impact of group events on individuals, and some with initiatives which individuals might take in the context of the group. Such a list serves the purpose of alerting practitioners to phenomena which occur or can occur in groups. In order to serve the further purpose of guiding the practitioner in decisions about how to make use of a group as a medium for help, it is necessary to place these features and processes into some kind of model which shows their relation to one another, the functions they may be serving for the group, and their facilitating or hindering impact.

In attempting to bring these diverse characteristics together into a coherent model, I propose to build from the concepts of norms and belief systems. I have already suggested that norms and belief systems are functional in groups in a simple economic sense but more importantly as safety-generators for members. Many norms and belief systems function to contain anxieties and fears. For example, if the members of a group fear that the therapist or worker will abandon them, they might establish a norm of behaving deferentially toward the therapist or worker. If the members of a group fear criticism from others, they might establish a norm of concealing feelings and experiences which they consider would put them at risk.

Why might group members experience fears which require the establishment of norms and belief systems to contain them? One can postulate that when persons enter groups designed to offer them some form of help they know that they will be expected (and they often expect themselves) to take certain risks which they do not ordinarily take: to try out new behaviours, to share experiences which they usually feel it necessary or prudent to conceal, or to acknowledge feelings which they usually hold at a distance. In the face of this, persons can be expected to act self-protectively. Since everyone is concerned to protect themselves, members of groups not infrequently act collaboratively, usually without being aware that they are doing so, to establish norms or belief systems which function to contain or alleviate fears which are elicited in response to external or internal pressures to take unusual risks.

We have now identified three elements and suggested some links between them: a norm or belief system, some fear or anxiety, and some felt pressure or personally-held wish to express certain feelings, share certain experiences or try certain behaviours. Norms and belief systems are features of the group as a whole. They carry weight because most of the persons in the group subscribe to them and operate in terms of them. Fears, felt pressures, wishes and hopes must belong to individuals, but if they were experienced by only one or two persons in a group they would not be powerful enough to require the establishment of mutually held norms or belief systems. The feelings which I am referring to are in some sense shared or held in common. Pressures which are externally imposed are felt by all or most of the persons in the group. Similar (not the same, but similar) hopes, wishes, yearnings, fears, anxieties and guilts may be held by all or most of the members of a group.

Rather than continue to speak in terms of norms and belief systems, I will introduce a new term, 'group solution', which is a wider concept than either 'norm' or 'belief system' but encompasses both. By arguments already presented, norms and belief systems can be seen to serve protective functions for the group. They 'solve' the emotional problem of how to stay in the group and confront own experiences and feelings without at the same time being overwhelmed by fear or guilt. Other forms of group solutions can be observed in groups. One of these is the mutually held and supported individual defence. Such defences as denial, rationalization, intellectualization, withdrawal and the like can of course be observed in individuals. At times, in a group, individual tendencies to erect particular defences come together, are mutually reinforced and come to characterize the group as a whole. *Everyone* denies, or rationalizes (etc.) and those who do not do so actively sit back and do not interfere with the defences becoming generally established by others. This dynamic is commonly referred to as a 'collusive defence'. In the language which I am introducing, it is a form of group solution. Another form of group solution consists of collaboratively maintained interactive patterns involving role differentiation. In scapegoating, for example, one person occupies the role of scapegoat while others attack him; in 'playing at therapy', one person assumes the role of the patient or client while others seek to help and advise him. These are two examples of a family of group solutions in which most of the members of the group are protected from self-acknowledgment or self-exposure by depositing risks on to one person in the group. Group solutions which involve role differentiation can work in other ways, as well. For example, a group might avoid confronting their angry feeling towards a worker or therapist by casting one person into the role of expert, encouraging him to do what they consider the therapist or worker ought to be doing but is not. In this example, one person is elevated into a highly respected position. He is better off, one might say, than the scapegoat, or at least feels less pain, but he too is being built into a group solution which fulfils a function for the group. Not all group solutions serve purely defensive functions. Some group solutions, whether they be norms, belief systems or interactive patterns, not only function to help members to feel safe in the group but also allow critical issues to be explored relatively freely and widely.

The concept of 'group solution' is one of a number of concepts which is built into a model of group functioning known as 'group focal conflict theory' (Whitman and Stock, 1958; Whitaker and Lieberman, 1964; Whitaker, 1982). This model is based on the work of Thomas French (French, 1952, 1954), who conceptualized individual dynamics in nuclear conflict terms, and within this utilized the concepts of 'disturbing motive' (by which he meant some basic impulse or wish), 'reactive motive' (by which he meant a fear or guilt which was in conflict with the disturbing motive) and 'solution' (which functioned to contain reactive fears and sometimes also allowed for the expression of associated impulses and wishes). This model is described more fully in chapter 8, where it is presented as a sometimes useful way of thinking about individuals in groups and seeing the connections between individual and group dynamics.

When French's basic ideas were transposed and extended to apply to the dynamics of groups, the model worked out like this: There are times in a group when one can observe the emergence of some shared wish, impulse or hope. In the language of the model, this is called the 'disturbing motive', after French, or often simply the 'shared wish'. If nothing stands against this, that is, if nothing stops it from being expressed openly in the group, then this shared wish, impulse or hope can emerge as a theme for discussion. Often, however, the shared wish or impulse is accompanied by some related shared fear or guilt which is in conflict with the shared wish and fights against its emergence. In the language of the model this is called the 'reactive motive', or more simply, the reactive or shared fear. The wish and the fear, taken together, constitute the group focal conflict.

When a group focal conflict begins to take shape in a group one also can see efforts toward dealing with the conflict in some way: in the language of the model, efforts to establish some solution to the shared conflict. The solutions which members find may focus almost entirely on the fears, abandoning for the moment any effort to satisfy the associated shared wish. Or, a solution may simultaneously deal with the fear and allow for some expression or satisfaction of the wish. In the terms of the theoretical model, a 'restrictive' solution deals with the fear at the expense of the wish. Fears are contained and members feel more comfortable but they avoid confronting the impulses or feelings which stirred up the fears in the first place. Restrictive solutions narrow the boundaries of a group and preclude useful explorations and experiences. In contrast, an 'enabling' solution deals with the fear and at the same time allows expression of the wish. Fears are contained and at the same time members can confront and explore the associated impulses and feelings. Under such conditions, wider explorations are possible.

In a group, a disturbing motive might involve a wish to be close to others, a wish to be nurtured and loved, angry impulses, a wish to have an exclusive relationship with the therapist or worker,

and so on. A reactive motive might involve fears of being abandoned, of being ridiculed, of being criticized, of losing control, of
being overwhelmed by own feelings, and so on. Restrictive solutions which one sometimes sees emerging in groups include talking
about trivial issues, blaming others for one's troubles, displacing
anger which belongs to someone inside the group on to someone
outside it, turn-taking, mutually maintained denial, and many
others. Enabling solutions which can arise in groups include
acknowledging that everyone present has faults, acknowledging
that feelings such as anger or envy are human and universally
experienced, seeing everyone in the group as basically alike, and
others.

Sometimes one sees a 'solutional conflict' emerge in a group.
This tends to occur during a period when a possible group solution
is emerging but is not yet firmly consolidated. Most of the
members are prepared to support or go along with a particular
emerging solution but one stands against it and tries to prevent it
from becoming established. By so doing he places himself in a
deviant position with respect to the others. It will be seen that a
group focal conflict model allows one to extend the idea of a
deviant member, earlier defined (see section 3) as one who rejects
a group norm or shared belief. A deviant member can now be
defined as one who cannot accept or refuses to co-operate with
an emerging group solution. An inability or unwillingness to go
along with a group solution can take the form of rejecting a norm
or of being unwilling to accept some emerging shared belief, but
it can also involve failing to support or fighting against some
emerging shared defence or declining to occupy some role which
the others are trying to press one into as a part of some group
solution.

The major elements of this model and their interrelationship
can be represented diagrammatically as follows:

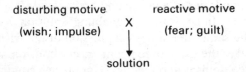

A group focal conflict model brings together the ideas of themes
as constructed through associative processes and successive stages
in development. Within the general notion that groups usually can
be seen to move through a formative, established and termination

phase, one can see certain shared wishes and fears, and associated solutions, becoming focal for a time, giving way to others, and these in turn giving way to still others. Groups often return to particular issues and themes again and again, in varying solutional contexts, tackling the theme in different ways and taking it varying distances. Certain kinds of restrictive solutions require attention from the therapist or worker, particularly if they seem to be doing harm to some one individual or if they become fixed as an unproductive style of operating in the group. A group which is working well tends to move from a preponderant use of restrictive solutions during the formative phase to a preponderant use of enabling solutions during the established phase. A group which gets stuck in its formative phase is one which finds no way to shift from some fixed restrictive solution.

The behaviour of individuals, the positions they occupy and the experiences they undergo can be seen in the context of a continually evolving and shifting pattern of emerging group focal conflicts and associated solutions. A person may fight a rearguard action against a particular solution becoming established. He may drift to the periphery of the group when an enabling solution allows some issue to be explored which he finds difficult. He may be thrust into a peripheral position by some dynamic of the group, as when a group deals with a deviant by encapsulating him, i.e. acting as if he is not there, as a device for proceeding with a preferred solution which the deviant member cannot accept. An individual may take the lead in establishing some shared defence. He may occupy a particular role in a group solution. He may be disliked for challenging some solution which everyone else requires or for making it impossible for some restrictive solution to work. He may be liked and favoured because he is a key person in maintaining some needed restrictive solution. He may experience support and gain courage during a period when an enabling solution is in operation. In the context of some powerful group focal conflict he may find it impossible to resist sharing in experiencing certain impulses or fears, and in consequence may experience massive threat. Because the group situation is fluid and touches upon individual concerns in different ways at different times, he may occupy all of these positions at one time or another and undergo a wide range of experiences.

Sometimes persons thrust themselves into the centre of a group because they have experienced a personal crisis outside the group or because a heavily charged special relationship with another member has surfaced. The latter is likely to occur within the context of some group dynamic. Certainly, the way in which it is explored in the group will depend on the prevailing character of group preoccupations and the nature of the solution in operation at the time. When an individual's centrality is a consequence of some personal crisis or emergency, in the first instance this has nothing to do with the group: it is his strong personal need which presses him to insist on having the group's time and attention. However, the manner in which the others respond to such a bid for help will depend very much on how that person's own situation resonates with the situations of others, the ways in which it may constitute a threat, and the like. What begins as an individual concern can build into a shared issue, or if it persists as an individual concern the manner in which others respond is much influenced by the state of the group, especially the kind of prevailing solution.

It will be clear that of the group-as-a-whole phenomena discussed earlier, norms and belief systems fit into the model as forms of solution. Moods and atmospheres will have a different meaning and function for the group at different times. A shared mood may function as a group solution, as when a prevailing mood of boredom is actually functional for a group in that it prevents exploration of some threatening issue. A shared fear, which in a group focal conflict model constitutes a reactive motive, can escalate in a group through processes of contagion. Panic may emerge when a group is suddenly bereft of a needed solution. How a therapist regards a particular mood or atmosphere and whether and how he seeks to influence it will depend on how he sees it as fitting into the dynamics of the group.

Whether a therapist or worker welcomes or deplores some particular level of cohesiveness in a group will depend very much on the function he sees it serving. At times a very high level of cohesiveness can constitute a restrictive solution. As an example, suppose that one judges a group to be caught up in a group focal conflict in which angry, hostile impulses toward fellow-members are in conflict with fears of losing support from one another. The associated restrictive solution is a high degree of cohesiveness which maintains mutual support and avoids the risks of allowing anger and hostility to surface. An optimum level of cohesiveness can function as an enabling solution in a group, but, as discussed earlier, what is optimum will vary according to the nature and requirements of the membership.

Earlier in this chapter a number of behaviours on the part of individuals were discussed which can (although they do not always) contribute to personal benefit. These included comparing oneself with others, observing others from a non-participant position, giving and receiving feedback and trying out new behaviours. All of these are more likely to occur in beneficial forms when a group is operating on some enabling solution than when it is operating on some restrictive solution. Consider that when a prevailing solution is restrictive in character the group will be operating within narrow boundaries and avoiding exploration of certain feelings or experiences which are important but which are not being allowed to surface. When this happens, there is a reduced opportunity for social comparison and for useful feedback, and less of significance for the non-participating member to observe. Under some restrictive solutions particular individuals may be urged to try out new behaviours but this tends to involve their being encouraged to risk themselves in order to protect others. If under these circumstances they experience severe threat, they may learn only that they were right and prudent all along to conceal certain feelings or avoid certain behaviours. As a part of certain restrictive solutions 'feedback' of a destructive kind is offered in the guise of 'helping'. For example what is commonly believed by members to be a form of help directed at one person is in fact projected blame or a displaced attack. This is a form of 'help' which is not helpful and may do harm. Social comparison can and does occur virtually all the time but under heavily restrictive solutions it may occur at a relatively superficial level and/or opportunities for following through may be limited.

During periods when a group is operating on some enabling solution, inhibiting fears are reduced, boundaries are wider, and more meaningful issues are likely to be explored more openly, more extensively and in greater depth. Processes of social comparison, feedback, spectatorship and behavioural try-outs are likely to go on in a more useful and constructive manner. It follows that a worker or therapist who helps a group work toward the establishment of enabling rather than restrictive solutions will at the same time be helping to establish a richer environment with more potential for personal gain.

There are times in the course of a group's life when an individual stands in a relationship to the prevailing group dynamics such that special opportunities exist for exploiting the situation for the specific benefit of that person. For example, when a person is in a deviant position in the group with respect to some emerging group solution, a special opportunity exists for exploring how it is that he cannot accept it. When a person is brought by processes of contagion to face some feeling he ordinarily avoids then there is a special opportunity for him to confront it and for others to help him to do so. When an individual finds a special person in the group who stands for someone or something important to him, then special opportunities exist for those most directly concerned (and for others as spectators or as active helpers) to gain new understandings or try out new behaviours. In general, it is the special resonances between individual, group and inter-personal dynamics which provide special opportunities for benefit over and above those accruing from social comparison, feedback and the like.

I consider a group focal conflict model useful when thinking about certain planning decisions, especially those concerned with designing and selecting for a group. One has to look to other frameworks and models as guides to other planning decisions and tasks, for example, anticipating the impact of a group on its organizational environment, or working out procedures for monitoring and evaluating a group. During the actual conduct of a group, the model is particularly useful for groups which rely on open discussion, where associative processes are given free rein. It can also usefully be invoked in groups which make use of topic-based discussion or activities, especially at critical moments when a group gets stuck or appears to be damaging someone. In all groups, however structured, the model can help one to be alert to special opportunities for benefiting individuals. In working with certain populations, especially when one has defined benefit in very specific and limited terms, a group focal conflict model is unnecessarily elaborate or only partially relevant. For example, some groups are composed of persons who cannot easily or consistently listen and attend to one another. In such groups associative processes are much attenuated and it may make sense only occasionally to think in terms of shared feelings or solutions. One can sometimes make partial use of the model, as when one sees similar defences aroused in different persons in response to external pressure. Although these emerge in parallel rather than as a consequence of collaborative processes, they present the therapist or worker with the same task of perceiving their function for members and thinking out directions and means for intervening.

An understanding of the dynamics of groups is an essential part of the knowledge base necessary to the planner and conductor of groups but it is not enough in itself. One certainly also needs an understanding of how group and individual dynamics connect and an understanding of individual members in terms relevant to the group. Further, a *theoretical* understanding of how groups may operate is no use unless one can find ways of applying and using that understanding in the face of real, concrete, unique situations. A general understanding pays off if and when it can help one to see what decisions and what courses of action make sense when actually engaged in planning and conducting a group.

Part II

Before the group starts

Chapter 3

Initial planning: fitting type of group and leadership approach to the patient or client population

This chapter deals with the first five decisions listed and discussed in chapter 1: deciding on the population with which one intends to work; deciding on which benefits one hopes to procure for persons drawn from the population; deciding whether or not a group is likely to be a suitable medium for helping persons drawn from the population to achieve those benefits; and if yes, deciding on the basic structure and character of the group and whether to work alone or with one or more co-workers or co-therapists.

The first two of these are preliminary to deciding whether or not a group experience is likely to benefit a population. Specifying a population with which to work can best be done by identifying explicitly the opportunities offered by one's work setting, the aims and requirements of one's organization, and one's own interests and levels of skill and experience. On this, I consider that no more need be said than has already been said in chapter 1.

Once a population has been identified, further planning decisions cannot be made until one has formed some opinion about the character of the population and has defined the benefits one hopes to procure for persons drawn from it. On the basis of this, one can make a preliminary decision as to whether or not persons from the population are or are not likely to make use of a group experience, or to put this conversely, whether the experiences generated by a group can reasonably be expected to facilitate their moving from their current state to a preferred state.

If it is reasonable to assume that *some* form of group experience might suit, then one is faced with the planning task which is the principal concern of this chapter: what kind of group, how structured and how conducted, is most likely to suit the patient or client population? A planned group experience which 'suits' must mean one which is likely to benefit persons drawn from the population, which they are likely to be able to use, and which is likely to seem plausible to them.

Whether to work with one or more colleagues or alone is a decision which is sometimes made for one by the policies of one's organization, but sometimes is within one's own power to make. If the latter is the case, it seems best to make a tentative agreement early, so that those likely to be working together can make planning decisions together. Decisions made mutually are of course more likely to work out in practice than are decisions made by one person and then imposed on or passively accepted by another. Further, while working out plans, prospective co-therapists or co-workers will also be testing out their likely compatibility. I shall return to this issue toward the end of this chapter.

At the beginning of chapter 1 a number of examples were presented of persons who might possibly benefit from some form of group experience. That list was by no means exhaustive, yet it provided a very wide range of examples of persons who come to or are sent to members of the helping professions in the hope of personal benefit. No single kind of experience could be expected to meet the needs of so diverse a range of potential clients, patients or group participants. It is clearly not appropriate to think globally about 'groups' being helpful to 'people'. Rather, we need some framework to direct us toward thinking about 'what people?' and 'what groups?' A potentially infinite list of populations needs to be reduced to a finite list of population categories. Then, a way of thinking about these categories is required which will direct us toward making sensible decisions about whether a group might prove useful or not, and if so, what type of group involving which leadership approach.

The categories of populations which I shall shortly set down are an abstraction from experience – my own and that of colleagues and students. They should be regarded as *a* set of categories, not as *the* set of categories.

After describing a number of population categories I shall define two concepts – 'frontier' and 'preoccupying concern' – which I consider provide useful guidance in initial planning. My intention then is to discuss each population category in terms of frontier and preoccupying concern to show how thinking in these terms can guide decision-making. I shall hold in mind as I go the possibility that it may sometimes be useful to compose a group homogeneously with respect to population, and sometimes heterogeneously.

The following categories of persons commonly appear amongst the patients or clients of social workers, psychiatrists or psychologists, or seek help from or come to the attention of other helpers:

(1) Persons who have been functioning adequately and who would be described as 'normal' by ordinary standards but who now face some threat to life or identity. In this category one might include persons facing major surgery or debilitating illness; amputees and other accident victims; burns victims; persons who have lost hearing or vision; and so on. This is a 'victims of fate' category.

(2) Persons who have been functioning adequately and who would be regarded as 'normal' by ordinary standards but who are in a 'linked-fate' relationship with one or more others and who are experiencing special stress in consequence of this. Included in this category are parents of mentally handicapped children; parents of children with physical handicap or chronic illness; spouses of persons with a terminal illness; spouses of persons with a chronic debilitating or life-threatening illness; wives of prisoners; adolescent children of alcoholics; parents or spouses of schizophrenic or schizoid persons living at home; and so on.

(3) Persons experiencing or anticipating some life transition. This category includes persons about to be discharged from psychiatric hospitals, Borstal or prison; persons entering an institution; older persons who have just retired or are about to retire from their jobs; children about to enter secondary school; recent immigrants; recently divorced persons; persons who have suffered serious material loss through disaster; and so on. Such transitions may occur through personal choice or may have been thrust upon persons by circumstances. Whatever the character of the transition, the persons concerned are faced with the task of reordering their world and their place in it.

(4) Persons who are functioning adequately from the point of view of an outside observer but who are anxious or depressed, functioning below their capacity or behaving repeatedly in self-defeating ways. This category includes many persons who come to out-patient clinics seeking help or who seek help from private practitioners. It may also include students in secondary or higher education who refer themselves or are referred by teachers because they are working substantially below capacity.

(5) Persons experiencing or beginning to emerge from serious breakdowns in functioning. Within a relatively short period of time such persons have become unable to function at home or at work in their usual ways. They may become acutely anxious, depressed, phobic, delusional, etc., to the point where they cannot carry on their ordinary activities. Such persons may be found in the reception wards of psychiatric hospitals, in the psychiatric ward of a general hosptial, or at home where they carry on with difficulty with the help of family members and/or a general practitioner.

(6) Persons who have lost or who have never acquired basic social or interpersonal skills, or skills-of-living. This category includes some long-stay psychiatric hospital patients; psychiatric hospital patients who have been discharged into a semi-protected environment such as a hostel or a half-way house; institutionalized mentally handicapped persons regarded as potentially capable of living in the community; some physically handicapped persons and some adolescents who have been in institutional care for long periods; some chronic offenders currently living in the community; and so on.

(7) Persons who characteristically and over long periods – perhaps a lifetime – function at some low and unsatisfactory level. Such persons can be found both inside and outside institutions. This category includes withdrawn schizophrenic or schizoid persons, 'drifters', some alcoholics, some chronic offenders, persons who repeatedly visit general practitioners with vague somatic complaints, and the like. In general this category includes those persons for whom the professionals who know them see little prospect for change.

(8) Persons who are regarded as problems by others because they are disruptive, unruly, break laws or offend commonly held standards, or are destructive in their relationships but who do not see themselves as having problems and who do not seek help of their own volition. Included in this category might be some adolescent and adult offenders, disruptive adolescents in secondary schools, parents suspected of having harmed their children physically, and so on.

Holding these categories to one side for the moment, I would like to develop the ideas of 'frontier' and 'preoccupying concern'.

'Frontier' refers to the fact that every person already has within his or her personal repertory certain personal resources, certain skills and understandings which form a base for making choices and plans and undertaking activities which move him towards his own life goals. Similarly one can imagine for any person skills, understandings and personal resources which are outside his current repertory and beyond his current capacity. The border or margin between what he already has and can do and what is just beyond him can be thought of as his 'frontier'. Some skills and capacities will be well established and well within the frontier; others will be far beyond the frontier; still others are just beyond the frontier: 'beyond his grasp but within his reach'.

The frontier obviously varies from person to person: some have very little in the way of skills, understandings and personal resources; some have much more. Most though not all persons have the capacity to move beyond current frontiers. For many it is important to try, for the current frontier is dysfunctional, unsatisfying, gets them into trouble or is dangerous to others.

The second concept or idea is 'preoccupying concern'. By 'preoccupying concern' I mean any issue, worry or situation which at a given time occupies most of a person's horizon and is never far from his thoughts. Usually such a preoccupation arises in response to some event or circumstance which is new to the person, which lies outside his life experience so far and for which his experiences to date have not prepared him. He may feel beset by worries or concerns which are more than he can manage or which are managed only at great cost. He may feel and be immobilized and may have lost his sense of being able to cope. A preoccupying concern may have been precipitated by a particular event such as the birth of a handicapped child or an accident which leaves a person with some loss of faculty. Sometimes a preoccupying concern can involve an event which has not yet occurred: for example, anticipated surgery or anticipated entry into an old people's home. An event could be positively sought after and anticipated with pleasure (for example, marriage or emigration) and still be a preoccupying concern. A preoccupying concern soaks up time and energy, and often confronts an individual with tasks or feelings which are beyond his current coping capacities.

Thinking in terms of frontier and preoccupying concern allows one to define 'benefit' as moving beyond the current frontier (or sometimes holding on to a current frontier in the face of threat) and/or facing and coping more satisfactorily with the preoccupying concern.

With respect to frontier, persons will benefit from experiences which facilitate movement into the area 'just beyond' their frontiers. If a situation generates experiences which are too far within a person's frontier he is wasting his time for he is investing time and effort in seeking to acquire what he already has. If a situation generates experiences which are too far beyond his frontier it will either intimidate him, fail to engage him or prove irrelevant to him. With respect to preoccupying concern, persons will benefit if they can face the concern, think through its implications and mobilize their energies to deal with it. They will not benefit from working on some issue remote from the preoccupying concern nor from being pressed to focus on the concern at a time when they are likely to be overwhelmed by doing so.

Whilst the discussion in the preceding paragraph has emphasized movement and change, it should be noted that for some persons under some circumstances the preferred state consists of not losing ground, that is, of maintaining their current state in the face of some threat. In such instances one is aiming not for change, but for helping persons to hang on to current personal resources and skills in the face of potential deterioration or retreat.

Each of the population categories listed earlier can be thought about in terms of frontier and sometimes also in terms of preoccupying concern. From this, one can consider whether or not a group is likely to be a useful and usable route towards achieving benefit, and if so, the kind of group experience likely to be suitable.

Category 1: Persons who have been functioning adequately and who would be regarded as 'normal' by ordinary standards but who now face some threat to life or identity

Included within this category are persons facing major surgery or debilitating illness, amputees, burns victims, victims of natural disasters, and the like. This category includes those persons to whom a catastrophic or devastating event has already occurred and who are thereby facing a changed future whose principal features can be predicted, and those persons for whom the catastrophic event has not yet occurred but can be anticipated.

With respect to those for whom the catastrophic event has already occurred, we require some understanding of what the catastrophic event is and how persons in general are likely to respond to such events. The catastrophic events being considered here all involve some form of loss: in a specific sense, loss of health, sight, mobility etc.; in a more basic sense, loss of one's former self. The loss has already occurred and is finite (i.e. not progressive). The future is definable in that it requires the person to somehow carry on in the face of the loss. The crucial feature of such losses is the assault on basic identity. The person cannot afterwards be exactly the same person that he was before, yet it also is true to say that he is the same person that he was before. His key task is to acknowledge the character and consequences of the loss whilst at the same time maintaining a sense of continuity of self in the face of irrecoverable loss. Such losses are a form of bereavement and the responses which one expects of persons are analogous to those which follow bereavement. The literature on loss (Janis, 1969; Parkes, 1972; Maris, 1974) suggests that reactions to such losses move, at a varying pace and with temporary regressions, through a series of phases from shock, immobilization, often disbelief and denial, followed by a period of working on and working through the loss which can lead to a reconstitution of identity and often a different but in some degree satisfying lifestyle. The working-through phase includes confronting the feelings of sadness, rage, despair, possibly relief, possibly unrealistic hopes for the future which may arise in response to the loss. It involves confronting the task of revising previously established lifestyles which cannot now be maintained, relinquishing certain cherished activities, standing in a different relationship perhaps with those to whom the person has been closest, and the overriding task of finding ways of maintaining a sense of identity, of self-esteem and of usefulness in the face of drastically changed circumstances.

What is the next most needed or useful experience for persons who have sustained this kind of loss? In the period when shock predominates and the person is likely to feel immobilized and drained of energy, he principally needs protection, support and opportunities to ventilate and repeatedly tell his story as often as he wishes. Such opportunities help a person to emerge from the period of shock. Once the person has emerged from this stage he may need further opportunities to tell his story but also needs to look toward the future, begin to imagine himself in it and begin to make plans and decisions.

When considering whether a group can be expected to provide a useful experience for a person who has sustained this form of loss, I suggest that a group is not suitable whilst he is in a stage of shock but could be quite useful to him once he begins to emerge from it. During the period in which shock predominates the individual does not have access to his full range of defences and coping devices. He is likely to fall back on such defences as denial, distancing himself from the event or clinging to unrealistic fantasies about the future. He is not yet in the position to confront the implications of the loss and to press him to do so in a way which does not take close and careful account of his immediate defensive requirements is a disservice to him. In a group, where much sharing, confronting and supporting one another in facing the implications of loss are likely to occur, there is no way for the conductor, other group members or often the person himself to protect him from the invasion of essential defences. The task of seeing a person through the period of shock can best, in my opinion, be undertaken in a one-to-one situation, where the helper has more direct control over events. He is in a position to note, moment by moment, what the person is and is not ready for, and can introduce comments and interventions closely in line with where the individual shows himself to be. In a group one has less control over what comes at a person as stimuli, and on these grounds it can be argued that a group experience should be avoided during the period immediately following loss.

On the other hand, a group can be very useful to a person who shows signs of emerging from the initial period of shock and now needs opportunities to reflect and to face the likely realities of a changed future. Here, some of the phenomena likely to occur in groups can facilitate this process. For example, exploring feelings associated with the catastrophic event and beginning to anticipate the future is facilitated by sharing and comparing with persons in a like situation. Sharing and comparing supports the defining and redefining of the self. Getting fears out where they can be looked at facilitates the reality-testing of fears and arms one for the future. The support from others which one can gain in a group ('I felt the same way'; 'If you stick with it you are likely to feel

better after a bit'; and the like) can also be useful. The confrontation with reality which a group can provide by exposing over-
optimism or avoidance puts a person in a better position to make
realistic plans. A group experience can also reduce an individual's
sense of isolation and of facing a uniquely difficult future. He can
express his concerns about the consequences of his loss and find
that others share them. He can see displayed in front of him the
diverse ways in which different persons facing the same situation
see their future and ways of coping with it. All of this suggests
that a group can be of considerable use in the working-through
stage.

Having come to this view, the next question has to do with the
sort of group and leadership approach most likely to provide a
useful experience. Several possibilities come to mind. Consider,
as an example, amputees who have recovered from the most
serious effects of physical trauma and who have emerged sufficiently from a state of shock to the point of being able to talk and
exchange with others. Perhaps they are still undergoing physio-
therapy or are learning to use prostheses, but are nearly ready to
be discharged from hospital. Several kinds of groups could be
beneficial: a time-limited open discussion group; a time-limited
series of sessions structured in terms of directed discussion and
role-playing; or a time-limited group organized around providing
information and practice in needed new skills. It seems right that
any group planned for such a population should be time-limited,
for while there are advantages to sharing reactions with others in
a like situation one does not want to encourage the establishment
of a revised identity built too closely on the handicap itself. If one
thinks of the first alternative – a time-limited open discussion
group – then one might provide for six or eight sessions for five
or six persons. The common preoccupying concern is likely to
carry the members quite quickly into telling their stories to one
another and moving on from there. One would wish to have
a preliminary individual interview with each person considered
potentially suitable, to provide an opportunity for him to opt out
if he is too threatened by the prospect of a group, or doesn't need
it because he has other forms of help available or proves to be
still in a state of shock. Once the group is assembled one would
probably start by saying something like 'This group has been set
up to give you an opportunity to talk to others in a comparable
position about whatever is concerning you now or what you expect

to happen in the near future.' One then sits back and waits for the discussion to develop, coming in either to help the members across blocks to the discussion or to make use of the material which emerges. One would try to facilitate exploring and sharing, at the same time seeing to it that each person retains in his own hands the decisions as to when and how to participate. Such a group takes on the character of a short-term psychotherapeutic group.

A second possible structure is a time-limited series devoted to directed discussion and role-playing. One might plan for four to six sessions. In the first session one might ask the group members to tell as much as they wish about how the accident occurred. In the second session they might be asked to discuss how each person feels about his current situation and who and what he expects to encounter upon leaving the hospital. The third session (or the third, fourth and fifth if the series is to be a longer one) might then be devoted to rehearsing through role-playing the encounters which members have indicated as likely and problematic. A final session might be reserved for dealing with 'left-over' issues. It will be seen that this is a more highly structured form of group than the first one.

A third alternative – a time-limited group organized around providing information and practising needed skills – could be contained within four or five sessions, and could include a selection from the following: a demonstration of caring for the prosthesis, a talk from someone who had suffered a similar loss a year previously, an outside speaker on government benefits for the handicapped, practice in carrying out customary activities with the prosthesis or devising new ways of doing so, replanning one's house or flat, taking practice trips outside the hospital, etc. Such a group is orientated toward practical issues, not the expression or sharing of feelings and experiences, but should be planned with some unallocated or loosely structured time (for example following input from a speaker) so that should anyone wish to use the group for such purposes he or she has an opportunity to do so. A leader who has this kind of group in mind has two choices: he can plan the sessions himself, or he can use the first session to engage in joint planning with the participants, placing alternative possibilities before the group but leaving it to members to suggest further possibilities and to choose amongst them. The latter has the advantage of placing control over events back into the hands of persons who are likely to have experienced a reduced sense of mastery or control. Once a structure is decided upon, the leader's task is to work within it, as discussion leader or master of ceremonies, as required.

These are alternative ways of using groups for the population concerned. Each could work. The structures are different and demand different leadership behaviours and styles. The first requires a conductor to provide a brief introduction (not always so easy) and then requires of him the readiness to sit back in order to allow the members time to develop the discussion. The conductor then needs to be ready to enter in, sometimes to facilitate the group getting across blockages and sometimes to utilize or emphasize the points being made for the benefit of individual members. The second alternative involves the conductor in more detailed pre-planning. Once the group starts his task is to use the structure but at the same time be ready to modify it if the group can't use it or if issues come up which the structure cannot contain (suppose one has planned a role-play and no one is willing to participate in it). The third alternative requires skills in helping a group to plan: encouraging the expression of opinion, testing consensus and the like. It also requires moving a group through a series of structured activities, keeping to time, leading the discussion where the structure calls for this, etc. All three alternatives require the conductor to be an active listener, alert to what is emerging, to signs that the structure can or cannot be used, ready to deal with the unexpected. Some conductors will feel a lessened sense of control over the situation in the first alternative and on these grounds may prefer not to use it. Note that the three alternatives require different patterns of activity from the conductor, and require him to be active or inactive at different times.

Category 1 also includes persons who are anticipating a catastrophic event which has not yet occurred: those who are facing major surgery, a debilitating illness, a terminal illness, and the like. The literature on bereavement and loss is again relevant and to this I would add Janis's (1958) work on persons facing surgery in which he develops the idea of 'the work of worrying'. Janis concludes that persons are in an optimum position to face surgery if they worry appropriately: that is, neither so much as to be immobilizing nor so little as to fail to anticipate reasonably realistically the experience which is to come. One must use the term 'reasonably realistically' in that while persons 'know' that they are facing surgery, or a debilitating illness, etc., they do not know such critical things as how much pain there will be, how much disability will result, how quickly the disabling illness will progress, and the like. Persons anticipating a looming threat are facing an unknowable and unpredictable chronic crisis with recurring experiences of loss and attendant shock. The next most useful experience is one which facilitates the work of worrying, in a way which is tolerable to (i.e. not devastating for) the persons concerned.

Can a group provide this? Groups certainly are used for persons in such situations. It is my opinion that while a group experience can be useful much thought should be given to individual circumstances before encouraging any particular person to join a group. A person's state of readiness needs to be judged closely, and the real possibility that a group could confront him with more than he can cope with thoroughly acknowledged and respected. For some persons, one-to-one support may well provide the next most useful experience. For other persons, contact with others in a comparable situation can lend support and courage in facing what is to come and in taking active steps on their own behalf. For example, patients may use the group to give one another permission to know more or to avoid knowing more about their illness; they might lend one another courage in confronting doctors; they might help one another to plan for their families; and so on.

A potentially useful group structure is one which allows each member to regulate his own exposure to the group. For example, one might provide a place and time in a hospital ward for a group to meet and then make it very clear (and mean it) that potential members have the option of attending or not. In other words, one creates the opportunity for persons in like circumstances to share and exchange but at the same time places permeable boundaries around the group such that individuals can come or not, or having come can withdraw again with no loss of face and no pressure on them to remain in the group. The underlying assumption is that persons will know or sense when contact with the group will be useful and when it will be too much to tolerate.

Looking back over this category as a whole it would appear that preoccupying concern is a more salient factor than frontier. The preoccupying concern is clear and defined. It overrides frontier in that a wide range of frontiers can be accommodated within the same group.

Category 2: Persons who have been functioning adequately and who would be regarded as 'normal' by ordinary standards but who are in linked-fate relationship with one or more others and who are experiencing special stress in consequence of this

Included are such persons as parents of mentally handicapped children, prisoners' wives, adolescent children of alcoholic parents, and the like. Such persons are likely to face similar problems, undergo similar experiences, be confronted with similar pressures. For example, they might be pressed into an unremitting caretaking role, feel stigmatized, be forced into assuming unfamiliar and unwanted responsibilities, or be faced with fewer resources in time or money than before.

These communalities amount to likely similarities in preoccupying concern, and make a group with its opportunities for ventilation, social comparison, and practical help and advice a potentially useful experience. At the same time individual differences need to be recognized. If the linked-fate situation is of recent onset, then the individual may be in a state of crisis and display the same response sequence as that already described for persons in category 1. If the linked-fate relationship has been in existence for some time the person may be in one of several positions: he may have come to terms with his situation and found ways of dealing with it such that he does not need help from any source; he may have settled into a way of dealing with it which is not ideal in the sense that it carries some dysfunctional consequences but which is nevertheless well established (for example, certain forms of denial); he may have a solution in sight but lack the material resources (money or other) to put it into practice; he may have hit upon a preferred solution which requires the co-operation of others to come into being; or he may be in a chronic state of grief, distress or disarray.

It is immediately apparent that the next most needed or useful experience will be different for persons in these different positions. Some neither need nor want help from a group. Some need to be directed towards sources of material support. Some could benefit from a group which works collaboratively toward some shared external goal; some could benefit from a therapeutically orientated group in which opportunities to ventilate, share and examine the realities of their situation are provided; some could benefit from a group designed to provide practical advice and social support.

To summarize, a group could be beneficial for those for whom the next most useful experience is either sharing and working on own feelings *or* advice and know-how in management *or* arranging for mutual services *or* coming together to effect change in the outside world.

Let us take the parents of a mentally handicapped child as examples. Alternative possibilities include: a time-limited psychotherapeutic group, a self-help group or a social-action group.

A time-limited psychotherapeutic group, of about twelve to fifteen sessions, would most probably be presented as an opportunity for parents to discuss and share with one another experiences with and problems concerning or related to their children. Such groups almost invariably also include giving and getting advice and managing, disciplining and training the child, of the 'Have you tried . . .?' variety. Some such groups keep strictly to discussing the child but others range farther into general family relationships, impact on the marriage, impact on other siblings, and so on.

A second possibility is a self-help group where the group is seen as going on indefinitely but where it is understood that the leader's role is a temporary one to help the members establish a structure which can then stand on its own. Members of such groups may decide to exchange services, provide time off, arrange outings for the children, and in general provide mutual support. The group worker's agreement with the members can be quite explicit: 'I expect to meet with you for the first five sessions only. That will give us enough time to work out some plans so that the group can carry on on its own if the members wish.' Sometimes it is helpful for a leader to remain available as a consultant after the initial period and this too can be made explicit at the beginning.

A third possibility is an action group whose efforts are directed towards effecting some change in the outside world. Perhaps the parents wish to campaign for better play facilities in their neighbourhood, or for the inclusion of handicapped children in ordinary schools, or for an increase in government benefits, or perhaps they wish to create a better understanding of the needs of such children in the general public.

Groups organized as primarily therapeutic, primarily self-help or primarily social action groups do not always stay within these boundaries. They may each maintain their principal thrust, but at the same time generate particular side-benefits. The central focus of one kind of group becomes the side-benefit or spin-off of another. For example, a social action group directed towards informing the public about certain forms of handicap can at the same time provide for quite a lot of discharge of feeling ('We want them to *know*').

It is possible to work out what kind of group might be suitable for whom through preliminary individual interviews. Or one might decide on the kind of group (or groups, if one were prepared to conduct several at the same time) one has in mind, and then recruit members by open invitation, for example to all the parents who bring their children to an assessment centre or clinic. The description of the group needs to be full and accurate, for one is relying on self-selection, and the parents need to know enough about the character of the group to make choices that seem right to them.

The three types of group just described require different styles of leadership. The first places the conductor in the stance of a therapist who facilitates the emergence of feelings and concerns of importance to the members and then attempts to utilize these for their benefit. The second and third alternatives involve the conductor in the role of consultant, facilitator or manager. As consultant, he tries to help the members to think through their own purposes and to erect a structure which suits them. The conductor's role in such a group may involve him in a certain amount of teaching or modelling – for example if he sees that the group needs to test consensus, he might say something like: 'We had better not go any further with this until we are sure everyone agrees to it.' By such a comment he both helps the group directly and offers a model for effective working. In the third kind of group the conductor's task may carry him beyond the boundaries of the group into negotiating with other groups on its behalf, or preparing group members for doing so.

Category 3: Persons experiencing or anticipating some life transition

This category includes recently divorced persons, persons entering or leaving an institution, recent immigrants, etc.

Both research and theory tell us that transitions, whether self-sought or imposed, typically confront persons with both stresses and opportunities for growth (Golan, 1981). In the terms being used here, the transition itself is the preoccupying concern, and preoccupying concern is thus bound to be a salient factor. Frontier may also be important, as for example when persons experiencing the transition of leaving an institution are mentally handicapped adults or long-stay psychiatric hospital patients. In such instances the transition is the preoccupying concern but frontier must also be taken into account.

Persons in a transition or facing one need an opportunity to talk out their feelings about the transition, think their way into a changed status or situation, and if possible retain control over the manner and pace of the transition. Some may profit from opportunities to identify and learn new skills which may be required, or from support through the transition period. They may need help in finding ways to replace or partially replace what they lose in consequence of undergoing the transition, and in fully exploiting what it is possible to gain from it.

Consider one or two examples. A group of men have recently retired and are now attending a day centre. In addition to the usual social and other activities offered, they might be invited to join a time-limited, four- or five-session group designed to encourage understanding of the transition they are experiencing and to facilitate planning for the future. The sessions might well be highly structured in terms of a combination of tasks and discussion. Suppose that in the first session they are asked to generate two lists: first: 'things I liked best about my job and miss most'; second: 'things I disliked about my job and am glad to be rid of'. Discussion and sharing of the first list can lead to a more explicit acknowledgment of what the person has lost: perhaps opportunities to exercise a skill, social contacts, the satisfaction of having a structured day with built-in signals of what constitutes productiveness. Discussion of the second list can bring into the open what has been gained. The task is really one of analysing or factoring out what was important about what has been lost and gained by reason of the transition. Once this has been done, a task for session 2 might be to review a typical weekday now that the person has retired. Again two lists might be generated by each person: 'what I enjoy' and 'what I don't like or what bores me'. From such lists both the persons concerned and the others in the group develop a sense of the person's preferred lifestyle. A third collaborative task might involve thinking through the activities and choices now available to the individual, with the aim of finding functional equivalents to the valued lost experiences whilst at the same time avoiding those the person is glad to leave behind him. Subsequent sessions could then be devoted to supporting persons in trying out new activities. While it is possible to conduct this kind of analysis and do this kind of planning through one-to-one consultation, there are certain advantages to using a group. For example, sharing feelings and experiences and offering and receiving views, opinions and encouragement can alleviate isolation and help persons to find their way into a new social group; it can help them to hold on to or strengthen a sense of identity through processes of social comparison; and it can provide experiences of helping and being of service to others. If, as is generally assumed, retirement is a dislocating experience for many, which can involve an assault on self-esteem and sense of identity, then these further benefits are substantial.

Another example within this category is that of the recently arrived immigrant. Many immigrants do not need a planned group because in the course of finding a job or joining relatives who have preceded them they enter natural groups which support them in handling the transition and adapting to the new culture. However many immigrants do not have such opportunities and for them a planned group could be useful. Take as an example a group of women who are wives and mothers. The next most useful experience might be one which provides information about how things are done in this new country and what is ordinarily expected, and how what was important to them in the old setting might be preserved in the new one. Without information about the new setting the person typically does not know what to worry about, so worries about everything, or deals with the new situation by seeking isolation. A group can look at 'how things are done here' and 'how things were done there'. If both these kinds of information are available in the arena of the group, then comparisons between the previous and the new cultures can be made and the transition better understood and coped with. The conductor of such a group must receive as well as give information; seek to understand the culture from which the women came as well as inform them about the new culture. The group thus becomes very much a matter of shared learning. Since one usually finds out about a new culture by stubbing one's toes on it, opportunities to talk about what puzzles or confuses, what alarms or horrifies and what amuses are sure to be useful. A possible variation on this kind of group is to compose the group of three or four immigrants and three or four natives, with the instruction to 'learn all you can about one another's countries'. The task of the conductor then is to guide the discussion.

Category 4: Persons who are functioning adequately from the point of view of an outside observer but who are anxious or depressed, functioning below their capacity or behaving repeatedly in self-defeating ways

Persons in this category often seek psychotherapeutic help voluntarily. Sometimes they describe themselves as being concerned about some particular issue: for example, failure to establish or maintain satisfying close relationships, intractable overweight, persistent failure to carry through work projects, repetitive nightmares, etc. etc. It is frequently the case, however, that the concerns presented initially, while real enough, fade into the background once therapy is underway, to be replaced by initially unstated but more cogent issues, or else the presenting concern takes its place within a wider pattern of self-defeating behaviours or problem-ridden relationships. Sometimes persons describe themselves in a less specific way, complaining of purposelessness, a sense of unacceptability, or a vague sense of unfulfilment. The common characteristic of such persons is a sense of the unyielding nature of their situation: either they are at a loss as to what to do or try, or else no matter what they do or how hard they try, they are still stuck with the same problem.

'Preoccupying concern' does not appear to be a useful concept to apply to this population. Although there may *be* preoccupying concerns, they are likely to be diverse and may fall into the background quickly once persons move into some therapeutic endeavour. The concept of 'frontier' is more applicable. If the dilemma is not being able to make use of their considerable resources on their own behalf, then this marks the frontier which needs to be crossed. From a current state where their own resources are inaccessible, such persons need to move to a preferred state where they can make use of them.

The most useful next step for such persons is an experience which will unlock the inaccessible capacities so that the person is released to take steps on his own behalf toward his own life goals. The next most needed experience (I would say) is a corrective emotional experience. This notion is embedded in a particular conceptual model which posits underlying intrapersonal and interpersonal dynamics which maintain patterns of self-defeating behaviour. The assumption is that the behaviour, however unsatisfying and self-defeating, is nevertheless functional in some important sense for the person concerned. Being grossly overweight, for example, though desperately unwanted, is preferable to some other state, unknown but greatly feared, which would be even worse. The unwanted characteristic or interpersonal pattern acts as a solution to some dilemma and is held in place by fear: fear of the consequences of yielding it up. The corrective emotional experience involves facing previously avoided feelings or experiences and thus testing out in action whether or not the feared consequence will in fact occur. Typically, the feared consequence does not occur or else does not occur in so massive a form as expected, or occurs and is bearable (survivable). By any of these routes, the unwanted characteristic or interpersonal pattern is shown to be unnecessary to psychological survival. Repeated testings (called 'working-through') confirm this, and the individual arrives at a position where he can yield up the behaviour if he wishes to (as he usually does).

A corrective emotional experience can (potentially) be achieved in psychoanalysis, in individual psychotherapy or in group psychotherapy. It is a process which takes time, and therefore one generally needs to think in terms of an extended series of sessions, perhaps of indefinite tenure, or else a generously time-limited group with a built-in agreement to assess each person's situation and arrange for a further series, and more beyond that if needed.

If such persons are brought into a group its management requires of the conductor a willingness to allow associative material to emerge from the group, which means a relatively inactive stance for much of the time and being prepared to hold back and not do the group's work for it. It also involves being prepared to be active in two major ways: first, intervening in order to help the group to be a facilitating environment (which means fertile ground for the corrective emotional experience to take place), and second, intervening on behalf of persons in the group to prepare the way for the corrective emotional experience, to nail it down and point to it when it comes, and to assist in the working-through which follows.

Category 5: Persons experiencing serious breakdowns in functioning or just beginning to emerge from such a breakdown

This category includes the acutely depressed, anxious, phobic, withdrawn, delusional, disorganized or fragmented person. Some of these persons display active psychotic symptoms and some do not. For some, their present state will be a first breakdown from previously adequate levels of functioning. For others it may be the most recent of successive breakdowns. For still others the failure in functioning has become apparent when they have not been able to take up the activities or fulfil the life tasks which their increasing chronological age leads others to expect of them. This population varies also with respect to likely prognosis. Some will regain previous levels of adequate functioning, or even improve on previous levels. Others continue to deteriorate, perhaps stabilizing in a state which makes life outside an institution difficult to maintain. Although very diverse, the persons in this category have in common the fact that they cannot, at least for the time being, maintain even a semblance of living, loving and working in their ordinary environments.

For this population it does not seem profitable to think in terms of preoccopying concern. There may be such concerns, but as with the previous category they will be highly idiosyncratic and do not easily form a focus for thinking about the next most needed experience. Frontier is a more useful concept. The frontier is the current level of functioning. What lies just beyond the frontier (and which one hopes is graspable) is the re-establishment or the development of capacities to enter into and find satisfaction in relationships with others and in work. I use the term 'one hopes' because for this population it is very hard to predict whether or not movement can be achieved. One's purpose in working with such persons is to provide them with every opportunity to mobilize such strengths as they possess on their own behalf.

Some persons in this category will be in a florid state and should not be taken into groups. They are unlikely to profit from a group experience and if they prove impossible to contain they will interfere with gains which others might otherwise achieve. However, florid states do not last forever, and persons emerging from such states can be considered potential group members along with others in this category.

I believe that the most useful kind of group for this population is a time-limited group of fifteen to thirty sessions, with an understanding that each person's situation will be reviewed at that time, and the possibilities held open of either discontinuing therapy, continuing in a group, or shifting to some other form of help or support. The reason for preferring such a structure is the difficulty in predicting from the individual's present state his capacity for reconstitution and growth. A group can be a testing ground for this, for the individual will show by his behaviour whether he can make good, partial, or no use of the situation. Even if the latter proves to be the case something is achieved by providing the group therapist or worker with a much fuller understanding of the person and hence with a better basis for making recommendations on his behalf.

In a therapeutic group of the open-discussion sort, there will be opportunities for ventilating about the events which led to the breakdown or the hospitalization, opportunities for reaching out to others, for being of help to others, for comparing own views of self and the world with that of others, for developing capacities for listening to and communicating with others, for thinking through ways of reorganizing a lifestyle if this seems necessary or useful, for testing out new behaviours in the group, etc. For some, experiences which can properly be called 'corrective emotional experiences' may occur.

The following variation of this structure is useful in institutional settings where the average length of stay is such that a group cannot easily maintain its membership over thirty sessions. In order to avoid a continually revolving door one can set up a group which meets twice a week for (say) seven or eight weeks as a closed group, tolerating drop-outs if they occur and not bringing new persons in, and then reconstituting the group for a further seven or eight weeks, retaining some members from the previous series and adding others to bring it up to strength again. The reconstituted group again goes on for a further seven or eight weeks and then is again reconstituted.

For many groups established with persons in this category the conductor's style can usefully be much the same as that adopted for category 4. However, if the composition is drawn from the more damaged or withdrawn end of the spectrum the conductor is likely to find that if he wishes to rely on open discussion, he must become more active in particular ways. If some personal resources and interpersonal skills are missing in the group the conductor will have to provide them. For example, he may have to play an active role in establishing links between one patient's offerings and another (he may frequently need to make interventions like 'John is telling us he felt depressed this week when he failed to get a job. Has anyone else had moments of feeling badly?') In other words in this sort of group the conductor cannot rely on the members listening to one another and building upon one another's offerings and therefore must be prepared (if he intends to rely on open discussion) to create and display these links himself. If the members are very anxious he may have to participate more of the time – not to reassure in any simplistic sense but to show by his behaviour that he is there and listening. If the group is disorderly and undisciplined he may have to be prepared to tell specific persons to be still, to listen, to allow someone to talk, etc. If one or more group members produce delusional material it will be useful if he can help members to pierce the possibly bizarre material and understand its import for the person(s) concerned.

Faced with this population, a therapist or group worker might decide not to rely on open discussion but to utilize a different structure: topic-oriented discussion, for example, or activity groups in which events-in-action can be used from time to time to underline issues of importance to individuals. These more highly structured groups provide a framework within which psychologically fragile persons may feel safe enough to operate. Such groups can be constructed to include escape hatches in the form of sanctioned absences or insulation from others through absorption in some activity.

Category 6: Persons who have lost or who have never acquired basic social or interpersonal skills, or skills of living

This category includes those who have become 'institutionalized' through long periods of living within a psychiatric hospital; those of low intellectual ability; those who for some reason have missed out on opportunities to acquire ordinary skills of living.

For this population, there often is no identifiable preoccupying concern, but there is a frontier. The 'just beyond' area includes a set of practical and interpersonal skills which if acquired could allow for independent or semi-independent living. The next most useful experience is one which facilitates the acquisition of such skills. As with the previous category, this population may include those who have already reached their limit and for whom no further progress can realistically be expected. It may also include those who can move substantially beyond their current frontier. As with the previous category, some persons will benefit from a group experience and some will not, but it may be difficult to predict this from observing present levels of functioning. The group, as before, becomes both an opportunity and a testing ground.

Persons in this category are likely to benefit from groups which have an educational or semi-educational character, in which skills are taught, demonstrated and practised. The skills may be practical ones or may centre around managing interpersonal encounters. The skills-learning aspects can be built into and around a social group or club, or into a structured series of sessions.

As one example, consider five or six women known to a social work agency who maintain poor standards of care of their homes and children. They lack skills in meal planning, shopping and meal preparation. These women are invited to spend an afternoon a week at the agency, which has a meeting room, a kitchen and a play room for the children, whom the women are invited to bring along. The afternoon is mainly social in character – a chance to be free of the direct demands of young children – but it always includes the planning and preparation of a light meal which is then eaten by the women, the children and the leaders attached to the group. The women work at the meal in pairs or threes, with the leader or worker functioning as consultant. A form of teaching is undertaken, mainly through providing a model and stating as one goes the steps and decisions involved.

Another example might be long-stay psychiatric hospital patients no longer actively psychotic who are considered potentially capable of living outside the institution, but who for many years have not handled money, used public transportation or shopped for themselves. A series of eight, ten or twelve group sessions might be planned which begins by introducing the members to the actual physical objects which they will need to use and understand in order to carry out these skills of living – money, tins of food, etc. –, proceed from there to role-playing exercises which provide practice in talking to a shopkeeper, getting on a bus and so forth, and finish with a number of outings in which the skills are practised in real settings outside the hospital. As always, the population must be judged carefully: if the persons in the group have difficulty in maintaining boundaries between self and others, then pretending to be someone else, as in role-playing, could be inappropriate. It is best in such instances to move directly to tackling real situations.

There are many variations of such groups and they are not hard to plan if one has the frontier of the persons concerned clearly in mind. Such groups require quite a good deal of pre-planning on the part of the group leader, a willingness to direct and instruct, and a capacity for shifting one's approach if the detailed structure one has worked out proves unusable by the persons in the group or if events show that either more or less time needs to be given to particular parts of the sequence.

Category 7: Persons who characteristically and over very long periods of time – even a lifetime – function at some quite low and unsatisfactory level

This category includes some borderline persons, 'burnt-out' schizophrenics, persons with chronic non-specific somatic complaints, etc. They may include persons in the previous two categories for whom groups as well as other helping efforts have had no effect, and where helpers who have come to know them have concluded that further change or movement is unlikely. This population could include persons in psychiatric hospitals who are unlikely ever to leave them; ex-psychiatric hospital patients living permanently in hostels; drifters who periodically seek refuge in shelters; or alcoholics who repeatedly come to a detoxification centre. Many such persons need support but are unwilling to get too close to those who wish to provide it. Others cling dependently to their doctors and supporters and in the end come to be seen as pests and nuisances.

As with the previous category, preoccupying concern is not a relevant concept, but frontier is useful. The frontier is similar to that for persons in category 6 and for some of the persons in category 5. The difference is that the prognosis is poor and that while a 'next most useful step' can be identified, there is no evidence that the person can or will take it.

For such persons, groups which support, supply and literally or psychologically feed the members can be useful in maintaining them at their current levels of functioning, and can sometimes make life more satisfying and enjoyable even if nothing which can be called 'change' occurs. Sometimes a group can make the difference between such persons being able to maintain themselves outside an institution or not. Sometimes access to a group can forestall or shorten periods of even greater decompensation.

It will be clear that psychotherapeutic groups as usually understood and constructed are inappropriate because they make demands that are too far beyond the frontiers of members of such a population. Groups designed to raise the level of practical and interpersonal skills may have been tried without effect. Time-limited groups are of no use because such persons have already displayed an incapacity to maintain themselves without support. The appropriate group is of unlimited duration, possibly running into years, with permeable boundaries, so that each member can make as much or as little use of it as he or she wishes and can regulate for himself or herself frequency of attendance. Here are some examples.

An overcrowded psychiatric hospital ward had living in it sixty women who had been in the hospital for anything from four to thirty years. Some half-dozen or so were able to engage in conversation with the nurses and attendants at least some of the time; others hallucinated much of the time, a few were catatonic, and quite a number were senile. Many were incontinent. The nurses decided to try a group which would meet twice a week for an hour. Meetings were held in an alcove which was open to the ward and had a piano in it. The nurses invited five women to come to the group and four attended the first meeting. Some chairs were pulled out from their customary place along the wall and placed in the centre of the alcove. The meeting was held in full view of the other women in the ward and within the hearing of those who chose or happened to drift nearby. The nurses found they had to be very active, to ask questions about interests, to make suggestions, to seek expressions of feelings. Many such efforts bore no fruit. The group persisted, however, and now and then two things happened: first, flurries of activity occurred which were sustained over two or three meetings and sometimes led to plans for excursions outside the ward. Second, the numbers who attended gradually increased. Some of the other women on the ward drifted into the group and a few who had been thought to be altogether unaware of anything going on around them came to sit with the group, though they said nothing, ever. No one was pressed to come or censured when they did not. Attendance varied from four to as many as twelve or fifteen. The group persisted in this way for several years. The nurses were satisfied with the group even though only a few persons could be said to 'progress', even a little. One of the spin-offs of the group was the benefit which accrued for the nurses and attendants, who felt for the first time that their work with the patients was having some effect, even if infinitesimal. The impact on staff was to shift attitudes and behaviour away from an exclusive concern with custodial care. This is a true story and I tell it at some length because it is an example of group work with a population which many would regard as hopeless and unrewarding.

Another example: a number of patients were attached to an out-patient psychiatric unit, referred there because no physical basis could be found for chronic somatic complaints of dizziness, fatigue, headaches, etc. They were exceedingly demanding of the psychiatrists' time, but showed no discernible improvement after extended therapeutic effort. The psychiatrists and others who had contact with them became impatient and began to wish to avoid them. A 'Tuesday afternoon clinic' was set up and some ten or twelve persons were invited to attend. The clinic operated for two hours and during that time the patients were invited to make use of a waiting room which was furnished with comfortable chairs, and tea and biscuits were served. Two therapists, not always the same ones, were on call, and anyone who wished to see one would tell the receptionist on arrival, and a twenty- to thirty-minute individual session was provided. While waiting for the therapist patients chatted to one another and ate biscuits and drank tea. Some patients came for the whole two hours and some for only part of it; some came every time, others only occasionally or for runs of sessions; some asked to speak to a psychiatrist and others did not, contenting themselves with social chat. Reliance on and a sense of support from the clinic seemed to develop, and the patients did not seem to mind seeing different therapists at different times. The patients' need for support, contact and emotional supply seemed to be met by this arrangement, and the burden on the therapists was much reduced. The group was continuous and was expected by all to be a permanent arrangement.

A final example: every morning in a detoxification unit those residents who were physically able to do so attended a forty-five-minute meeting first thing in the morning. During this meeting newcomers were greeted and introduced, and familiar faces who were in yet again for drying out were welcomed. The meeting was devoted to discussing how the various persons intended to use their day – either by participating in some of the activities provided at the centre or by trying for a job or making outside visits. The meetings were set up to be planning meetings, individually geared, and never looked beyond the day itself. Membership varied day by day though there were many repeaters. The group seemed to provide social contact, encouragement to make and carry out a plan for the day, and a sense of being known and supported by the staff of the clinic.

Many variations of these deliberately interminable groups can be designed, in such a way as to lend strength, support and some enhancement of life satisfaction to the members whilst not overburdening the staff responsible.

With respect to all of the populations discussed so far, one can reasonably make the assumption that the benefits which one has in mind as an outsider, as a member of one of the helping professions *looking at* a population, will coincide, near enough, with the benefits which those same persons are likely to wish to procure for themselves. Whatever language one uses to oneself to define 'benefit' for a population, one can imagine stating the benefits one has in mind in plain language likely to make sense to the persons concerned. One also assumes that the *route* one has in mind – i.e., the kind of group experience – will seem plausible to those concerned. In instances where one cannot be sure that a particular kind of group experience will seem a plausible route toward benefit one can build choice into one's plan such that prospective members can choose or devise experiences for themselves. Another way of putting this is to say that although the planning is being done by the prospective conductor of a group and therefore must be done on the basis of *his* judgments and opinions about a population, one of the factors which he takes into account is his best guess about what persons in the population can acknowledge about what they want for themselves, and his best guess as to what they will see as reasonable and potentially useful rather than irrelevant, impossible, or bizarre. Later on in the course of planning, when specific persons are identified as possible members for a group, one can check this out directly with them. At this point one has to rely on one's own best judgment, based usually on previous experience with the population.

One further population category is to be considered:

Category 8: Persons who are regarded as problems by others because they are disruptive, unruly, break laws, offend commonly held standards, or are destructive in their relationships, but who do not see themselves as having problems and who do not seek help of their own volition

Persons in this category might include violent offenders, unruly adolescents, parents suspected of physically harming their children, and the like.

With respect to persons in this category, one cannot assume that one's own ideas about what is needed, about what will constitute 'benefit', will be acceptable to and make sense to members of the population. In fact, one can assume the opposite: that they will either see no problem at all attached to themselves or their situation, or else that they will have wishes and hopes different from or at variance with those which a worker or therapist thinks they should have. Given this gulf, one certainly cannot make the further assumption that a group which is planned on the basis of one's own views about benefit is likely to seem plausible to the persons concerned. Such persons are commonly said to be 'unmotivated', which usually means that they don't want to engage in the kind of group which the conductor regards as potentially useful.

I have made the point earlier that a frontier can be identified for everyone. It follows that one can identify 'frontier' for persons falling into this category, whether one is thinking of the adolescent of low intelligence who has offended unskilfully and almost unwittingly and is now angry and resentful at finding himself in a correctional institution, or the able young executive or engineer whose friends are concerned about his increasingly bizarre behaviour but who himself sees nothing wrong, or the teacher who successfully rationalizes his destructive impact on his pupils, or the parent with an explosive temper whose children are at risk.

With respect to this population category there is a preoccupying concern but it is not located in the prospective patient or client. It is located in the therapist, social worker, colleague or friend – the person who is suffering, sees others suffering, or who is aware of problems which the person concerned does not recognize. Those who can be said to have a preoccupying concern are in a difficult and usually frustrating position, for they may feel that if only they could get the person into some form of help, some good might come of it, for that person and for others. This leads to the commonly held view, which I shall later challenge, that it is necessary to 'motivate' people.

Supposing one makes the assumption that a group could benefit such a person if only he or she would come into it, and supposing one is right. What then? For some persons in this category there is no way to bring them into groups or into any other kind of helping relationship. The patterns of behaviour, the lifestyle, the way in which the self is seen, the structure of defences preclude this. The persons concerned may receive any suggestion that help is needed as ludicrous or offensive.

Persons in this category are sometimes brought into groups through coercion, persuasion or deception.

Coercion can occur when the therapist group worker or institution has real power over the persons concerned and can require them to attend groups. For example, a drug abuser has committed an offence and has been given a choice by the court between a prison term and a treatment centre. He 'chooses' the treatment centre. Or, an adolescent offender is placed on a probation order by the court and happens to live in an area where supervision is carried out through the use of groups. Or, a docile and uncomprehending long-stay psychiatric hospital patient is told by a psychiatrist to go along to a group and does so. None of these persons sees the point of a group nor would they enter it voluntarily.

Persuasion can be no more than a seemingly more gentle form of coercion. The conductor's power in this case is his presumed greater experience or expertise. Coercion and persuasion may well bring persons into a group but they cannot guarantee that those persons will engage usefully in the group experience. In fact, resentments and fears may be stirred up which make useful engagement unlikely.

Deception occurs when the conductor misrepresents to the potential member the nature of the group in the hope that once the person is in the group he will be able to make use of it as the conductor hopes. A not infrequent form of deception is that in which the group is represented as a social club or an activity programme while the conductor privately intends that it should have a therapeutic character. This form of deception is tempting when a therapist or worker is keen to include an 'unmotivated' client, but it is a mistake. At the very least the group leader and the members find themselves working at cross purposes on different assumptions about the character and point of the group. More seriously, such deceptions cannot by their nature be maintained and then the fact that deception has occurred interferes with the establishment of trust in the group.

In working with persons within this population category it is sometimes possible to start with a kind of group which makes sense to them rather than the kind of group the leader most wishes to establish. Most frequently this means starting (without reservations and with commitment) with a social group or some sort of discussion group. In the course of such a group interactions will occur among members and some spin-off benefits of the sort the leader hopes for may occur. It is useful to build into such a group a review period after a stated number of meetings, and at this point the conductor may put it to the group that some portion of their future time might be reserved for another kind of group effort. Having had some experience together the members may be more likely to see the point or at least be less puzzled or frightened.

Following the course of action just described does not involve 'motivating' the person. Urging a therapist to 'motivate' a person sounds like good advice until one thinks about it. Then one realizes that the actual process of 'motivating' someone tends to involve some form of coercion or deception. This often 'works' in the sense that some unmotivated persons come into groups. However, I consider that the consequences of coercion and deception are so likely to interfere with the effective use of the group that it should not be practised.

In the course of discussing these various population categories and the kinds of groups which might be planned for them, I have referred to the kinds of demands likely to be made on the therapists or workers concerned and the approach or leadership style likely to be required. Returning now to the issue of single or multiple leadership, it will be clear that one must take into account the nature of the group as well as the preferences of the staff persons concerned.

In my experience, in groups which rely on open discussion, members find it difficult to tolerate more than two therapists, or at the very most, two therapists and a non-participating observer who sits outside the circle of the group. This has to do with the kinds of fantasies which typically arise in groups about the presumed feelings and attitudes of the therapist, his power, and how he might use it. Certain fears – of being criticized or found unacceptable by the leader – often arise, and the patients or clients may then assume that the therapist will use his power to abandon or expel them, or simply disapprove. When such fears emerge, a group of seven or eight persons can easily feel outnumbered and intimidated by three conductors. If one anticipates that the group is to have this character, it is best to keep the number of staff involved down to two or one.

Other kinds of groups are planned to be somewhat larger and make use primarily of activities. For such groups three or even more conductors may be useful, particularly if the group is expected to work for part of the time in sub-groups, and if it is thought that the presence of a leader is required for each. Even so, one should think out with care just how many persons are really necessary. There is sometimes a tendency to oversupply a group with leaders, perhaps in the hope that disruptive or destructive interaction may thereby be forestalled. It is doubtful whether a multiplicity of leaders helps with such problems: it can make matters worse by communicating to the members that the leaders see the group as a potentially explosive place, or by intimidating the members by bringing in so many persons with power and authority.

One of the advantages of co-leadership, and it is a substantial one, is that someone is available with whom to talk about the group following each session who has shared in the experience. This can be a great facilitator of work with a group. Inevitably, there will be sessions where one or another or both of the conductors of the group feel confused, feel that they have failed to see the thrust and point of the discussion, consider that they have made errors or missed opportunities, and the like. The chance to talk over these issues is an invaluable source of clarification and support. A co-therapist or co-worker can also be helpful during the sessions themselves. What is missed by one may be detected by the other, and one conductor may subtly cue the other into noting important events in the group which he might otherwise miss. When one worker or therapist feels at a loss and withdraws the other may feel able to take responsibility. An error made by one may be retrieved by the other. These potential advantages cannot be achieved unless the two persons concerned trust one another and are reasonably congenial in their approach to the group. Providing these favourable conditions prevail, then co-leaders can gain a great deal from working together. They can feel free to reveal themselves to one another, make critical comments, confess to confusion, point to areas of disagreement and conflict, etc., without fear of being attacked or shamed and without the need for defensiveness. If this is not the case, then all of the potentially negative consequences of co-leadership are likely to emerge: during the sessions themselves each may see the other as 'spoiling' the group and leading it in undesirable directions. If the two conductors provide conflicting signals to the group, as they may well do, then the members themselves become confused and disoriented. If conflicts between the persons conducting the group remain unacknowledged, then their mutual hostility, mistrust or reserve will find a way to 'leak' into the group, with consequences which are both unrecognized and unintended, and which because of their covert character cannot easily be worked on. If the two leaders do not get on reasonably well together, post-group discussions are likely to be either sterile or conflict-ridden.

All of this clearly indicates that persons who are thinking of working together should make as certain as possible beforehand that they can trust one another and adopt reasonably compatible stances towards the group. They can do this during the planning stage through discussions in which they share their views about what they hope the group can accomplish, how they expect to function during the sessions, their attitudes towards a variety of possible problem persons and situations, and so forth. This will go a long way towards helping them to predict whether they can work usefully together. Later, during the actual operation of the group, it will be essential to engage in post-session discussions. If this is not done, private conceptualizations of events and inevitable points of conflict remain unexamined and the consequences for the group of using co-therapists or co-workers are likely to be negative rather than positive.

The question arises as to whether co-therapists or co-workers should agree to adopt different positions, roles or stances towards the group. If the two differ markedly in status or experience, this should be acknowledged between themselves and in the group. For example, if one is a student and the other an experienced therapist, then this should be acknowledged. (It will be apparent anyway and will influence how the two behave in the group, so it is best not to make it a secret.) They will need to agree which of them is to make any initial opening statement, and accept that whoever does this is likely to be seen as senior to the other. Beyond this, I believe that it accomplishes little to agree beforehand about who will do what, or take which attitude. In the event, the most powerful factor influencing this will be the flow of group events, not prior agreements. The most important differences between any two conductors will stem from how each experiences the events of the group, and how each is experienced by group participants.

Should one of the therapists be male and one female? It is sometimes assumed that this is an advantage, on the grounds that the group is more likely to simulate a family, or that participants will be exposed to wider opportunities for change if one male and one female person is available to relate to, or function as a transference figure. Sometimes one certainly sees participants using a male and female therapist in these ways. One also sees participants using therapists of the same sex differentially, for example, when one female therapist is seen as the mother and the other as a sexually attractive peer. It is an open question as to whether co-therapists need to be of different sexes or the same sex in order for such phenomena to emerge. Participants in groups seem to use the raw material available, and similar phenomena may well emerge regardless of the sex of the therapists. However, I know of no evidence for this, and opinions among therapists and workers differ on this point.

There is little else so unpleasant as trying to work with an uncongenial co-leader. I once worked with someone who proved to have an entirely different threshold from mine with regard to hostility. He regarded some of my interventions as unnecessarily cruel and potentially damaging to the members, while I considered the same comments as necessary and non-hostile statements about what was going on in the group. This led to numerous instances in which he tried to undo what he saw as the potentially damaging effects of my comments, whilst I felt frustrated and angry at seeing my efforts thus undermined. No amount of post-session discussion settled the issue and it proved impossible to work together.

It is also possible for two conductors to be so congenial, so like one another in thresholds and stance that they collude in avoiding particular issues in the group. Together, without at all realizing it, they restrict the issues or areas which may be explored in the group, and thus reduce its potential effectiveness. Co-leadership works best when the two leaders are clearly different persons, with different strengths and sensitivities, but where they share certain basic stances and values concerning the group. If such is the case then the group is more likely to be a generally useful experience for the participants, and becomes both a pleasure and a source of continuing learning for the leaders.

I have known of groups in which different conductors alternated in 'taking' the group on different days of the week and have been assured by those who have tried it that group members soon adapt to this arrangement. However it is hard to imagine such a group maintaining continuity and momentum, and it is a practice which I would think it best to avoid.

The principal error which it is possible to make when planning a structure for a group is mismatching, or failing to find a workable fit between the character of the population, a structure, and a leadership approach. The prospective group conductor plans a group which is either too far beyond or too far within the frontiers of the patient or client population, or irrelevant to the preoccupying concern. He may plan a group which is excessively threatening or baffling to the members by expecting them to engage in activities or express themselves in ways which are beyond them.

He may plan too rigidly and fail to allow for revision of his initial estimate of the frontier or preoccupying concern if events prove him to have been mistaken. He may plan a kind of group which seems plausible to him but implausible and irrelevant to prospective members. He may plan for one kind of group whilst secretly hoping it will turn into another, with resulting confusion and disappointment for all.

Errors involving failures to find a reasonable fit between patient or client population, type of group and leadership style seem most frequently to take the following form: the prospective group leader expects too much of his population. That is, he expects them to be able to work far beyond their actual frontiers. For example, inarticulate, withdrawn persons may be expected to talk freely in a minimally structured therapeutic group which relies for its success on relatively open and free-flowing expression of feelings and sharing of experiences. Or, the conductor expects a group of mothers of mentally handicapped children to talk about their deepest concerns involving guilt, lowered self-esteem and the like and is disappointed when they wish 'only' to talk about problems in managing their children, even though the latter is very much their preoccupying concern. The converse error, in which a leader plans a group which is too far within a population's likely frontier, is usually so ludicrous that it does not occur. Persons who are functioning adequately by ordinary standards but who are experiencing depression or anxiety and repeatedly engage in self-defeating behaviour are rarely encouraged to enter groups designed to teach them how to shop or use the buses.

It seems likely to me that errors in matching occur most frequently in consequence of a set of beliefs and values which holds that *real* group therapy or group work is long-term, 'deep', gets at painful and unrecognized feelings, and aims for the radical reconstruction of personality. Such assumptions about what 'real' group therapy is all about appear still to be quite widespread. They have a tenacious hold on many practitioners, some of whom will have been trained by persons who have emphasized such an approach. This kind of group is certainly appropriate for some populations: in the classification put forward in this chapter it is appropriate to persons in category 4 and some persons in category 5. Some groups designed for persons in categories 2 and 3 may also move into such realms. But this type of group is far too heavily idealized. There are many persons who potentially can benefit from groups for whom such an approach is no use at all. It is a disservice to such persons to attempt to impose such groups on them. Further, any attempt to do so leads to frustration and a sense of failure both for the members and for the group worker or therapist concerned.

When errors concerning fit are made, they usually come to light during the first few sessions of a group. They can be retrieved, providing of course that the group worker or therapist recognizes them as errors. How this can best be done is discussed in chapter 9, on the formative phase of a group, where the issue of avoiding the irredeemable collapse of structure is examined.

In the foregoing, I have put forward the two concepts of 'frontier' and 'preoccupying concern' and indicated how they can be used to assess a client or patient population and form a basis for deciding whether a group experience is suitable and if so, what kind of group might be planned. I have been working from an unstated assumption that one always starts with the patient or client population with which one intends to work. It is the patient or client population which is the 'given' in the situation. The population is as it is and must be taken as it is. All else can be planned, adapted, and designed. Groups of various sorts can be established and the therapist or group worker can select from his repertory of leadership styles those which may be expected best to suit the persons concerned. In practice of course a given group worker or therapist may come to realize from experience that he prefers to work with certain kinds of populations rather than others, or that his preferred leadership style best suits a particular and limited range of client or patient populations. He then may seek to concentrate his efforts with those populations. His starting point is himself. Yet, this can be seen as a variation on the procedure already described in that once the worker has a particular population in mind that population again becomes the given from which he works out his plans.

The populations discussed here have included only those which can in some sense be regarded as including patients or clients, but some of the group structures suggested could be applied to other populations, for example to those who are themselves helpers or caretakers, or potential ones. One thinks of support and/or training groups for houseparents in a corrective institution for adolescents or a residential facility for old people; of groups designed to help prospective adoptive parents or foster parents to explore and test their commitment before making final decisions; of groups of a semi-training, semi-therapeutic character for social workers, psychiatrists, psychologists or others who are in a programme of professional training. I believe that the same guiding principles of preoccupying concern and frontier can be applied to these non-patient populations.

I hope it is evident that there is nothing particularly sacrosanct about the population categories put forward in this chapter. In particular, it should be noted that if a group worker or therapist is working in a setting in which the population is already defined or restricted it is entirely possible and useful to look inside such a population, making finer distinctions than I have made here, but again applying the concepts of frontier and preoccupying concern as a basis for thinking out potentially useful designs or structures for groups.

Suggested exercises

For practice in designing groups suited to particular patient or client populations one might first of all identify population categories relevant to one's own work setting, describe each in terms of frontier and preoccupying concern (if applicable) and then design one or more groups which can plausibly be expected to benefit persons drawn from each population.

If one wishes to gain experience in planning for populations other than those in one's own work setting, one might engage in the same exercise with respect to one of the following:

(a) male prisoners with a background of violence who are about to be released from prison approximately six weeks hence;
(b) unemployed youths with little likelihood of getting a job in the near future;
(c) persons who have recently lost their vision;
(d) socially isolated physically handicapped persons living in the community;
(e) chronic complainers who frequently visit their general practitioners who appear to be suffering from no physical ailment (assume that you have been asked by the general practitioner to assist with these persons);
(f) a group of mentally handicapped adults who have been living in a residential facility for a long time, but where a change in policy means that they will soon be discharged to live in the community;
(g) any other population.

Another approach to understanding the link between character of the population and design of group is to start from one of the many descriptive accounts of groups to be found in the professional journals. With respect to any one of these, one could think out the current state and the preferred state of the patients or clients concerned, in terms of frontier and of preoccupying concern, decide whether or not the group designed for the population suited it, and whether an alternative design might suit it as well or better.

For practice in making a decision about co-leadership two colleagues or fellow-students might engage in an exploratory discussion aimed at testing their probable compatibility as co-therapists or co-workers. They would need to have some form of group generally in mind, e.g., activity-based group for adolescents, etc., and address themselves to such issues as what they would be aiming for in terms of benefit, how they see themselves operating in the group, problems they anticipate, group situations which in general they find comfortable or threatening, what each would expect of the other, etc. Such an exercise can be conducted in a work setting in which one intends to begin work with a group in the near future, or in a class or in-service training effort where one is thinking of an imagined future. In the latter case it can be useful if partners do not know one another well, since this will facilitate starting from no formed assumptions about how the other is likely to work. This exercise also helps each person to make his or her own stance more explicit.

Chapter 4
Taking the work setting into account

A great many persons who work with groups do so within some organization, institution or agency, whose mission, policies and practices are bound to affect their work. Persons and organizations outside one's own work setting may also have an impact: for example, the courts and the way they operate, the alternative forms of care available for a population (children in care, old people, alcoholics, etc.), or the policies of referring agencies. Persons who work from an independently managed centre or a private office may be dependent on colleagues or institutions for referrals. In some circumstances neighbours need to be counted as a significant part of the wider environment, because their attitudes have an impact on how a group can operate or because the operation of the group impinges on them in some way. The significant wider environment can be defined as any organization, group or person outside the group itself which is likely to affect the group or be affected by it.

Up to this point in planning, the character of the work setting has influenced decision-making primarily by making certain patient or client populations available and precluding access to others. On the basis of an understanding of the population with which one has decided to work, one has by now thought out a structure for a group and given thought to the implications for leadership style. At this point one will have a sufficiently clear image of what the group will be like once it is in operation, and of what further planning and preparation is required to get it started, to anticipate how the group is likely to affect and be affected by the wider environment. Before final plans are made it is sensible to take that wider environment into account. In particular, one can look at features of one's own organization

101

which may limit or channel the ways in which the group can operate, whether and how the operation of the group may affect the current policies and practices of one's own organization, the demands which the group is likely to make on colleagues, and whether and how the group is likely to disturb or be disturbed by other persons, groups or organizations.

A significant feature of any work setting is its boundary with the outside world. All organizations or institutions or individuals working 'alone' maintain some sort of boundary between their own work setting and persons, organizations, or groups lying outside it. The nature of that boundary, who belongs inside it and outside it, and who decides when persons stay inside it and move outside it has a substantial influence on how one can go about conducting work with groups.

Many institutions, including psychiatric hospitals, general and medical hospitals, prisons, Borstals and the like operate on clear-cut boundaries between the institution and the outside world. This is expressed in formalized criteria and procedures for admission and discharge. A patient, prisoner or inmate is usually definitely 'in' or clearly 'out' of the institution. A consequence of this is that if one is working with a group drawn from the population of such an institution the point of discharge or transfer is likely also to be the point at which the person must leave the group. There are exceptions to this, for example in psychiatric hospitals to which an outpatient department is attached, or general medical and surgical hospitals where a social worker may, at his or her discretion, continue work with a patient after discharge back into the community. Often, however, the boundary between the institution and the outside world is fixed and impermeable. This can sometimes lead to conflict, as when criteria for discharge from the institution (e.g. maximum hospital benefit) are different from the criteria the practitioner would like to use in decisions as to whether or not a person is ready to leave a group.

If the boundary of an institution is very firmly drawn it is likely to mean that the experiences of moving into the institution from the outside environment, and moving out again, are in themselves important transitions. These offer opportunities for the use of groups to ease the transition and take advantages of opportunities for learning and change arising from transition experiences.

A therapist, group worker or leader is bound to occupy some position with respect to the boundary of the organization: inside or outside, central or peripheral. In some instances and in a certain sense the group worker and other staff are themselves inmates of the institution along with patients, prisoners or residents. This is most likely to be the case where staff live in or near to the institution, and the institution is physically or psychologically isolated from the community. Perhaps this is an advantage, in that staff are in close contact with residents and can get to know them in many life contexts. However, staff in this position can become almost as isolated from the outside world as patients or residents and thus be in a poor position to facilitate contact with the outside world or provide preparation for moving into it. In extreme contrast to this, a group therapist or worker may have little to do with the institution apart from coming into it to conduct a group, for example if he is an external consultant who is not otherwise a part of the institution. This creates problems of its own which principally have to do with fewer avenues for understanding and empathizing with the situation of group participants, and with limited opportunities for communication with resident staff.

Organizational policy sometimes sets definite limits, in terms of weeks or months, that a person is likely to be available for membership in a group. In hospitals, prisons and some other settings the average length of stay is closely tied to the mission or purpose of the institution and is virtually a given from the point of view of anyone wishing to undertake work with groups. Clearly, likely length of stay will be different in the reception ward of a mental hospital, in an orthopaedic ward in a general hospital, in a maximum security unit in a prison, in a prison for petty offenders, or in a social work agency with no control over its intake and hence internal pressure to close cases as quickly as possible. Average length of stay and variations in length of stay do not necessarily generate problems for the group therapist or group worker, providing he has information about this ahead of time and can take it into account in his planning. If one knows, for example, that patients or residents enter from time to time in cohorts, and stay for, say, four weeks, then one's plans can take this into account. If one knows that patients or residents enter one by one scattered over a period of time and that average length of stay is two months, then one can develop a plan which accommodates to this.

Problems arise when length of stay cannot be predicted or when varying and inconsistent criteria are applied when patients/residents/inmates are discharged or transferred. A therapist or group worker is clearly at a disadvantage if he designs a group structure which in order to be effective must meet for, say, twenty sessions and then finds that a majority of the members are discharged after six or eight. He has set up expectations in the patients which cannot be met and harm may be done if issues and feelings have become exposed which cannot be dealt with in the time available. Difficulties also arise when decisions about length of stay are made by different persons on the basis of different criteria, or when they are made abruptly, with little notice. Such practices create conditions which are incompatible with effective work with groups and are a source of conflict between group therapists and the administration of the institution or other staff. The most extreme instance of this occurs when a group worker or therapist is not consulted or informed about plans for discharge or transfer and hears about it only when someone fails to turn up for a group session. This is bound to generate stress and distress for the members of a group who find that one of the members has disappeared unexpectedly. Moreover, it is quite possible that the person so precipitously removed may have reached some critical point in the group and that opportunities to follow through are abruptly cut off.

Thus, whether or not a group can achieve its potential will depend very much on the locus of power within an institution or organization and how that power is used, and on the nature of the communication channels within the organization. Problems arise for the conductor of the group when he has little or no power, *and* when existing practices undermine what he is trying to achieve, *and* where communication channels are faulty or blocked.

All organizations and institutions have some policy about communicating with other staff about patients/residents/inmates through written records or case conferences and reviews. These requirements are unlikely to create a problem for a group worker or therapist unless he feels that he is being pressed to breach confidentiality or fears that group members, knowing of these requirements, will censor their participation in the group in some dysfunctional way. He may well find ways to accommodate to these requirements without doing harm to persons in his group. A fuller discussion of how this may be done is provided in the next chapter, where record-keeping is discussed as one of a number of detailed planning tasks. If however the conductor of a group cannot see how to meet institutional or agency requirements without doing harm to persons in the group, then clearly he is in a state of conflict with others in the organization and is faced with either abandoning his plans or attempting to influence and change the institution's policies.

Policies about length of stay, criteria for discharge and record-keeping are some of many which influence how a group can be planned and conducted. Other policies (official or unofficial, acknowledged or unacknowledged) which may have an impact include those which define or restrict the status and role of particular categories of staff, those which lead to more time being invested in some categories of patients/residents/inmates than others, those which encourage the admission of particular categories of patients/residents/inmates, and training policies.

The discussion so far has had to do with how certain features of a work setting may influence, limit and channel the kind of group work which can be undertaken. It is also the case that conducting a group may have an impact on the work setting, either creating problems for it or revealing that certain existing policies and practices require amendment if work with groups is to be a feature of the organization. This is particularly likely to be the case where working with groups is a new venture or where one is interested in introducing a new form of group work.

For example, helping agencies and institutions commonly employ some device for calculating workloads and seeking to make them equitable among staff. In some instances these derive from the days when only one-to-one forms of help were employed. In some social work agencies, for example, allocation of work is according to the number of individual clients or families on any given worker's list. Simple head-counting is sometimes modified by categorizing clients or families into those requiring short-term intensive, long-term intensive, and long-term non-intensive attention so that weightings can be assigned and individual workers can be helped to maintain balanced case loads. The introduction of group work can present a problem by rendering this system obsolete.

Where work allocation is by caseload, few staff have enough persons in their own caseloads to make up a group. They therefore seek referrals from colleagues. Entirely apart from whether or not such referrals are forthcoming, issues often arise as to whether the patient or client then 'counts' on the group worker's caseload or remains in the caseload of the referring person. Many settings have not worked out a way of dealing with this. They sometimes accommodate to it by regarding work with groups as an activity which one can choose to engage in in one's spare time but which is not taken into account when assessing workload. This clearly places the group worker at a disadvantage because the time-consuming character of working with groups is not recognized, and working with groups retains the status of an 'extra' activity.

In addition to publicly declared and acknowledged goals, institutions and agencies (or more accurately, their top administrators) are likely to hold certain further goals which have a bearing on work with groups. For example, an important but possibly unstated goal may be that of maintaining the institution's reputation in the community. The administrators of a psychiatric hospital or a Borstal may want their patients or residents to remain inconspicuous in the community or at least to be on their best behaviour and bring credit to the institution when they venture outside it. It is understandable and proper that administrators hold to this goal because they are concerned among other things with the long-term survival of the institution. It is often the case that those lower down the organization's hierarchy – the conductors of a group among them – are less centrally concerned about the institution's reputation and are therefore more ready to risk it. This can generate conflict when the operation of a group requires taking patients or residents out into the community with some degree of attendant risk. Should some event actually occur which threatens the reputation of the institution, the operation of the group can fairly be said to have harmed the institution. Overt conflict may erupt and administrators may use their superior power to restrict the ways in which the group can henceforward operate.

When problems arise within organizations and institutions these typically have to do with imbalances with respect to the relationship between task, power, information and responsibility. For example, if a group worker or therapist assumes responsibility for the members of a group but does not have power to decide about or influence the timing of transfer or discharge, then an imbalance exists between power and responsibility and a problem ensues for the conductor of the group. The superintendent of a hospital or the head of an agency is responsible for the long-term survival and the reputation of the institution or agency, yet has no power over how individual members of staff carry out their day-to-day work. The conductor of a group has assumed responsibilities for members of the group and may have adequate power to carry out those responsibilities, but he may lack relevant information, as when ward staff know about crises on the ward but communication channels do not exist for conveying that information to the group worker or therapist. Some imbalances can be redressed by careful attention to organizational policies and practices but some are inherent to organizations because their very character and size require some differential distribution of tasks and responsibilities amongst staff. It is difficult to get the balance right and to keep it right.

The operation of a group often makes demands on colleagues not directly involved with the group, or requires their co-operation if the group is to proceed smoothly and be effective. A group worker or therapist may rely on colleagues for referrals, or for co-operation in the form of not disturbing him or the group while it is in session, or for ensuring that group members are available during the times the group is scheduled to meet, or for consultation and informal support. Whether or not such co-operation and support is forthcoming will depend very much on whether colleagues' attitudes are generally positive or generally negative towards the idea of working with groups. If attitudes are generally positive then colleagues will support one's efforts, and if they do not or cannot one usually can find out early just what is standing in the way and take it into account in planning. Negative attitudes may stem from worries and reservations about presumed harmful effects of groups or an awareness that the operation of a group may in some way impinge harmfully upon one's own work or status, an awareness that the operation of the group may create problems for the organization which would not otherwise arise (for example with respect to allocating workloads or sharing responsibilites for clients or patients), or a prevailing view that working with groups is second-best to individual therapy, case-work, or family therapy. Sometimes negative attitudes about groups are shared by prospective group members, who are then reluctant to join a group.

Where negative attitudes are out in the open and expressed directly, one usually can find ways of dealing with them, by providing further information, making opportunities for reservations to be aired and if possible resolved, for identifying the ways in which the conduct of a group is likely to interfere with existing procedures and to try to avert problems arising from this, and so on. It is when negative attitudes remain covert that problems tend to arise: referrals are promised but never materialize; patients or clients are mysteriously unavailable when the group is due to meet; negative attitudes on the part of colleagues get communicated to members and these emerge as a problem within the group; and the conductor of the group develops an uneasy sense that his colleagues have adopted a critical set towards his work and are watching from the wings, waiting for him to make some terrible error. Under these conditions it is difficult if not impossible to conduct effective work with groups. It is like driving with the brakes on.

An interference fit between the operation of a group and its wider environment is most likely to occur within one's own organization or institution, but sometimes it occurs with reference to other organizations or with neighbours. If one is going to make use of premises belonging to some other organization for one's work with a group, then the needs and preferences of that organization need to be taken into account. If one is working within a children's home or assessment centre, then opportunities for alternative forms of care within a wider care system, and attitudes about them, will have an impact on one's work. If referrals come from another agency, then the policies of that agency will bear on one's work.

It is easy to assume, when one is planning and hoping to conduct some form of group, that any obstacle in its way or any indication of reservations about it is a form of resistance and that those who resist are somehow the villains in the piece. In fact, those who resist setting up a group may be protecting some overarching goal of the organization or some policy or practice which serves a useful function for the organization. When one sees a conflict looming, or identifies some person or some policy as spoiling one's efforts, it is a good idea to look carefully at the likely consequences of carrying out one's plan, for the organization and its policies, for colleagues, and for others concerned. At the same time one needs to look at the nature of the constraints which features of the wider environment are likely to place on the operation of the group. One needs to arrive at a point of view about whether or not effective and satisfying work can be carried out under the prevailing conditions of organizational structures and policies, level of support and receptiveness among colleagues, practices and attitudes of relevant others, and one's own position with regard to task, responsibility, power and information. If one considers that, given all these environmental factors, useful work can be accomplished, then one goes on with one's plan or a modification of it. One might come to the view that the operation of the group as planned will generate unacceptable costs to one's organization or colleagues and decide to abandon the plan on these grounds. If one judges that serious costs to the organization will not ensue but that one cannot operate effectively and satisfyingly under prevailing conditions then the only choices are to abandon one's plan or defer implementing it until one has tried to influence some aspect of the work setting.

It follows that a group therapist or worker may be faced, under some circumstances, with a task which in itself has nothing to do with planning and conducting groups: that is, taking action to try to influence some aspect of his work setting. He may find himself wishing to influence organizational policies or practices, attitudes held by colleagues, or the stance of one powerful person. It is often possible to influence a work setting, even from a position of little power, so it is well worth thinking through what may be involved. Influence attempts involve two stages which may need to be repeated many times: a thinking-out or diagnostic stage and an action stage. The thinking-out stage involves seeking to understand the problem as fully as possible; forming hypotheses as to what factors or forces may be holding the problem in place; then identifying those actions which are within one's power to make and those actions which are not; then anticipating (still as an internal process) possible consequences of alternative courses of action, particularly in order to avoid making things worse; and then deciding on action. The action stage involves trying something, and then noting what happens in consequence. If the action one takes achieves the results that one wants then of course one can consider that one's attempt to influence the organization has been successful and one can proceed with one's plans for the group. If, as is more likely to be the case, the action leads to some consequences which do not fully achieve one's aims then one must go back to the thinking-out stage and undertake a further analysis, this time with the benefit of new information acquired through observing the consequences of the action step. The second look is likely to suggest further action.

The above is a statement, in prose, of procedures for analysis and action-taking suggested by Kurt Lewin and called by him 'force-field analysis' (Lewin, 1951). Lewin's scheme is a powerful one for helping to develop an understanding of a problem situation and identifying possible courses of action. The key terms in Lewin's approach are 'force-field', 'quasi-stationary equilibrium'; 'goal'; 'restraining forces'; and 'driving forces'. Lewin borrowed these terms from topology and sought to apply them to human situations. Figure 4.1 is commonly employed to show the relationships amongst these factors:

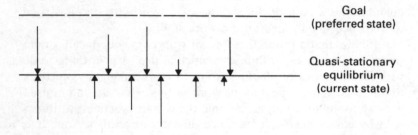

Goal
(preferred state)

Quasi-stationary
equilibrium
(current state)

Figure 4.1

In this diagram the solid line represents the quasi-stationary equilibrium. This is the situation as it is now. Part of one's task when using this device is to define the situation as it is now in as accurate and succinct terms as possible. Since the scheme is applied to situations where one is dissatisfied with something, the line representing the quasi-stationary equilibrium may well be defined as 'not getting referrals', or 'group sessions are interrupted', or 'I don't feel free to seek consultation from colleagues', etc. Lewin regarded such a situation as being in a quasi-stationary equilibrium in that the situation is more or less stable but varies a bit from time to time because various forces bearing on the situation tend to fluctuate.

In the diagram, the dashed line parallel to the solid line showing the quasi-stationary equilibrium is the goal: that is, the state of affairs which the group worker or therapist would like to achieve. It too needs to be defined as accurately and as concisely as possible. If one has defined the current state with care this is not difficult to do, for the goal is likely to be something like 'receive more referrals', 'stop the interruptions', 'feel free to approach colleagues for consultation', and so on.

Lewin represented what he called 'restraining forces' by arrows pointing downward on the equilibrium line. These are the forces existing in the situation which push the equilibrium away from the goal towards an even worse situation than the current one. Lewin represented what he called 'driving forces' by arrows pointing upwards towards the goal. Arrows differing in length represent forces of varying strength. Some forces operate in direct opposition to others and can be shown in the diagram as pushing against one another. Lewin assumed that any situation always included forces pressing in both directions and that it was the outcome or resultant of these forces which held the quasi-stationary equilibrium (the undesired current situation) in place. The entire diagram is referred to as 'the force field'.

In this scheme the first step toward influencing a situation is diagnosis, which I have earlier called the thinking-out stage. This involves specifying the quasi-stationary equilibrium, the goal, and all the restraining and driving forces which one can think of which might be operating in the situation. For example, if the current situation is a lack of referrals one might assume that driving forces in the situation are the basic good will of colleagues, a mutual interest in benefiting clients or patients, and the verbal expression of support. One might assume that restraining forces include pressures on time, worries that one might lose contact with own clients, fears of the possibly destructive impact of the group on clients, and so on. If one takes this as an example of using force field analysis then the diagram would look like Figure 4.2.

Note that in theory the quasi-stationary equilibrium will move nearer to the goal under two conditions: first, if one or more of the restraining forces can be weakened or removed; and second, if one or more of the driving forces can be strengthened or if new driving forces can be introduced.

In practice, planning for action involves identifying those forces which can and cannot be influenced and investing one's time and effort in the former and not in the latter. In our example pressure of time on colleagues may be an extremely important restraining force but it may be entirely outside one's power to influence it. If one judges this to be the case then it is a waste of one's time to work on that particular factor. On the other hand, if one judges that a powerful restraining force is worries on the part of one's colleagues that once their clients join the group they will lose touch with them, then this may be something that it is within

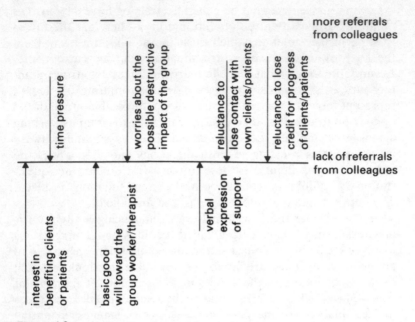

Figure 4.2

one's power to do something about. A further step in planning is to predict to oneself the likely consequences of certain influence attempts. In particular it is important to consider the possibility that introducing new driving forces may generate new restraining forces and in effect lead to no change or even make matters worse. For example, supposing that one suspects that an important restraining force is one's colleagues' concern that they will lose credit for any progress made by clients on their caseload if the clients join a group and then show improvement. Supposing one then considers introducing a new driving force into the situation consisting of reassuring colleagues that this will not occur. As the colleagues may not have been acknowledging this fear one may, by referring to it, stir up resentment toward oneself (a new restraining force), thus moving farther still from the goal. One can forestall making errors of this sort by attempting to think out the consequences of any particular piece of action ahead of time.

The final step in planning is to decide which force to attempt to influence and to think out a procedure for doing so. Lewin took the view that it was a better tactic to attempt to remove or weaken a restraining force than to strengthen a driving force or introduce a new driving force. The reason for this is a somewhat technical one, namely that the more forces operate in a situation the more tension there is in the system and the more difficult it will be for the quasi-stationary equilibrium to shift. If one removes forces then there is less tension in the system and a greater likelihood of movement. Suppose, in our example, that the worker or therapist has decided that the restraining force having to do with worries about the possible destructive impact of the group are important and amenable to influence. He might decide to ask for staff time in which both potential benefits and potential negative effects of groups could be aired and explored. His hope, of course, is that unrealistic fears could be dissipated by this means and that realistic fears could be acknowledged and their consequences guarded against.

The worker or therapist has now moved to the action stage in which he sets in motion the action he has planned, carries it out and then observes the consequences. Lewin has another diagram to display this process, which I will call Figure 4.3.

Every sequence begins with observing events in the real world, followed by assessment of them in order to devise a plan (this can be done with the help of a force-field diagram), followed by putting the plan into action, followed by observing the consequences in the real world of doing so, followed by re-assessment, and so on. The ongoing spiral emphasizes the likelihood that a single sequence of diagnosis and action is unlikely to lead immediately to a desired result. It is usually the case that re-diagnosis and further action is required. One may find, on the basis of

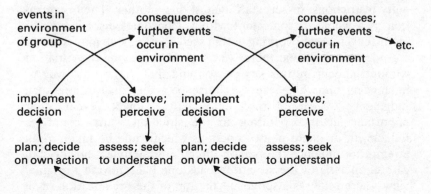

Figure 4.3

the additional information acquired through trying something and seeing what happens, that one's original diagnosis was basically correct but that one's action brought with it unforeseen consequences which led to a net situation of no change by generating further restraining forces. Or one might find that additional restraining forces operate in the situation of which one was not aware. The force-field diagram needs to be redrawn at each successive re-assessment stage, taking additional information into account. Sometimes the new information suggests that the force field should be reconceptualized in some way. For example, suppose that a discussion with colleagues intended to explore possible positive and negative consequences of working with groups reveals that worries about loss of contact with own clients is a powerful factor. One might decide to redraw one's diagram so that the quasi-stationary equilibrium is defined as 'potential loss of contact with own clients' and the goal line is defined as 'no loss of contact with own clients'. It would then be possible to enter those driving and restraining forces which one thinks might operate on this new quasi-stationary equilibrium. Perhaps this new diagnosis leads one to invent new channels of communication between self and colleagues. Working out a force-field analysis on paper is an exercise which can be done collaboratively with colleagues. If this is done one is less likely to overlook important forces which may be operating.

Some problems in organizations seem to be generated by the behaviour of one person who is in a position of power. He or she characteristically and frequently blocks action, sabotages plans, offers misleading information, states own opinion as fact, imposes petty restrictions, or sets staff against one another. The organization as a whole or some unit within it becomes disordered and inefficient. If one is working within such a setting one may come to feel, despairingly, that there is no way of improving the situation without influencing this key person and that there is no way of influencing him. One can of course be wrong in forming such judgments. A careful force-field analysis might reveal other important factors operating in the situation which could be influenced, or might point to actions which could be taken in an attempt to influence the person directly. Sometimes, however, a careful analysis of the situation leads one back to one's original view: there really is a spoiler at the top of the organization or in some critical power position within it. G. Whitaker has called such persons 'pathogenic leaders' and suggests reasons for their acquiring and staying in positions of power (G. Whitaker, 1982). He argues that such persons cannot be influenced, either by direct attempts or by 'human relations' or semi-therapeutic efforts, but that a combination of internal arming and structural solutions can help. Internal arming means establishing internal attitudes which insulate oneself from the destructive impact of such persons, thus avoiding immobilization, despair, etc. Structural solutions include such devices as minuting decisions so that there is a public record of them and the person in power cannot so easily reverse them, making use of voting as a device for making the weight of staff opinion clear, creating clear communication channels within the organization, and so on. These ideas can be blended into Lewin's device of force-field analysis. For example, if one perceives that the head of an organization or unit utilizes 'divide and conquer' tactics with staff and that these operate to maintain an attitude of resistance to anything new, one might introduce a new force in the form of initiating communication to expose and test rumours. In Whitaker's terms one is introducing a structural solution; in Lewin's terms one is weakening the impact of a restraining force by introducing a new driving force.

In general the consequences of undertaking an analysis of the relevant wider environment and of trying out actions suggested by such an analysis are one of three: one might oneself come to see that resistant behaviour is an expression of justifiable concerns and that group work should not be undertaken in the setting or at least not in the form originally planned. It is difficult when one feels to be the victim of incalcitrance on the part of others to entertain the possibility that they could be right and oneself could be wrong. However sometimes persons have good reasons for resisting change, and it is well to be aware of them. A second possibility is that one's plan stands up to analysis and is unlikely to do harm, that some of the forces operating in the situation can be influenced and that in consequence the work setting becomes more receptive for group work. A third possibility is that the forces operating in the situation are both powerful and uninfluenceable. Some problems are intractable. This occurs less frequently than one is inclined to believe but it certainly can happen. If this is the case then one either goes ahead with plans under adverse circumstances, or abandons one's intention to conduct groups in the setting, or leaves the setting.

Sometimes problems arising from the nature of the setting are not apparent at the time when one is planning the group, but only emerge after the group is underway. Happily, it is not too late to undertake an analysis of the situation and to take action to improve it. An analysis of the wider environment can be undertaken at any stage of one's effort, and action suggested by the analysis can be taken.

It is unrealistic to expect a perfect fit between one's plan for a group and its wider environment. If potential problems are acknowledged at the planning stage, these can be dealt with more often than not. In the course of planning, it is well worth one's time to interrupt planning for the group itself long enough to examine with care the wider environment in which the group will necessarily have to operate, in order to forestall the emergence of problems later on.

Suggested exercises

Anyone wishing to gain experience with force-field analysis as a diagnostic device can do so by following the procedures described in the second part of this chapter, applying them to any situation in which a current situation (quasi-stationary equilibrium) and a goal can be specified. The scheme can be applied to individual and group as well as to organizational situations. Thus, someone who now smokes but wishes to stop could work out a force-field analysis in which he or she attempts to identify all the driving and restraining forces operating in the situation, then notes those which could be influenced or those additional forces which could be introduced. Anyone working within a staff or team characterized by low morale could take 'low morale' as the current situation or quasi-stationary equilibrium and 'increased morale' as the goal, and undertake a force-field analysis. And so on. It is best to develop an exercise based on one's own experience since it is only then that one has access to information which should find a place in Lewin's scheme as a driving or a restraining force.

Chapter 5

Further planning: making detailed decisions about the structure of the group and the policies one intends to follow

This chapter examines the further and more specific planning decisions which can and should be made before specific persons are invited to join the group and before the group actually meets for the first time. It has to do with such issues as the size of the group, when and where it shall meet, the duration of sessions, and the like. Quite a number of such detailed planning decisions must be made, and many of them are interdependent.

The further planning decisions to be discussed here are:

1 What physical setting best suits the group one intends to work with?
2 How many persons should be included in the group?
3 Should the group be long- or short-term, closed or open and time-limited or not?
4 For how long should each session go on?
5 How frequently should the group meet?
6 In how much detail should the first and subsequent sessions be planned?
7 Should members be involved in planning?
8 What contact or communication will need to be maintained with colleagues not directly involved with the group?
9 What records should a therapist or worker keep for his own use?
10 What rules can and should the conductor make, for members and for self, before or at the start of the group?

I shall take up these points one at a time, showing links as I go, and in every case making the assumption that the person or persons who are to conduct the group have already thought through general characteristics of the population and have made basic decisions about the type of group likely to suit it. Further, I shall assume that issues having to do with the work setting have been explored and worked out. The conductor is now at the point where he expects to begin working with a group in the relatively near future.

A therapist or worker may of course acquire a group in ways other than starting a new group from among a pool of clients or patients. He may, for example, enter an ongoing group as a student, observer or co-leader; he may take over a group from a previous leader; he may be 'given' a group which has been assembled by someone else; he may 'find' a group in the sense that the group already existed and had a life before it became defined as a client or patient group. If a therapist or group worker begins with a group in these other ways, then some or all of the detailed decisions just listed will already have been made by others. Certain further decisions face a practitioner who acquires a group in one or another of these other ways. They include:

11 How can the transition be planned and managed when a new conductor joins an existing group?
12 What choices are open to one and what decisions need to be made when one is 'given' a group or when one 'finds' one?

Sometimes different kinds of groups are formed into a programme which may also include individual psychotherapy or case work. When such is the case an additional planning task is:

13 How can components of a programme be planned so as to avoid overkill, dilution and confusion, or undoing?

1 What physical setting best suits the group one intends to work with?

The character and purpose of the group and the intended leadership approach may influence the choice of physical setting in quite direct ways. For example, is equipment required? Should the group meet in a kitchen, lounge or workshop? Does there need to be open space or props for role-playing? The physical setting is a form of communication to the members as to what is and is not expected, how they are regarded, and what relationship the therapist or worker hopes to establish with them. For example if the conductor has in mind a group with permeable boundaries such that persons feel free to attend or not, and free either to drift to the periphery of the group or to locate themselves in its centre, then a corner of a larger room or a room with an open door helps to communicate this. If the group is to be a work group engaged in some form of planning either for selves or in order to influence the outside world then chairs arranged around a table communicates 'this is a place to work'. If the conductor then sits at the head of the table this communicates 'I am in charge' or 'I am in a special position'. If the conductor takes a seat along the side of the table this communicates 'I wish to be one of you'. If the group is to be a therapeutic group relying on open discussion then a reasonably comfortable room with chairs arranged in an open circle is a concrete expression of the hoped-for openness. A closed door emphasizes the private, confidential and personal character of the discussion. A conductor may sometimes wish to offer nurturance to a group, and might decide to display this in a concrete way by reserving a corner for tea and biscuits, or coffee and cakes.

Any physical setting or arrangement may generate trust and ease for one population of persons, discomfort and mistrust for others. What does elegance communicate? What does shabbiness communicate? An aspect of the physical environment is the clothing worn by the worker or therapist. Shall he wear informal clothing or a white coat? What does he wish to communicate, and what meaning is likely to be attached to his choice of clothing by the persons in the group?

The general point is that physical setting deserves consideration. It is not, however, an overriding factor, and if the setting is less than optimal for the kind of group one has in mind this should not be allowed to interfere with getting started with a group. Many less than optimal settings can be overcome by the spirit of the group.

2 How many persons should be included in the group?

The number of persons to be included in a group depends very much on the type of group one expects to conduct. Generally speaking a group should be large enough to allow the structure one intends to use to operate. An activity-based group, for example, where sub-groups are expected to engage in different activities for some of the time can be rather larger (twelve or fifteen or eighteen) than a group which expects to rely entirely on face-to-face interaction and discussion (about six to nine). A group needs to be large enough to allow the special features of groups to emerge. This tends to mean a minimum of five or six persons, since pairs and trios have dynamics of their own and fours and fives may not include the diversity in membership needed to support one's helping efforts.

Therapists or group workers who work with groups which rely on open discussion seem to agree that six to nine members is about right. If the group gets much larger than nine it almost always separates out into a core group of persons who participate actively and peripheral members who remain mainly spectators. If the group is much less than six the richness of interaction is less and the group becomes a less useful environment for change. Fulkerson, Hawkins and Alden (1981) have reported that in groups of four or less norms tended to become established which worked against the therapeutic process. I have known conductors who reduced the size of their groups to three or four in the hope that the group would thereby become more manageable. It is doubtful whether it does. It certainly becomes less useful.

If one is conducting a group with permeable boundaries to which everyone from a rather large population (for example, up to sixty if it is a large ward in a mental hospital) is invited to come, then one cannot control the size of the group. On the other hand, this kind of group is deliberately planned to allow for a fluctuating core of actively participating persons with a fluctuating group of persons who occupy a peripheral, spectator position.

3 Should the group be long- or short-term, closed or open, and time-limited or not?

These are related issues. Long-term groups will almost certainly have a 'slow-open' character. That is, members are expected to commit themselves to the group for an extended but indefinite period. Their departure from the group is determined by their readiness to leave it rather than by a specified time limit. When a person leaves such a group, a new person is usually brought into it, to maintain the numbers. Departures from the group do not happen very often and the membership is stable for long periods. It changes slowly, from time to time: hence, the term 'slow-open'. Such an arrangement is appropriate for groups in which major reconstructive work is hoped for for the members (category 4 and some persons in category 5, discussed in chapter 3). It is also appropriate for groups whose purpose is to offer ongoing support to persons for whom substantial personal change is not expected (category 7 in chapter 3). Such groups may go on for years, though the membership is likely gradually to shift.

'Slow-open' can, I suppose, be contrasted with 'fast-open', in which some members leave the group and others enter it every few sessions. Such an arrangement may be an advantage in groups designed to help persons through particular kinds of transitions, for example into or out of an institution. Experienced persons who have been in the group for a time can benefit newcomers. Since the business of the group is to facilitate dealing with losses and gains associated with transitions, a shifting membership can keep these issues in the foreground. In most groups, however, frequent goings and comings interfere with the helping process. The members of the group continually have to cope with departures and arrivals. It is difficult for a useful set of norms to become established, and the members' energies become bound up in handling their feelings about persons leaving and entering, or else they defend against such feelings by reducing investment in fellow-members or in the group generally. If the setting in which one works faces one with a high turnover one can maintain a group as a closed-membership group for a specified period of time, tolerating periods of low membership as some persons leave, and then build up the numbers again all at once, dealing at that time with a reconstituted group made up of 'old' and 'new' members. This provides periods of relative stability in which members may have to deal with some persons leaving, but not with new entrants.

Some groups, for example skill-development groups, or those set up to deal with crises associated with personal disasters or with stresses generated by linked-fate relationships, can usefully be both short-term and closed. Members are expected to stay the course. Should there be a catastrophic loss of members, then of course this becomes a problem for the group to deal with and may displace earlier agreements, but barring this infrequent occurrence, the closedness of the group maximizes the likelihood that a useful helping atmosphere can be established and maintained over a relatively short period.

A time limit can be useful where one wishes to build in a specific review point. Here, patients or clients know from the start that at a given time, *x* number of sessions hence, all will be involved in an evaluation of the group, their own part in it, and their own situation at that time. A time limit can also be useful if one anticipates, or hopes, that a group of persons, in consequence of having had one kind of experience together, might come to a point of readiness for another type of group experience. It is also indicated when one judges that a group could help persons face some crisis, but where one does not want to encourage the person to build their life or identity on that crisis or its consequences (as with many persons in category 1, chapter 3).

With some kinds of populations one has a choice between a time-limited structure and an open-ended one. There are advantages and disadvantages to both arrangements, and it is hard to recommend one over the other. A time-limited group, provided it is generous enough, has the advantage of a built-in period of evaluation which is known in advance. Members generally take the fixed number of sessions into account and pace themselves, often making better use of the time than when it stretches indefinitely before them. The time-limit communicates: 'Much can be done in the time available. We will abandon no one, but take a look at where we are after *x* number of sessions and see what else, if anything, is required.' A group which is open-ended communicates: 'We have a great deal of time at our disposal and will be as thorough and take as much time as required for each person here.' There is much to be said for both communications.

I see no advantages in a group being both long-term and time-limited. If a long period is seen as appropriate (more than twenty-five sessions or so) this constitutes an acknowledgment that substantial time is required for either support or working through. One cannot predict, for individual persons, just how long will prove to be long enough. So, an assumption made at the beginning that a group should last for two years, or five years, or eighteen months, has a flimsy base and may encourage members to delay the start of real work.

4 For how long should each session go on?

For groups which rely on open discussion, experience suggests that an hour is too short and an hour-and-a-half is long enough. An hour-and-a-quarter is manageable. Group sessions need to be somewhat longer than individual sessions as it so often takes the group a little while to warm up and find an issue or theme. On the other hand a group which goes on for much longer than an hour-and-a-half is likely to accommodate to the time available and not use it any more fruitfully than a somewhat shorter period. Other group structures might require either longer or shorter times. For example, some groups involving skill development may include time-consuming activities or a sequence of different types of group experience, and will need more time. A group designed to include discussion, preparing and eating a meal, followed by an activity could easily require from two to three hours. For some populations and purposes, thirty minutes is time enough – for example if one is working with mentally handicapped persons where attention span is short, or with very damaged or regressed mental hospital patients where only short periods of close contact with others can be tolerated.

5 How frequently should the group meet?

A group may be designed to meet either three or four times a week, twice a week, once a week, or once in every two weeks. Some very short-term groups may meet daily for three or four days.

The frequency of meetings has an influence on the intensity of the experience for the members, the importance the group takes on for them, and the sense of continuity members can sustain concerning the group.

One's choice of frequency must depend on the benefits one hopes to procure and the character of the population with whom one intends to work. A group which meets three or four times a week over a period of time is likely to generate intense experiences. The very frequency of the group communicates that the group is seen as an important part of the ongoing life of the persons in it. Groups which meet twice a week acquire nearly the same level of intensity, groups which meet once a week rather less and groups which meet once a fortnight less still. The ratio between time spent in the group and time spent elsewhere, then bears some relationship to the intensity of the experience and to how important the group becomes to its members. One sometimes wants and sometimes does not want the group to be a very intense experience. One sometimes wants and sometimes does not want the group to take on major significance in the life of the person. I have heard practitioners unquestioningly accept the view that it is 'better' for a group experience to be more rather than less intense, and more rather than less important in the life of the person. This is an unwarranted assumption. Some persons, for example, might be overwhelmed by too intense an experience. For some populations, (for example the physically handicapped) one might not wish to encourage the group to become a dominant reference group for the members. In skill development groups one might consider it disadvantageous to encourage the view in members that it is only in the group that new skills can be practised safely, and might therefore space group sessions in such a way that ample time is available to practise skills in the world outside the group.

The frequency of meetings, or to put it another way, the duration of the space between meetings, influences the sense of continuity which members can maintain about the group experience. If one regards it as important to the work of the group for members to maintain a sense of continuity, and for the momentum of one session to feed into the next, then one is safest with meetings of twice a week as a minimum. Many but not all persons can hold to a sense of continuity when the group assembles weekly, and if the interval is longer than this, there tends to be a sense that the group is starting over each time. For some purposes, this 'starting over' feature is not a handicap, but then the design must include some device for establishing a focus for each session.

Intensity, importance and continuity need to be kept in some sort of balance. One might consider, for example, that for a particular population continuity and moderate but not high intensity are indicated. In that case, a frequency of once a week might be about right. For another population one might consider that continuity would be useful but that it is undesirable for the group to become too important in the lives of the members. One might then decide to meet once a fortnight (to reduce importance) and strive for continuity by some means other than frequency – for example by mutually planning for a series of sessions.

One sometimes hears of group workers or therapists who reduce frequency in the hope that they can conduct more groups and thus reach more persons. This is a mistake, for the principal criterion ought to be what will facilitate the work of the group for the population one intends to work with. If one is concerned about reaching more people, then the best route to this is to increase one's efficiency, by being as sure as one can be of planning a group which suits the population.

6 In how much detail should the first and subsequent sessions be planned?

Groups of different structures require vastly different degrees of detailed planning for the first and for subsequent sessions. If one intends to make use of open discussion, then one needs only to think out how to open the first session. Beyond this, one intends to make space for themes, issues and concerns to arise from the interaction of the members, and then to make use of these as seems appropriate, aiming always to maintaining the group as a viable helping medium and finding and using special opportunities to benefit members.

If one has in mind a group which is to be based on topic-orientated discussion, then a plan needs to be devised for the first session and for some or all of those which are to follow. One might identify topics ahead of time for the whole series (taking care to build in some unallocated time so that members can shape each topic in ways that suit them and pursue other issues important to them that one didn't think of oneself). Or, one might devise topics to be discussed during the first few sessions, and then schedule a planning session in which members are invited to suggest further topics. Still another possibility is to list a number of possible topics and ask members to choose among them in the course of the first session. Or, one might make no decisions about topics oneself (apart from the fact that there are to be some) and build the task of identifying and selecting topics into the first session as a matter for everyone to decide. Whatever procedure is followed it is important to allow space in the form of a certain amount of unallocated time so that members can use the time and the structure flexibly and creatively in their own interests.

Some groups are structured to make substantial use of games, exercises, role-playing or activities. Where this is the case, substantial detailed planning is required. As with topic-oriented groups, one might plan the first session only, the first few sessions, or the whole series, and one might or might not arrange for shared planning.

A large literature exists which describes virtually endless varieties of games, exercises, etc. which may be used in groups (see comments on selected references to this chapter). The games and exercises which I have used and/or read about seem to me to fall into particular categories, each with its own character, purposes, and likely consequences:

(a) The game, activity or exercise is something to be done for its own sake, for its intrinsic appeal to those who participate in it. The purpose of the activity is pleasure and enjoyment (table tennis, canoeing, mountain-climbing, etc.)

(b) The game, activity or exercise is expected to generate interactions between participants which can then be utilized as a basis for interventions on the part of the conductor directed towards benefiting individuals. For example in a competitive team game one side wins and the other loses: this becomes a basis for discussing the feelings which persons experience in the course of the game and when they know the outcome. Or, two boys who are working together at building a boat get into a quarrel: this is used as an opportunity for looking at how each handles anger.

(c) The game, activity or exercise constitutes a rehearsal in a protected environment for something the individual wishes to do or will have to do later in the outside world. It may involve role-playing or a try-out in the real world with the support of a companion or helper. Skill-development groups usually make use of rehearsal activities and games.

(d) The game, activity or exercise is analogous to something else and is intended to be an easy or palatable step toward understanding that something else. For example the well-known tower-building game, in which teams build a tower from old newspapers is meant to be analogous to real-life decision-making. The hope is that participants will see more clearly than they otherwise might how decisions are made in groups and the manner in which they themselves usually participate. Another example is the KIM game where members leave the room one at a time and are shown, individually, a tray of miscellaneous objects. It is presented as a memory game and when the group reassembles members are asked to arrive at a consensus about what they have seen. For two persons one of the objects is switched, so that an obstacle to consensus is built in, unknown to the participants. The ensuing discussion is meant to show how group pressure can lead persons to shift their perceptions. This game is meant to be analogous to peer-group pressures which influence the perceptions of individuals. Its purpose is to generate insight in the members about the character and power of such influences.

(e) The exercise, game or activity is an alternative route, often a more systematic route, towards something which could otherwise occur in open discussion. For example, in a card-sorting exercise, a pack of cards, each bearing descriptive words or phrases are provided to members of a group. The members examine the cards and take turns in placing them face down in front of others in the group whom they think the card describes. When all the cards have been distributed each person examines the pack in front of him and by this means gains information about how he is perceived by others. This device is intended to provide interpersonal feedback, although I would argue (see chapter 2) that this is a misuse of the term.

(f) The game, exercise or activity is meant to make something which one expects or hopes to happen anyway, happen faster. These are commonly called accelerating devices. Some examples are getting-acquainted games, trust-building exercises and self-disclosure games.

(g) The game or exercise is something which is meant to help persons to empathize with others with whom they interact and whose points of view they do not ordinarily take into account. An example of this might be a role-playing situation in which someone is asked to take the role of their own mother or father, a policeman, a teacher, etc.

As a guide to deciding whether or when to use some particular game, exercise or activity one can usefully ask oneself and try to answer the following questions:

(i) What experiences is the game, exercise or activity likely to generate for those who participate in it? Depending on their character, games or exercises may place persons in close physical contact, keep them at a physical distance from one another or place physical barriers between them. For some participants they may generate an experience of winning; for others, an experience of losing (or of being quick or slow, clever or stupid, strong or weak). A game may require co-operation or encourage competitiveness. It may overface a person with more than he or she can handle or be well within his/her scope. It may require much or little skill. It may encourage fantasy or keep fantasy contained. It may or may not encourage self-revelation. Because games and exercises are usually highly structured (when activities are not highly structured we call them 'play') they tend to influence or press participants into particular forms of experience which can be predicted in advance.

(ii) What are *all* the consequences of utilizing the device, including both intended and unintended likely consequences? When using a game or exercise one intends that some beneficial consequence will follow: that is one's reason for using it. However a game or exercise may have further consequences which may be unintended and welcome, or unintended and unwelcome. The KIM game, for example, shows participants something about group pressures but also demonstrates that the conductor is prepared to practise deception on the members.

(iii) Are the likely consequences the same or different for different participants? In many games, exercises and activities the outcome is different for different persons: someone wins and someone loses; some are shown to be strong in comparison with others while others are shown to be weak; someone is deceived while others are not. Some games and exercises generate enjoyment and pleasure for some and distress for others. For example some persons enjoy and others cannot tolerate the close physical contact which some exercises require.

(iv) Are any of the likely consequences for the members in general or for specific persons likely to be damaging in character? The KIM game, for example, involves deceit and is therefore likely to erode participants' trust in the conductor of the group. The card-sorting exercise described earlier *can* be damaging depending on how the game goes. Note that whilst the game is going on no one in the group, neither the members nor the leader, has any control over the character of the 'feedback' which is building up for the various persons in the group. The kinds of opinions which are being expressed about particular persons only becomes known after all the cards have been distributed, when each person picks up the cards which have been placed before him. If he experiences these as devastating, inaccurate, or unbearably inconsistent with his own view of himself, there is no way for him to protect himself or for others to offer protection. There has been no opportunity for him to provide the rest of the group with cues as to the impact of the feedback while it was accumulating and when they could still take his reactions into account and adjust their own behaviour.

(v) If any of the consequences are likely to be damaging can the device be modified so as to forestall these? If the answer to this question is 'yes' then the implied course of action is to make use of the device in a modified form. If the answer is 'no' then the appropriate course of action is not to use the device.

(vi) Does the device allow for choice on the part of the participants? Can persons freely opt out of participating if they wish to? Can persons choose different roles or different ways of participating within the structure of the game? Some games offer true choice. Some games offer no choice. Some games allow a phony choice in that opting out carries loss of reputation or status within the group.

(vii) What preparation or follow-up is required in order for potential benefits to be achieved and potential damage to be averted? It is well recognized that in role-playing activities it is important to allow adequate time for 'de-roling' – that is, for members to discuss the feelings stirred up in them while they were in role and their reactions to the behaviour of others. Games and exercises can generate or release feelings which persons ordinarily avoid and find it difficult to handle. Time and follow-up support is necessary for dealing with these and for providing necessary recovery time.

(viii) In what ways could the device go wrong and if it does, what can or should the conductor do? Some games and exercises only accomplish their intended purpose if everything goes exactly as intended and if everyone participates exactly as wished. In the real world this sometimes does not occur and the game collapses or begins to teach 'lessons' that were not intended and which may even contravene the group worker's intentions. When this occurs the group worker needs to think quickly in order to make positive use of the unexpected.

Sometimes one sees games, exercises or activities used in ways which primarily serve the needs of the conductor of the group rather than of the members. If he is anxious about what might occur under unstructured conditions or is worried about filling up the time, he may use games or exercises simply to meet these fears. This leads to a 'bin' approach: one reaches into one's bin of games and selects one, any one, as a time-filler or an avoidance device. In fact, games and exercises are very powerful devices which if well selected and well used can contribute directly to achieving the benefits one has in mind for members of the group. In order for this to occur, however, games, exercises and activities need to be chosen with care with the specific situation of the persons with whom one is working in mind, and with an awareness of the full range of possible consequences.

Potentially beneficial effects of exercises and games can be summarized as: providing pleasure; providing practice in a protected situation for learning to do things not currently in the repertoire of the participants; providing practice in a protected situation for anticipating how one might feel and what one might do in a forthcoming inevitable but feared interaction; and reducing fears by making opportunities for persons to try new behaviours which they have previously avoided or had no opportunity to engage in but which are potentially within their range. Potentially damaging effects include: exposing a person to feelings he cannot manage; exposing a person to self-recognitions which he finds intolerable; making explicit to a person opinions about him which damage self-esteem or threaten identity and which may lead him to leave the group; placing persons in failure situations; destroying or impairing trust between the conductor of the group and the participants.

7 Should the members be involved in planning?

This depends on such factors as whether or not the members have the necessary skills to engage in planning, whether or not they have relevant information or experience to draw on as a base for planning, and whether or not the activity of engaging in planning can in itself be expected to help members to move from some current state to some preferred state. Some persons cannot engage in collective planning because they do not have the skills, understandings or experience required. A regressed group of long-stay patients is unlikely to be able to plan an activity-based group. Persons to be seen in a psychotherapeutic group on an out-patient basis are unlikely to have the experience required to make good decisions about the frequency of sessions or policies about open or closed membership. The therapist or worker, who *does* have the experience, information or skills, must be the one to make the decisions. Sometimes the members or potential members are the best persons to make particular decisions because they have the necessary information and experience and the therapist does not. For example, the parents of handicapped children may be in the best position to decide about the kind of group which would best meet their needs, or the frequency with which the group should meet. Sometimes the potential members should be the ones to make certain decisions because that fits the purpose of the group – for example, perhaps the whole point of the group is to contribute to developing skills of planning and decision-making. In such a case it makes sense to reserve certain decisions for the group members to make when the group convenes for the first time. Even so, it is the therapist or worker who decides which decisions to make himself or in conjunction with colleagues, and which decisions to reserve for the total group membership. Thus, it is the conductor of the group who retains responsibility for deciding how planning decisions are to be made.

8 What contact or communication will need to be maintained with colleagues not directly involved in the group?

If the person who is conducting a group is working from a private office there may be no externally imposed requirement for him to communicate with colleagues about what goes on in his group, although he may choose to do so for reasons of his own, for example to support his own learning or to help guard against errors. More often than not, however, a therapist or group worker is in a position where he or she is required to communicate with colleagues in certain ways. It is sometimes the case that the patients or clients who are particpating in the group are also being seen by someone else individually, in a therapeutic or case work relationship. Two persons share responsibility for the patient or client and the question arises as to what kinds of information, if any, should be exchanged. In many settings the group therapist or group worker is expected to provide information about the group or persons in it to colleagues through verbal reports in case conferences or by written reports inserted into records. Apart from this, a group therapist or worker is likely to wish to maintain communication with certain others in the organization if those others have power over the patients, e.g. to grant weekend passes or to discharge or transfer them. In virtually all organizations or institutions a good deal of informal, casual information exchange goes on. A therapist or group worker may well wish to think over beforehand whether he wishes to seek or avoid opportunities for casual communication, and to consider his stance should colleagues express interest in or curiosity about the group.

If a client or patient is simultaneously a member of a group and is being seen by someone else individually, then agreements need to be reached about what (if anything) needs communicating. In my view opportunities for communication should be established from the beginning. These can then be used much or little depending on how the therapies evolve. The several therapists concerned may become aware that the patient is using one situation to avoid working in the other, or playing off one therapist against the other, or there may be indications from the way the patient is operating in one or the other setting that the therapists are working at cross purposes. If any of this occurs, then the therapists should make use of opportunities to communicate. If none of these special situations arises, it still seems a natural thing for the therapists to wish to compare notes from time to time as to how the patient is utilizing the group situation, developing in the individual contacts, and bringing material from the individual sessions to the group and vice versa. It is, however, important that the group therapist not use material communicated to him by the individual therapist in group sessions (and vice versa). The reasons for this are straightforward: any person undergoing two forms of therapy at the same time can be expected to use them differently. He may feel able to reveal certain experiences in individual sessions which he is not ready to reveal in the group. He may be working on the same problems in both settings but in different ways which involve differing patterns of disclosure.

These need to be respected. Betrayals of confidence across the two settings are likely to generate mistrust in the patient and be counter-productive.

As with co-leaders in groups, problems do not appear to be created if the group conductor and the individual worker or therapist have a congenial and mutually trusting relationship. The arrangement does not work well if the colleagues concerned are mutually distrustful or if each takes a proprietary attitude towards the client or patient, wishing to view any progress as a consequence of his or her personal intervention.

Sometimes one sees groups so arranged that some people in the group are also seen individually by the group leader while others are not. It is hard to defend this arrangement. Almost inevitably, feelings of jealousy and resentment of preferential treatment are stirred up. Some persons are provided with an escape hatch from dealing with issues within the group and others are not. Some persons are provided with individual support and others are not. It seems a better policy either to see no one individually or to see everyone individually. The same point holds when all of the persons in the group are seen individually by someone but some are seen by the group therapist and some by another colleague. This arrangement, too, brings with it inherent problems which are better avoided.

In many institutional or agency settings a group therapist or group worker is expected to share information about persons in his group by providing verbal or written reports. Where ultimate responsibility for a patient or client lies with the institution or agency this is an entirely legitimate requirement. I emphasize this because some group therapists resent such demands and take the view that everything that happens in a group should be confidential. This attitude fails to recognize the nature of one's responsibilities to one's agency or institution or the locus of power within it. If a therapist or worker accepts that he must communicate about the persons in the group, he still has decisions to make about just what should be communicated. By virtue of his special knowledge he can exert 'fate control' over the persons in the group. That is, his opinion as to a person's readiness for discharge, weekend leave, privileges, transfers within the institution or to another institution will carry weight. Some practitioners experience distress over being in such a position. One of their worries is that patients or clients will restrict their participation if they know that reports are to be made based on their behaviour in the group. Some group therapists or workers are reluctant to tell group members about the sorts of records being kept for fear that this will so inhibit them that they will not make use of the group at all. One needs to keep in mind that patients and clients are usually well aware that some form of record is being kept. This being so, patients may censor their participation more if the nature of the record-keeping is not made explicit than if it is. Fears of the unknown are typically worse than fears of the known. Patients and clients do of course exercise control over how they participate and what they reveal. This is as it should be and will be. Group members need to make their decisions on the basis of fact, not fantasy. Factors bearing on self-censorship – including record-keeping – should be made known to group members. I have considerable confidence that persons in groups can find ways to utilize the group situation and that if they feel obliged to keep some secrets this is not necessarily critical, because other content can serve the same dynamic purpose.

Whether or not official records are kept the group leader is faced with deciding whether or not to offer information in casual contact with colleagues and how to respond to casual enquiry or active curiosity. Total secrecy about a group when it is conducted in an institutional or organizational setting seems dysfunctional. Secretiveness generates or exacerbates suspicions in colleagues about what may be going on. This is not to say that it is appropriate to gossip about a group or give extensive rundowns over a cup of tea. But why not say, for example, that the group now seems to be moving ahead after a difficult start, or that a particular patient left the group in an upset state, or that some recent disturbing event in the setting has had a particular impact on the group? In close-grained settings staff function more effectively if there is open communication of this sort. The guiding principle seems to be the commonsense one that if the information is relevant to future actions concerning the patients then it should be shared. The only conditions under which one might have reservations about sharing are those where there are low levels of trust within the colleague group. If this is the case then a problem exists within the organization or institution which deserves attention entirely apart from its relevance to work with groups.

Sometimes the group conductor may be aware that his colleagues have reservations about the value of group work. This awareness is certain to influence the information he is prepared to share. The best tactic, in my experience, is to be open and accurate when sharing information about the group – that is, to communicate both one's pleasures and one's disappointments: the exciting, productive sessions as well as the difficult ones. Accurate, honest communications rather than selective and hence misleading reports are most likely to contribute to the development of realistic views about groups.

9 What records should a therapist or worker keep for his own use?

A group worker or therapist may well wish to keep some form of written record for his own use, over and above that which his organization requires of him. Purposes which may be served by keeping records include wishing to improve one's own understanding of groups and one's own behaviour in them, making available to oneself full information which can form the basis for written insertions into officially maintained records, or undertaking formal research in order to gain knowledge about particular features of the group or the effectiveness of the group.

For increasing own learning there is nothing more useful than taping sessions and re-listening, or, if this is truly not possible, making detailed process notes as soon after the close of each group session as possible. 'Tape' could mean video-tape or audio-tape. If a group relies mainly on talk, then audio-tapes are almost as useful as video. With an audio-tape as a base it is usually not difficult to recall non-verbal behaviours which accompanied the verbal interaction. If a group uses role-play, sculpting and the like then a video-tape is necessary. The great advantage of a tape is that is is a faithful and accurate recorder, and unlike people is never tempted to select some features of a session and ignore others. The disadvantage is that it takes an hour-and-a-half to listen to or watch an hour-and-a-half session: using tapes can become a time-consuming affair. Despite this there is a lot to be said for allowing oneself the experience at least occasionally of listening to or watching one's own group. If time is limited one can listen to a smallish sample and still gain a great deal. One almost always grasps aspects of the interaction which one missed while the session was going on. One can develop a better understanding of one's own leadership style. If the listening or watching is done co-operatively with a co-leader the learnings multiply because there then exists the opportunity to compare two impressions of the same events.

Sometimes group therapists or group workers tell me that their patients or clients would not tolerate a tape. While this is sometimes the case I believe that it is so less frequently than leaders tend to assume. The best way to test out whether or not a group really can tolerate being taped is to try it. If the tape recorder and microphone are clearly visible and the therapist sets it up in a matter of fact way at the beginning of a session then one of three things will happen: either the members take no notice and get on with their discussion; or the members take up the issue of being recorded as an explicit concern; or the members seem to ignore the tape but the interaction reveals indirectly that they are concerned about it. If either of the latter occurs, then it is appropriate to take this up with the group, inviting members to air their concerns about the taping and related or underlying issues. Much more often than not, in my experience, worries are alleviated and it becomes possible and acceptable to tape the sessions. If an explanation is requested or seems required something along the following lines can be offered: 'I want to understand the group better as it goes along and to understand myself as a group therapist better, so I plan to tape the sessions and listen to some parts of them in between our meetings.' The response to such a comment tells the therapist what more, if anything, needs to be said. Sometimes therapists say that members of a group will be more forthcoming if sessions were not taped. There is no way of testing this: one is left with one's own opinions. I believe that if taping generates substantial concerns these will soon become apparent either directly or in indirect, symbolic terms. If the issue is then explored in the group one can soon form a judgment as to whether or not the members have found a way to deal with their concerns. If the members display an abiding fear of being taped, then of course one should abandon the idea.

If for whatever reason it is impossible to tape a session then process notes are useful. I often suggest that people make process notes by dividing sheets of paper down the middle vertically so that a verbatim log can be kept on the left side of the page and one's impressions, reactions and interpretations of what is going on can be noted on the right hand side of the page. The reason for this is that it can be difficult to discipline oneself to produce a descriptive log which is not coloured by personal interpretations and reactions. The divided page helps. It takes a little experience with process recording to realize that a presumably descriptive statement such as 'the group engaged in trivial discussion' is in fact an interpretation. A process recording can never be as accurate as tape, of course, but it is far better than relying on unguided recalled impressions. It is an instructive exercise for two co-therapists to produce process recordings independently and then to compare them. Much information is gained about differences in perspectives on group events.

If one's purpose is to have material on which to base reports to staff or official records for the agency or institution, then a rather different kind of recording may be useful. For example one might set down a brief summary of the events of the group, including successive topics taken up, notable events (quarrels, outbursts, challenges to the leader, periods of depression or apathy, and the like), and follow this with brief notes about the ways in which each person in the group entered into the discussion or activity and seemed affected by it. One would also wish to keep straightforward records of attendance and tardiness. It is also useful to make a note of events occurring in the environment which have had an impact on the group. Such a record is not presented to other staff or entered into the patient's record in the form in which it is made, but forms a basis for such reports or entries.

If one intends to conduct formal research then one needs to devise a research design before the group starts. The design then tells one what kinds of records should be kept and what kinds of data should be collected (see chapter 6 for a full discussion). One cannot decide to undertake formal research after the group is underway because most research topics require one to collect data either before the group begins or at its very start. If one misses the opportunity it is lost forever.

10 What rules can and should the leader make, for members and for self, before or at the start of the group?

Before starting the group it is useful to think through the kind of rules one may make for oneself and for the group.

There are, in my view, certain rules which one should make for oneself and then stick with. These include never missing a session, starting and stopping on time, deciding whether or not and on what basis to see group members individually outside the group sessions, and possibly some others having to do with intended conduct during the group itself.

Some conductors are rather casual about missing or postponing group sessions. They may, for example, ask a colleague to take a session because they expect to have to attend a meeting, or they may change the time of the meeting at short notice (especially in residential settings where patients or clients are available much of the time). Sometimes members are not informed of absences or postponements until they arrive for a session. Any such behaviour on the part of the therapist or group workers is an error because it communicates to the group 'other things are more important than you'; 'I do not really care about you'. Such attitudes work against the helping process. It is unreasonable to expect group members to develop trust in a therapist or worker if he or she does not demonstrate commitment to the members of the group. I have heard it argued that to inform a group of prospective absences before they arrive would create anxiety and lead them to miss the session. This is a spurious argument. Necessary absences, announced in advance, do not generate more feelings than can be dealt with within the group. Even unexpected but unavoidable absences if explained and accounted for tend to be accepted by members providing that they do not occur too often. (From time to time in this book I make points which seem to me to be so obvious that they hardly need mentioning. The importance of avoiding absences is one of them. I include it because I have observed or heard about casual attendance, postponements, and the like, far too often.)

Persons who conduct groups express different views on the issue of starting and stopping on time. In my view, it is always appropriate to start on time. For some populations it is important also to stop on time; for others it is appropriate to allow some flexibility in the stopping time. Beyond a five-minute period of grace at the beginning of the session I see no reason for delaying the start of a group to wait for latecomers. This merely communicates to the members that the group is a casual enterprise and that a casual attitude towards it is acceptable. One cannot force people to arrive on time, but one can allow the natural consequence of lateness to occur – that is, missing the first part of the session and incurring whatever reactions arise from other members of the group. The issue of stopping on time is somewhat different. In groups composed of relatively intact persons where open discussion is the vehicle, I would almost always stop on time, again allowing about five minutes for flexibility. Not infrequently in such groups the most interesting and valuable discussion seems to occur just before the end of the session. Stopping on time comes as a gross interruption of valuable discussion. Yet, consider that when the members of a group get involved in something absorbing and potentially valuable just towards the end they are probably doing one of two things: either testing out the leader's commitment to them ('Do you or do you not value us enough to give extra time?') or invoking a collusive defence against involvement in the group (the members only get down to real issues when there is very little time to develop them). Either of these issues can be taken up with the group and dealt with within the time allotted. To respond by extending the time is collusion with the members in dealing with an issue through acting-out. Like all acting-out it keeps the issue in the realm of the unmentionable or the unexaminable. As with all rules, circumstances alter cases. Under exceptional circumstances one might extend a session in order to deal with some unexpected crisis, but this is likely to occur only rarely.

In groups which are highly structured it is usually unnecessary to run over time if one has judged with reasonable accuracy the time required to move through a planned set of activities. In less structured groups with more damaged or immature persons it might sometimes serve one's purposes for the group to run over, if one judges that these persons will only understand and become convinced of the therapist's commitment to them through very concrete expressions of this, in this case being willing to give more of one's time. Even so, there are other ways of communicating commitment in concrete terms and if one judges this to be necessary they can be planned into the design of the group.

It sometimes happens during the course of a group that one or more of the members will seek out private contact with the leader at some point or another before, after, or between sessions. It is as well to think out one's policy about this beforehand. My own views on this have changed over the years. At one time, when I was working mainly with psychotherapeutic groups, I operated on a fairly firm rule about this, quite quickly referring members back to the group itself. I have since become more flexible, seeking each time to think out just why a person is seeking an individual contact, and responding accordingly. A person who is in a real emergency is in a different position from one who is seeking to bypass the group or form a special relationship with the therapist. What is regarded as a 'real' emergency is a matter of opinion, but it will surely include a bereavement, or being the victim of a criminal attack. Such emergencies happen rarely, but when they do it seems appropriate to see the person for as long as seems required for him or her to feel better able to cope with it. Towards the end of such a contact it is a good idea to suggest to the person that he or she tell the group that there had been such a contact and say as much about it as he or she wishes. If the person seems to be using the contact in an effort to bypass the group – that is, to deal with some matter in the safer context of a one-to-one relationship rather than to risk raising it in the group situation – then it is appropriate to hear the issue out with little comment and then suggest that it be taken up in the group. If the person claims that it could not possibly be revealed in the group, then this, of course, can become the subject for discussion. If a member of a group comes to the therapist or worker privately with what appears to be a pseudo-problem, or one that could easily have waited a day or two for discussion during the group, this may be an instance of a member seeking a special or favoured relationship with the therapist. Here too, it is best not to engage with the person at length but to make an early recommendation that the issue be brought up in the group. Whatever the reason for a person seeking individual contact it is an error to allow such contacts to go on in secret from the other members. Apart from the fact that it never seems possible to maintain such secrecy, placing any one individual in so special a situation is bound to have repercussions in the group and generate problems which would not otherwise occur.

So far, these are rules which a group worker or therapist may make for himself. Making rules for the members is an entirely different matter. What rules, if any, should one make about tardiness, absences, confidentiality, outside contacts amongst members, the group breaking up into sub-group discussions, etc? All such behaviours belong to persons other than oneself and therefore are not in one's direct control. One can choose to announce to a group, 'in this group we shall not have outside contacts', or 'people are expected to come on time', but it is folly to expect that such a declaration necessarily is followed by compliance. It is quite appropriate to tell a group in the beginning that the group's work will be facilitated if people come on time and avoid absences, if one wishes to do so. However, such a comment had best not be regarded as a rule, but as a statement of one's own views about conditions which will facilitate the work of the group. It refers to the conductor's preferences; whether or not it becomes a norm for the group is another matter. If a conductor regarded non-compliance with such stated preferences as breaking a group norm, this would be an error since a group norm in fact has not been established. Norms can be established only by the group members themselves over a period of time, through direct discussions leading to consensus or through behaviour which displays common attitudes toward tardiness, absence, breaches of confidentiality, and the like.

With reference to confidentiality, some therapists make an explicit effort to establish this as a group norm at the start of the group, and others do not, preferring to wait for the issue to emerge. My own preference is to say nothing, on grounds that the issue will emerge if it becomes a problem for the group. A declaration on the part of the leader about confidentiality is a pious hope and both he and everyone else knows it. The same general point can be made about outside contacts amongst members.

11 How can the transition be planned and managed when a new conductor joins an existing group?

A change in leadership may occur in a group conducted by two persons where one of these drops out and a new person is brought in as co-conductor, or in a group with a single conductor in which a new conductor replaces a previous one.

When one knows about a projected change ahead of time, the two persons concerned (the old and the new) can enter into discussions in which the old leader informs the new one about the group and the new leader shares his expectations about the group and his own role in it.

If the new person is to join (rather than replace) an existing therapist or worker, then the two of them can test their likely compatibility in much the same ways in which two colleagues would do who expect to start fresh with a group. It is helpful to inform group members two or three sessions beforehand that a new leader is about to join the group, so that they can digest this information, have time to express their feelings about it, and prepare internally for the forthcoming change. Some leaders seek the members' permission beforehand and abide by their decision. In either case, members know about the change before it occurs. The new and the established therapist can agree ahead of time as to whether the existing leader of the group is to introduce the new leader or whether the new person is to introduce himself. Something should be said, in the interests of reducing unnecessary confusion and maintaining a sense of safety in the group.

If a new conductor is to replace (rather than join) an existing conductor, a decision will need to be made as to whether or not there is to be a period of overlap when both leaders are present. On balance, I think it best to avoid this. There should be of course a period, again, of two, three or four sessions during which group members know of the impending change, and can express such feelings as they may have, especially about losing their leader, and exploit the situation for what can be gained from it. Whether this should be a shorter or a longer period depends on the overall life of the group: shorter if the group is brief and limited; longer if it is an extended group. As the new person cannot possibly be like the old one, it seems better to present the members with successive tasks (coping with the impending loss of one therapist or worker; finding ways to know another) than to expect them to deal with both tasks simultaneously.

Under special and rare circumstances a therapist or worker might have to join a group as conductor with no opportunity for prior notice to the participants or for personal preparation for the task. This could only occur when a group is being conducted by a single therapist or worker who suffers some family emergency, sudden illness, or even dies. If this occurs, one's only course of action is to inform the members of the circumstances which have made the change necessary, and respond to what then emerges as best one can. The event is likely to produce a crisis for the group, for they have had no time to anticipate the loss of their conductor and no time to prepare internally for the change. When the new conductor first walks into such a group, he knows only that he must try to help the members through this crisis. Later he can enlist the help of the members themselves in his task of getting oriented to a group which has a character and history of which he knows nothing.

12 What choices are open to one and what decisions need to be made when one is 'given' a group or when one 'finds' one?

Sometimes a worker or therapist is 'given' a group which has been planned by someone else. This might occur when someone higher up in the hierarchy of an organization plans a group and then assigns it to someone lower in the hierarchy, or when a new appointee is expected to fit into an already established programme by taking on one part of it. Many persons who begin their work with groups by this route feel that they have no choice and that their involvement with the group is a fait accompli: hence the common use of the term 'given'. Not so. It is important to remember that one can say no. In particular, one would wish to review all the decisions made about the group – the basic one discussed in chapter 3 and the detailed planning decisions in this chapter, and decide whether or not one regards the group as planned to be viable. Can the group, given the set of decisions already made, be reasonably expected to survive and to benefit its members? If one's answer to this is 'no' then it is reasonable to request that certain issues be re-examined.

Sometimes a leader 'finds' a group in the sense that the group already existed and had a life of its own before it became defined as a client group. This might be the case when one sets out to work with a group of adolescents who already constitute a gang or a friendship group, or a group of persons drawn from a ward or house who already have had a good deal of interaction with one another, or with students from a course who already know one another and where a group experience is to be a part of their training. The would-be conductor is a newcomer. The members have already had substantial experience together: as a group they will have established a whole range of norms, and as a group they share a history. However, although these persons are already formed into a group, they have not been a *helping* group. They, together with the person who is to be the conductor, face the task of transforming themselves from a group of colleagues/ friends/fellow residents into a group geared to achieve personal benefits. Certain planning decisions (size of group, membership) have already been made. Others (venue, duration of sessions, etc.) can be made mutually with members. Of special importance will be the ground rules on which the group is to operate, since the norms which support the work of a helping group may be quite different from those which evolve in a group of friends, acquaintances or colleagues. Examining these and seeking to establish new ground rules is an important early task for 'found' groups.

Up to now, I have been discussing a group as an isolated event. It is sometimes the case that a group is part of a larger programme which may include other groups of differing types and/or individual case work or psychotherapy. This is most likely to be the case in a residential setting. In a therapeutic community, in particular, patients may be involved in a variety of groups in the course of a day or a week and in addition have individual therapeutic sessions. In planning any particular component of such a programme the question of relationship among components arises.

13 How can components of a programme be planned so as to avoid overkill, dilution and confusion, or undoing?

In making detailed planning decisions for groups which are to be conducted within some larger programme one needs to take into account the impact which particular parts of the programme may have on one another and their collective impact on patients or clients and on staff.

One hazard is overkill: it is possible to design a day or a week with so much presumed therapeutic interaction of one sort or another that neither patients nor staff have private time in which to think through or digest experiences or to find relief from the demands of constant interaction. Another hazard is inadequate differentiation. For example, successive groups planned to occur on the same day are intended to be a planning group, a therapeutic group, a ward administration group, etc. The same persons attend all these groups and in operation the boundaries between them become blurred and both the patients and staff become unclear as to the functions of each group. The programme loses point and incisiveness. Both patients and staff may become confused and the overall effort is diluted.

Different parts of a programme can prove to be an interference fit. That is, one finds when putting an apparently plausible programme into operation that participants – which could mean patients or staff – use one part of the programme to undo the potential effectiveness of others. This can occur, for example, when an individual avoids confronting some issue in a therapeutic group by acting it out in a ward administration group. If probable interference fits can be anticipated at the planning stage, such problems can sometimes be averted. If not, certain planning decisions will have to be re-made later, in the light of experience.

This calls to mind a general point which can be made about most of the detailed decisions discussed in this chapter. Except where one decides to reserve a decision until it can be made mutually with members, decisions are made ahead of time by the conductors of the group. Indeed, some of them must be made ahead of time (e.g. venue) in order for the group to come together at all. Decisions can only be made on the basis of information available at the time: planning decisions are best guesses about what is likely to work in the future on the basis of what is known in the present. When planning decisions are put into practice new information becomes available. In the light of this new information decisions can be re-examined and some may require revision.

In addition to the detailed planning decisions discussed in this chapter, two more planning decisions remain to be made: how to arrange for monitoring and evaluating a group, and by what means to identify a membership. These are discussed in chapters 6 and 7 respectively.

Suggested exercises

To gain experience in making detailed planning decisions one might carry one of the exercises suggested at the end of chapter 3 (first two paragraphs under Suggested exercises) to further completion by constructing a checklist composed of detailed planning decisions 1–10 and arriving at decisions with respect to each.

If one has a special interest in utilizing games, exercises or activities in work with groups one might make a tentative plan for a first session or a series of sessions for a specified population and then test the suitability of the plan by, first, answering the questions (i) through (viii), posed in section 6 of this chapter, and second, forming a judgment as to whether or not the plan is or is not likely to facilitate achieving the benefits one has in mind for members of the group.

One might also like to select a number of games, exercises or activities from one of the many handbooks and guides available (see Selected References for chapter 5, page 405) and explore its character and likely consequences by applying the same set of questions to each.

Chapter 6

Deciding by what means to monitor the group and assess its functioning

Continuing attention to monitoring and assessing a group serves one's overall purposes by providing information which can be taken into account when making decisions and planning action. I take it for granted that a therapist, group worker or leader should continually monitor and assess any group with which he or she is working: as it goes along, as a guide to action whilst actually conducting the group; and afterwards, to help in decisions about subsequent groups. Monitoring is noticing: watching, listening, trying to make sense of what one sees and hears. Assessing is checking events against intentions. At least three time scales or time units are involved: successive events while a group is in session; each individual session taken as a unit; and the series of sessions which comprises the life of the group. Some forms of monitoring and assessing require pre-planning. Thus, thought needs to be given to this issue before a group starts.

Monitoring and assessing the events of a group while it is in session is a matter of getting into a definite habit of maintaining an internal dialogue with oneself during sessions, noting just how the group is moving, what issues it takes up, where it gets stuck, the stance which each person takes toward successive events, and the like. No pre-planning or special equipment is required. One needs an attitude of mind and skills in observing and in making sense of complex and shifting situations. I shall reserve a full discussion of this form of monitoring for chapter 8.

A group worker or therapist may also wish to take as a time unit each session of the group. Here, he or she seeks to review each session as it occurs, considering its overall character, how it developed, what happened to or for particular individuals, how oneself as worker or therapist participated and what followed from one's participation, whether the group as presently functioning is working towards achieving the benefits one had in mind when setting it up, and if not what is standing in its way. This kind of monitoring and assessing must be planned for ahead of time, first to reserve the time required for doing it, and second to arrange certain aids to monitoring and assessing such as taping, or pre-specifying periodic reviews for particular purposes, or planning for particular forms of information-gathering.

A third time unit is the series as a whole. The therapist or group worker will almost certainly wish to review the whole effort, to form some view as to whether the group fulfilled the purposes he had in mind for it, and whether, if further groups are to be conducted, they should be planned in the same way or differently. Post-group reviews need to be planned beforehand to be sure of gathering the information required. For example, in order to assess whether change has occurred one needs information about a person's state at the start of the group. In order to evaluate particular devices or activities which one has built into the structure of the group, one has to gather information about their impact soon after they occur in the series of sessions.

None of the above is, or needs to be, formal research. Sometimes but certainly not always one might wish to design and carry out formal research, over and above informal forms of monitoring and assessment. Usually one undertakes formal research either to satisfy one's own curiosities about certain features of the group and how it works (if they cannot be satisfied by informal means) or in order to influence and guide future action – one's own or that of others – for example, by checking out the costs and benefits of conducting a particular kind of group.

In this chapter I shall first discuss informal monitoring and assessment, either after each session or after a series is completed, and associated decisions about the budgeting of time, record-keeping and report-making. Following this, I shall consider formal research directed towards evaluating outcomes, understanding processes, and assessing costs and benefits. This book is for practitioners, not research workers. For those practitioners who see a big gap between practice and research, or even see these two activities as an interference fit, I would like to show how, by relatively little additional pre-planning and later work, the ordinary task of informal monitoring and assessment can be transformed into small-scale formal research.

1 Informal monitoring and assessing

If one is to review a group session by session, the most obvious requirement is time. Very nearly of equal importance is a helper – a co-conductor, observer or colleague with whom one can discuss events and test impressions. Such reviews can be greatly aided by some form of recording or record-keeping, although these are not absolutely necessary.

In practical terms post-session reviews require reserving a period of time after each session for discussion with one's co-therapist, co-worker or observer, or if there is none, with a colleague who agrees to function as a listener and consultant. A minimum time requirement is thirty minutes or so, immediately following each group session, or, if this is not possible, sometime during the following day. If one makes use of someone who has not been present in the group, then additional time needs to be allotted, since some of the time will have to be spent in reporting events.

Ongoing monitoring and assessing generates such substantial benefits that it is well worth the time involved. Post-session discussions constitute feedback to the therapist or worker about the group. This generates immediate benefits: the therapist or worker is likely to become aware of events occurring in the group, and their import, more explicitly and accurately than is likely if he does not make a deliberate effort to review the session. This awareness can then be utilized (in fact, inevitably *will* be utilized) in guiding his interventions in subsequent sessions.

Both immediately and in the longer run, post-session discussions help the therapist or worker to develop and sharpen his skills of observation and his capacity to understand events arising in groups. As this occurs, he is likely to experience fewer periods of confusion and to be more likely to see, confront and capitalize on situations arising in the group.

The simplest form of post-session discussion is an open discussion based on the recollections of those present, or based on the therapist's or worker's verbal account to a colleague. Such an approach does however run the risk of selective recall – remembering what was dramatic or pleasing or difficult, and losing track of the rest. It can therefore be useful to think out ahead of time the issues one wants to be sure to examine. These might include how the group as a whole is moving and developing; how specific members are participating; and what one is doing oneself. With reference to the group as a whole, for example, one might ask 'Is what is happening in the group right now telling me that my original assessment of frontier and/or preoccupying concern was correct? Or incorrect?' 'Has the group got stuck in some unproductive interpersonal pattern or in some restrictive solution? If so, what can I do about it?' 'What was the prevailing mood?' 'Is the level of tension so high that useful work is unlikely?' And so on. Some questions have to do with the particular stance which individuals take in the group and the manner in which they participate: 'Is anyone getting left out in this group? Why?' 'Did anyone seem particularly worried or distressed today? In what way? In response to what?' 'Does this suggest action on my part for next time?' 'Did the session seem particularly important to certain persons? Who and in what way? Is there a way in which I can follow up on this? What opportunities should I look for?' 'Is anyone presenting a special problem to the group? Should I be doing something about this? What?'

Another category of questions has to do with oneself rather than with the group or the members specifically. One can and should ask: 'What did I say or do in this session and did my behaviour have the consequences I intended?' 'Was my timing right, or did I intervene prematurely or let things run on for too long?' 'Have I been silent when I ought to have intervened?' 'What were the consequences of my spontaneous comments? Looking back, to what do I now think they were a response?' 'Have I been playing favourites? Why?' 'Have I been ignoring or excluding someone? Why?' 'Have I been colluding in some shared defence or restrictive solution?'

If two co-therapists or workers are involved, some questions can be directed to how they function together, and to the differences and similarities between them. 'Did we see things the same or differently?' 'Were we working towards different goals or on different assumptions, and if so what were they?' 'Did we get in each other's way? How?' 'How did each of us feel towards the other in the course of the session? In response to what events?' 'Were we being seen or used differently by the group members?' 'Were there times when one saw something the other didn't, or where one rescued the other?'

Such questions look at specific interventions in short runs of events. Each leader can also ask questions about his or her own participation which take a somewhat longer view: 'Looking back over a run of sessions, under what conditions do I find myself most active? Least active?' 'What do I tend to worry about?' 'Are there things I consistently run away from?' 'Whom do I like and whom do I dislike in this group? How can I explain this to myself?' 'Do I consistently make the same kind of error?'

Monitoring can be supported by various forms of record-keeping. One could, for example, decide to write a brief summary of each session, or two co-therapists or workers could take turns doing so, or, for some or all sessions, each could produce a summary independently, so that these form the basis for comparing perceptions and judgments about the group. If two persons keep records by dividing a page vertically and recording down the left side the events which actually occurred, in sequence, and down the right side own feelings and reactions and hypotheses as to the possible import of the events, then these form a useful basis for comparing the perceptions and imposed meanings of those concerned. One might also consider identifying in advance points in the life of the group when individual members will be reviewed for how they are participating in and benefiting from the group (or not). One might decide to tape the sessions and use some of these tapes as a basis for discussion. As tape-listening is a time-consuming activity, one might agree beforehand to tape certain sessions only, or to tape all sessions but listen to only specified ones. Another aid to record-keeping is to prepare some sort of form beforehand, perhaps listing out issues or questions which one considers particularly important to keep in mind. These then constitute guides or reminders to the worker or therapist to attend to particular points during each post-session discussion.

The kind of records which one decides to keep depends partly on what one wishes to learn oneself from the post-session discussions, and partly on whether one's purposes have to do solely with the workers or therapists concerned, or whether they also include making reports to others or conducting formal investigations. If the purpose relates to those directly responsible for the group, then the whole point of the post-session discussions and of any supporting record-keeping is to ensure that one uses the events of the group as feedback to oneself in guiding own action, and in sharpening one's skills of observing and intervening. If this is one's purpose, then there is no particular need to be systematic or consistent in the form of record-keeping. On the contrary, it is a definite advantage to try out different forms of record-keeping and to use the post-session discussion times differently, sometimes listening to tapes, sometimes comparing written summaries, sometimes comparing one's own written account with the tape of the session, and so on. If one's purpose includes making a report to others, either during the life of the group or afterward, then record-keeping needs to take this into account. Most probably one will wish to be somewhat more systematic in recording – for example, making sure that there is a written summary of each session, or making sure that the participation of each member is reviewed at regular intervals.

It is distracting, both for the person conducting the group and the members, to take notes while a group is in session. One's attention inevitably is divided, and since much in a group depends on catching non-verbal behaviours and using non-verbal behaviour oneself (eye contact, posture and the like), trying to take notes distracts one from the primary task. Note-taking can also be a message to the group: 'My notes are more important than you.' So, record-keeping generally has to be done after the session ends – the sooner the better – or by a non-participating observer, or by an audio- or video-tape. These are not mutually exclusive, and it can be a positive advantage to use several.

In addition to reviewing and assessing each session, one will almost certainly wish to review the whole group effort after the group finishes, looking at what each person seems to have gained, and whether each person has gained as much as one thought was possible at the start of the group. It is useful also to consider the way in which the group developed and the character it came to have, and to judge whether there was anything about the group itself – such as the persistence of collusive defences, or the members failing to find a way to cope with a difficult person – which got in the way of the group achieving its full potential. For some kinds of groups it is useful to build in an evaluation period during the final session of the group. In that case, members' opinions as to personal gains and the usefulness or otherwise of the group can be joined to one's own views about the value of the group experience.

The group will have been based on some structure, whether that of open discussion, topic-oriented discussion, or exercises and activities. Whatever its structure, one would wish to consider whether or not the structure worked as intended, whether some persons found it more useful than others, and so on. In virtually all groups, some members gain more from the experience than others; indeed some may seem not to have gained at all. It seems important then to examine as best one can what might account for such differences. Perhaps the persons concerned were different in some important ways in the first place; or they came to occupy particular positions in the group which then influenced the ways in which they could be reached by or use the experience. Or the therapist or worker was more interested in some than in others and attended to them differently. One might also wish to look at outside fortuitous events or calamities in the lives of the persons in the group, in order to identify possible extra-group influences on their experiences.

It is important to plan the nature of the post-group review ahead of time, since it is frequently the case that certain records needs to be kept or certain information gathered in order for the review to take place. After the group finishes is too late, for example, to ask members how they saw their problems when the group began, or what they expected from the group, or to ask others (for example ward staff or houseparents) how a particular person usually interacted with others or what his prevailing mood was before he entered the group. Recollection is too likely to be coloured by subsequent events. If one wishes to evaluate a particular group structure, especially one which has involved a series of activities, exercises or games, or one which included some special once-only activity (such as a weekend away), one would probably wish to ask members quite near to the time how they experienced an event and what they thought they gained from it. Asking them at the end of the group is also useful, but tends to elicit different information.

Some particular questions which one can ask oneself after the group finishes and which can guide assessment include: 'Did members benefit in the ways I hoped for?' 'Who appeared to gain from participating in this group, and who did not? Can I think of any explanations for this?' 'Looking back, was the structure right for the group, or would some modification of it, or a different structure altogether, have been a better fit with the frontier and/or preoccupying concern of those in it?' 'Would a different leadership approach on my part have yielded a better result?' 'Were there particular turning points in this group, after which things got better, or worse?' 'In what ways did and did not the co-leaders get along together, and did this influence how things went?' 'Did the group get stuck in some collusive defence or restrictive solution? If so, what prevented moving out of it?'

A post-group assessment can be conducted informally through general discussion among those concerned, or one might decide to structure it a bit more by making use of questions like the above as a guide to discussion, or one might decide to formalize the review by turning questions like the above into a questionnaire to be filled out by co-leaders and/or observer (if any). In some settings, it is possible to ask others besides those who have been concerned with the group to fill out such forms – for example, ward or hostel staff – and it is also possible to construct parallel forms which can be filled out by the group members themselves.

Some of the records kept in connection with post-session discussions can be used for post-group reviews. For example, if one has recorded one's opinions about specific members at intervals throughout the life of the group, then these statements can be brought together to form the basis for a post-group review.

Some of the discussion so far raises the question of what shall be held to be useful sources of information? Possible sources are oneself and those others who have functioned as co-leaders or observers, the persons who have actually participated in the group as members, and others who know the persons or are in a position to observe them in their daily lives outside the group. It can be useful to seek information from several different sources, to see how they fit and mesh. There is of course a sense in which all information from whatever source is true and correct. Information derived from different sources ought to and indeed must make sense, each in terms of the other, but it would be simplistic to assume that they must coincide, or that there is something wrong if they do not. It is not justifiable to assume that one source of information is better or more accurate than another. Rather, one needs to recognize that any information is from one person's particular perspective. Looking at different perspectives against one another is more likely to increase understanding than looking at just one.

Some practitioners worry that their own views will be 'too subjective', by which they mean distorted or biased, or serving own personal purposes. Amongst a number of definitions of 'subjective', the *Shorter Oxford Dictionary* offers the following:

(i) Relating to the thinking subject; proceeding from or taking place within the subject; having its source in the mind.
(ii) Existing in the mind only; illusory, fanciful

Judgments made about the group and the persons in it are bound to be subjective in the first sense; they need not be subjective in the second sense. If each person who is observing and making judgments about the group ties his judgments to observable events, then these judgments will of course proceed from 'the thinking subject', but they need not be illusory or fanciful. Indeed, some of the devices suggested earlier are designed to minimize distortion and to reveal differences in perspective. For example, comparing one's own summary of a session with a tape reveals omissions and distortions; comparing one's own observations and judgments with that of others reveals differences in perspective. Arguing out differences is a route toward reducing distortion.

Another question which is sometimes asked is whether one should engage in such extensive discussions and reviews (which after all are very time-consuming) each time one conducts a group. Perhaps one is conducting a number of groups at the same time and the overall investment of time becomes prohibitive. Or, as one gains more experience, detailed reviews seem less necessary. If one's purpose is ongoing learning for oneself, then one might choose to engage in close forms of monitoring and assessing with at least some of the sessions of some of the groups which one conducts, perhaps choosing to examine those sessions which one has found particularly puzzling or interesting. As experience accumulates one comes more and more to internalize the process of monitoring and assessing, and therefore might not always need to make a special point of regular reviews. Even so, regular reviews of some portion of one's work are a form of insurance that one is still paying attention properly, and help one to avoid falling into bad habits of either observation, meaning-placing or intervening. If one is trying something new in the way of structure, or working with a client or patient group with which one has not worked before, then regular discussion and review is likely to be particularly useful.

If one's purpose is training others, then regular discussions and reviews of the sort suggested here are a very good route to learning for less experienced persons. If one's purpose is to guide further decisions, particularly with regard to the investment of time in further groups, then regular monitoring and assessing is important, to avoid making decisions on general impressions only.

2 Formal assessments and investigations

One sometimes wishes to undertake more formal and rigorous forms of research, addressed either to evaluating the group, or to understanding some of the processes which go on in the group, or to working out the return on investment of one's efforts with groups, that is, examining costs against benefits.

Evaluating the group

Much of what has been suggested in the preceding section *is* evaluation, of an informal sort. Most practitioners who have monitored a group throughout its life and reviewed it carefully afterward develop quite a sound understanding of the success or otherwise of the group and of its impact on the clients or patients in it. They are likely to be aware of major errors, if any have been made. They are likely to recognize that some persons have gained more than others and to have some plausible ideas about reasons for this. Why, then, engage in formal evaluation research? There seem to be two possible motivations: the first is to learn more than can be learned by informal methods, and the second is to demonstrate the value of the group to others, through a visibly rigorous and systematic evaluation. In the latter case, a further motivation is likely to be persuading those with power to continue to support a group programme.

If one's major reason for undertaking formal evaluation research is to prove to someone else that the group is worthwhile, then the best advice is not to bother. The need to prove worthwhileness already suggests that someone who has power to make decisions is unconvinced of the usefulness of groups. If this is the case, formal research findings are unlikely to change his views. For technical reasons, to be discussed shortly, it is very difficult to conduct evaluation research completely satisfactorily. Questions can almost always be raised about the findings and design faults can be identified. (If all else fails, a sceptic can claim that too few subjects were studied.) Sceptics can always find grounds on which to dismiss positive research results. One need only consider the reverse situation to be convinced of this. A practitioner is far more likely to base future decisions on his own experiences and impressions than on the results of some formal study. If his direct experience tells him that some persons do gain from their experience in a group, a formal evaluation study which has produced negative findings is unlikely to stop him from wishing to work with groups in the future.

If this is so, then if one is faced with someone who doubts the potential value of groups the best route towards influencing him is not through conducting formal research, but through opening up the issue for discussion. By this means one can understand better the nature of his reservations and worries and seek to reduce them, or work out what would, for him, be a reasonable test of his reservations. One needs to hold in mind that research rarely if ever 'proves' anything. Rather, it can support or fail to support certain assumptions and hypotheses; it can help to ensure against jumping to conclusions on the basis of partial or unsystematically examined evidence, and it can generate information and understandings not available by other means.

Although I am dismissing evaluation research when it is undertaken to prove something to someone else, I am not dismissing it altogether, because such research can help one to understand more clearly than can general impressions, who benefits and who doesn't, and why. An investigation which examines such a question can guide both practice and policy by suggesting what sorts of persons were able to make use of a particular group structure, by identifying lost opportunities in the group which could be watched for another time, by seeking to identify events which got in the way of persons using the group as well as they might, etc. Evaluation research can be designed to yield far more information than whether the group was 'successful' or not. Many groups are a mixed bag as far as success is concerned. Some persons benefit and others do not. Usually the therapist or group worker already knows this, from his observations of the group. What he needs to know is what can account for the different outcomes of the group for particular persons.

Evaluation research seems to fall into two main categories: 'outcome' research, and 'process-outcome' research. The first is addressed to the question of what changes, if any, occur for persons who have participated in a group. The group itself, or what has gone on in it, is not examined. The group remains a 'black box' which is not investigated specifically but is assumed to have been the critical variable influencing change. The second kind of evaluation also seeks to identify the changes, if any, which ensue from a group experience, but it does so in connection with an examination of events within the group or of the experiences which individuals have undergone while in the group. The group is no longer a black box, but a box which is opened then looked into for events and experiences which can plausibly be linked to outcomes.

If one is to invest time in designing and carrying out evaluation research, it is more profitable to undertake process-outcome research rather than merely outcome research, because the former yields more information.

Both forms of evaluation research require one to specify and then find ways of measuring outcome variables, that is, criteria which one accepts as indicating desired and undesired outcomes. Both forms of research must include some means of testing whether changes have occurred in respect of the outcome variables, and both utilize some device for plausibly claiming that any changes which occur have to do with the group experience and not with some other event. Outcome research usually tries to accomplish the latter by making use of control groups and/or by establishing a base-line for each person in the group. Process-outcome research may or may not use control groups or seek to establish base-lines, but in any case will try to show how experiences or processes within the group are associated with different outcomes.

1 *Identifying outcome variables.* An initial task in designing evaluation research is to identify one or several outcome variables relevant to the population one is working with. Key outcome variables will be the hoped-for benefits identified early in the planning process. In other words, what was specified early in planning as hoped-for benefits on behalf of the patients or clients with whom one intends to work can be specified later as outcome variables. One conducts a piece of evaluation research to find out whether or not what one hoped would occur did in fact occur.

In addition to the benefits one hopes to achieve (now specified as outcome variables) one may wish, for some groups, to identify outcome at another level which has to do with certain further consequences one hopes will ensue if the primary benefits are achieved. For example, one might hope that long-stay psychiatric hospital patients become able to maintain themselves outside the institution; one may hope that youthful offenders do not re-offend; one may hope that alcoholics stop drinking; one may hope that chronic complainers take up less staff time. These further consequences may be built into an evaluation study as outcome variables: indeed it is often the case that the administrators of an agency or institution have been willing to invest in a group programme because they hope for just such outcomes. However, from a practitioner's point of view such outcomes as these are the further consequences of personal benefits, which I have suggested earlier can usefully be defined in terms of persons moving beyond current frontiers or coping more satisfactorily with preoccupying concerns. This point becomes clearer if one thinks for a moment of the consequences of defining hoped-for benefit as preventing readmission or re-offending, etc. Goals defined in these terms cannot provide a guide for planning: they are too removed from the immediate experience of the persons concerned. One has to look for other things as hoped-for benefit which, if achieved, would then contribute to avoiding further admissions, etc. More-over, if one were primarily interested in, say, preventing re-offending, there are shorter routes to this goal than conducting a group. One could for example impose a curfew on young people or redefine what shall be regarded as an offence. The general point is that if one utilizes readmission rates, re-offending rates, etc. as outcome variables one should certainly not stop there but also seek to identify outcome variables in terms of originally specified hoped-for benefits, linked to one's conceptualization of frontier and preoccupying concern. With respect to youthful offenders, for example, one might have considered at the planning stage that many young offenders lack skills in handling angry feelings and that impulsive striking out at others gets them into trouble with the law. In that case, skills in managing anger is one of the hoped-for benefits, and success should be measured in terms of whether or not members show evidence of developing such skills. At the same time one might have considered that youthful offenders suffer from low self-esteem, or lack sources for self-esteem other than offending. If so, then one also hopes for increased levels of self-esteem, and will regard the group as successful if enhanced self-esteem not linked to offending can be demonstrated. One has now identified two outcome variables – increased skills in managing anger, and increased levels of self-esteem – to which one could add not re-offending.

Another kind of outcome variable has to do with what members of groups hope for on their own behalf. These may or may not coincide with what the therapist or worker, from his perspective, hopes for. Or, members and group conductors sometimes hope for the same outcomes but place different emphases on them. For a group member, for example, getting rid of nightmares might be a prime aim; from the group conductor's point of view nightmares, while not unimportant, may be seen as an aspect of something else, for example, developing satisfactory ways of managing anger.

One usually also wishes to design an evaluation study in such a way that it can 'catch' unanticipated outcomes: those which one did not specify at the beginning as hoped-for benefits but which nevertheless occurred. It is not unusual to observe spin-off benefits in groups. For example, one might not set up a group for young offenders in order for them to function as sympathetic helpers to others, but gaining such experiences could well be one of the spin-off benefits which the group generates for them.

Sometimes benefits occur for persons who are not the primary beneficiaries and may not even be members of the group. Usually although not always these will be other family members who are not directly concerned but nevertheless benefit from changes which occur in the group members themselves. For some kinds of groups it is appropriate to include outcome variables which pertain to these indirect beneficiaries.

With some kinds of groups (e.g. elderly mentally infirm hospitalized patients) one does not necessarily expect positive change but sees the group as a holding operation, forestalling further deterioration. In such instances, stability (i.e no change) can reasonably be accepted as an outcome variable, and the group regarded as effective if one can show that without the group, deterioration would likely have taken place. An outcome variable need not always emphasize change, but it does need to refer to and express the benefits one hopes to achieve.

2 *Assessing whether or not change has taken place.* Because one is always comparing what persons were like before the group experience with what they are like afterwards one always needs at least one pre-measure and at least one post-measure: pattern

and frequency of offending before and after, level of self-esteem before and after, level of morale before and after, and so on. Some outcome variables are easier to measure and quantify than others. For example it is easier to assess whether or not a client re-offends within six months than whether a client handles anger more effectively than before. However, 'easy' is not the same as 'important'. All too often one finds in published evaluation studies that the researcher has restricted himself to outcome variables which are easily measured and quantified, and hence responsive to being expressed in statistical terms. If the variables so identified turn out to be trivial, then much is lost. More satisfactory designs seek to identify a range of outcome variables, some of which can be readily quantified and others not. They may also seek to measure the same variable by different means. Ideally, 'hard', quantifiable data forms a framework for qualitative data, such that the former contributes discipline to one's findings and the latter provides richness and detail. To return to our earlier example, one might wish to assess the pre-group position of the adolescent with regard to offending in terms of number and type of offences over a certain period of time (hard data). With regard to the management of anger one might wish to elicit and analyse anecdotal accounts of episodes which stirred up anger, or one might decide to administer some projective device such as TAT cards or a sentence completion test (soft data). With regard to self-esteem, one might use a paper-and-pencil test of self-esteem (hard data) and observations of the adolescent in interaction with his peers (soft data). The same devices would need to be used following the close of the group. Some outcome variables, by their nature, must be assessed over a period of time (for example re-offending). Some outcome variables need to be measured several times – immediately after the group finishes, six months later – in order to establish that the change is a stable one rather than a temporary effect.

3 *Demonstrating that outcome is related to the group experience.* It is always possible that any changes which occurred between the time of entering and the time of leaving a group could have come about through something other than the group experience itself. One therefore needs some grounds for arguing plausibly that it is the group which has been the agent of change rather than some other experience or event.

It is of course neither possible nor desirable to isolate persons in groups from other life experiences. Amongst all these simultaneously occurring life experiences, of which the group is only one, how can one demonstrate that it is the group which has made a critical difference? In outcome research, two devices are commonly employed: one is to make use of a control group; the other is to establish a base-line for each person against which change is measured (each subject becomes his own control). In process-outcome research these devices may also be used but in addition, and primarily one seeks to show that outcomes are specifically linked to critical events within the group.

A control group is a group of persons who are as similar as possible to the persons actually undergoing the group experience. The difference is that the members of the control group do not undergo the group experience. The same measurements are taken of all persons in both groups, at the same times. If the control group shows negligible change while the persons who have had a group experience show considerable change, then it is plausible to assume that it is the group experience which has had the impact.

The task for the researcher is to select a control group which is comparable to the experimental group. Since no two persons are alike this is of course impossible in any detail. One can relatively easily match a control group and an experimental group on such variables as age, sex, education, number of offences, type of offence, and the like. It might be at least as important, but will certainly be more difficult, to match them on other variables such as the offender's attitudes towards the offence, or level of hope about the future. To take another example, if one is dealing with hospitalized patients, one could identify a control group on the usual factors of age, sex and education, and add to these number of years in the hospital, frequency of leaving the hospital grounds, and average number of contacts with family per month or year. It would be more difficult to match persons for the quality of contact with relatives, or attitudes and feelings connected with being outside the hospital, although these variables could be equally or more important. Sometimes each member of a group is matched with a specific other person, to assure closer matching of the control and the experimental groups. It is always a matter of debate as to whether a control and an experimental group can be adequately matched on factors which really matter.

When a control group is used, a further assumption is made

that the members of the experimental group and of the control group are likely to be subject to, overall and on average, the same additional extra-to-the-group experiences. These additional factors are then assumed to cancel one another out to the point where they can be disregarded. The larger the number of persons in both groups, the more defensible is this argument. Where one is dealing with small numbers, it is questionable whether this assumption can be justified.

A second way of seeking to assure that it is the group experience which has been the critical factor influencing change is to identify a base-line for each person in the group against which change can be measured. In order to do this, one assesses each person not only at a point of entry and point of exit but at some earlier point. For example, suppose one plans to conduct a group with long-stay psychiatric hospital patients. It would be possible to assess them at a pre-entry point (P) which might be some three or four or six months before they are taken into the group. One would then measure them again at the point of entry (E) and at the point of exit (X). Such a design allows one to compare a period of non-intervention (P to E) with a period during which help has been offered in the form of a group (E to X). If one can show that a person has been stable from P to E, but shows change from E to X, this supports the argument that it is the group which has made the difference. The assumption is that although real-life events go on throughout the overall period (P to X), the principal difference between the period P to E and E to X is the group. Of course it is always possible that some very influential event occurred for some or even all of the population during the period E to X – perhaps they were all moved to splendid new quarters. Common sense tells one to check for such factors, both for the population as a whole and for individual persons. If one is dealing with large numbers, one makes the assumption that extra-group events are likely to be distributed over the whole period, and that their effects would be equally felt during the two periods P to E and E to X and can therefore be disregarded.

Under some circumstances it is impossible to use this device because it is not reasonable to assume a period of stability preceding the initiation of the helping effort. In the example concerning adolescent boys, for example, if the boys are in a period of rapid physical and emotional development, as is likely to be the case, then one cannot reasonably expect to demonstrate stability during a pre-group period. One can think also of situations where a pre-group period of stability is logically impossible – when, for example, a group has been set up for parents of recently diagnosed mentally handicapped children, or for women whose husbands have recently been sentenced to prison terms.

In process-outcome studies one attempts to link outcomes with particular processes which have occurred within the group or with particular features of the group. If change can be shown to have occurred when certain processes or features were present and not to have occurred when they have not, then one feels a certain confidence in maintaining that it was these processes or features which were related to outcome.

For example, suppose that a social worker, in the course of conducting groups for adolescent boys, notes that the boys fall into two main groups – the aggressive, boisterous ones and the withdrawn, fearful ones. He may begin to wonder whether both groups benefit equally from a group experience, and if benefit would be likely to increase if groups were composed homogeneously of one or the other type of boy. This could be tested in a study by identifying outcome variables and finding ways of measuring them and then constructing several groups in which the composition is varied (homogeneous-aggressive; homogeneous-withdrawn; and mixed), taking care to assign boys of each type randomly to the three kinds of group, or else matching them; and assessing members in terms of the outcome variables at the point of entry and the point of exit from the group. If results showed, for example, that withdrawn boys who participated in the mixed group showed more positive change than withdrawn boys who participated in the homogeneous group, then one could plausibly claim that group composition was a factor influencing outcome. This example is an instance of process-outcome research where a feature of the group (i.e. composition) is examined.

To take another example, suppose one is working with persons with recently acquired physical handicaps, and has developed the notion that benefit is associated with active rather than passive participation during the group sessions. On the basis of assessments of outcome, members could be divided into a high-gain and a low-gain group. One would then require measures of active as against passive participation – which could be simple number-of-contribution counts if the group has been structured to allow each person an equal opportunity to contribute, or perhaps the number of comments offered which refer to the self and own situation. If a different structure is used, for example if the group makes substantial use of role-playing, one could count the number of times specific persons volunteered to role-play their own situations or to engage in active practice for situations they expected to encounter outside the hospital. One's original guess would be confirmed if the high-gain members also participated markedly more actively in the group. This example is an instance of process-outcome research where an aspect of process (extent and nature of participation) is examined.

Process-outcome research may have an essentially exploratory character. Suppose one has judged, on specified criteria, that certain persons in a group have benefited whilst others have not. Providing that full records have been kept of the sessions, it would be possible to review the sessions, searching for any events or experiences which differentiated the high-benefit and low-benefit persons, even if one had no definite ideas about possible differentiating factors beforehand.

Some process-outcome studies, such as that just referred to, require extensive burrowing into the material of the sessions, and close examination of moment-by-moment events over a period of time. They are necessarily small-scale studies. While one must be cautious about generalizing from them, they have the advantage of allowing one to examine complex and subtle processes for their possible relation to outcome.

3 Cost-benefit analyses

What is the balance between the costs incurred when conducting groups and the benefits which ensue? Conducting a group requires allocating resources to it, and both practitioners and administrators sometimes want evidence that the results achieved warrant the necessary investment of resources.

Ideally, a cost-benefit analysis should permit both costs and benefits to be expressed in comparable quantitative terms. A consideration of the nature of likely costs and benefits reveals that this may be difficult or impossible to achieve, and that a cost-benefit analysis which acknowledges the real nature of the situation will have to include quantifiable and unquantifiable, tangible and intangible, short-run and long-run costs and benefits.

The 'cost' side of things is usually both easier to determine and easier to measure in quantitative terms. Conducting a group requires staff time, and staff time costs money. The amount of money involved can be calculated easily in terms of percentage of a staff member's time, which in turn can be expressed in terms of money. If the group effort involves more than one member of staff, or involves bringing someone in from the outside, then this too can be costed in terms of money. Conducting a group requires space, heat, perhaps equipment, perhaps consumables in the form of coffee or tea. Planning for groups may require correspondence and memos, hence secretarial time, stationery, etc. All of these costs can be expressed in terms of money and one can specify them accurately.

Another form of cost is termed 'opportunity costs'. While a member of staff is engaged in planning, conducting or evaluating a group, he cannot be doing other things. Some other activities are given up or foregone so that the group effort can be undertaken. These other activities are lost opportunities, for the staff member and for the institution or agency. Lost opportunities may be a significant cost of conducting a group, but they are harder to quantify. Some agencies have schemes for assessing workloads (one group = so many individual clients) and in such instances a number can be attached to opportunity costs, but whether this is an entirely satisfactory way of assessing these costs is debatable.

One can also imagine less tangible but no less important costs. For example, if a group programme is an innovation in an institution, perhaps tension rises amongst staff, who feel they are engaging in a risky activity. Or perhaps an uneasy competitiveness is stirred up amongst staff about whose efforts are really benefiting the clients or patients concerned. If a group, for example on a psychiatric ward, generates periods of heightened anxiety amongst the patients, then disturbances may arise which would not otherwise have occurred. These are all possibilities. If a group experience turns out to damage a patient or client, then this surely should be counted as a cost. These kinds of costs are difficult if not impossible to measure, and are often a subject of debate among personnel.

On the whole, costs tend to be closely tied in time to the actual life of the group. They are, for the most part, immediate and visible, and do not run on into the indeterminate future.

Costs, whether they are assessed in terms of what is done

(conducting a group) or not done (foregoing the opportunity to work with *x* number of individuals or families), and whether they are tangible or intangible, mean little in themselves. They take on meaning only in relation to what is gained by incurring the costs.

It is more difficult to be precise and accurate about benefits than about costs. The major benefit which one hopes for is, of course, benefit to the persons who participate in the group, as defined early in the planning stage. The discussion earlier in this chapter about outcome variables has already illustrated that working out and then actually quantifying benefit is not always a straightforward task. Some benefits can be quantified (*x* number of months without re-offending; fewer days absent from school) but many others are essentially qualitative in nature and a matter of judgment (level of self-esteem; improved interpersonal skills). Ingenious devices exist and can be invented to express qualitative benefits in quantitative terms. Opinions differ as to whether these are or can be entirely satisfactory.

The question also arises as to who shall judge benefits: the enthusiastic practitioner, the sceptical colleague, the patient or client? Each perspective may carry its own biases.

Some benefits to patients or clients may not be apparent immediately but may emerge over quite a long time span. Some benefits which can be seen immediately after a group experience do not persist. Consider, for example, a group which has been planned to help persons through some life transition. Some of those in the group seem more distressed and less capable when the group finishes than when it began, but if one followed them over a period of time one might see recovery and stabilization, and then an increased capacity to face further transitions. Others might show immediate gains but later, when deprived of the ongoing support of the group, lose them. Still others might show immediate gains which persist over time. One's assessment of benefit would vary substantially depending on just when it was made. An assumption that benefit is tied in time to the point at which a group ends is not warranted. Very long-term benefits are understandably lost sight of in most evaluation or cost-benefit studies.

In addition to benefits to the patients or clients directly concerned, benefits may accrue to others. For example, in consequence of participating in a group designed for parents of handicapped children, one mother lost some of her single-minded devotion to her handicapped child and began to invest more time in her other children, with probable long-term benefits for them. This is an example of a longer-term, spin-off benefit which accrues to someone other than the intended beneficiaries of the helping effort.

Spin-off benefits should certainly be included in any cost-benefit analysis. They can accrue to the patient or clients themselves, to others in their families or networks, to staff directly or indirectly concerned, or to the institution or agency. For example, one of the benefits of a programme of group work in a long-stay ward in a psychiatric hospital was a visible increase in the level of morale of staff. The nurses on this ward came to feel that their efforts in working with a population often regarded as beyond help could bear fruit and that they themselves were worthwhile persons engaged in useful work. Clearly, this benefited not only the staff concerned, but those in their charge.

One of the benefits of a group programme might be a long-run saving of time. For example, a group programme in a psychiatric hospital could conceivably reduce readmission rates or lengthen the period of time between admissions. If so, then the saving of staff time over the longer term should be regarded as a benefit to be set against the immediate investment of staff time in the running of the group.

Having made some assessment of costs and benefits one must of course set them against one another and form some overall judgment as to whether benefits outweigh costs. The clearest picture can be obtained if one seeks to set down all costs and all benefits: quantifiable and not quantifiable, short-term and long-term, direct and spin-off, clear-cut and debatable. One then forms a judgment as to whether benefits outweigh costs or vice versa. It is to be expected that many but not all costs and only some benefits can be expressed in terms of numbers, and that opinions within a staff may well differ as to what properly constitutes a cost and what properly counts as a benefit. Nevertheless, by setting down as complete a set of costs and benefits as one can, and quantifying where possible, one gets nearer to answering the question as to whether or not the effort has been worthwhile.

4 Transforming informal monitoring and assessing into small-scale formal research

Formal research need not always be elaborate and time-consuming. Nor does it necessarily involve highly developed and specialized skills in instrument-construction or statistics. Sometimes, by relatively little extra effort and time, one can build on what one will be doing in any case, either in the course of conducting a group or monitoring it informally, to extend one's effort into a respectable small-scale study.

For example, suppose that one is conducting a group intended to help young male prisoners develop certain social skills, such that when they present themselves to a prospective employer (for example) they are more likely to be received favourably. Suppose further that one has in mind the use of role-playing as practice in participating in job interviews and that one intends to use video feedback for some of the time. It would not be difficult to design into the programme two different but parallel forms of role-play and introduce them into the programme during the first and the final sessions. Tapes of these could constitute primary data for assessing pre- and post-levels of social skills. One would need to work out specific indices of social skills (for example, maintaining eye-contact, avoiding distracting mannerisms, speaking clearly and concisely) and ask independent judges to utilize these as dimensions for rating level of skill. One would need to take care to conceal from the judges anything which might reveal which role-play occurred early and which late in the series.

To take another example, suppose that one is conducting a group for mothers of mentally handicapped children, and hopes that they will find ways of coping with the experiences of rearing such a child at less personal cost to themselves. One could devise a relatively straightforward sentence completion test and administer it before the group starts and during the final session (e.g. 'My son/daughter is . . .' 'The thing that worries me most is . . .' 'When I talk to others about my child, I . . .' etc.) Such a device could even be built into the group experience, for example, after the mothers have completed the sentence completion test a second time during the final session, one could redistribute the first one, invite members to compare their pre- and post-responses, and encourage discussion and sharing. If one also taped the final session one might acquire useful information about the features of the group which the women saw as making a difference to them.

Many other examples could be cited. Perhaps I should re-emphasize, however, that *formal* studies of whatever kind are not essential to the effective conduct of group. Some means for monitoring and assessing is however essential if one is to acquire useful feedback about one's efforts.

Suggested exercises

In a sense this entire chapter constitutes a set of suggested exercises. The best way to gain experience in setting up a monitoring scheme is to plan one for a group with which one intends to work. If one does not expect to work with a group in the near future but nevertheless wishes to gain experience, one could take as a base one of the groups designed as part of a chapter 3 exercise and further developed as part of a chapter 5 exercise, and then work out a suitable scheme for monitoring that group.

Chapter 7

Forming a membership: selecting and preparing members, and composing a group

One further set of decisions and tasks faces a group worker, therapist or leader before he or she can actually begin to work with a group. These involve identifying actual named persons who are to be members, testing their willingness and readiness to join the group, and engaging in preparatory work with them if one sees this as necessary or helpful. As one engages in these tasks a group composition is being constructed or identified. Under some circumstances it is appropriate to allow a composition simply to happen as a by-product of membership-formation procedures; under other circumstances, composing a group can be taken on as a further task.

In chapter 1 the point was made that after all planning decisions have been made except those concerned with forming a membership, it is well to pause and decide finally whether or not one is prepared to commit oneself to working with the group one has been planning. Before this point, specific persons have not been approached and no harm can be done to them if one decides after all not to proceed. Once one informs potential patients or clients about a group and certainly once they agree to enter it, it is too late to withdraw from the enterprise without possibly doing harm, since one will have raised expectations and made implicit promises which one is then bound to keep. If one engages in the final planning tasks to be described in this chapter it should be on the basis of an internal decision to stick with the group come what may.

In forming a membership one is aiming for two things: first, the inclusion of persons likely to benefit and the exclusion of persons whom one judges could be damaged by the group or likely to be unmanageably disruptive; and second, a composition likely to provide both support and challenge to the members when the group comes into being. In other words one is trying to assemble a group which is likely to survive and flourish.

The discussion is presented in four sections: selection, composition, preparation, and the uses of a preliminary interview.

1 Selection

Some persons should not become members of groups. They include those who are so highly threatened by the prospect that they cannot be expected to function in a group and could be damaged by it; those who are too disorganized and potentially disruptive; and those who are so caught up in personal crisis that they are unlikely to gain from a group or to function effectively within it.

The highly threatened person. It is important to distinguish between the highly threatened person and the one who has anxieties and worries about entering a group which can be articulated and faced. The latter are suitable candidates; the former are not.

While some persons are eager to enter a group, many experience qualms, worries and reservations. Many persons who are frightened at the prospect of entering a group are aware that in a group they will be in an exposed position. They are afraid that others in the group will be critical or unaccepting, or they fear that they will show up badly in comparison with others. Such persons usually have some sense of what it is they are worried about and can say something about it: 'There are things I could never say' 'They'll all know better than me' 'How can other people with problems help me?' A preliminary one-to-one interview can be used in part to acknowledge and discuss such worries and reservations. Exploration of concerns, seeking to understand explicitly just what they are, acknowledging and respecting them often is sufficiently reassuring to tip the balance and bring the person to the point of readiness to try the group. Occasionally, however, one encounters a person whose fears seem to be on another scale altogether. Such a person is alarmed at the prospect of a group in some gross, profound and often inchoate way. He may be able to say only: 'I couldn't', and repeatedly 'No, I never could.' When invited to explore and give examples, he cannot, and his alarm remains unabated.

Such persons may well be sensing something in themselves which would truly make a group experience intolerable. They seem somehow aware that their defences could not stand up against the forces that can emerge in a group: that they would be swept up by group affect, or pressed to reveal more or express more than they could tolerate, or forced to face the unfaceable before being able to bear it. Of course they do not say this in so many words. What one actually sees is protracted inarticulate panic. One judges that underlying this panic is profound fear of losing the self under the impact of group forces. When faced with this rare but intractable, gross, massive fear, it seems best to accept it and find some alternative for the person concerned. Such persons, if pressed into a group, could be damaged by the experience and end up worse off than before. One needs to judge whether the fear a particular person is displaying can be allayed through exploration and examination of it or whether further pressing will only exacerbate the fear. The clearest indicator seems to be whether or not the person can articulate the fear. If he can articulate it there is a reasonable chance that he can develop some sense of potential mastery over it. If he cannot, it remains inaccessible to him and retains its power.

The disorganized and/or potentially disruptive person. Some persons are characterized by extremes of internal disorganization such that they are confused about self, are self-absorbed to the point of hardly being aware of other persons or of events around them, or perceive the world in fragmented or distorted ways. Some such persons are silent and withdrawn. Others display such behaviours as never sitting still for long, continually entering and leaving rooms, breaking into the conversation of others with idiosyncratic and often incomprehensible statements. They may be verbally violent, prone to physical violence, or simply voluble and out-of-touch.

If a person cannot make himself understood by others or cannot hear others, he may still benefit from some kinds of groups – particularly those which make little or no demands for inter-personal interaction but instead provide for human presence through parallel or highly structured activity. Other kinds of groups, particularly those which require verbal interaction, are less likely to be suitable.

The internally disorganized person who is also silent and withdrawn is unlikely to be disruptive to others in an unmanageable way. If such a person is brought into a group he may well become the recipient of fantasies on the part of others simply because he remains unknowable and is an easy person on to whom to project hopes and fears. He may become an object of concern to others. These reactions on the part of others are manageable and can be exploited to the benefit of all concerned. One or two such persons might be included in a group if one were reasonably convinced that they could maintain needed defences in the face of group forces.

In contrast, the disorganized person who is active and voluble may be disruptive in a pervasive and unmanageable way. If he cannot sit reasonably still in a chair, if he walks about or repeatedly leaves and re-enters the room, if he is hardly able to stop talking even in response to the strongest and clearest of signals, if his outpourings are so exclusively a product of his internal preoccupations and fantasies that he cannot hear others and cannot even begin to see his impact on them, then it will be very difficult to contain him in a group or stop him pre-empting the therapeutic possibilities of the group for others.

Many persons emerge, over a period of time, from such extreme states, and then become amenable to being helped in groups. It seems best to wait for such emergence, or to provide other forms of help to facilitate such emergence before bringing such persons into a group.

I hope it is clear that I am not implying that all potentially difficult persons should be prevented from joining groups, nor even that persons who (for example) are hallucinating or delusional should necessarily be excluded. Many such persons profit from a group experience and can be contained within a group. The core criteria are the capacities to sit still, listen, and hold still for others for some part of the time.

Persons caught up in acute crises. It has already been suggested in chapter 3 that many persons in crisis situations can profit from a group experience once they emerge from the initial phase of shock. While still in a state of shock usual defences and coping devices are temporarily unavailable or so reduced that the person is barely able to maintain himself through essential daily routines, or may be in an acute state of anxiety or depression which is so all-encompassing that there is no energy to spare. Personal resources are at a low ebb and defences thin. Rather than a group, such persons need time and space around them so that they can begin to recover themselves, or else individual support where the help-giver can be closely in touch, moment by moment, with what the person needs and can use and tolerate. After such persons have emerged from the acute phase of reaction to crisis it is possible that the further work of recovery can be facilitated by an experience in a group.

With respect to the highly threatened person and the person in an acute stage of reacting to crisis, an underlying assumption is that needed defences should be respected and that individuals who sense that they could be damaged by a group (which really means that they sense that defences could be invaded and shattered) should not be pressed into one. This is a somewhat difficult point to make clear because there is no doubt that one of the routes towards personal change in group situations is the challenge to defences which can lead to persons seeing how it was that certain defences had to be erected and perceiving/experiencing that the defences are no longer essential. Thus, challenging defences could be a good thing whilst invading or shattering them is not. One is trying, perhaps, to make a judgment about that elusive notion called 'ego strength'. Is, or is not, the person in a state to survive and make positive use of the challenge to defences which is likely to occur? If one's best judgment is that the individual will not be able to bear such challenges or if the individual senses this in himself then it is better not to have him in the group because the therapist or group worker is not in a position to control closely the nature of the challenge or its impact on vulnerable individuals.

With respect to all three kinds of persons I am acknowledging the power of the forces which can operate in groups and their destructive potential for particularly vulnerable persons.

2 Composition

Under some circumstances a group therapist or group worker is in a position to compose or assemble a group: that is, to decide what combination of persons to bring into a given group. Questions then arise as to whether a planned composition is any more likely to support a group effort than a random composition, and as to whether some set of concepts can be invoked to guide decision-making in this matter.

In order to approach this issue I would wish to suggest that any group, in order to be successful, has to find some way to make use of the group structure set up by or for them. If we assume that the group has been so planned that its structure is a good fit with the frontier and/or preoccupying concern which characterizes the population, then we can begin to look at those features of the group situation itself which will facilitate persons utilizing the structure. In general, persons are likely to make good use of a structure which is generally suitable if they experience levels of safety and mutual trust which enable them to feel free to express and expose themselves and take part in the activities laid down by or for the group. In other words the group will proceed best if the persons in them are prepared to participate and take whatever risks that participation brings with it, without erecting collusive defences (in group focal conflict terms, restrictive solutions) against the experience.

Some compositions contribute to and support and make more likely the positive utilization of the opportunities a group offers than others. While attention to composition cannot guarantee an effective group it can tilt the odds toward effectiveness and is therefore worth consideration.

Composition has to do with the relative homogeneity and heterogeneity of the group with regard to a spectrum of factors, which could include any human characteristic but in practice tends to include such factors as age, sex, race, problem or symptom and mental or psychological state. I will comment on these factors but also suggest other dimensions which seem critical to the subsequent operation of a group.

The discussion in chapter 3 has suggested that it can often be useful for the members of a group to be generally similar with respect to frontier and/or preoccupying concern. However these guiding principles take us only a limited distance when actually composing a group because their application produces groups whose members have a common cutting edge but may be either similar or quite different with respect to further dimensions critical to the operation of the group.

One such further dimension can be called 'preferred mode of expressing affect'. People differ in how easy or difficult they usually find it to express anger, warmth, support, challenge, dependency and the like. One can say they 'prefer' one or a few affective modes over others. Homogeneity of preferred affective mode limits the usefulness of the group, for it leads to the establishment of prevailing moods or behaviours involving hostility, or warm cosiness, or passive reliance on the leader. In any such instance certain areas of human experiencing may persistently fail to be explored, because there is no resource within the composition to press for its exploration. Rather better is a composition which includes diverse modes of expressing affect. Such a group is not so likely to get stuck in just one mode or a limited range of modes, and stands a better chance of becoming a flexible and varied instrument.

A related dimension is that of 'preferred defence'. Most persons have recourse to a range of defences, but certain ones may be preferred in the sense of being resorted to most frequently. A composition which is homogeneous with regard to preferred defence again limits the usefulness of the group, for the individual propensities quickly gain mutual support, become a way of life for the group and are then very difficult to shift. In group focal conflict terms, similar habitual individual solutions gain support and reinforcement through interpersonal interaction, and become firmly established as shared restrictive solutions. One need only think of a group composed mainly of intellectualizers, or mainly of suspicious paranoids, or mainly of persons who withdraw when under threat to be convinced of this point.

Sometimes an individual defence takes the form of some conviction or belief, e.g. 'I am in no way responsible for my behaviour because it is controlled by forces outside myself which compel me to do bad things' or 'I cannot influence my own fate because I am a victim of society.' If there is a diversity of such beliefs represented in the group's composition, then challenge, exploration and testing is more likely to occur. But if all hold to a similar view, then that view gains firmer plausibility through the weight of consensus. If the leader is the only one to hold an alternative view, it becomes almost impossible to examine the belief *as* a belief, for it tends to acquire the status of an incontrovertible fact.

So far I have suggested that a group composition which is heterogeneous with regard to preferred affective mode and preferred defence is desirable. There is a further dimension, which can be called 'level of vulnerability' where *homogeneity* is desirable. As this is an unfamiliar term it requires explanation. Level of vulnerability has to do with how likely it is that the group may 'get to' a person in ways which he cannot tolerate and which lead him to panic, to flee, to experience dysfunctional anxiety or to intensify defences to the point where he becomes unreachable. These consequences are either damaging to the person or insulate him from the group. In either case one wishes to avoid them if possible. A person in such a position can be described as having a high level of vulnerability. This feature of persons is not directly related to seriousness of the disturbance or to psychiatric classification. One can imagine persons who can be regarded as seriously disturbed who are not particularly vulnerable because they allow events to wash over them or because they have established powerful and intact paranoid systems which operate as insulating defences. On the other hand one can imagine less disturbed persons who because of the structure of defences and of coping strategies are in a more vulnerable position. Apparently well-functioning but brittle persons are an example of this. Members of groups whose composition is relatively homogeneous with respect to level of vulnerability are able to move at roughly the same rate. It may be a faster pace or a slower pace but it is one which is tolerable to the members. Imagine on the other hand a group in which one or two persons experience massive threat because the others are prepared to move quickly into expressing certain feelings or sharing certain kinds of experiences when they are not. Or, imagine a group in which the general pace of exploration is much slower than necessary for one or two individuals, who are ready to move much faster. In the first example the individual is made dysfunctionally anxious; in the second he is held back from the movement he could otherwise make.

With respect to age, sex and race, composition should be consistent with purpose. If one applies the guidelines set down in chapter 3 concerning frontier and preoccupying concern, one ought to get to a composition which is about right with respect to these variables. It is obvious enough that a group planned for mothers of mentally handicapped children will be composed of women; that a group designed for persons about to leave a psychiatric hospital will be mixed with regard to sex, age and probably race; that a group designed to develop practical skills for long-stay mental hospital patients will be likely to include persons in early or later middle age; and so on.

One comment can be made of a cautionary nature: it is undesirable for a composition to include only one woman, or one man, or one non-white, or one much older or much younger person. There are two reasons for this. The first is that the person can rather quickly be cast into a stereotyped role by the other members. The much older person may be cast into the role of sage or has-been; the much younger person into the role of inexperienced brash adolescent; the woman or man into stereotyped sex roles; and the lone non-white into stereotypes of blacks, aborigines, etc. The second reason is that the person in a unique position has a ready-made defence available to him should the others point to some characteristic which the person finds unacceptable. The West Indian can say 'You are saying that because you are prejudiced against West Indians'; the woman can say 'Naturally, none of you can understand me.' If at least two such persons are present in any group both the tendency to stereotype and the tendency to use the social role defensively is less likely to occur: both the individual and the group will benefit. In group focal conflict terms, it is too easy for the exception in the group to become locked inside some restrictive group solution which requires him to behave in some particular way or be seen in stereotyped terms.

Years of formal education does not appear to be a relevant factor when composing a group. Groups can accommodate a wide range of level of education. In fact, there can be an advantage in diversity, in that the tendency toward intellectualization that one sometimes sees in lengthily educated persons may be challenged by those who insist on plain language.

It will be clear from the above that psychiatric classification, as such, is not a primary consideration when composing a group. The variables of preferred affective mode, preferred defence and level of vulnerability are more sensitive indicators.

These various considerations lead to certain rules of thumb concerning composition. Within any general category of client, patient or member population (understood in terms of frontier and preoccupying concern):

1 Aim for heterogeneity in preferred mode of affective expression;

2 Aim for heterogeneity in preferred defence;
3 Aim for homogeneity with respect to level of vulnerability;
4 Avoid including only one member of any minority group.

Of the factors which one might hold in mind when composing a group, those easiest to recognize are of course age, sex and race. One does not even have to meet the person to get such information. Getting an impression of preferred affective mode, preferred defence and in particular level of vulnerability is more difficult, and can only be done by direct contact with the person or by making use of the judgments of colleagues who know the person.

When actually composing a group it is usually the case that one or two persons at a time come to the attention of, and perhaps are seen by, the person who is assembling the group. Over a period of a few weeks, the leader begins to see the shape his group is taking. If he accumulates two or at most three rather withdrawn individuals he will know to seek out more verbal, aggressive ones. If he has gathered two or three rather rebellious, hostile persons, he will know to seek out some leaven for his group in the form of rather warmer or mediating types, or those less concerned with challenging persons in authority. If he sees that the persons selected so far are at one range of level of vulnerabililty, he will reserve the person who deviates substantially from this for another group. And so on.

In some settings a therapist or group worker is faced with a pool of prospective patients or clients who are already substantially restricted in range or type of person. Perhaps one is working in an alcoholics' unit, or a unit for drug abusers, or a residential unit for delinquent adolescent boys, etc. Whilst it is undoubtedly true that some populations are relatively more homogeneous than others, I believe that there are few which cannot generate a reasonable diversity in composition, although it may take more time in some settings than in others to assemble a group. One needs to keep in mind that a population which is homogeneous in regard to a diagnostic category or type of problem is not necessarily homogeneous along the dimensions being emphasized here. For example, a group of delinquent adolescent boys whom one might assume to be rather heavily loaded towards hostile rebellion is, as persons who work with such individuals well know, a more heterogeneous population than that stereotype would have it. Drug abusers, alcoholics, psychiatric hospital patients, prisoners, the mentally handicapped, are also likely to be quite diverse along the dimensions which I am suggesting are most important.

Some writers on groups suggest that random selection and composition, simply taking whoever comes, is likely to be just as effective as the greatest care and planned effort. This can be the case, depending on the nature of the pool of potential group members from which one is drawing. If this pool is already homogeneous with regard to level of vulnerability, and heterogeneous with regard to other factors, then random selection can be expected to generate a useful mix of persons. It must also be acknowledged that one's judgment about such factors as preferred mode of affective expression, etc., cannot be perfect and in any case can rarely if ever be based on full information. Whilst accepting all of this, I would still prefer to monitor a group's composition in the ways suggested in this section, on the grounds that composition has a powerful influence on how a group operates. Attention to composition can at least avoid certain difficulties, although it cannot in itself guarantee an effective group.

In some work settings one cannot select or compose, for example because one does not wish to exclude anyone currently resident on a ward or any adolescent currently resident on a housing estate. Then, one either includes everyone, or extends an open invitation to all potential members, leaving the group's composition to be a product of individual choices. The latter can be a sensible course of action, since persons who feel excessively threatened by the prospect of participating in a group can select themselves out. It will not, of course, allow control over composition. When arriving at a composition through random selection or open invitation it is still possible to monitor the composition by taking note of the four composition variables listed a few pages back: preferred affective mode; preferred defence; level of vulnerability; and minority members. What kind of a group is it shaping up to be, and is it a 'good-enough' composition or one likely to present difficulties? If the composition looks to be 'good-enough' then there is of course no problem. It is sometimes possible to accommodate to an unfavourable composition by modifying the structure of a group. For example, a group structure with permeable boundaries can accommodate a wider range of vulnerability level than can a group with tight and impermeable boundaries. To take a concrete instance, a psychiatric ward might well include persons who are very diverse with respect to level of vulnerability, with some patients barely able to face leaving their beds and others out in the community much of the time, preparing for discharge. By arguments already put forward these should not all be in the same group. If for some reason they must be, then an arrangement whereby absences, tardiness and leaving the room early are tolerated serves to protect the more vulnerable members. Where potentially disruptive persons must be included in a group, a structure with pre-planned shifts in type of activity may be useful, or a structure which includes periods of working in sub-groups, so that disruptive persons can be contained for part of the time in separated sub-groups. Such lines of reasoning are simply further applications of ideas already presented in chapter 3 concerning frontier. In that chapter, before one had specific persons in mind as prospective members, one could think only in terms of population. At this stage in planning, the same ideas can be applied to individuals.

Institution or agency policies and structures have a powerful effect on the nature of available pools of potential group members. Institutions often have policies and practices about who enters the institution and how persons are allocated to sub-units (wards, houses, prison wings) once they are admitted. A frequent practice is to place newcomers in a reception ward or house and then after a period of time disperse them to other units within the institution. Where this is the practice, it would be possible to conduct short-term transition or orientation groups with newcomers, without concerning oneself with either selection or composition. Apart from the direct benefit of easing the transition into the institution, such groups provide useful information about each person about level of vulnerability, preferred defences and preferred affective mode. When the time comes to reassign persons to other units within the residential facility, one has an information base for decision-making. If groups are then to be utilized with the total population of a ward or house or drawn randomly from it, then the pool is such as to make more likely relative homogeneity with regard to level of vulnerability and heterogeneity with respect to other factors.

If one has decided to work with an already existing group, then of course the composition is fixed. One cannot influence it and does not wish to influence it, since working with the composition is a key part of the task. An understanding of the composition and of the functions served by it becomes a basis for one's work, but this understanding can be left to evolve as one works with the group, since it does not affect pre-planning decisions.

3 Preparation for participation in a group

What is 'preparation'? What is it for and is it always necessary? Preparation must mean trying to get persons who are not yet ready to participate in the kind of group one has in mind into a state of readiness for participation. Lack of readiness could mean insufficient skills to cope with a particular kind of group or worries and anxieties about the group likely to make it difficult for the person to engage in the group.

Lack of readiness related to lack of appropriate skills should not really arise if one has undertaken planning with care. If, for example, one has judged frontier carefully and designed one's group with this in mind, then the demands made upon the person by the group should be a close-enough match with that person's capabilities. If they are not, then one has planned the wrong kind of group or misjudged frontier.

Sometimes, as indicated in the first section of this chapter, one encounters persons with fears and worries about participating in a group. From the point of view of selection, one has to make a judgment as to whether these fears can be alleviated or managed enough for the person to enter a group, or whether they are intractable fears which contra-indicate group membership. From the point of view of preparation, if the fears are open to alleviation then it is to the person's advantage that some degree of alleviation occur before the group begins to meet. Such preparation makes it easier for the person to move into the group and reduces unnecessary or dysfunctional anxiety and suffering. One or two preliminary individual interviews can be used both as a basis for selection and as an opportunity to prepare persons for participation.

I use the term 'to seek to alleviate fears' rather than 'to reassure' because the latter term seems in common usage to confuse what the therapist or group worker does with what the patient or client feels. Workers or therapists who say 'I reassured him' sometimes mean 'I told him not to worry', or 'I told him his fears were unnecessary or groundless.' Such statements tell us only what the worker or therapist said; they say nothing about how the recipient of the statement then felt. It is a reasonable guess that following such 'reassurance' the recipient does not necessarily feel less fearful. He may, instead, consider that he was not taken seriously, or was not understood. Feeling less fearful does not come about through being told that one's fears are groundless or by being instructed not to worry, but rather through the route of being taken seriously and helped to state and specify fears. Once stated, fears can be examined for their likelihood of being realistic: that is, is what is feared actually likely to happen? It is often possible to help a person to name his fears, along the lines of 'If I say, do, or experience thus and thus, I will then feel devastated (ashamed, embarrassed, etc.)' or 'If I say or do thus and thus, others will say or do so and so and then I will feel devastated (ashamed, embarrassed, etc.).' If he can do this, he will have been explicit enough to ask himself the further question 'Will I really feel that badly?' 'Are others likely to respond in the way I fear, and if they do, will I then find that intolerable?' Often fears are exaggerated or the person finds strength to face them once he gets a clearer notion of what they are. If after exploration it still seems plausible that what the person fears could happen, or if he considers there is no real way to test or predict, then the person can be invited to consider what he might do in the face of his fears: 'What would you do if the worst happened and people laughed at you (thought you were a terrible person, wanted to have nothing more to do with you', etc.). By such means a person can sometimes think through to possible reactions or strategies, and thus gain a greater sense of potential mastery over the situations he predicts might occur. Along with this comes a greater sense of being ready to enter the group.

Under some circumstances preparation is neither necessary nor sensible. If a group is very short-term, a preliminary interview may invade the time which might more usefully be spent in the group itself. Very short-term groups are likely to be highly structured or directed to some quite specific purpose. In such instances the structure serves to contain fears, and preparation which has the purpose of alleviating fears is not so necessary. Some persons are not able to imagine themselves into a group experience. In such a case a preliminary interview cannot serve a preparatory function. It would be better to design a fairly structured group in which the first session or two constituted preparation for the series, by involving members in representative but manageable activities.

Preliminary interviews and their multiple functions

It will be clear from the preceding discussion that one or a few preliminary interviews can serve several purposes. It or they can:

1 provide a testing ground so that both the leader and the prospective member can arrive at a decision as to whether or not a group is likely to be useful and manageable for the person concerned;
2 provide the leader with enough information about the person to judge how he would fit into the developing composition of the group currently being planned; and
3 prepare the prospective member for the group by providing opportunities to express and explore curiosities, expectations and fears.

A preliminary interview seems to move through several stages, which reflect the fact that the functions it is meant to serve follow one another in at least a rough order. One wants first to learn enough about the person to decide for oneself whether a group might be a potentially useful and manageable experience. One therefore will wish to get to know the person in the first instance without reference to the possibility of his participating in a group. If on the basis of what one hears one decides privately that a group is not suitable one can quietly drop the idea of a group without ever mentioning it, thus saving the person from any suggestion of being rejected or found wanting. If one decides that the person might benefit from a group experience, one then wishes to know how he takes to the idea. His response to the offer of a group typically provides further information as to general suitability, particularly with respect to the character of fears about the group experience, and also provides opportunities to explore expectations and worries. As one observes how a person presents himself and interacts, notes what he says about expectations and fears, notes how he predicts he might feel and behave in a group, one is gaining more information about level of vulnerability, preferred affective mode and preferred defences which one can then fit into what has already been decided about membership. One might consider that the person is likely to complement the composition as worked out so far, or at least fit into it. Alternatively one might consider that the person will overweigh the group in some direction, and that another group should be found for him. Finally, supposing that participating in the group currently being organized makes sense to both the interviewer and the prospective group member, a commitment can be made by both to working together along with others in a group.

As it is often useful to begin in a general way, seeking to get to know the person without in the first instance particular reference to a group, one might begin by asking 'Can you tell me a bit about how you came to be in this hospital?' or 'Can you tell me what you see as the main thing you need from your contact with the Family Service Unit?' or (supposing the individual has been seen extensively by others): 'I know that you have talked already with Doctor (or Mrs, or Mr) so and so, but I wonder if you would mind telling me a bit about yourself and how you see your present situation?' In fifteen or twenty minutes, the individual is likely to provide a picture of where he currently stands. At this point the interviewer can say something like 'One of the possibilities here is meeting in a group with other people who are in a similar situation/have some of the same problems.'

Under some circumstances it is intrusive or unnecessary to begin by asking for personal details. For example, in a setting in which a group is an additional, optional service, one might simply say 'We are organizing a group for single parents (parents who bring their children here to the assessment centre', etc.). Where one does not wish to place choice for entering the group into the hands of the potential members one might simply declare; 'It is our policy here to conduct short-term groups for persons who are about to be discharged from the hospital. I would like to invite you to join such a group. It meets on . . .'

By whatever route, one gets to a point in the interview where the possibility of a group is mentioned. The person may react with eagerness, or more likely, reservations. His first response might be 'I wouldn't like it' or 'I would find it difficult', stated either matter-of-factly, or with some degree of alarm. Invited to say more about his feelings, a person may be able to describe and articulate them quite clearly, or he may simply restate, in a frightened, desperate or inchoate way that he simply couldn't manage it, doesn't know why, etc. If an individual can get no distance toward explicating his fears and they do not abate, then this seems an indication that the fears are both massive and intractable. The therapist may then say, 'Well, I can see how you might not take to a group. There are other possibilities. For example . . . .' This sort of response is meant to offer the individual who truly cannot face a group a genuine opportunity to opt out without in any way being reproached for wishing to do so. For those who are able to specify and from thence discuss and explore worries, the next part of the interview can be devoted to such exploration.

I should perhaps emphasize that by exploration I do not mean persuasion. From time to time someone asks me 'How do I sell a group to a prospective member?' If this means 'How do I persuade someone against his will to enter a group?' the answer is 'Don't.' Nothing is gained in the long run by persuading someone into entering a group who sees no point in it or who is profoundly frightened of it. In the face of a reluctant or worried person it is better to set oneself the task of informing the person about the group, and helping him to identify and explore his reservations, so that both the conductor of the group and the patient or client can make a sensible decision about whether or not he or she should enter the group.

Whether a person's initial reaction to the possibility of joining a group is reluctance or eagerness, further exploration is in order. What lies behind the eagerness or the reluctance? What is wished for, and what is feared? Clues soon emerge from the statements the person makes or the questions he asks. Some not unusual questions and statements include: 'How many people will come?' 'Who will the others be?' 'I could never talk about my problems in front of others.' 'Listening to other sick people will make me worse.' 'Perhaps it would help us to get started if I tell everyone how I manage my child.' 'How long will it take to get rid of my nightmares?' 'How can talking in a group help me?' 'Do I have to come?' 'How can you be sure a group will help me?' A response can be offered to all such questions and statements. Straightforward questions about how many, when, how long, can be answered factually. Questions about who else will be there can be answered in general terms, e.g. 'The others will be persons who like you have come to this clinic for help and who feel themselves to have various kinds of problems, with studying, or parents, or boyfriends and girlfriends. Everyone will be fairly near to one another in age'; or, 'The others will all be persons who like you are ready to leave the hospital, but who because of an accident or illness won't be able to lead the same kind of life as before. The particular handicap and what led up to it is likely to be different, but everyone will have that kind of problem in common.'

Some questions reveal unrealistic expectations. A group therapist or group worker cannot be sure that a group will help a particular person, nor rid him of unwanted symptoms or problems. The answer to many such questions is 'I don't know' or 'I can't offer you any definite promises or guarantees.' One can go on to explain 'We don't know yet what your nightmares are all about, and we don't know how quick or easy it will be to understand them.' A person who indicates that he wishes to be the centre of attention can be told 'It certainly will be helpful to hear from you and from others.'

Questions like 'Do I have to come?' are queries about the therapist's power, and should be answered factually. The answer might be 'Yes, it is a condition of being on this ward that everyone is expected to come to this group.' On the other hand, if the group is differently structured the answer might be 'We hope you will come regularly, but we find it best to encourage each person to make that decision for herself.' Similarly, one sometimes gets questions about what sorts of records will be kept, and these too can be answered factually.

Sometimes the questions a person asks or the statements he makes reveal something about the position he will seek to establish for himself in the group, and the conditions under which he is likely to feel safe. He may say 'I couldn't talk at first' or 'Will you always be there?' This makes an opportunity for a bit more exploration. The therapist or worker can ask what might make it difficult for him to talk, or why it would be important to him that the therapist always be present. Such explorations often reveal particular fears. The therapist can then acknowledge such fears, suggest that the person is unlikely to be the only person to have them, and give permission to the individual to operate in his own preferred way (e.g. 'I can see that you are the kind of person who would prefer to sit back a bit at first and decide for yourself when to start talking'). Such acknowledgment and permission is often sufficiently anxiety-reducing that the person feels able to enter the group despite certain worries about it.

Some questions are very hard to answer, either because it is difficult to find a shared vocabulary, or because so much time would be required, or because the therapist or worker does not himself have an explanation. A prospective member who asks 'How can participation in a group help me?' is asking the same question which theorists have been asking for decades, and although individual theorists may feel they have gone some way towards answering such a question for themselves, certainly no one has answered it to the satisfaction of the field in general. In any case, the person who has asked the question does not want a treatise on alternative explanations for therapeutic gain in groups. It seems best to say something simple, for example, 'It seems to have something to do with being able to talk things out, and the sharing. Of course there's no guarantee, but many people do find it helpful.' Or, 'Well, we know that a lot of people your age feel a bit unsure of themselves when it comes to things like meeting strangers, or applying for a job, so we consider that having a chance to practise such things could help.' Or, 'Well, take an example, getting into trouble sometimes follows from getting angry and just hitting out. Well, everyone gets angry, but different people do different things when they get angry. Sometimes seeing what others do and hearing what they say about it, and comparing your way, helps to see other possibilities.'

All of the above is to say that an individual, by his initial response to hearing that a group is a possibility, will provide information as to expectations, worries and curiosities, and this in turn provides a basis for decisions about selection and composition, and at the same time constitutes useful preparatory work. With regard to the latter, the person may seek and receive orientation to the group experience. He may seek and receive permission to be the kind of person, in the group, that he predicts he will be and wishes to be. The end position is one in which the therapist or worker is able to say either 'It does seem from what you are telling me that a group is not the best idea for you right now so we should consider other possibilities' or 'I wonder how you feel about joining the group we are starting in two weeks' time' or 'Although you do still have some reservations about joining a group, and I do think I understand them, I would like to encourage you to come into this group' or 'Right, then, we start next Wednesday . . .'

Suggested exercises

One can gain experience in conducting preparatory interviews through engaging in role-playing. If a colleague is prepared to play the part of a prospective group member, then one can conduct an interview designed to test his/her interest in and readiness to join a group. The person may either be himself in such an interview, in which case one needs to have in mind the kind of group which he might plausibly enter, or else he may take on the role of some particular client or patient with whom he has worked.

One can gain an appreciation of differing compositions and their impact by recollecting groups with which one has worked in the past and retrospectively reviewing their compositions, in terms of the preferred affective modes, preferred defences and level of vulnerability of members. This should help one to see the impact of varying compositions. One can also review previous experience with the aim of identifying persons whom one judges in retrospect should not have become members and seeking to think out what contra-indicating factors were present.

Part III

During the life of the group

Chapter 8
Listening to and observing groups and conceptualizing what one sees and hears

In taking on the task of conducting a group, a therapist, group worker or leader has assumed the special responsibility of saying and doing that which will most help the group to become and remain a positive medium for help and most help each person who participates in the group to benefit from it. Internal work consisting of keeping in touch with and trying to make sense of the events of the group forms a basis for carrying out this task. Necessary internal work can be factored out as:

to develop, refine and expand one's understanding of each person in the group;
to keep in touch with the dynamics of the group as a whole while it is in session and as it develops over time;
to keep in touch with one's own feelings and to note one's own behaviour and its consequences; and
to perceive connections between group and individual dynamics.

Watching, listening and thinking go together. Placing meaning on events is an inescapable feature of watching and listening. Perceptual selection is inevitable and one is bound to make judgments as one goes along, some of them hardly noticed, about what is worth noting and what is not, and how events fit together. Another way of stating this is to say that as a group therapist, group worker or leader listens, watches and participates he is bound to be operating on some internal model which guides his observations and suggests possible meanings. The internal model may be more or less explicit, more or less in line with articulated models already available in published work, but it is certain to be *there*.

Many group leaders operate mainly intuitively and do not try to make explicit to themselves what they are or should be listening for. Some resist the idea of thinking too explicitly about what they see and hear and what it might mean for fear that explicitness will reduce spontaneity. In my view, no matter how great one's natural ability, it can be more effectively developed and deployed if one has some ideas in mind about what to attend to as a group session proceeds. Informed intuition is better than uninformed intuition. This is not meant to turn conducting a group into an intellectual exercise, depreciate the value of 'soaking up' the flavour and atmosphere of a group or rule out spontaneous comments. Thinking *and* feeling are involved in watching, listening and meaning-making. If one takes a stand against thinking in order to ensure spontaneity one increases the risk of distorted or filtered listening. If one overvalues a cognitive stance one increases the risk of missing significant events and of forcing events rigidly into some conceptual framework.

In a group, a great deal happens all at once. Persons talk, do or do not build logically on the thread of the discussion, interrupt, change the subject, behave 'characteristically' or 'uncharacteristically', become irritated, get upset, make jokes, dreamily withdraw, etc., etc. Members form alliances, make friends and enemies, shift alliances, support or don't support one another, support or don't support the conductor of the group, and when responding to others display sympathy, impatience, boredom, anger, bafflement and many more feelings. The general atmosphere of the group may be depressed, excited, sullen, flat or other. The conversation may be orderly, focused, scattered, halting or hard to follow. The interaction sometimes involves undertones of affect which seem inconsistent with what is being talked about; topics may shift in unexpected ways; long periods of laboured and apparently fruitless discussion may occur. When the structure planned for a group involves discussing successive topics, periods of involved work during which everyone sticks to a topic may be followed by a drift away from the topic, or a topic may be resisted altogether. When an activity, game or exercise is involved, members may work hard at it, resist it or slip into chaotic behaviour. The group leader or therapist may feel pleased, despairing, confused, excited, impatient or angry with the group. He may find himself approving of some individuals and disapproving of others, feeling that one person is 'spoiling' the group while another is 'helping' it. If he has a co-leader he will have equally complex, diverse and shifting feelings about him.

How is a conductor to make sense of such many-faceted events? While all this is going on, how is a leader, therapist or worker to keep in touch with group, self, every member of the group and the connections among them? Without question or doubt, this is a demanding task. Not the least reason for its demandingness is that no part of this task can be pursued independently of any other part of it. One develops a better understanding of individuals, for example, by noting how each contributes to and reacts to group-level phenomena. Many of one's own feelings and behaviours are reactions to particular persons or to events in the group. Group-level dynamics are a product of the interaction amongst the persons in the group. Keeping in touch with all these aspects of the group is an admittedly difficult task, probably never fully mastered, yet it is a learnable skill: one can get better at it through experience. In the discussion which follows I shall try to acknowledge the intertwining and interdependence of different aspects of the observing task as I go along, yet bring first one aspect and then another into the forefront of discussion.

Developing, expanding and refining one's understanding of each person in the group

In many though not all groups this begins at the planning stage. For all groups, it continues throughout the group's life. During planning one may begin to develop an understanding of individual members through personal contacts or through discussions with colleagues who already know them. Such understandings, however, are bound to be limited. A much fuller understanding of each person can begin to develop once sessions begin, based on noting what the person says about himself, how he presents himself non-verbally, and how he interacts with others and participates in the group.

In a group, the information which a person provides about himself through the content of what he says is likely to occur in bits and pieces, widely spaced, in and among general group discussion or participation in activities. In a discussion, an individual may begin a personal account and get interrupted. He may provide only hints by saying 'It's the same with me' or 'I have never felt that way.' Occasionally a person offers an extended and ordered personal account of his life or some major aspect of it. But it is not really possible for the therapist or worker to develop his knowledge through interviewing the person, as he might expect to do in one-to-one interaction. In a group one never *only* speaks to an individual, even when addressing someone directly. One is always also saying something to or for the group. Should the therapist pursue any sustained form of history-taking in the group, he risks generating undesirable consequences, for example, neglecting others, placing others in a passive, listening role, or conveying that one person is his favourite. Further, following up on what one person is saying about himself is likely to pre-empt the development of some issue or theme of potential importance to all or most of those present, and to preclude the social comparison and/or receiving and providing feedback, which are important routes towards benefit.

On the whole, then, anything which resembles systematic history-taking is ruled out. Rather, the conductor of a group relies on noting what it is that each person says about himself or herself from time to time and in different contexts. He may ask occasional questions which lead to clarification or expansion, but even so for the most part he is in the position of accepting information rather than pursuing it. The information which comes his way is likely to appear in scattered, fragmentary and unordered forms. The group conductor needs to develop the knack of holding such bits of information in mind and fitting each new bit into a gradually expanding picture of each person. He must do this, of course, for each of the persons in the group. It is as if he reserves space in his mind for each person, and as new information comes his way he adds it in, gradually expanding, correcting and refining his emerging picture of each individual.

The *content* of what a person says about himself or his life or how he views himself or others is by no means the only source of information available to a group worker or therapist. In fact, while a group is an imperfect medium for learning about a person through what he says *about* himself, it is a superb medium for learning about a person through noticing the manner and pattern of his participation. This includes presentation of self and cueing behaviour, responses to particular others, participation in total group phenomena, and overall participative patterns.

Presentation of self seems to me inseparable from cueing

behaviour. An individual presents himself in a particular way in a group: by how he dresses, how he enters the room, how and where he sits, how he says what he says, the context in which he chooses to speak, and the like. For example, a middle-aged man arrived for the first session of a newly formed therapeutic group, moved a chair out of the circle into a corner of the room, sat down and folded his arms across his chest. He said nothing for the first ten minutes of the session when he confirmed the message conveyed by his behaviour and posture by saying 'I'll come but I won't speak.' In a planning group, a young woman was the first to speak, and dominated the group for some time, offering a detailed plan to the group in an authoritative manner. In a time-limited group for mothers of mentally handicapped children, one of the women offered to get the group started by providing an account of her son's difficult birth and early years, and proceeded to do so in a manner which allowed no interruption and called attention to her patience and skill in handling him. All three persons were presenting themselves as particular kinds of persons and offering cues about how they wished others to respond to them. The first man communicates: 'I am my own man, here against my will, don't press me or approach me.' The young woman communicates: 'I am an able person who knows exactly what we should do. Listen to me and do as I say.' The mother of the handicapped child is saying 'Think of me as a patient, caring, good mother.' The signals and cues which persons send forth in a group say, in effect, 'think of me as *this* kind of a person, not *that* kind'; 'behave toward me in *this* way, not *that* way.' Messages, signals and cues are sent through posture and non-verbal behaviour as when a person shows that he is or is not prepared to get involved in the group, demands a central place in it or is frightened by it. Signals and cues are also conveyed through the tone of voice adopted: imperious, self-confident, ingratiating, etc. Or, cues may be contained in the stance adopted with respect to what is happening in the group. A person may, for example, disown a general mood of anger or depression or try to move the group away from it, or he may refuse to accept some generally held group opinion. Messages are sometimes conveyed by what is going on when a person tries to change the subject, or by what it is he allows to run on.

Some of these interpersonal messages exert a strong pull on others to respond in a particular way. For example, someone who acts weak and helpless is putting pressure on others to help him or to be sympathetic. Someone who seeks to dominate is putting pressure on others to be passive and submissive. Someone who makes himself ridiculous is inviting others to laugh at him. Some cueing behaviours are quite complex. There is, for example, the 'yes, but . . .' person, who presents a problem with every appearance of one who wants to help, elicits advice, and then says 'Yes, but that won't work because . . .' or 'I've tried that and it didn't work' or 'Yes, perhaps, but I forgot to tell you . . .' He then complains that no one is helping him with his serious and pressing problems. The message is complicated and possibly includes 'I have terrible problems'; 'no one helps me'; 'no one here is any good.' It is hard for others not to respond with suggestions and advice; it is hard for others not to feel badly at not having helped or angry with the person for putting them in such a position. A young woman in a group told amusing stories in which she invariably had done something foolish or embarrassing, and then in the midst of the laughter which followed would suddenly say in a depressed tone, 'It's a terrible problem for me really.' The others suddenly and unexpectedly found themselves in the position of laughing in the face of tragedy, and tended to feel chagrined and ashamed. It can take some time to catch on to complex interpersonal patterns. Sometimes the person concerned sadly or bitterly complains about the responses he receives from others, not recognizing the part which he himself plays in eliciting them.

Many further instances of self-presentation and cueing could be mentioned. One person may seem particularly skilled in getting others to feel that they have victimized him. Another may display friendly interest in someone and then suddenly reject him or let him down. Individuals may present themselves, or cue others to see them as: a helpless victim of fate; a person who never gets angry; the champion of the underdog; the victim of injustice; a strong person who is always in control; ever-helpful; important, all-knowing, and superior; a person of no use and worthy of no respect; a person to whom the opinion of others means nothing; a 'good', model person; the 'I don't care what you think of me' sort; and so on and so on.

Sometimes a person displays repeated behaviours which do not particularly function as cues though they may tend to elicit characteristic responses. For example, a person may frequently display angry outbursts and feel sorry afterwards; or talk endlessly and appear oblivious to the unreceptivity or restlessness of others; or get sulky and withdraw; or express anger in subtle and indirect ways through sarcasm or hostile jokes; or speak cryptically.

A person also reveals himself by how he responds to particular others in the group. For example he will respond in his own way towards those who are aggressive, demanding, helpless, sarcastic, older, younger, more educated, and so on. There will be some he admires, some he dislikes, some he is envious of. There may be someone in the group who frightens or intimidates him. Why? It can be revealing to note how different persons respond to those who tend to be silent. Some persons are ready to leave them alone while others cannot bear silent individuals but continually press them to reveal themselves. Some assume that a silent person is hostile, others that he or she holds but is concealing wisdom or magical help.

One of the persons to whom each patient or member responds to in a particular way is of course the therapist or group worker. The conductor of a group can learn a good deal about a person (and about himself) by noting the feelings and behaviours which that person displays towards him and tends to elicit from him. For example, a person may be suspicious of or mistrustful of the leader, or he may constantly try to please him, or he may expect marvellous and impossible things of him, or he may try to form a special relationship with the leader and push others out. The leader in turn may feel more sympathetic towards some one person than towards the others; he may see some one person as spoiling the group; he may dislike someone, or find someone baffling, or especially interesting. A leader's own feelings can be a useful guide to developing an understanding of individual group members, providing he keeps it in mind that the feelings and opinions stirred up in him by others also reveal something about himself. One needs also keep in mind that how a person behaves with the leader is not necessarily an indication of how he behaves with others, since the leader occupies a special position in the group.

It is useful also to notice with whom a person forms an alliance, or towards whom he displays a consistent dislike. Often an alliance helps an individual play out some preferred interpersonal pattern. The individual has found someone else in the group who will help him to maintain a preferred interpersonal role or stance. Dislikes can occur because someone in the group is ready to move into areas which an individual experiences as threatening, because someone resembles a person who has been threatening or destructive in the past, or because someone's behaviour prevents a member from occupying some favoured role in the group.

A further source of information about individuals, rather different from those discussed so far, is observation of how the person contributes to or responds to total group phenomena: to mood and atmosphere, to prevailing themes, to emerging norms. For example, how does a person behave when the general atmosphere is one of anger or distress or depression or elation? Does he withdraw from, participate in or instigate such moods? Does he keep them going or try to shift them? Particular themes emerge in groups from time to time or may be introduced by the leader: how I behave when I get angry; what I am looking forward to most and what I most fear about going home from this hospital; what I find most painful about my handicapped child; the hardest thing to bear about my husband being in prison; etc., etc. What is the person's stance toward such themes? Can he tolerate exploration within the theme? Does he try to turn the group away from it? Does he take it seriously or try to trivialize it?

Patterns of participation shift in groups. How does an individual behave when two or three persons dominate the group for a time? How does he behave when someone is absent? Is he suspicious, guilty, concerned or pleased? How does the impending absence of the therapist affect him? If there is a shift towards greater intimacy in the group is he frightened or pleased? If there is a shift toward freer expression of anger or dissatisfaction, what is his response then? What is his overall participation pattern? Is he generally silent, or generally active? Does he participate mainly at the specific invitation of others? Does he come alive only towards the end of a group session?

A group worker or therapist is likely to develop some part of his understanding of individuals in the group through a direct process of empathy: of sensing or 'knowing' how another person feels in consequence of feeling or having felt similarly oneself. 'Empathy' is interestingly defined in the *Shorter Oxford Dictionary* as 'the power of projecting one's personality into, and so fully understanding, the object of contemplation'. This definition raises questions as to how 'fully' one person can ever understand another by this means and to what degree projection in the psychological sense may be involved, with attendant risks of distortion.

Everyone is familiar with the internal sense of 'I know just how he feels' or 'I'm glad I'm not in his shoes', which signals empathy. It is a useful route towards forming hypotheses about how others may be feeling, but it is well to be cautious about making assumptions about what must be so for others made on the basis of what one thinks one would feel oneself in similar circumstances.

These various routes towards understanding persons combine over a period of time to build a picture of each person in the group. It should be emphasized that one is always forming ideas about a person from incomplete data. At the beginning one has had minimal opportunity to observe, yet one begins (one can hardly help it) to develop ideas about what the person is like. These ideas should be held loosely, so that one is ready to modify and discard, if need be, and certainly to elaborate and develop one's picture as time goes on, since new situations and hence new information continually arise during the life of the group. Although one is bound to form first impressions, it is particularly important to hold to these as hypotheses only, since persons typically display only a part of themselves in the beginning, as a reaction to a new situation. To assume that one has learned something about the whole person from his behaviour at the start of a group is a serious form of jumping to conclusions.

So far the discussion has referred to what can be observed about an individual when the whole group is interacting together. In many forms of group work one's opportunities for observing individuals extend beyond this into other interactive situations: sub-group activities, mealtimes, the drive home in the mini-bus. If this is the case then opportunities for observation expand. One can ask oneself whether a person behaves differently or seems to feel differently in different situations. For example, does he seem more at ease in a more structured or a less structured situation? Does he prefer periods when the leader is actively directing things or when the members are making their own decisions? Does he prefer solitary activity to activities which require interaction? Are certain routines more stressful to him than others – for example, saying goodbye, getting up, changing from one activity to another, moving from a non-competitive to a competitive sport? In a residential setting or a club setting where certain rules and routines are a part of the group experience, one can ask a further set of questions: does the individual characteristically break rules or fail to conform to routines? Does he respond to explanations? Does he expect punishment if he breaks rules, and if so, what kind? Do you as leader constantly feel that you have to notice his reactions and take special care to 'handle' him? What does the handling involve? How does he react when he wins, loses, is left out, gets his own way, doesn't get his own way? Does he get into trouble? Is he always 'good'? If he gets into trouble, what is it about? Does he find it difficult to accept corrections or remonstrances from others? Even when one's principal contact with group members is in the more contained environment of a room with a circle of chairs one sometimes has opportunities to observe these extra-group interactions. For example, when the time is up, does the individual go off by himself or does he chat with others? How does he react when he meets you, the conductor, by accident in the corridor or in the road? And so on.

All of these are opportunities for observing and hence for understanding individuals but they will not all be available in the same group. It will be clear that the structure and character of a group limits and channels what can be observed. If, for example, a group is set up for therapeutic purposes and relies on open discussion, then there will be many opportunities to observe how a person seeks to establish a theme, joins in on an emerging theme or tries to evade or modify one. There will be little opportunity, however, to observe him in other kinds of interactive situations, for example those involving activities, and no opportunity to note what sort of activities he seeks out for himself. A group which uses role-playing to provide practice in social skills provides opportunities to note how a person engages in a planned exercise but reduces opportunities to note the position he seeks out for himself in a less highly structured group.

In general, one wishes to develop an understanding of each person in a group so that one can be alert to situations arising which are specifically relevant to the person and which offer special opportunities for personal gain, to situations likely to generate intolerable stress for an individual, and to the possibility of a person getting stuck in some limited form of participation which insulates him or her from useful experiences within the group. In short, one wishes to develop an understanding of each person which will help one to ensure that the group situation is being fully exploited on his behalf rather than only partially utilized.

The *kind* of understanding likely to be necessary and helpful will vary from group to group, depending on how one has conceptualized the 'preferred state' to which one hopes to help members to move. For example, if one is working with long-stay psychiatric patients and has defined the preferred state as 'being able to handle tasks of ordinary day-to-day living outside the hospital environment', then it will be useful to be aware of each person's current level of functioning, the practical skills which each feels comfortable with and uneasy about, and the responses of each to opportunities to practise skills. It is not relevant to the worker's or therapist's purposes and therefore he does not need to know whether the person has lost skills which he once had or whether he never developed them in the first place, nor how long the person has lived in a de-skilled state, nor details of personal history. If one were searching for a model which could offer a frame into which one's developing understanding of each person could be fitted a relatively simple model would suffice: one which helps one to identify a profile of skills and factors which could block skill acquisition. To be useful, a model need not include notions about how schizophrenia develops, nor processes by which institutionalization may develop.

In a group planned for women whose husbands or co-habitees have just been sentenced to prison terms, where one has defined the preferred state as 'facing and finding ways of coping with a changed personal situation', it is relevant to one's purposes and therefore useful to know something of the family circumstances, each woman's personal, interpersonal and financial resources, and her feelings about and responses to her predicament. It is usually not necessary to seek to understand her current experiences in the context of life-long patterns of coping or how these emerged in the first place in her family of origin. A useful model would include some ideas about impact of transitions and how persons are likely to behave in the face of them, and an understanding of a range of defensive reactions and coping devices. In such a case one would also need a body of information (as contrasted with a conceptual framework) having to do with financial and other resources available to women in such a situation. In groups composed of persons with long-standing interpersonal problems one may have conceptualized the preferred state as 'being able to exercise choice over behaviour and discard self-defeating behaviours'. If so, one is likely to wish to understand as fully as possible how each person feels and operates in the here-and-now of the group; features of his current life outside the group; significant features of his past life, including experiences within his family of origin; and connections between all of these. This includes an understanding of the abiding wishes and fears and guilts which have become a part of that person's personality and the ways in which past history still remains an influence in current relationships. For such persons a model is required which includes some notions about the functions which the self-defeating behaviour is fulfilling, factors and processes holding it in place, the interpersonal situations in which it is elicited and displayed in current life, and probably the interpersonal contexts in which the self-defeating patterns emerged earlier in the person's life. It is obvious that a model which emphasized, say, a profile of practical skills would be largely irrelevant, and certainly inadequate.

The general point being made is that different kinds of understandings are required and different models of the person are useful for different groups, depending in particular on the kinds of benefits one is hoping to achieve on behalf of members.

When a more elaborated model seems indicated, considerable choice is open to a practitioner. I prefer French's nuclear conflict model (French, 1952, 1954) in part because it facilitates seeing connections between group-level and individual dynamics. In this model the key concepts are *nuclear conflict, focal conflict, disturbing motive, reactive motive* and *solution*. According to French's line of thought, nuclear conflicts become established in consequence of early experiences, usually although not invariably within the family of origin, and remain important in adult life. A nuclear conflict includes a disturbing motive (some core wish or impulse – for example, a wish for nurturance or closeness, or angry feelings towards a parent) which is in conflict with a reactive motive (some abiding fear or guilt, such as a conviction of being intrinsically unworthy of love, or a fear of abandonment should one's feelings of anger be recognized). As a way of dealing with a nuclear conflict, an individual establishes one or more solutions which serve to contain the fears and sometimes also allow for some expression or satisfaction of the wish. A solution might involve, for example, denying that one needs close relationships, or finding indirect ways of expressing anger, or forming a close relationship with someone who can express anger *for* one. The nuclear conflict maintains its power in adult life, but the disturbing and reactive motives sink out of awareness. The individual may be aware of habitual patterns (a tendency towards sarcasm, love affairs which never last, a tendency to accept blame when things go wrong, etc.) which in terms of the model function as solutions. He is unlikely, however, to be more than dimly aware of the underlying wishes and fears which require the maintenance of the solution. In adult life, the nuclear conflict does not emerge in its original form. Rather, *focal* conflicts emerge which are resonant with but not identical with the original muclear conflict. The individual experiences wishes and fears which are basically the same as those involved in the nuclear conflict but which are coloured by the current situation which has recalled or re-elicited them. In response to the emergence of these wishes and fears he is likely to invoke habitual solutions, which again will be coloured by and adapted to the features of the contemporary situation.

The nuclear conflict is internalized – that is, the wishes and fears involved are experienced as real and as part of the self. They develop in the first place in the matrix of early experience. The infant and young child experiences the common human needs for nurturance, closeness, acceptance, etc. These are initial 'disturbing motives'. If they are reasonably met by the environment a nuclear conflict does not develop. However, if their satisfaction is consistently thwarted, then the thwarting factor, which exists as a reality factor in the environment, stands in opposition to the disturbing motive. As repeated experiences occur of some disturbing motive thwarted by some reality factor some internalized fear or guilt becomes established which combines with the wish or impulse to form a nuclear conflict. An example which I have used in the past (Whitaker, 1982) can be diagrammed as shown in Figure 8.1.

Usually, persons develop more than one solution to the same underlying conflict. Certain of these may operate to the person's advantage. They allow some gratification or expression of the disturbing motive and are seen in a positive light by others. Certain of them may operate to his disadvantage, making it more difficult for him to achieve the satisfactions which he seeks. The underlying wish and fear, being internalized and lost to awareness, are carried into current situations and relationships where the likelihood of the feared consequence (e.g. rejection or abandonment) is remote. Because the reactive motive retains its power, the solution is invoked where the realities of the situation do not require it. The person acts the clown with persons who do not

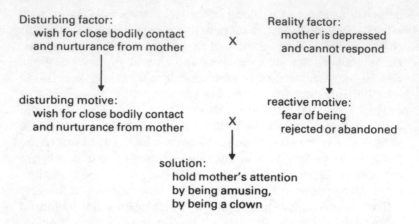

Figure 8.1

need him to be one in order to elicit the response he craves. Perhaps this means that in adult life he gets close only to those who for reasons of their own need a clown in their lives. Perhaps his clownishness alienates some persons who could provide him with the intimacy which he still seeks. The manner in which an habitual solution is expressed in adult life is influenced by maturation as well as circumstances. A small boy may think it very funny to stand on his head. As an adult, he may tell sophisticated stories, but the same basic solution is operating, and is fulfilling analogous functions.

Some solutions are defences in the usual sense of the term (denial, rationalization, avoidance, etc.) but others take the form of habitual ways of presenting the self, or preferred interpersonal patterns, or even whole lifestyles. Some solutions require partners or particular environments in order for them to be carried out, and account for some of the choices which persons make, for example, of marital partner or occupation.

Solutions may be maladaptive or adaptive in character, in the sense of interfering with or facilitating the pursuit of life goals. One of the advantages of this model is that it calls attention to the strengths as well as to the weaknesses of an individual, for few persons are characterized only by maladaptive solutions. Although developed for use with psychoanalytic patients, the model can be applied to persons regarded as functioning adequately, since many persons can be described in terms of some nuclear conflict to which they have established mainly adaptive solutions.

In adults who present themselves for psychotherapy, an habitual maladaptive solution is often presented as an unwanted symptom: 'I am overweight and can't control it'; 'my relationships with women never last more than a few months'; etc. The symptom, the complained-of behaviour, can be understood in terms of the function that it is fulfilling for the person. The model suggests that the symptom, however unwanted, is linked to an underlying internalized conflict, and functions to alleviate reactive fears.

Many persons function quite well and do not experience undue anxiety or distress as long as life circumstances permit them to operate on favoured solutions. A crisis or transition, however, may deprive a person of a needed solution. Consider as an example a long-distance truck driver who had to give up his job when kidney failure required him to use a dialysis machine twice a week. This man began to experience severe psychological distress. His job proved to have functioned as a solution for him, helping him to maintain a needed distance from his family and a self-image of being his own man. His illness forced a change in life style which not only deprived him of this necessary solution, but also forced him into a position (his wife operated the machine during his twice-weekly sessions) which exacerbated underlying fears concerned with being at the mercy of untrustworthy others. Were this man to become a member of a short-term helping group for persons with recently acquired handicaps, his therapist would be better able to make use of the group on his behalf if he understood the function which his previous occupation had fulfilled for him.

A person who has been deprived of an habitual solution is in a position where underlying fears are no longer being contained. The group, one hopes, can constitute a safe environment in which these fears can be confronted. Where a person is clinging to a maladaptive personal solution, a group constitutes a contemporary situation which may at certain times resonate with the abiding nuclear conflict, and re-elicit the feelings involved in it in the form of a derived focal conflict. If work can occur on the focal conflict in its derived form, then the opportunity exists for the person to confront his fears and test whether, whatever their origin, they are realistic ones in his current life; and to test whether his adult strengths can be brought to bear, whatever his earlier inability to manage his fears. If he can confront his fears and experience them as unrealistic or exaggerated or else as reality-based but manageable, then the fears lose their potency and the need to maintain the habitual maladaptive solution lessens or is done away with.

I find it useful to hold this model in mind for persons who are behaving in self-defeating ways and are anxious or depressed (category 4 in chapter 3) and for many persons emerging from breakdowns in functioning (category 5). It is also useful for some persons who are facing transitions or caught in a linked-fate relationship (categories 1, 2 and 3), where one might see the transition or relationship as robbing them of a needed personal solution, or the linked-fate relationship precluding the establishment of satisfactory solutions. The model is usually not relevant to persons displaying low levels of practical and interpersonal skills (category 6) or persons who function chronically at some low, unsatisfactory level (category 7). It is occasionally relevant to persons who break laws or offend commonly held standards (category 8), in instances where it is plausible to assume that the behaviour functions as a solution to some underlying conflict. However, it should be applied cautiously to such persons because so many other factors could be involved, some originating outside the person himself (e.g. an unsuitable school curriculum).

When one is concentrating on developing an understanding of individuals in groups, the individual is in focus and the group is context. It is also possible to attend to the group-as-a-whole as a phenomenon in itself. Since the group is the vehicle which one is attempting to use to benefit persons, maintaining an understanding of its character and functioning must be an important part of one's monitoring task. One needs to be able to judge when a group is working well and when it is not; when one should address oneself to its functioning and when one need not. A second aspect of the internal work which a therapist or worker carries on while conducting a group necessarily is the following:

Keeping in touch with the dynamics of the group as a whole while it is in session and as it develops over time

Without forgetting that the group could not exist were it not for the persons in it, one can nevertheless look at group-level phenomena and successive group events somewhat independently of the meaning of those events for the persons engaged in them.

The issue of *what* one can observe about the group as a whole has already been taken up in chapter 2, where a number of special characteristics of the group were discussed. To recap briefly, it was suggested that the following group-level phenomena occur in groups: group moods and atmospheres, including emotional contagion; shared themes; norms and belief systems, including the possibility that some of these may take the form of collusive defences; the development of a group over time; and degree of cohesiveness. A group focal conflict model was then put forward as a container for these features of groups. I shall not restate that model, but point out that it utilizes concepts parallel to those put forward by French in his nuclear conflict model, modified and extended where required in order to render those concepts relevant to the operation of a group.

Our concern here is how a group worker or therapist can grasp these group-level events, while the group is going on and while he is discharging his responsibilities as conductor of the group. Certain group-level phenomena (especially moods, atmospheres, shared fears) may be grasped through direct and seemingly instantaneous experience. Other phenomena (especially covert themes and components of a group focal conflict) may be understood through attending to associational processes in groups. Still other phenomena (especially the norms and shared beliefs, and degrees of cohesiveness) are best grasped through noting patterns and consistencies in behaviour amongst members.

There are times when one seems to grasp certain phenomena occurring in a group intuitively, that is, virtually instantaneously, without being aware of thinking about them. The *Shorter Oxford Dictionary* defines intuition as 'the immediate apprehension of an object by the mind without the intervention of any reasoning process'. This certainly occurs and when it occurs it is often accompanied by a strong conviction that one is right. Processes of resonance, contagion and empathy may all be involved. A therapist's or worker's own feelings may 'resonate' with those being expressed by members and he may then be alert to minimal cues offered by non-verbal and para-linguistic behaviours or he may respond similarly to triggering events. He 'knows' what is happening because he feels what is happening. Or, a therapist or worker may get caught up in processes of contagion. Because he is capable of depression, elation, anger, etc. himself, and because they are always present in him in a latent form, when these affects or others catch fire in a group he experiences them himself by the same processes which operate for anyone else in the group (see Redl's ideas about contagion, described in chapter 2). Or, the therapist or worker 'understands' through processes of empathy. Just as the conductor of a group may consider that he understands an individual through empathizing with him in his situation, he may feel able to understand a number of persons or even a whole group by the same means. I am not sure how distinctive these processes are. Certainly resonance, contagion and empathy all involve direct in-touchness between the personality/experiences/feelings of the conductor of the group and of others present.

A second route toward grasping group-level phenomena has to do with receiving the successive events occurring during a session as elements in a free associative process. How it is that overt and covert themes can become established in a group through associative processes has already been described in chapter 2. Such processes are easier to observe within some group structures than others. A group which proceeds by open discussion with the general remit to discuss whatever is important to members deliberately removes obstacles to an associational flow. In a group in which topics have been planned the discussion is supposed to be *about* something and the overt theme is prescribed. Nevertheless further themes, either overt or covert in character, can emerge in, through or in addition to the prescribed theme by the same processes. The same thing can be said about groups structured in terms of exercises, games or activities. Free-associative processes occur within the structure, or break through it, and become quite visible at times. It is only in the most highly prescriptive of structures where associative processes may be precluded or curtailed by the structure.

When listening to an associational flow, one often notes that as the 'conversation' proceeds, a member responds to only a part of what has just been said. That is, he receives selectively, and either ignores certain bits of what has been said as if they had not occurred at all, or else recasts what has been said in terms which make sense to him, and responds to that. Whoever speaks next does the same. Each person brings his own self to the interaction, and much filtering and re-interpreting goes on. In addition to those who are participating actively, that is, actually saying something, others are also participating, showing by their posture,

evidence of attention or inattention, etc., how they may be responding internally to the evolving events of the group. As such a run
of interactions proceeds, one can begin to see that a particular
thread is maintained through diverse contributions to the
conversation.

It can take some time for a theme to emerge clearly. A clear
expression of some concern expressed by one person is not of
course a shared theme. One has to wait to see how this is built
upon over a period of time before one can judge whether that
person was expressing something important to others besides himself, or whether it was entirely idiosyncratic, or whether some
aspect of his contribution was relevant to others in the group.

As one listens and watches, one develops hypotheses about the
possible import of what is being said. Thinking now in group focal
conflict terms, it is often the solution which first emerges clearly.
For example, suppose that parents of mentally handicapped children begin a group session by discussing the accomplishments of
their normal children. Virtually everyone joins in on this and it is
clearly a shared theme, overt in character. From a group focal
conflict point of view one is most likely seeing the operation of a
restrictive solution. That is, everyone knows that they have joined
the group in order to explore feelings and experiences around the
handicapped child in the family. Hence, focusing only on the
normal children is an evasion: in group focal conflict terms a
restrictive solution. When one sees such a theme emerging, one
might speculate that the members cannot as yet bear to say
anything about feelings and experiences concerning the handicapped child. However, the group has as yet given no clue as to
just what is making this so difficult. As one waits and listens, one
most likely begins to hear clues. Perhaps someone says 'Of course,
my handicapped child never gets praised by my relatives for
anything he accomplishes' (an *individual* concern, so far, which
could have to do with resentment towards relatives, or disappointment on behalf of the handicapped child, or personal disappointment in having own hopes thwarted). This comment then might
be followed by someone saying 'It makes me angry when people
can never find anything nice to say about Sally. I think it hurts
her feelings.' (This is also an individual concern, which shares
with the previous comment anger towards others and sympathy
with the child.) Suppose a next comment is 'People don't understand that a mentally handicapped child has feelings just like

anyone else.' (An individual concern, like all others, but now one can begin to speculate that the *shared* feeling is anger at those who don't understand.) One would then continue to listen to see if this hypothesis is supported by subsequent events. Let us suppose that it is, but that a new element comes in: someone says 'Unless you have a handicapped child yourself, I think it *is* hard to understand.' At this point the therapist might recollect that he is the only person present who does not have a handicapped child, and wonder if the members are concerned about whether *he* is likely to fail to understand their children, and by extension them and their feelings. Let us suppose that the next minute or two supports this view. By now one might feel reasonably confident about one's developing understanding of the situation, and might represent it (to oneself) in group focal conflict terms as shown in Figure 8.2.

Sometimes the sequence of associations is mainly non-verbal. In a group which Morton A. Lieberman and I once conducted the patients, all from a male psychiatric ward, entered the room in ones and twos, as usual. The first to enter sat against a wall opposite the two therapists, who were sitting with one or two vacant chairs between them. The next person to enter sat beside the first, and the next two moved chairs so that they too were sitting against the wall next to the first two. Others did the same, until seven patients were arrayed along the wall, opposite the therapists. The first verbal comment was a joke: 'This is a line-up' (i.e. a police line-up). From this sequence of events both

disturbing motive:
    wish for their children to be
    valued, and by extension for   X
    themselves to be valued

reactive motive:
    fear that the therapist will
    not be sympathetic to their
    feelings ('not understand')

solution:
    talk about the
    accomplishments of
    their normal children

which gives way to:
    complain, and at the
    same time implicitly
    ask for reassurance

Figure 8.2

therapists formed the view (though neither said anything at the time) that the patients felt that the therapists were opposed to them or after them in some way, or that they (the patients) felt guilty about something. As in any such situation one would have to wait to see how the interaction develops before forming any further or more definite views.

Sometimes a flow of associations is couched in terms which suggest that the overt content is expressing a covert theme in symbolic terms. For example, the members of a group nervously shared the opinion that the building in which the group was meeting had been built with inadequately reinforced concrete, and that similarly built buildings had collapsed. A therapist or worker listening to this might form the view that the members shared some worries about the inadequate underpinnings of the group (or competence of the builder-therapist?) In group focal conflict terms a reactive fear might be present about the dangers of the group or the inadequacies of the therapist, very much masked by a restrictive solution involving expressing feelings in symbolic terms. One would have to wait to see how such a conversation developed to get a clearer view of the feelings involved.

When working with very disturbed persons in a group, one may find that powerful internal preoccupations interrupt or apparently interrupt the associative flow. For example, in a group composed mainly of persons just emerging from florid psychotic states, one member suddenly turned on another and said in an angry tone: '*You* don't understand what I am talking about.' Later, he was able to explain that he was responding to something which had been said some twenty or twenty-five minutes earlier. During the intervening time the patient had retreated into himself, not hearing what was being said and preoccupied only with his own concerns. These private concerns finally burst out without regard to what was going on currently in the group. The patient's statement came as an interruption, yet it was also a response, albeit delayed, to events in the group. In another such group, a patient launched into a long story about how his employer had persecuted him and arranged for his admission to a psychiatric ward because of suspecting him of a crime which he did not commit. At the time this seemed to the therapist to be entirely outside the associational flow. However, during this time the members of the group had been developing a theme about whether or not the therapists could accept them, particularly if they were to reveal more of themselves. The comment about the employer, although delusional in character, fitted this theme in that it had to do with being blamed and the bad consequences which could then follow.

In general, the skill of listening to/watching an associative flow involves a consistent but 'light' or unlaboured attentiveness. By this I mean noting but not listening too ponderously to each individual contribution, allowing oneself to 'hear' what is happening at levels including but also additional to the manifest content of a conversation. In arriving at possible meanings, it is important not to foreclose too quickly: one needs to hold hypotheses in mind loosely, waiting to see if ensuing events support or disconfirm them, or require modification. Making use of an associative flow to understand group-level events requires above all giving a group room for such flows to emerge, and avoiding dominating the situation to the point of actually interrupting the flow.

A third route towards understanding certain group-level processes is through noting regularities in behaviour and patterns of behaviour over a period of time. Many significant norms and shared beliefs are never made explicit: one becomes aware of them by noting what members typically do and say or never do and say. For example one might note that being on time seems to mean coming about five minutes late, or that members never interrupt one another, or that anger is expressed towards one another but never at the leader, or that everyone agrees that they are the victims of injustice and are not to be held responsible for their own behaviour. One might note that the members seem very skilful at giving each person an equal period of time in the centre of attention, and conclude that this is an operating norm for the group. One can catch on to restrictive solutions which involve role differentiation by noting how members co-operate in keeping certain forms of interaction going, for example, maintaining one person in the role of patient while others function as therapists, or attacking one person for harbouring unacceptable feelings. One becomes aware of degrees of cohesiveness by noting what persons consistently say about the group (e.g. it is or is not important to them) and how they behave, especially when someone crosses the group's boundaries. Members of cohesive groups are more likely to see entering and leaving the group, absences, etc. as noteworthy events than are members of less cohesive groups.

In addition to trying to be in touch with group-level phenomena as they develop within sessions, one can reflect on the events of a group between sessions, and also try to see broader patterns which emerge over a series of sessions. Post-session reflections often suggest meanings for events which escaped one at the time. Alternative meanings come to mind or one is helped to see alternative meanings by a co-worker, co-therapist, observer or consultant. In long-term groups one sees productive patches, unproductive patches, members returning to and re-exploring earlier themes. Just as one can hold inside one's head spaces for each member of the group, one can also hold space for the earlier history of a group. For example, one might see a restrictive solution emerge which members have utilized earlier in the group's history, or one might see an earlier theme re-emerge in a new context and be explored in a new way. Part of one's understanding of the evolution of a group is to see connections between later and earlier themes: how earlier ones paved the way for later ones; how later ones expand upon earlier ones. In other words, one sees, hears and makes sense of events in the group at both the micro-level of successive events within sessions and at the macro-level of events across several or a whole series of sessions.

Why try to keep in touch with group-level phenomena? Essentially because there will be times when one wishes to influence them and times when one wishes to utilize them for the benefit of individual members. Most persons who conduct groups have in mind an image of a well-functioning group and a poorly functioning group. A well-functioning group is one whose members work hard at matters important to them, who utilize rather than fight against the structure planned for the group, who develop a sense of mutual trust, who display a minimum of self-censorship and resistance, who offer mutual support yet challenge one another in a non-destructive manner, and who engage in wide-ranging explorations and sharings. A poorly functioning group displays opposite characteristics, and may tend either towards the flaccid and the pallid, or towards dysfunctional levels of internal conflict. The behaviour of the conductor of the group is one factor of many which influences the character and course of a group. Although he cannot determine how things go, he can at times influence it. It follows that if he is in touch with group-level features of the group he will at the same time be forming judgments as to how well the group is functioning and whether or not he should try to influence it. Beyond this – and this is the second point – there will be times when the dynamics of the group resonate with the dynamics of individuals in ways which create special opportunities for benefiting the latter. If the therapist or worker is alert to group-level phenomena (and of course has also developed an understanding of each person in the group) he is in a better position to catch such moments and make use of them.

Keeping in touch with one's own feelings and noting one's own behaviour and its consequences

It has already been pointed out that one's own feelings can be indicators of or guides to appreciating the feelings of others and understanding certain total-group phenomena. Further to this, it is important to keep in touch with own feelings because if they are unacknowledged or ignored they may emerge in unintended and unnoted ways which work against one's general hopes and intentions for the group and/or for particular persons in the group.

What feelings might one experience, as a worker or therapist, while a group is in session? Even before a group begins, one is likely to harbour certain hopes and fears, for oneself, for persons in the group and for the group enterprise in general. Once a group begins to meet, specific events may stir up certain worries, hopes and preferences. There will be times when the issues and themes with which members of the group are struggling resonate with powerful concerns of one's own, and one is then especially vulnerable to one's own feelings getting in the way of the task.

Especially if working with groups is a new venture within an agency or institution, the worker or therapist may have staked a good deal on its success: his own reputation, and the likelihood or not that working with groups will become an established and respected part of the organization's work. Hopes may be high and worries substantial. If work with groups is well established an inexperienced therapist or worker may feel he or she has a lot to live up to. Conducting a group is often a curiously public enterprise, even when sessions are held behind closed doors. Perhaps it has to do with the number of persons involved and the fact that in many settings one will have received referrals from colleagues who retain primary responsibility for the patients or clients in the group, and have an interest in how the group is going. Therapists and workers are also rightly aware of the complexity and demand-ingness of the task. Based on his experience in training group therapists, Meyer Wiliams identified a number of what he called 'fearful fantasies' amongst trainees: encountering unmanageable resistance, losing control of the group, excessive hostility breaking out, acting out by group members, overwhelming dependency demands, and group disintegration (Williams, 1966). I do not believe that these fears are restricted to inexperienced persons, although increased experience does help to remind one that such fantasies rarely materialize. Experienced as well as inexperienced therapists and workers can worry: 'What if no one comes next time?' 'What if no one says anything?' 'What if they gang up on me?' etc. Such fears do not, in themselves, cause problems, but the defences which the conductor of a group erects in the face of them shapes his behaviour and restricts it in ways likely to reduce the usefulness of the group for members.

Feelings, sometimes quite powerful feelings, are bound to be stirred up in a therapist or worker while a group is in session. It is hard to avoid feeling angry with someone who seems to be spoiling a group or especially pleased with someone who seems to be helping it. It is hard not to feel injured when under attack, frightened when someone is out of control, worried when members seem pushed into more than they can handle, triumphant when persons achieve something really important to them, hopeless when a group gets stuck in an unproductive patch, help-less when one is confused by events and hasn't a clue as to what is going on, or exhilarated when a group goes well and then disappointed when it doesn't keep up its good work.

Certain inner experiences and feelings have to do with how the issues and themes arising in the group may resonate at times with the problems, hopes, fears, and characteristic defences and security operations of the therapist or worker. I find it easiest to discuss this in group focal conflict and nuclear conflict terms. If a prevailing group focal conflict resonates with a nuclear conflict which has been a significant part of the conductor's own life and life course, then he is likely to experience the same impulses or wishes and the same fears as do the members, as intensely as they do and at the same unacknowledged level. Under such circum-stances he is likely to try to institute his own preferred solutions in the face of this, which it will be remembered could be some defence in the ordinary sense of the term but could also take the form of seeking certain alliances in the group or trying to establish certain norms or atmospheres. If he succeeds in doing this he will not be able to help the members because he has insulated himself from acknowledging the impulses and fears which are preoccupying them. If his preferred personal solutions coincide with those which the members are seeking to establish as shared solutions, he is likely to fall into colluding with the members in maintaining a restrictive solution (collusive defence). If this happens he is in a position from which he cannot help the members to shift away from a restrictive solution: on the contrary, he is working hard to help them to maintain it. The only way for a therapist or worker to avoid getting into such a fix is to be aware of his personal vulnerabilities, such that when such resonances begin to occur he is forewarned and can discipline himself to stand outside his own concerns enough to maintain a helping stance. The positive side of such resonances is that they help the therapist or worker to empathize with the feelings of the members. However, empathy can be utilized positively only if one can at the same time retain one's stance as a helper (The idea of *stance* is developed more fully in chapter 14.)

As conductor of a group one cannot avoid having feelings, sometimes quite strong ones, about what is going on in the group. More precisely, one could avoid them only by distancing oneself enough to lose touch with the group, and if one did that one would not be in a position to help either the group or the members. Certain feelings, especially anticipatory fears, are less likely to occur if one acknowledges their existence and considers ahead of time whether or not they are realistic. Often they are not, or at least they are exaggerated. Events which one fears may happen do not occur as often as one expects and when they do they usually can be managed. One can forearm oneself by thinking out ahead of time how one might cope with a feared situation should it arise. Having said this, many powerful feelings are unavoidable, nor would one wish to avoid them. What one wishes to avoid are certain of the behaviours which one's feelings could lead one into, in particular immobilization or errors. The best way to avoid these dysfunctional consequences of own feelings is to take on as an internal task noticing one's own feelings as they surface in response to group events. One then has a better chance of staying in control of whether and how they are expressed in action. It is by no means easy to keep in touch with own feelings (probably impossible to do so consistently) but like any other skill it can be developed and one can get better at it with practice. A consultant can be a great help with this. It is not unusual to become aware of certain feelings only after a session ends and perhaps after unacknowledged feelings have already led one into some error. This is not so serious, since errors can usually be retrieved if they are recognized. Certainly it is far better than never acknowledging the feelings at all.

Turning to one's visible behaviour in a group, the things that one does and says have consequences. Getting into the habit of noticing the consequences of what one does and says is another part of the self-monitoring task. What happens after one has intervened in some way constitutes feedback to oneself which can guide subsequent behaviour. If, for example, one has said something intended to encourage more persons to participate, and the conversation then becomes more general, this tells one that one can sit back and allow the conversation to proceed. The group does not need further interventions along the same lines. If one has attempted to reassure a group and then notes that the members seem just as anxious as before, then one might give thought to how it was that one's intervention did not work as one had hoped. Perhaps what one thought was reassurance actually conveyed veiled criticism or condemnation. Perhaps the members were so beset by fears that one's comment was not heard. If one has offered an interpretation intended to unblock the group and it is totally ignored, one might come to the view that the interpretation was ill-timed, or perhaps that it contained some additional message, such as 'You are not behaving as I wish.' If one has been silent for a considerable period of time and notices that persons in the group are getting restless and directing glances one's way, one might judge that one's persisting silence is generating a feeling of uneasiness in the group. Perceiving this as a consequence of one's behaviour would very likely lead one to find a way to become more active in the group. In general, what follows an intervention or a bit of behaviour, and the meanings which one can plausibly place on what follows, help one to see what one might then do or say.

As a guide to action one cannot do without feedback from the group, and the most useful form of feedback is noticing what happens as a consequence of one's own behaviour, moment by moment as the group proceeds. Noting consequences is a kind of habit, an attitude of mind which can be cultivated and developed with practice. In the longer run the habit of self-observation can facilitate an understanding of one's own style, of the experiences one characteristically seeks or avoids, of repeated errors, and the like, all of which contribute to improving one's functioning in groups.

Perceiving connections between group and individual dynamics

Connections between group and individual dynamics have necessarily been referred to again and again in the course of discussing how one may develop an understanding of individuals, note group-level phenomena, and keep in touch with one's own feelings. Each person in the group, by his or her behaviour, influences the character and course of a group, and the events of a group simultaneously have an impact on persons. Resonances can occur between the impulses, hopes, wishes, fears and guilts developed and shared at a group level with the impulses, hopes, fears, etc. important to individuals. Restrictive solutions established in the group can support or challenge the defences and personal solutions preferred by members.

Persons can influence a group by displaying resistance to the course of events, for example by interfering with the exploration of some theme, by refusing to accept some norm or otherwise shared belief, or by declining to co-operate in some solution which require their active participation in order to become established. Even a silent person can be said to be influencing the group if his silence can plausibly be taken as acquiescence. Or, his silence may powerfully influence the group if it becomes a repository for the fantasies of others. In group focal conflict terms, an individual might contribute to the establishment of some solution, fight against the establishment of a solution, be the first to be ready to abandon a restrictive solution, or be the first to acknowledge reactive fears. Individuals are by no means merely passive recipients of group forces, as those who fear the power of group pressures towards conformity might assume. Individually and collectively they take an active part in shaping the character of the group.

At the same time, the group has an impact on persons. In the context of a group exploring some theme, an individual may feel safe enough to confront experiences and feelings which he ordinarily avoids. If group conditions maintain persons in a 'safe-enough' position they may feel able to try out new behaviours. At times group forces prevent an individual from maintaining some preferred personal defence because it is inconsistent with a shared solution which everyone else is pressing for. Sometimes a person is carried into realms of usually avoided feelings through processes of contagion. He may become the target of group forces which have a destructive impact (for example if he occupies the position of scapegoat or becomes the target for displaced anger). Or, group forces may encapsulate him in some position which insulates him from experiences which could otherwise occur. If group forces facilitate the exploration of some meaningful issue in ways which go beyond his usual limits, or if group forces interfere with the operation of usual defences, the situation may be ripe for a corrective emotional experience. That is, in the context of group events, he may acknowledge feelings or express behaviours which he has always assumed would bring catastrophe in their wake, and find that the feared catastrophe does not occur.

Resonances can occur between the wishes and fears involved in a group focal conflict and wishes and fears important to an individual. When such resonances occur for members they constitute special opportunities for personal gain. For example, suppose the group as a whole is caught up in, say, a wish to be the therapist's special favourite versus fears of being rejected by fellow-members. Suppose further that this resonates with a long-standing personal dynamic for one or more members of the group. A special opportunity then exists for those persons to explore this theme in terms specifically relevant to themselves. The group dynamic both supports and challenges the individual.

Active participation is not required for there to be connections between individual and group dynamics. Often, a theme or issue which is being explored by some of the persons in the group is important in highly personal ways to a member who is not participating at all. He is in a spectator position, but the very fact that he is witness to something which connects with his own concerns is, for him, an important experience. In particular he may be hearing how others cope with a situation similar to one which faces him, or he may observe that others 'get away with' (do not bring retribution or other negative consequences upon

themselves) behaving in some way which he himself never dares
to do. This kind of connection between individual and group is
not visible to anyone else. A therapist or worker will either not
be aware of it at all or else will simply be guessing about a
connection on the basis of what he understands about persons in
general or this person in particular.

All of the above refer to connections which can occur. Some
of them are visible enough so that a therapist or worker can
perceive them if he or she is tuned in to the possibility of their
occurring. Others occur inside persons and are not visible to
others. If the conductor of a group is already in the habit of noting
group-level dynamics and has been developing an understanding
of each individual in the group by means already described, and
if he is furthermore aware of the kinds of connections which may
occur, then he or she is in a good position to be alert to connections and probable connections. As a basis for intervening, perceiving connections is of central importance, since there are times
when the conductor of the group, by emphasizing these connections or encouraging persons to explore them, can greatly enhance
the usefulness of the group for particular individuals.

All of the internal work discussed in this chapter goes on at the
same time. Each task is a part of every other task. One can choose
by an act of will to focus one's attention on some one member or
on the group as a whole or on some strong personal feeling but
if one does so one is merely choosing which, for the moment,
shall be figure and which ground, which shall be placed in the
forefront of attention and which allowed to recede into the background. When actually participating in a group what usually
happens is that one is gaining impressions about everything at
the same time, though some facets of the group may be more
prominently in focus than others. This is as it should be, for these
aspects of the group are inextricably linked, and any single event
usually provides information about all of them.

Only a fraction of what one thinks to oneself while conducting
a group actually emerges as behaviour which is visible to others.
Some of one's thinking will have been in the form of tentative
ideas which have had to be discarded in the light of subsequent
events. Some of what one might have said does not need to be
said because members of the group do it for one. Some of what
one feels and thinks, if expressed, will only interfere with the

useful operation of the group. Acknowledging all this, there are times when a therapist's or worker's active participation crucially affects the development of a group or its usefulness for individual members. No better basis for intervening exists than listening and observing with care and trying to make sense of what one sees and hears.

Suggested exercises

A good way to develop observation, listening and meaning-making skills is to observe a group which one is not responsible for conducting. If this can be done from behind a one-way screen this is an advantage, because it means that others can observe at the same time and one can compare notes as one goes, or else one can take private notes about what one thinks is going on and compare them afterwards. Failing this, it is sometimes possible to arrange to be a non-participant observer, sitting quietly in a corner while the group is in session. In either case it is possible to compare one's own impressions later with the person(s) actually conducting the group. The advantage of being a non-participating observer, especially if one is inexperienced, is that one is not preoccupied by the responsibility of conducting the group and can turn one's attention freely to the observing/listening/meaning-making task. The opportunity to compare one's own understanding of events with that of others, afterwards, is useful because one does not expect everyone to develop the same views, and comparisons help one to see what one has emphasized or over emphasized, missed, etc., and reveals alternative ways of viewing the same events.

If one is unable to observe a live group, video-tapes are useful, audio-tapes somewhat less useful (and often hard to follow). The same exercise of comparing impressions and formulations can be followed. An advantage of tapes is that one can stop and restart them. This means that a group watching and/or listening to a tape can stop it at intervals and discuss the import of an episode while it is still fresh in mind. Replaying episodes where there has been disagreement between observers offers further opportunities for learning.

Chapter 9
The formative phase of a group: character and purposes

This chapter is the first in a series which focuses on how a therapist, group worker or leader may best conduct a group while it is in session. This and succeeding chapters confront the issue of what one might say and do, when, and to what purpose, while in face-to-face interaction with a group and its members.

All groups are different, and each group continuously evolves and changes. An intervention which makes sense at one point may be entirely inappropriate at another. Yet guidelines can be offered, based on an awareness of one's purposes and an understanding of the situations, problems and opportunities likely to arise during successive phases of a group's life.

Toward the end of chapter 1 a number of instrumental purposes were listed which had to do with the conduct of the group while it is in session. If pursued, these can be expected to contribute to the realization of one's overall purpose of benefiting members by making as full use as possible of the potentials of the group as a medium for help. These instrumental purposes were:

to seek to conduct the group so as to maintain a general sense of safety at a level at which members feel safe enough to stay in the group and to take personal risks;

to seek to avoid the irredeemable collapse of structure;

to work toward the establishment and maintenance of norms in the group which support it as a positive medium for help; (in group focal conflict terms, to work toward the establishment and maintenance of enabling rather than restrictive solutions);

to utilize events occurring in the group for the specific benefit of members;

to avoid doing harm; and
to discern and think out how to retrieve errors.

The first three of these have to do with maintaining conditions in the group likely to facilitate effective work. They are addressed to the dynamics of the *group*. In groups, much of the benefit which accrues to individuals derives from interactions among peers. The therapist or worker can do much to increase the likelihood that these interactions will be fruitful if he attends to and seeks to influence certain features of the group as a whole. The next instrumental purpose calls attention to direct work with individual members which a worker or therapist may undertake with the group as context. It emphasizes seeing the relevance of particular events to particular patients or clients, and intervening actively to exploit such situations on behalf of specific persons.

These first four instrumental purposes are interrelated, in that it is impossible to pursue any one of them without affecting the others. Any one of them can be pursued in a way which either supports or subverts the therapist's or worker's overall purpose in conducting the group; any one of them can be pursued in ways which could either support or work against certain of the others.

A group experience can harm as well as help. Errors can be made which limit the usefulness of the group. The final two instrumental purposes call attention to these possibilities. Discussions of them are meant to help practitioners to avoid harmful consequences and to either forestall errors or to detect them when they occur and perceive ways of retrieving them.

These instrumental purposes are important throughout all phases of a group's life, but each takes on a particular character and relative importance depending on whether the group is newly formed, well-established, or near to the end of its life. In this chapter I shall discuss these instrumental purposes as they pertain to the formative stage of a group, taking into account how all concerned are likely to feel when a group first begins to meet, and what is likely to seem most important to them at the time.

Conducting the group so as to maintain a general sense of safety at a level at which members feel safe enough to stay in the group and to take personal risks

If the members of a group do not experience the group situation as a safe-enough environment they will not stay in it; they will either flee literally, or insulate themselves from the experience psychologically. If either of these things happens, the likelihood of benefit is destroyed or diminished, for everyone or for some. Questions then arise as to 'How safe is safe enough?' 'How safe is too safe?' 'What is unsafeness?' I suggest that feeling 'safe enough' means experiencing a degree of ease, trust, and confidence in self and others which makes it possible to stay in the group and begin to take risks in it. This does not imply comfort or absence of all threat or challenge. 'Too safe' is sinking so comfortably into a customary and preferred interpersonal position that nothing new is experienced or tried. 'Unsafeness' is feeling so perturbed and alarmed at the bad things which could happen that the only way one can protect oneself is to get away.

Persons do not stay in groups unless they get personal pay-offs, but at the start of a group, persons will stay with a group in the *hope* of personal pay-offs providing that they do not feel grossly threatened. Pay-offs occur through taking personal risks. 'Risk' by dictionary definition is 'hazard, danger; exposure to mischance or peril' (*Shorter Oxford Dictionary*). Entering a group is a risky step for most people, almost by definition. In all of the kinds of groups discussed in chapter 3, and they were many and various, persons are being asked, implicitly or explicitly, to expose themselves to unknown others, to confront aspects of themselves which they may ordinarily try to avoid, to try out new behaviours which have been outside their repertory to date, to open up to examination their customary views of self and of the world. All this adds up to a challenge to one's sense of self which is bound to be disconcerting, at least, and is often experienced as hazardous.

Although most people experience entering a new group as a risky step, exceptions occur. For example, some persons feel reasonably safe within a structure in which definite activities are prescribed and the leader moves the members through these activities – perhaps because such a structure is familiar through previous experiences with doctors and teachers, or because responsibility for behaviour lies elsewhere than in themselves.

Although most persons feel unsafe, initially, within open structures which offer few guidelines as to where to start and how to
proceed, now and then one encounters someone who prefers this
more open structure and fears the control implied in more highly
structured groups. Some persons fear the consequences of early
self-exposure, yet enter a group with such powerful needs to
ventilate pent-up feelings that this need overrides concerns about
safety. These exceptions do not alter the main point – that the
weight of affect at the beginning stages of a group tends toward
a sense of threat.

Much of what happens at the beginning of a group can be
understood in terms of the persons in it striving to find a comfortable or manageable position in the group, striving to be allowed
by others to occupy that position, or striving to combine with
others to construct a safe environment. Of course, what is safe
for one is not safe for another, and during the initial period of a
group one not only sees efforts on the part of members to bind
together to establish conditions of safety, but also collisions and
conflicts between members as each tries to negotiate a position of
safety in the group.

As this implies, members can be expected to do much of the
work involved in generating safety themselves. Exceptions occur,
as when a person with poor personal control or an overwhelming
need to ventilate a personal concern moves impulsively into self-
revelations and expressions of feelings which leave him or her
feeling exposed and under threat, and which frighten others by
displaying the vulnerable position which persons can get into in
groups. When this occurs, the general level of threat rises sharply
and the sense of safety diminishes. For the most part, however,
members find ways to band together to establish a sense of safety
in a group. They may do this in a way which makes it difficult for
anyone actually to benefit much from the group. For example,
group members might render the group a safe place by supporting
one another in intellectualizing, or by discussing matters of no
real concern to them, or by filling up the time with constant
challenges to the conductor of the group to explain how the group
can be of any use. If this sort of thing happens, then members
feel safe enough to stay in the group but in accomplishing this
they have greatly diminished the potential usefulness of the group
or have even rendered it useless.

In group focal conflict terms, supporting one another in intellectualizing, discussing matters of no real concern, and many, many other patterns of interacting constitute restrictive solutions. It is not at all unusual for such restrictive solutions to arise at the very beginning of a group (as well as, from time to time, later) because of the overriding need to survive and feel safe in the group, which tends to take precedence at least temporarily over the wish for personal gain.

When a restrictive solution is established are the members making the group 'too safe' or are they simply doing what they need to do to feel 'safe enough'? I am inclined to the latter view. It can easily be the case that the members can feel safe enough to stay in the group *only* if they intellectualize, or discuss matters of no importance to them, or adopt some other device which insulates them from the potential impact of the group.

If such a situation arises then the conductor of the group and the members are in a state of potential conflict. The conductor of the group wants the members to stay *and* to take risks. The members wish, for the moment at least, only to survive. It is prudent, in my view, not to push a group too hard over this issue at the very beginning. Feeling safe enough to stay in the group is of primary importance when a group first forms. After all, if members experience so much threat that they flee from the group then there will be no group and no chance of potential benefits. A bit later in this chapter, when discussing how a group may shift or be helped to shift from some restrictive solution to a more enabling one, I shall point to processes which can lead to the break-up of a restrictive solution and to ways in which the conductor of a group can help these processes along.

Avoiding the irredeemable collapse of structure

A group must work to some kind of structure, whether this is planned for it or built by it. Otherwise, chaos and working at cross-purposes occurs. During the planning stage one tries to design a group likely to suit the needs and capacities of the persons who are to join it. However, neither the conductor of the group nor anyone else can be absolutely certain about how, or even whether, a planned structure will work in practice. It is only when the group starts to meet and the persons in it actually begin to interact that the suitability of the structure is put to the test.

From the very beginning, events begin to reveal how the

members of a group take to the structure planned for it. Perhaps the members quickly show that they can work within the structure and that it makes sense to them; perhaps they challenge it openly; perhaps they work within it for some of the time but at other times drift away from it; perhaps they simply ignore it.

In order for a group to survive it is not necessary for the members to hold to the originally planned structure. What is necessary is that *some* usable structure is established, or to put it another way round, it is important to the group's survival to avoid the irredeemable collapse of structure. Of course it is easier and more pleasing to the leader, and the group can get down to work more quickly, if the members take to the structure as originally planned. Sometimes this happens. Other possibilities, however, are that substantial obstacles to working to the structure are encountered, or that the planned structure proves to be altogether unworkable.

One of the conductor's tasks during the opening period of any group is to look to the information and evidence provided by successive events in order to judge how or if the structure is taking hold and to do his best to forestall the collapse of structure. In terms of actual behaviour this may mean doing nothing (if the originally planned structure is working, or if the members simply need time to work their way into it) or it may mean intervening so as to remove obstacles to its working (if for example the members need to learn certain skills to make the structure work or if certain shared fears are getting in their way) or it may mean renegotiating a structure with the group members so that a usable structure can be found (if there is clear evidence over a period of time that the original structure cannot work).

If a therapist or worker tries to force the group to hold to a structure which events reveal is truly unworkable, then one of three consequences can be expected to occur. One of these is that the sense of being unsafe increases. Members don't know how to use the structure or are afraid to use it, yet are being pressed to do so by the very person to whom they look for help and support. Under such circumstances the sense of safety could easily fall below levels which make it possible for persons to remain in the group. In other words, the conductor is working towards, or thinks he is working towards, one of the instrumental purposes attached to the beginning stage of the group whilst losing track of and sacrificing another. A second possible consequence is that the members display an outward conformity to the structure without using it in a meaningful way. They find a way to fake it. If this occurs, necessary risks will not be taken and personal pay-offs cannot occur. A third possible consequence is that the structure works, or appears to work, only as long as the conductor keeps pushing it. For maintaining an appearance of the structure working, the conductor and the group pay the price of locating the responsibility for the group's operation in the hands of the conductor of the group instead of where it belongs, as a shared responsibility for all.

It follows that one of the errors a therapist or worker can make early in a group is to insist on holding to the originally planned structure beyond the point where its essential unworkability has been firmly demonstrated. The opposite but parallel error is to fail to give the original structure a fair chance: to fail to give the group enough time to test it or to fail to help the group to do the work which is required to overcome the obstacles which are getting in the way of using the structure. The question remains, of course, as to how best to differentiate between a structure which is irretrievably unworkable, and one which requires further effort in order to work. In making this judgment I believe that it is helpful to re-examine the relationship between the structure which has been planned for the group, and frontier.

If the members are unable to use the structure, then one has misjudged frontier. If the members are unable to use the structure but could relatively easily do so with further explanation, preparation or training, then one may have misjudged frontier to some degree, but the current structure can probably be modified, or its full use temporarily postponed while the necessary further preparation takes place. If the members have erected defences against a structure which they are technically capable of utilizing, then one has judged frontier correctly but the members need to overcome initial fears in order to use the structure as intended.

Now and then it is blatantly clear from the very beginning that a mismatch has occurred between frontier and structure. For example, a group was set up in a geriatric ward in a psychiatric hospital with the intention of helping the members to reminisce, thus providing pleasure and creating an opportunity for members to review their lives and if possible to find continuity and meaning in them. The patients, when they arrived, proved to be far gone in senility and/or deafness, and incapable of participating in the kind of group which had been planned. Selection had been placed in the hands of the nursing assistants on the ward, who proved to have negative feelings about groups, and who found a way to express their resistance by providing an unsuitable collection of patients for the group.

As a further example, consider a group composed of ex-psychiatric hospital patients, where the stated purpose was to forestall readmission. (Nowadays I would consider this to be an altogether unsuitable purpose, since it has nothing to do with the members' frontier and/or preoccupying concern.) A structure was planned for this group which involved open discussion. However, rather than discussing their feelings and problems openly as was hoped, each member acted as if there were no one else in the room except himself and the therapist. Each directed questions at the therapist: 'Should I go on taking these tablets?' 'Will I be seeing my doctor tonight?' Despite various attempts on the part of the therapist to encourage the members to listen to one another and converse together, this never happened. No sustained interpersonal interaction occurred. It was the persistence of this pattern over a period of some meetings which eventually convinced the therapist that he had misjudged frontier, and that the members of this group could not make use of the planned structure.

It is entirely possible that the interactive pattern, 'Speak only to the therapist', is functioning as a restrictive solution in a group whose members are technically capable of listening to one another and of sharing feelings and experiences. How can one tell the difference between 'cannot' and 'are frightened of'? Sometimes one gets clues from the nature of the questions being addressed to the leader. If the members ask 'How do we know that coming here will help us?' or 'What should we be talking about?', they are showing that they understand what the structure requires of them. The very fact that the first person plural is used indicates that they are aware that they are participating in a collective enterprise and perceive themselves as members of a *group*. This suggests that although there is work to be done before the structure can be utilized fully, members are potentially capable of using the structure.

Although threats to the structure can occur later on in the life of a group, it is at the very beginning that a group is most vulnerable to the possible collapse of structure. If the structure collapses and is not replaced by an alternative structure which suits the frontiers better, then either so many persons drop out that the group is no longer viable or it continues in a limping fashion which cannot be expected to offer much to the members.

The two instrumental purposes discussed so far – maintaining an adequate sense of safety in the group and avoiding the irredeemable collapse of structure – are centrally important at the beginning of a group, since the group's internal viability depends on achieving them.

Working toward the establishment and maintenance of norms which facilitate effective work: in group focal conflict terms, working toward the establishment and maintenance of enabling rather than restrictive group solutions

A group will be a more effective medium for help if the members can establish norms which support a readiness on the part of members to express themselves freely and frankly and to try out new behaviours. In group focal conflict terms, this means operating on enabling rather than restrictive solutions for as much of the time as is consistent with maintaining adequate levels of safety.

During the early sessions of a group it is to be expected that the members' interest in rendering the group a safe environment may lead them to establish restrictive solutions of one form or another, in response to the pressures which the structure, and simply being in a group with unknown others, place upon them.

As long as a group operates on a restrictive solution the members will feel safe, but they will be operating within such narrow boundaries that little in the way of useful exploration, social comparison, feedback, etc. can take place. It is therefore part of the therapist's or worker's task to monitor this aspect of the group's functioning and look to ways of helping members give up restrictive solutions in favour of enabling ones.

Restrictive solutions which one may see arising during the beginning phase of a group include: support one another in intellectualizing; get one member of the group to expose himself, thus allowing all others to feel safe; express personal concerns indirectly or in symbolic terms; remain silent; talk about the problems of someone not present; interact only with the leader, ignoring all others; withdraw into solitary activities (if the structure allows for this); talk about 'problems' which are not one's real concerns;

fill all of the available time by challenging the value of the group or the competence of the leader; disown one's problems, that is, deny them or blame them on some outside agent; talk only to one's neighbour (i.e. do not face the whole group).

When a worker or therapist perceives that a group is operating on some restrictive solution the initial decision which faces him is whether to intervene at all – i.e. whether or not to interrupt and try to influence the group process. Some guidelines are: do not intervene if any attempt to influence the situation is likely to be fruitless; do not intervene if it is likely that in the course of operating on the restrictive solution, forces will be set in motion likely to lead to its abandonment or revision; intervene if you judge you can accelerate the process with little risk to the group; intervene if the solution has gone on for so long that you judge it could become a fixed way of life for the group; intervene early if the restrictive solution appears to be doing harm to some one person in the group.

Some restrictive solutions are so consistently and tightly maintained that any attempt to influence the situation is doomed to failure. If the members are collaborating very effectively in, say, discussing their problems in general terms or blaming outside agents – that is, if there is no chink in the maintenance of the solution and no one at all shows signs of thinking or operating differently – then the conductor of the group may correctly judge that the members so need to maintain the solution that efforts to shift it simply will not work. One can test this out if one wishes by some low-risk intervention such as a read-out of events, e.g., 'So far we are talking about the problem of loneliness in very general terms.' If the response to this is a flurry of comments about the pervasiveness of loneliness in modern society, then the leader might as well sit back and wait until the monolithic character of the restrictive solution begins to yield. He will not win against the power of such group forces. If he tries to press a group out of a tightly maintained restrictive solution he will succeed only in setting himself up as the group's enemy: in group focal conflict terms, tipping the group into an episode of solutional conflict, with himself as deviant.

A group focal conflict model argues that a restrictive solution fulfils a function for a group in that it operates to contain associated but unrecognized shared fears. It follows that if the members of a group are to give up some restrictive solution they will do so most readily if the associated fears can be alleviated. The question then arises as to the processes by which this might occur.

Often (not always) the interaction which occurs during the time that a restrictive solution dominates a group leads to the abandonment of the restrictive solution without specific intervention from the therapist or worker. This can occur either because operating on restrictive solutions involves the members in interactions which lead to the alleviation of associated fears, thus rendering the solution unnecessary, or because continuing to operate on a restrictive solution over a period of time stirs up feelings of resentment or impatience in one or more members and this leads them into behaviours which break up the solution. As an example of the first process consider a group which is discussing someone not present and known to only one member (someone's cousin, say, who is described as *really* having problems). The therapist or worker judges that the pursuit of this theme constitutes a restrictive solution which, as long as it operates, protects group members from self-exposure and from whatever bad consequences they fear would follow upon self-exposure (most likely, fears of criticism or rejection). However, while discussing this problem-ridden cousin, suppose that the members express sympathy towards him, acknowledge that peculiar or bad behaviour can nevertheless be understood, and come to agree that his problems are not necessarily an indication of terrible mental illness. What is happening is that while they are speaking about someone outside the group and thus protecting themselves they are also testing out in indirect ways whether or not persons in the group can take a sympathetic view towards those with problems. As events show this to be the case, fears of being criticized or rejected for having problems abate. The members may then come to the point of being able to abandon the restrictive solution, replacing it, perhaps, with a more enabling solution, such as 'agree that having problems doesn't mean that a person is crazy'.

As an example of the second process, consider a group which has encouraged one of its members, John, to tell his story at length, thus protecting everyone else from self-exposure. Perhaps John feels flattered at first and co-operates happily, but as time goes on he feels more and more at risk in the group and eventually refuses to go on. If this happens, the restrictive solution, 'get one person to talk' cannot continue because it requires John's co-operation and he has come to the point of being unwilling to continue. The restrictive solution must necessarily break up, although it might be replaced by some other restrictive solution rather than by an enabling one.

Both these examples call attention to the fact that a period during which restrictive solution is in operation is not static, but that some development or evolution is occurring during this time which often leads to a group shifting away from a restrictive solution on its own. It follows that a therapist's or worker's best move can be to do nothing, at least for a time, but to wait and see if the group, without any help or nudging, can move away from operating on some prevailing restrictive solution.

Some restrictive solutions cannot be expected to yield in consequence of forces operating within the group. For example, a prolonged silence which has been functioning as a restrictive solution is likely to become harder and harder to break. Moreover, nothing is going on between members which could function to alleviate associated fears. The conductor of the group might consider that the level of anxiety is mounting in the group to the point where some might feel compelled to flee. Under such conditions a group worker or therapist would need to take active steps to help members to break the silence.

The conductor of a group would also wish to intervene early if he judges that one person in the group is likely to be harmed if the group continues to operate on a restrictive solution. This is most likely to be the case where the restrictive solution requires role differentiation, and one person is occupying a particular central role in the solution. This occurs, for example, where one person is being scapegoated or where one person is being encouraged to spill out his feelings, seems to be getting anxious and yet cannot extricate himself from this position. Restrictive solutions which do not involve role differentiation, but instead consist of the collaborative maintenance of some shared defence (e.g. blaming an external agent, mutual avoidance) are less likely to do active harm.

One would also wish to intervene if one thought that some restrictive solution was becoming established as a permanent way of life in the group. I believe that this happens less often than therapists and workers fear. Because a particular pattern goes on for thirty or forty minutes or most of a session does not mean that it will go on forever. One can rely with some confidence on the fact that while members experience fears which require the establishment of a restrictive solution, they usually also wish to utilize the group on their own behalf. If anything at all can go on during the time the restrictive solution dominates the group which tends to alleviate underlying fears, then the solution becomes less necessary to the members and the push from the associated wish comes into play. If a restrictive solution persists into a third or fourth session in an unaltered form then I would be inclined to look to the possibility that the leader has been colluding with the members in maintaining it or that the members are incapable of working to the structure.

If the conductor of a group decides to try to influence a group away from operating on some restrictive solution, it is a better strategy to try to alleviate associated underlying fears than to challenge or attack the solution directly. A direct attack on a needed solution can increase the general level of threat, perhaps to intolerable levels. It can intensify the associated underlying fears which the restrictive solution was containing, and thus lead the members to cling even more tightly to the established restrictive solution. It can generate new fears which lead the members to shift to some other even more intractable restrictive solution.

If on the other hand the conductor of the group can do something which leads to the alleviation of associated underlying fears, the restrictive solution will become less necessary to the group. If this occurs, the members are in a position to give up the solution because it no longer serves a function for them. A full discussion of what might be tried under different group circumstances is reserved for the next chapter, where a number of examples of early restrictive solutions are discussed.

All of the discussion so far, having to do with safety, with structure and with the character of the solutions which become established in the group have to do with the survival of the group and its survival as the *kind* of group within which benefit is likely to occur for individuals. Attention has been directed primarily toward the group rather than to specific persons in it. The next instrumental purpose turns to specific group members, regarding the group as context.

Utilizing events occurring within the group for the specific benefit of individuals

If a group can come to operate for most of the time on enabling solutions, then many of the benefits which derive from social comparison, receiving and using feedback from others, exploring own feelings and concerns, and trying out new behaviours, will occur without specific help from the therapist or worker. However, there are times when a therapist or worker can intervene to make sure that some one person is really taking in and registering some event or experience which the conductor judges to be of particular importance or where the conductor intervenes to assure that some situation of special relevance to the individual is fully exploited on his behalf. The question arises as to how a therapist or worker can best pursue this instrumental purpose during the formative phase without at the same time working against establishing the group as a viable medium for help.

There are times when utilizing a situation for the specific benefit of one person in the group can interfere with one's primary interest of supporting the development of the group's internal viability. Consider the following example: early in the first session of an open-ended therapeutic group, before a clear theme had emerged, one young woman (Jane) said to another (Barbara) something like: 'What are *you* doing here? You're beautiful!' To this, Barbara replied with feeling: 'Hah!' The therapist judged that Jane carried about with her an assumption that beautiful women don't have problems, and that the very presence of a good-looking woman challenged this assumption at the very start of the group. The therapist could have taken this as an opportunity for direct work with Jane, encouraging her to look at the experiences which have generated this assumption and how she feels now that it has been challenged. However, had he done so he would have supported a particular structure in the group – conducting one-to-one therapy with an audience – which he did not wish to see established because it would tend to pre-empt free exchanges among members. Further, he would have communicated to the others: 'One person here has said something important and worthy of my attention; others have not.' This could generate anger, loss of interest or fears of being abandoned in the other members of the group, and thus interfere with the group becoming a helping environment for all. To place one person in a central position at

the beginning brings penalties as well as possible benefits: perhaps
the person would be helped by the therapist's individual attention,
but perhaps also she would be placed in an excessively exposed
position and become dysfunctionally anxious. Perhaps she would
become the target of attack or resentment by the others. These
are high prices to pay for the benefits which direct focusing might
bring. Consider also that for Jane, some benefit has already
occurred. She is unlikely to have missed the point that beautiful
women can have problems. Meanwhile, the therapist has learned
something about her. He can hold on to this bit of understanding
until a better opportunity arises in the group for its exploration.
By 'a better opportunity' I mean a time when the group as a
whole is engaged in a discussion which bears in some way on this
issue: the assumptions which each makes about self or others, or
how each feels about his/her physical appearance, or what
particular persons in the group mean to each member. Opportunities then arise for *all* the members to undertake personal explorations within the theme. Within such a context, Jane's feelings
about physical beauty might well resurface, or if they did not the
therapist could remind her of her earlier comment. Another,
better intervention open to the therapist at such a time would be
a question to the members in general: 'Why *did* people come to
this group?' This might have opened the way for Barbara to
explain what problems she feels to have despite being a good-
looking young woman, and for Jane and others to share their
personal concerns. Such an intervention does not focus on any
one person but encourages the establishment of a theme to which
all (including of course Jane) could contribute.

Consider another example: a situation was described earlier in
this chapter in which one group member, John, discussed his
personal problems and was encouraged to do so by others. It was
suggested that this could function in the group as a restrictive
solution. If the therapist or worker were to join in with the
members in enquiring about and commenting on John's problems
he would be colluding in supporting a restrictive solution in the
group and would probably prolong it. Even if John were in some
sense benefiting (which may or may not be the case), encouraging
the others to continue to concentrate on him works against the
longer-term interests of all concerned.

Consider one further example: early in a group for mothers of
Down's syndrome children, the discussion turned to the anger and

hurt which these women experienced when strangers stared at their children. One member, Cynthia, had been silent but then began to cry. The therapist turned to Cynthia and said: 'I guess you are showing us that this is important to you as well.' Cynthia acknowledged this and told a distressing story at some length. The others listened with sympathy, asked encouraging questions, and brought in similar stories. In this case, the therapist briefly turned his attention to one person in the group in order to make room for her to share her experiences with others. This was done in the context of a general group discussion of a shared theme. Others as well as Cynthia benefited from this: Cynthia expressed feelings which she had been holding back; others found opportunities to compare feelings and experiences. Cynthia's participation was not extraneous to a shared theme nor could it be regarded as part of a restrictive solution. This intervention was also a communication to the group that tears can be faced and accepted.

These examples are meant to draw attention to the importance of taking into account context and the likely consequences for all concerned when deciding whether or not, and how, to pursue opportunities arising in the group for benefiting specific persons. During the formative stage of the group, if one pursues such opportunities too eagerly, without regard to the full consequences of doing so, one risks interfering with the development of the group as a viable medium for help. Later on in a group's development the risks which follow upon focusing on individual members (even, at times, extended focusing) are less, for reasons which I shall detail in chapter 11.

This line of argument leads to the position that one need not be too concerned to be 'therapeutic' in a specific sense at the very beginning of the group. If one can help the members to feel safe enough, and if one can hold to or find a usable structure, then the group will survive. If one can see the group through its initial tendency to operate on restrictive solutions, then it will survive with a good potential for helping its members. Once the group is past its often shaky beginnings, a whole range of opportunities for benefiting individuals will arise and can then be pursued with less risk to the viability of the group.

Avoiding doing harm

The principal harm which can occur for individual members during the formative stage has to do with their being exposed to experiences which overwhelm them. Persons bring their own fears and vulnerabilities to a group. If they are pressed to participate in ways which generate excessive threat, if they cannot stop themselves from plunging into experiences or revelations which overwhelm them with unmanageable feelings, if as spectators they hear and see things which abruptly jar their sense of who they are and what the world is like, then harm may ensue. Another way of saying this is that harm can follow upon 'too much too soon' in the way of assaults on identity or the invasion or bypassing of needed defences. While it is true that in many kinds of groups benefits cannot occur unless aspects of identity are challenged and revised and dysfunctional defences given up, one's aim should be to help this to occur in a way and at a pace which allows each person to assimilate such charges without experiencing utterly unmanageable anxiety and the collapse of essential defences.

If persons experience gross assault on the self they will either stay in the group but close themselves off from the experience, or stay in the group while at the same time experiencing near-intolerable anxiety and dread, or drop out. Any of these responses renders the group useless to them, although of course if they remain in the group the opportunity is there for later recovery. Persons who drop out may do so with little harm to themselves if they leave at a point where they are still sensing the *likelihood* of unmanageable assaults on the self but where these have not yet occurred. Such persons sensibly protect themselves by physical flight. One might say that they experience harm in the form of dashed hopes and a lost opportunity, but no more. Some persons who drop out, however, have already experienced profound disturbance and take these feelings with them into arenas in which no help is available to them.

The likelihood of damaging consequences occurring for individuals can be reduced if care is given to planning (especially getting the structure right for the population and allowing escape hatches for persons who sense that they will be grossly threatened by participation in a group) and to the conduct of the group (especially allowing persons to find their own way into this new situation). However, just occasionally a situation arises where the greatest care cannot avert such consequences. This occurs when the vulnerability of a person remains invisible to the therapist, the person himself, or anyone else concerned until after the damaging impact has already occurred.

Some ways of conducting a group increase the likelihood of casualties of this sort. Aggressive, invasive, over-managing approaches increase risk. Some leaders find such approaches tempting, possibly because members' responses to them can be quite dramatic – a lot seems to be happening because strong feelings are being expressed. Allowing persons to find their own way into a group, offering more gentle challenges and adopting a 'paving the way' approach makes for a slower and less dramatic start, but I believe that it pays off in the end because it helps persons to develop a secure base from which to explore issues important to them.

Discerning and thinking out how to retrieve errors

In the course of this chapter, a number of references have been made to errors which a therapist or group worker is vulnerable to making during the formative phase of a group.

Some errors have to do with the structure of a group. The group conductor might either hold to the original structure too long, in the face of compelling evidence that it is proving unsuitable, or he might be ready to give up on the structure too soon, before its potential usefulness has been fully tested. One form which the latter error can take is a kind of 'fast-follower' approach on the part of the leader: the moment that the structure is challenged by one person through a suggestion that the group proceed in another way, the leader is ready to co-operate, only to find that someone else then supports the original plan. The leader again switches his support, and then finds another, different challenge arising from another quarter. Everyone becomes confused. The leader is in fact interfering with the associational flow. A better approach is to sit back and allow enough time for the members to explore the structure, to the point where everyone can see the weight of opinion in the group. Such explorations amount to trying a structure on for size, and often make it possible for members to use the structure originally planned, even though it has been challenged in various ways.

Another error having to do with structure involves supporting, through one's behaviour, a structure which one does not in fact wish to become established in the group. For example in response to pressures from members the conductor of a group might fall into concentrating on one person for a lengthy period. This supports one-to-one interaction between the conductor and one person at a time – a structure which I suggest is unsuitable to a group, where one wishes to make room for peer interaction to occur. Another such error simply involves talking too much (which means more than the planned structure requires), thus reducing the opportunities for members to engage with one another.

Another kind of error has to do with behaving in ways which erode the sense of safety in the group. Adopting a leadership style which is aggressive, invasive or over-managing has already been mentioned in the previous section. Even when one does not intend to operate in this manner, however, one can inadvertently introduce interventions which tend to intensify threat to dysfunctional levels. A therapist or worker might, for example, be unintentionally punitive if by implication he chastises a group for operating on some restrictive solution or for failing to work to the planned structure as the therapist hoped. In group focal conflict terms punitive interventions can intensify reactive fears or introduce new reactive fears, thus making it more difficult than before for members to yield up restrictive solutions. Another way in which the conductor of a group can negatively influence the sense of safety in the group is by pressing too hard or too soon for the abandonment of a restrictive solution which is still needed in order for members to feel safe enough to stay in the group. I believe also that one should be extremely careful about the kinds of accelerating devices or exercises which one introduces, in case these invade or bypass needed defences.

A therapist or worker might also commit the error of standing in the way of a group becoming a more useful medium for help by colluding with some restrictive solution and thus keeping it in operation for longer than necessary from the members' point of view. This might happen, for example, if the conductor becomes intrigued with the problems of one person whom the others have been keeping in the centre of attention for defensive purposes, or if the conductor himself fears the consequences of exploring certain issues or themes and supports the group in restrictive solutions which involve avoidance or intellectualization.

The inadvertent display of favouritism, that is, conveying that one person is more interesting or more worth investing time in than others, is an error which has multiple consequences. The person so favoured may become the target of attack by others and persons not favoured may lose heart and withdraw investment from the group. In group focal conflict terms one would say that when the conductor of a group displays favouritism he risks stimulating reactive fears of abandonment or loss of support which would not otherwise exist. Members of the group either react with anger towards the therapist or to the favoured person or else erect restrictive solutions which would not otherwise be required.

Errors are more easily avoided if one is alert to the possibility of their occurring. However, errors cannot be avoided altogether and it is fortunate that providing one has recognized an error as such, it can almost always be retrieved. In seeking to retrieve an error it is sometimes helpful to acknowledge the error openly, especially if one judges it useful to call the members' attention to some shift in the manner of one's own participation. For example, one might say, 'I think I've been talking so much that I haven't given others a chance to come into the conversation, so I'll stop for a bit now.' The acknowledgment of an error need not and should not include self-blame. A leader who conveys 'I have just made a terrible mistake' undermines the members' sense that they can rely on him and confronts the members with the task of dealing with one of the leader's own problems. In contrast, the calm and frank acknowledgment of an error demonstrates that the leader can acknowledge errors whilst still accepting himself and does not confront the members with having to deal with an extraneous (to them) problem.

One need not always acknowledge an error openly in order to retrieve it. If in the course of one's internal monitoring of the group one realizes that one has been colluding in some restrictive solution it is possible simply to stop doing so. If one sees from the reactions of the members that one has been pressing them too soon to give up some restrictive solution, then one can simply subside for a while and allow the conversation to proceed.

Some errors are more difficult to retrieve than others, and sometimes one has to give the group time to recover from an error one has made. For example if one has been punitive or shown favouritism then one may have to make room for an extended run of interactions during which similar errors are avoided, in order to provide time for the members to deal with the feelings which one's error has stirred up.

While one clearly should do what one can to avoid making errors, equally clearly one is bound to make errors from time to time. *Providing* one recognizes them as errors, not only can they usually be retrieved but the manner in which one acknowledges and retrieves them can often provide a useful model for the members of the group.

While actually conducting a group there is no way to stop the action in order to give leisurely thought to these various instrumental purposes and to how they might be pursued under prevailing circumstances. It is only the printed page which allows us to consider them one at a time at our leisure. Nor can a therapist, worker or leader pursue the instrumental purposes discussed in this chapter directly. He cannot, for example, say to himself 'Let's see now, I will now make the group a safe-enough place for the members', and then do it. The conductor of a group is faced with events which proceed inexorably on a time-line. The first session begins at some specified time and goes on minute by minute until the time comes for the session to close. The members then disperse until the next scheduled session. In the course of a group's minute-by-minute operation a therapist, worker or leader will take certain initiatives, some of which can be pre-planned. For much of the time, however, he will be responding to events arising in the group. How holding instrumental purposes in mind may guide behaviour in particular situations is illustrated in the chapter which follows.

Chapter 10
Getting started: opening a group and responding to what happens next

When a new group assembles for the first time, the group worker, therapist or leader is faced with a number of persons gathered together into a room who expect him or her to do or say something to get the group started. The conductor of the group will of course be aware of this ahead of time and can think out how he intends to open the group. This is the last decision which he can make at leisure, because what he says and does next will necessarily be in response to what emerges in the group.

This is the case for groups of varying structures. For example, in a group which has been planned to rely on open discussion, a therapist or worker might make a brief opening comment, or choose to say nothing at all. In either case, he then waits for something to emerge from the group. His next decisions have to do with when and how to respond to what emerges. If a group is structured in terms of pre-designated topics, then the therapist or worker is likely to refer to this in an opening comment, hope that what follows relates to the topic, and again decide when and how to participate further when he sees and hears what emerges from the group. The leader of a group whose structure involves activities or exercises will have done considerable detailed planning. He will not only provide an opening, but will have a schedule of events in mind, and will expect to intervene at intervals to move the group along from one part of its task to another. Even in the most highly structured of groups, however, that which is important and real to members must and can only emerge from the members themselves. Exactly what will emerge cannot be predicted ahead of time, and in all groups, however structured, the therapist, leader or worker will be faced with having to respond to the unpredictable and the unexpected.

Returning to the very first moments in the life of a group, what might a therapist or worker say or do to get the group off to a good start? Assuming for a moment that it is the group worker or therapist who makes the first comment, the following are some examples.

(For an out-patient group):
I have talked with each of you individually but this is the first time we are meeting as a group. We expect to meet on Tuesdays and Fridays for an hour-and-a-quarter each time and during that time use this group to discuss matters of concern to the persons here. The idea is that by reflecting on one's own experience and that of others, and hearing the views of others, some benefits will occur.

(For a long-stay ward in a psychiatric hospital):
This is our first session together. We are going to have six in all and each one will be devoted to some particular activity. This time we are going to make a map of this ward and then of the building and the hospital grounds and tell each other what parts of it each person knows and goes to. (The leader would then begin to involve the patients in the task.)

(For parents of mentally handicapped children):
I am Mary Johnson. I am not a member of the staff of this clinic but I've been asked by staff to come in to conduct some group discussions for interested parents. This is the first of twelve sessions. We will meet in this room every Tuesday night at this time. We will expect to go on for an hour-and-a-half. Everyone here signed up for the group but this is the first time I have met you personally. Perhaps some of you already know one another from bringing your children to the clinic. I hope that by bringing people together who have had to face similar situations it may be possible for everyone to gain something by sharing experiences and thinking out together what it means to have a mentally handicapped child in the family.

(For a group of young offenders, aged 14–16):
I would like to welcome you all to Hawthorne Center. We are going to meet for two hours every Wednesday night for the

next twelve weeks, and we expect also to go away for a camping weekend towards the end of that time. We expect to spend the first hour-and-a-quarter or so each time in any activity which appeals to you. If you look around you will see lots of possibilities. After that we will all get together to talk over what you have been doing and what you would like to do next time. Mike and Jane and I will circulate around and will be glad to help people get started if they want us to. I'll call everyone back together at about 8.15.

(For a group of orthopaedically impaired patients soon to be discharged from hospital):
This is the first of four one-and-a-quarter-hour discussions which have been planned in order to help you to anticipate what may happen after you leave the hospital and to think about the best ways for you to cope with your new situation. Everyone here has a physical handicap of one sort or another, relatively recently acquired either through illness or accident. Today, we have it in mind to talk about the events which brought you to the hospital. What happened?

These examples have in common the fact that they restate for the group what members may know already, offer minimum necessary information about the structure of the group, and sometimes refer to the conductor's hopes and intentions in bringing the group together. If the structure requires some very specific activity, then the opening statement includes any directions or guidance which may be necessary. Such an opening relates to the instrumental purposes discussed in the previous chapter in the following ways: it informs or reminds persons of the structure and explicitly or implicitly invites them to operate in terms of it, and it supports a sense of safety by demonstrating that the therapist intends to be active, involved, and *there*. Such openings also preserve choice, in that they leave it open to each member to decide how he or she will participate. This makes room for each person to seek his own position in the group and so enhance his personal sense of safety. Making room for each person to engage in the group in his or her own way also creates opportunities for the worker or therapist to begin to get to know persons by noting the choices they make.

There are two logical alternatives to this kind of opening: the therapist or worker could say less, including saying nothing at all; or he could say more.

For many of the kinds of groups discussed in this book it is inadvisable to say less or nothing because to do so increases fears and erodes the level of sense of safety. Some persons are too fearful, unskilled or inexperienced even to start to work to a structure without some direction, encouragement or permission from the therapist. For some persons, the very sound of the leader's voice is reassuring since it conveys in however nascent a way that he is committed to the group and available to it. Some therapists begin a group (most likely it is a long-term therapeutic group intended to be intensive in character) by saying nothing at all. The intention, I think, is to increase anxiety levels and so elicit primitive material quickly. In my own view, the anxiety level is likely to be high in any case in such groups because patients know they are expected to reveal material and express feelings ordinarily censored or suppressed. An opening in which the therapist is silent increases anxiety levels still farther, perhaps to the point where patients defend themselves by closing off and restricting unnecessarily.

The second logical alternative is to say more than the examples suggest. The 'more' that could be said might have to do with rules, reassurances, introductions, directions, additional information and short cuts.

Rules. A leader may consider that a group will be more effective if members come regularly, come on time, maintain confidentiality, avoid contact with one another outside the sessions, etc., and therefore may seek to establish these practices right from the start by setting down rules which he expects the members to follow. The problem here is that the therapist or group worker can *state* a rule, but he has no real power to enforce it. Such practices can only be sustained if norms develop in a group to support them, and this can occur only under two conditions: either a norm is so thoroughly established in the world outside the group that all members can be expected to bring it into the group with them, or else a norm becomes established through interaction amongst the members if and when the issue surfaces as important. Thus, a norm about confidentiality may well become established in a group but it will be because one or several members are particularly concerned about it and introduce it as an issue, or because someone violates implicit assumptions about confidentiality and thus renders it an issue for the group. If a leader tries to make rules in the beginning, he should also acknowledge to himself that his declaration of a wish that something be so does not ensure that it will be so. Further, one needs to keep in mind that listing out a large number of rules in the beginning can convey 'You must do as I say or I will disapprove of you' and this is a message which the conductor of a group is unlikely to want to convey.

Reassurances. A group conductor who is concerned to reduce or minimize initial worries about the group or who fears that members may leave if they do not see quick results may be tempted to offer reassurances. He may tell the members that such groups have proved beneficial in the past, or that they need not worry about gossip because everything said in the group will be held in confidence. It is doubtful whether such statements really function as reassurance. To be told that the group will help them is an empty promise, in that neither the conductor nor anyone else knows at the very beginning whether the experience will really prove of benefit. The conductor hopes so and he has grounds for thinking so, but to make a promise about it goes beyond his powers, and group members will know this. He can say 'I intend to do everything I can to help to make this a worthwhile experience for everyone here', which is a promise he can keep, but he cannot say much more. Telling members that others have benefited from similar groups rarely if ever reassures, since so many persons are ready to believe that they, unlike others, are beyond help. Reassuring members about confidentiality does not work because members will be well aware that while the conductor of a group may be able to control his own tendency to gossip he can control no one else's. Gratuitous offers of reassurance raise the question of who needs to be reassured, and to whom the reassurance is directed. Perhaps the therapist or worker is essentially trying to reassure himself. I think it is better to allow initial reassurance to derive from a clear and not too elaborated statement about the group and how one sees it proceeding followed by a confident move to operate in terms of the planned structure.

Introductions. Should one introduce oneself or others? Presumably the group members already know who the group worker or therapist is. If not, the conductor should introduce himself. If there is a co-leader or observer then certainly that person should be introduced, to avoid unnecessary confusion as to his or her position and function in the group. Should one also introduce members? Sometimes yes, sometimes no. One might judge that excessively high initial levels of anxiety could be reduced if members at least heard one another's voices once, or were able to put names to unknown faces. If so, one should introduce members, or provide a way for them to introduce themselves. For some populations, however, forcing even this much self-exposure could be threatening. If one judges this to be the case, then one might decide to wait for persons to introduce themselves in their own way. If one is working with a group with ordinary social skills, then instructing them to introduce themselves could pre-empt a relatively easy and safe way to get into interacting on their own.

Directions. With respect to directions, it is clear that some structures require more directions from the worker or therapist than others. Some groups require frequent further directions in order to facilitate moving through a series of exercises or activities. The number and kind of directions, clearly, should fit the structure. A sensible rule to follow for oneself is to avoid offering any directions which the members could provide for themselves.

Information. Group members need to have certain kinds of information in order to orient themselves to the group and have some basis on which to participate. Often, as pointed out earlier, the therapist's or worker's introductory statement will include a statement of what the group is for, for how long it will meet, who the conductor(s) is/are, some indication of how the conductor expects to proceed, and sometimes something about the nature of the membership. This is probably an adequate information base. If someone who is expected to be a member is absent, this might be mentioned. A question sometimes arises as to whether a conductor should offer information about the records he intends to keep or the fact that he is taping the group. Such decisions can best be made on the basis of considering whether the members need the information in order to get started, whether commenting on it is likely to increase or decrease the general sense of safety, and whether failing to comment on it amounts to deception. If I were taping, I would make the machinery and the act of taping perfectly visible and then might or might not comment on it. If I were to comment it would certainly be brief: 'I'm taping these sessions because I often find it helps me to understand what is going on if I can listen afterwards' (or whatever). To dwell on the point and certainly to offer verbal reassurances amounts to an instruction that members ought to be worrying about the tape. To conceal the fact that one is taping is an error because it is deception, and deception damages trust and hence a sense of safety. With many groups the best policy can be to make the taping evident but then not to comment at all, but to allow the concern, if there is one, to emerge in the interaction. Commenting on record-keeping is unnecessary if, as is usually the case, members know about it already or are likely to assume it.

Short cuts. Short cuts and accelerating devices – that is, devices for helping members to move more quickly into the kind of discussion or interaction which one hopes for – can, in my opinion, be either useful or damaging. One should, as with all else, make one's decision on the basis of the most likely consequences of introducing any such device. A well-thought-out introduction is of course in itself a short cut. Many other devices can be utilized. They usually consist of some exercise, game or special instruction.

Consider, as an example, an instruction in which each member is asked to tell the others about some personal characteristic or experience about which he or she is ashamed. This device places pressure on persons to reveal themselves and is intended to help members move more quickly into discussing issues which are personally important to them. Different persons are likely to feel differently about such an instruction: some may welcome a nudge toward self-exposure, some may resent it as intrusive, and some may be fearful of complying yet feel they must. In response, some may reveal something and then later become anxious about having done so, others may reveal something and then experience relief, and still others may trivialize the exercise by joking or by faking a response. For those who are fearful but feel compelled to respond, defences are bypassed and the person later feels exposed and in a hazardous position. For those who respond trivially the device has succeeded only in mobilizing defences. In both cases individuals are likely at least for a time to feel wary of the conductor of the group. Because this device can place some persons in a worse rather than a better position to make use of the group it is one which in my opinion should be avoided.

Consider another, different example of a short cut. Ruth Cohn, in a discussion of her theme-centered interactional method, suggests as one of several ground rules for participants: 'Be your own chairman. Speak or be silent as you want to be and be aware of your own agenda.' Cohn emphasizes that being one's own chairman is not at all the same thing as 'doing one's own thing', a phrase which tends to convey that one is not responsible for the consequences of own behaviour. Cohn says, ' "To be my own chairman" means to include what I feel like doing into the givens of the reality situation: other people, time-space factors, aids and obstacles, and my own contradictory needs, wishes, goals, and so on' (Cohn, 1971, p.263). This ground rule encourages persons to assume control over their own participation and to make choices about participation in the light of inner and outer realities. This special instruction encourages the utilization of coping devices, including such defences as the person senses he or she needs to employ in any given situation. By sanctioning the use of such defences as the person senses to be necessary, persons are more likely to feel in control and hence safe. A likely consequence is a *reduction* in the utilization of defences.

These two examples stand in marked contrast to one another, with respect to the character of the short cut and the consequences of employing it. In the first example the conductor of the group assumes control and requires a definite response from each member. In the second example the conductor of the group places control in the hands of the members, who are invited to express or censor themselves as seems best to them. In my view the first kind of device should be avoided while the second could be useful, for reasons already provided.

Getting-to-know-one-another or breaking-the-ice games are sometimes introduced into groups. For example the members of a group might be asked to toss a ball back and forth among them, each time naming the person to whom they throw the ball. The game is meant to help members get to know one another's names quickly. Such a game can be useful providing it is likely to be experienced by members as fun rather than as a pointless or demeaning exercise. Perhaps it is for this reason that such games are most commonly used with groups of children or young adolescents.

In general, if a short cut or an accelerating device is likely to contribute to feeling safe-enough within the group, if it facilitates using the structure planned for the group, if it is likely to seem plausible and acceptable to members and if it is unlikely to result in damage to individuals, then one may feel confident about using it. Otherwise, the device should be avoided.

Before moving on from this discussion of how a therapist, group worker or leader may open a group, it seems worth mentioning that the longer the therapist or group worker goes on with an introductory statement, the more time he takes away from the group members to start engaging with one another. Overly long introductory statements (I know of one which went on for forty-five minutes, including much detail about the history of group therapy) are likely to be an indication of the therapist's anxiety rather than a helpful and necessary input for the group.

Assuming that it is the leader who makes the opening comment, he will sooner or later stop speaking and then something else will happen. The something else which then happens cannot be precisely predicted, but whatever it is the leader's subsequent behaviour must take it into account.

A group could, and in my experience now and then does, immediately get down to useful work within the struture planned for it. When this happens it is likely to be because the therapist has estimated correctly the frontier and/or preoccupying concern of the population he is working with and has designed a suitable structure and because the persons in the group are particularly ready to take risks (often because they are desperate for an opportunity to share experiences). In a group which starts smoothly it is also likely that the therapist's or worker's opening comment has steered the members towards working to its planned structure and has avoided stirring up unnecessary fears. Such a combination of factors makes for an easy start.

A group could also, in theory, collapse within minutes into chaos or into a contagion of fear which leads members to flee from the group. I have never known this to happen and can imagine it happening only if really gross errors were made during the planning stage and if the opening comment had been such as to sharply intensify anxieties about the group.

What is more likely than either an entirely smooth start or a disastrous one is a run of events which suggests that the members are trying but finding it difficult to work together usefully. Perhaps the opening comment is followed by a long and increasingly awkward silence; or by a rather wooden and unenthusiastic compliance in a planned exercise or activity; or by desultory conversation on some topic of no apparent relevance to the members; or by one person talking directly to the worker or therapist as if no one else were there, with others silent; or by aggressive challenges to the leader's competence. These and other forms of less-than-optimal starts are not unusual. In fact, they are almost to be expected if one bears in mind that so many persons experience entering a new group as threatening in some degree.

In the discussion which follows I shall describe a number of possible responses to a therapist's or worker's opening comment, consider ways in which these may be understood and suggest interventions which can be tried:

(1) *In a group in which the therapist or worker intends to rely on general discussion among the members, his opening comment is followed by a long and increasingly anxious silence.* If this occurs, it is a reasonable guess that the members are feeling uneasy or confused, but as long as the silence persists one has no way of knowing just what feelings are present nor whether they are shared or diverse and idiosyncratic. The therapist or group worker is faced with deciding whether or not, or how soon, to break the silence. Generally, one hopes that the members can break the silence themselves, since this would be consistent with one's hope that members will engage with one another rather than rely on the conductor. This consideration argues in favour of waiting. At the same time one does not want the silence to run on for so long that the sense of risk increases and it becomes less and less likely that one of the members will feel able to speak. Some persons can tolerate longer silences than others, so the kind of population one is working with is a factor. Because a silence can seem so much longer than it actually is, it is useful to sit where one can see a clock and remind oneself unobtrusively that a silence which feels like a very long time has in fact gone on for only two or three minutes. This helps to forestall a too-early intervention, that is, one which comes during a period in which there is still a good chance that a member of the group will break the silence. During a silence one can be alert to non-verbal indications of increasing tension, which show that the sense of safety is beginning to erode and that a comment from the worker or therapist is required.

If one of the members has been able to break the silence then the problem has of course disappeared. If this does not happen one can try directing a question to the group: 'It is hard to get started. How is that?' Or 'What is making it difficult to talk?' Such questions usually make it possible for someone to say something, perhaps: 'We don't know where to start', or 'I had a lot of things to say before I came but somehow I can't remember any of them', or 'I thought you would be telling us what to talk about.' If any such comment as this is made one might extend a non-verbal invitation to others to speak by glancing around the room or one might enquire as to whether others feel the same or differently as the person who has spoken first. Often, this is all that is required in order to encourage a more general discussion. A problem still exists of course but now it is a *defined* problem: the members had expectations of the therapist which are not being fulfilled, or no one can think of anything to say, etc. The situation is entirely different from that of a general silence. If a further silence ensues I would again allow sufficient time for someone to find something to say but if the silence again runs on one might begin to express one's own thoughts to the group. For example one might say 'I have been thinking that it might be very hard to start because no one is quite sure of what sort of start is appropriate. Well, we could start by talking about how each person feels now, or by talking about what brought people here, or by introducing ourselves.' Such a comment provides guidance without imposing any single direction on the group. It still leaves the members choice as to how to begin. In my experience silence does not persist through and beyond such interventions unless one has thoroughly misjudged the capacities of the members.

When a therapist or worker is faced with a long initial silence he should consider the possibility that he himself has raised the level of anxiety by something in his opening comment. If, for example, he has indicated that he expects members to talk about difficult or painful experiences he may have created a too-high threshold for participation. If he thinks he has made such an error he could retrieve it by saying something like 'I have just been thinking that by saying that we will get the most from the group by talking freely about personal problems I may have made it hard to begin. I think that we could begin with virtually anything, even the weather, and see how we feel as we go.' Such a comment has some chance of retrieving the error because it gives the members permission to find a less threatening way in which to begin.

There are certain ways of breaking an initial silence which are well to avoid. For example, engaging with one person or calling on one specific person to talk is likely to break the silence but at the same time it indicates to the group that the therapist prefers to proceed by one-to-one interaction. Comments which convey reproach, blame or impatience are also to be avoided. A therapist is sometimes vulnerable to making unrecognized critical or reproachful comments because of his own anxieties at the start of a group. If he fears that the group will never get started or that he will fail in his task and be liable to criticism from colleagues, then he may feel angry at a group which finds it difficult to start. Anger can leak out in such comments as 'It will be hard for us to get anywhere if people don't talk.' Comments of this kind can stimulate fears of disapproval, retribution or abandonment from the therapist or worker, or can intensify such fears if they are already present.

(2) *In an open-discussion or topic-oriented group the opening comment is followed by casual or desultory conversation on some topic of no apparent relevance to the members*. The members begin to talk about something that was on television the previous night, or football, or the hospital cafeteria, etc. The therapist or worker quite understandably considers that the group was not brought together in order to pursue such topics as these and may therefore feel that he ought to help the group move on to something which concerns them more directly. However, I am going to argue that in the first instance the best thing to do is nothing at all. The reason for this is the likelihood that while the members are talking about an apparently trivial or off-target topic they are in fact interacting with one another in ways which accomplish useful work. For example, during the first session of a group of psychiatric in-patients the members spent thirty or forty minutes talking about baseball. The discussion turned to which team the various members favoured or supported. During this discussion members acknowledged that different persons supported different teams, that each of the teams mentioned was good in its own way, and so on. The discussion about baseball constituted a low-risk way of testing out whether individual differences with regard to preferences and opinions would be tolerated within the group.

The members were interacting in such a way as to increase the general sense of safety. In this group the members shifted into a discussion of more personal concerns on their own, after one person eventually said 'We didn't come here to talk about baseball.' In this situation and others like it, it would be against the members' interests if the therapist interrupted this useful process and prematurely pressed the group to talk about 'important' matters.

An apparently trivial or off-target topic can sometimes constitute a metaphor for the group. In group focal conflict terms metaphoric discussions can express shared wishes and fears and the stance which members take with respect to them. For example, another in-patient group began by discussing the kind of phonograph record in which a number of different musical selections are brought together for the purpose of providing relaxed listening. They speculated as to whether selections brought together in this way really fitted together, would meet the taste of anyone who purchased the record, could include some 'junk', and so on. A therapist or worker listening to this might form the hypothesis that while not aware of it themselves the members were really expressing some hopes and fears about the group: will the members of the group fit together? will the combination make sense and be pleasing? will the group serve its purpose? etc. The members are ventilating their anxieties, albeit in symbolic terms. If as the conversation proceeds someone says 'Records like that can be a really good buy' and several others agree, one might consider that the interaction has allowed members to feel more comfortable and optimistic about the group.

In both these examples one would say in group focal conflict terms that the members were operating on the restrictive solution, 'talk about a safe, impersonal topic'. The topic is only *apparently* irrelevant. In one case (the phonograph record) the content is a metaphor for the group. In the other case (baseball) the discussion offers opportunities to express individual differences in safe terms and to test acceptance and acceptability. Some groups may need to operate on this level for extended periods of time, or even deal with some issue entirely in metaphoric terms, in order to maintain an adequate level of safety.

As conductor of a group one can sometimes usefully participate in the conversation at the same level as the group members. Such comments do not challenge the group to change the subject or to talk in other terms. They either underline the good work which is already being done or develop the theme in ways likely to reduce shared fears. For example, in the group which was discussing baseball, one might say 'Many people insult one another about their favourite teams, but we are saying here that it is understandable that people have their own favourites and that every team has its good points.' This extracts from the general discussion that aspect of it which the therapist or worker judges is helping the group to reduce shared fears, and emphasizes it for the members. In the group discussing the record one might say something like: 'I find that such records can be enjoyable. I can enjoy each selection even though they are different.' By such a comment the conductor joins in the metaphor and by his comment communicates his willingness to appreciate each member of the group.

Sometimes one judges that it will be difficult for a group to move forward unless the members can discuss the feelings implicit in symbolic material directly and that members are potentially capable of doing so. In that case one can try a series of interventions which one hopes will lead step by step to the acknowledgment and direct exploration of feelings. For example during the discussion about the phonograph record one might say something like: 'I guess it makes one wonder about combinations of things and persons and how they work out.' The intention is to encourage the members to discuss other combinations and how they work, but it does not press them to think in terms of the group. If the members do not respond to this one could try a follow-up intervention, e.g., 'I think this happens in other situations too, for example, a football team is a combination of persons, isn't it?' If the members are able to explore the general issue in further ways one might later say 'What about here? We have a combination of persons right here.' If the members respond to this they are now exploring their hopes and fears about the group in direct terms. In the course of such an exploration they can consider or be helped to consider whether and how their fears are realistic. The general strategy is to try to detach the discussion from the symbolic material without immediately attaching it to the here-and-now experience in the group. These are low-risk interventions because they are unlikely to lead to the intensification of fears and because whilst encouraging movement they nevertheless allow members to move at their own pace. If at any point the members

do not respond to one of these interventions, the worker or therapist can simply sit back and allow the group a little more time.
None of these interventions is an interpretation in the sense of
suggesting meanings to the members. They do however direct the
members towards considering meanings, and try to allow them to
do so in their own way.

A series of low-risk interventions can be contrasted with a single
intervention which by interpretation presents a meaning of the
indirect or symbolic material to the group. For example, one
might say 'When you are talking about records made up of
different selections you are really expressing some worries as to
whether the combination of persons here in this group will prove
to be worthwhile or not.' This is a high-risk intervention. In one
step it places before the members an interpretation of events
which they have not considered up to then. Whether or not such
an interpretation is accepted depends on whether or not it seems
plausible to members, and this depends on the timing of the
interpretation within the associative flow. If everyone who has
spoken so far has supported the discussion at a symbolic level,
then there exists in the group no readiness to hear the interpretation. On the other hand if even one person begins, say, to be
restive or to wonder why the group is discussing records, then the
interpretation could make sense at least to that person and so find
some support from within the group. One would then say that the
timing was right. Not only does the timing have to be right in order
for members to accept and make use of such an interpretation, but
a premature interpretation can leave a group worse off than
before. If the interpretation leads members to see the therapist
or worker as prone to making outlandish assumptions about the
'real' meaning of their discussions and especially if they experience
implied criticism, feel 'caught out', or feel dangerously exposed
to the power of their own feelings, then the level of threat in the
group is likely to rise sharply. A shift into a period of chaos could
follow, or a shift into a further restrictive solution. Sometimes
one sees a therapist or worker compound the error of having
introduced a premature interpretation by regarding any ensuing
bafflement or protest as an indication of resistance which in itself
constitutes 'proof' that the interpretation was correct. If this view
is pressed on the members, it may well drive them into some still
more intractable shared defences which are much harder to deal
with.

I am not arguing against the technical correctness of the interpretation about phonograph records, since to me it seems a
reasonable construction of events. The question is whether to hold
to this interpretation as an internal hypothesis or to express it to
the group. I would argue that because errors in timing are easily
made and can have negative consequences that this is a high-risk
intervention. Moreover, it is often unnecessary since one can
usually get to the same point through a series of low-risk interventions. A series of interventions rather than one single global interpretation has the further advantage that at each step the conductor
can note how the members respond to his interventions and on
the basis of this can judge readiness and adjust his pace.

It is sometimes useful to point to connections between symbolic
material and here-and-now experiences *after* the members have
moved beyond the off-target or symbolic discussion on to direct
sharing of their here-and-now feelings. One might, for example,
find an opportunity to say something like: 'Remember when we
were talking about phonograph records? That was the first hint,
perhaps, that we were wondering whether *this* combination of
persons could be a good one or not.' One is not intending to
influence the current situation, which no longer needs influencing,
but makes the comment in the hope that if members come to
understand that symbolic material can pertain to here-and-now
concerns, then the next time that some symbolic discussion occurs,
they might be ready, sooner than before, to query its import.

(3) *The opening comment is followed by one person talking directly
to the worker or therapist as if no one else were there, while others
remain silent.* If this happens, either the members are incapable
of listening to and engaging with one another or they misunder-
stand what is expected of them or they are experiencing certain
fears and reservations about the group and are making use of this
interactive pattern as a restrictive solution.

Often one can rule out the possibility that the group members
are incapable of listening and engaging one another because it is
an implausible assumption given one's general understanding of
the population. Apart from this, the only way to develop a firm
view about what might underlie this pattern is to assume a basic
capability to interact and try certain interventions to see if the
members can shift into engaging with one another. In theory, one
could break up this pattern simply by avoiding responding to
anyone who addresses the leader directly. The problem with this

as a strategy is that it may leave a vacuum which the members find it impossible to fill (except with silence), and that it is likely to be received by the members as an indication of lack of interest or of rejection. Some form of response is required. One might respond briefly and then look around expectantly to see if others can join in. If they do not and the first person continues to address himself to the therapist, one might again answer briefly and then say something like 'Jerry is telling us that he has been looking for a job this past week and he's worried about not having found one. What about others?' Or, 'I have been wondering how others have been feeling while Jerry and I have been talking.' Such interventions are likely to lead to more general discussion if the members are capable of it. Sometimes however one finds that the first person to talk subsides and another takes his place. The members begin to take turns in addressing questions to the therapist. The interaction then takes the form of a star with the therapist or worker in the centre. If this happens, an intervention which can be tried is a read-out of events, e.g. 'Since we started today, first one and then another has been asking me questions. No one has talked yet to one another.' In response to such a read-out someone might say 'Well, you are the one who has the answers' or 'How can other people in trouble help me?' If others join in, then a conversation has developed. If not, one can ask whether others have been feeling the same way. Whatever follows provides information to the therapist and to everyone present about the expectations or fears or puzzlements of the members. These can then be examined. By this time the initial pattern has shifted. Sometimes, in response to a read-out one gets a 'so what?' kind of response. One can then follow it up with a question or further comment, e.g. 'I've been wondering how it is that everything comes to me.' If the pattern does not change in response to these various comments then one might begin to conclude that it is unrealistic to expect the persons in the group to interact directly with one another. The course of events in the group reveals that one has misjudged frontier and planned a structure which the members are incapable of using. This then requires a rethinking of frontier in the light of new information, and finding a way to establish a new structure for the group.

(4) *The opening comment is followed by an extended abstract or intellectual discussion*. No one links this discussion to their own situation. For example, the members talk about the plight of

the single parent, or loneliness, or the sense of the lost self in contemporary society, etc. As with discussions about apparently trivial topics, the interpersonal *events* which occur (for which the topic is only a vehicle) may lead 'naturally' to more personally related discussion. It is sensible therefore to avoid interrupting such a conversation for a considerable period of time, to allow such processes to occur. If a therapist or worker wishes to intervene he might try extracting from the conversation its emotional quality, and putting this before the group, e.g. 'We have been reflecting on how hard loneliness is to bear' or 'You are saying that people just don't understand what single parents are up against.' Such a comment sometimes acts as a stimulus to the group to shift into more personal discussion. Perhaps it reduces fears by displaying understanding and acceptance. If the intellectualizing is not abandoned, one can wait for a bit and then introduce an intervention which goes one step further, e.g. 'What about this loneliness? We have been saying that it's pretty universal. Has anyone here *not* experienced it?' This intervention attempts to sanction the feeling of loneliness and reduce the fear of owning it. If the group continues in the same manner one could try: 'What bad thing would happen if we talked about our own feelings of loneliness?' This intervention avoids putting direct pressure on the members to abandon the solution of intellectualizing, but invites them to examine the fears which may underlie the solution. One or another of these interventions is likely to lead to a shift from a pattern of intellectualizing providing that it is not too firmly fixed in all the members of the group as a favoured personal defence. Should this be the case (and this means that the therapist is facing a difficult composition) the therapist is in the position of being the only person present who wishes to depart from an otherwise acceptable and indeed preferred way of interacting. In group focal conflict terms the group is in a state of solutional conflict, with the therapist as deviant member. From this position, it is difficult to be useful to the group. The therapist has become the group's antagonist. If a therapist or worker sees that he is the only one pressing the members in a direction in which no one wants to move, then it is best to join the members rather than to quarrel with them. By 'joining' I do not mean colluding with the restrictive solution by beginning to intellectualize oneself. Rather, one can join the group by acknowledging the preference for intellectualizing in a sympathetic way and putting the issue to the group as a shared problem for all to address: 'I can see that everyone enjoys talking about this issue in very broad terms. Yet we also want our discussions to have meaning for each person here. How are we going to manage this?' Such an intervention can shift the situation from one in which the therapist is (or soon will be) the group's adversary to one in which all are facing the same problem.

(5) *The opening comment is followed by direct, aggressive challenges to the leader's competence.* One or several members ask 'What has your training been for conducting groups?' or 'How many groups have you led?' Such attacks do occur from time to time and it is as well to be forearmed against them because they can be disconcerting, particularly if the therapist is in some way unsure of himself. Probably the best reply is to give matter-of-fact information in a neutral tone and then wait to see what happens. One might say, for example, 'This is the third group I have conducted in this hospital. Before this my experience has been with . . .' or 'This is the first group of this type that I have conducted.' This could be followed by a question: 'In what way is this important?' Whatever follows should provide the therapist or worker with more information about the members' feelings. For example, if the challenge persists and members begin to ask 'How could you possibly handle a group like this?' one could enquire as to what sorts of things they think might emerge that would be difficult to handle. This kind of intervention seeks to get the members' fears out into the open where they can be examined. It is a fair guess that an attack on the therapist or worker so early in the group masks shared fears about the potential dangers of the group and worries about the therapist's or worker's capacity to cope with them. A defensive reaction on the part of the therapist (which is easy to fall into) should be avoided because it constitutes a demonstration to the group that the therapist is *not* capable of handling difficult situations. Such a response increases rather than alleviates fears.

(6) *The opening comment is followed by anxious questions about record-keeping, the use of tapes, or case conferences.* This kind of response to an opening is easy to deal with if the therapist is not obliged by his agency or institution to enter information into formal records or contribute to case reviews. One simply says so

and then enquires as to how it is that this has been a concern. If one is obliged to provide information formally to colleagues I think it best to provide clear and concise information to the members of the group, e.g. 'As you probably know, each patient in this hospital is reviewed every six weeks or so. At those times I will be expected to express my opinion. I intend to do that without going into a lot of detail about what happens here.' If group members press further, for example by asking whether the therapist or worker would reveal particular kinds of information, I would answer these questions too, but try to find an opportunity soon to ask how it is that it is important to know this. I believe also that it is useful to acknowledge openly that group members are bound to take the fact of record-keeping, case notes, etc. into account when participating in the group. One might say 'I think it is important that each person here decides for himself or herself what to say and what not to say in this group. You will know better than anyone else what it feels OK to talk about.' Such a comment makes it clear that control over self-revelation is in the hands of members (which is where it lies in any case). It tends to have a freeing effect. I have argued earlier (in chapter 5 when discussing communicating with colleagues about the group) that self-censorship occurs in any case and is likely to be greater under conditions of uncertainty and rumour than under conditions of clear and accurate information.

When a therapist or worker is required to keep or contribute to formal records, he or she has real power over members in the form of fate-control. It is tempting, sometimes, to try to conceal one's real power or to offer false reassurance, out of a fear that the members of the group will censor their participation heavily if one does not. This amounts to deception, which is never advisable because it is virtually certain to come to light and to reduce the level of safety in the group. Patients already know or will soon find out all about case conferences and written records. A therapist who resorts to deception shows that he is not to be trusted and is inclined to avoid difficult situations. If the patients come to see the therapist as someone who cannot be relied upon this does far more damage to the group as a useful medium for help than the self-censoring which patients may engage in because they have been told clearly how information deriving from their participation in the group is to be used.

Problems around record-keeping would disappear if formal

records were accessible to clients or patients and if they attended reviews. In some settings open access to records is already established as policy. In others the costs and benefits of introducing open access could be explored with colleagues.

With respect to taping sessions I have suggested earlier that if tapes are to be used the apparatus had best be made entirely visible so that if members are concerned about taping their worries can be aired. The line of reasoning is the same as that just presented. (See chapter 5, section 9, for a fuller discussion.)

(7) *In a theme-centred or open-discussion group, the opening comment is followed by one person talking about his problems while others question him and act as therapist or helper*. Particularly when this occurs at the start of a group this interactive pattern is likely to be functioning as a restrictive solution for the group. One person is prepared to talk about himself and all others are thus protected from putting themselves at risk. This is a pattern which clearly requires the co-operation of everyone in the group. It is incorrect or at least an over-simplification to think of it as involving one person monopolizing the group. Even if the person who is in the centre of the group's attention appears to be benefiting, a therapist or group worker is unlikely to want this pattern to persist because opportunities for others to benefit are precluded or restricted.

As with some other restrictive solutions already discussed, it seems best not to interrupt for a time in order to give forces within the group, likely to lead to the pattern breaking up, time to emerge. One possibility is that the person who is in the centre of attention notes that he is the only one who is revealing anything personal and begins to feel uneasy. He may then stop talking or ask someone else to talk. If he does this the pattern is broken because its maintenance requires his co-operation. Another possibility is that as the discussion goes on others notice that no bad consequences have followed upon self-disclosure. This has a fear-diminishing effect. As fears diminish, wishes and hopes to have one's say and be helped are likely to surface. Others may begin to feel left out and deprived rather than simply relieved at avoiding the hazards of self-disclosure. If this occurs they will shift away from functioning as helpers to one person and again the pattern will be broken.

Sometimes one wishes to intervene in such a situation rather than to wait for intra-group dynamics to emerge and have their effect because the pattern seems to be going on for an unnecessarily long time. In such circumstances one might try a simple read-out of events: 'Since we began today Robert has been telling us about his problems and others have been questioning him about them and trying to help him.' Sometimes such a read-out is enough in itself to lead to a shift. At other times the read-out is ignored or met with the assurance that all are satisfied and benefiting. If this happens it is a signal that the group is not ready to move from the pattern just yet. One would then sit back for a further period before intervening again. If members look puzzled or query the point of the comment one could try something like: 'I have been wondering how Robert and others feel about what has been happening.'

One also would wish to intervene if one judges that the person in the centre of attention is beginning to experience considerable distress yet is unable to extricate himself from the position the group is holding him in. Under these circumstances a useful intervention is to redefine the situation as a problem for the group (which is what it is): 'Why is it important to others that Robert talk about his problem?' This is an attempt to put an alternative version of events before the members, intended to direct them to considering what function Robert being the centre of attention might be serving for them. Thinking in group focal conflict terms, one is naming a restrictive solution (without labelling it as such, of course) and inviting members to consider why it is necessary to them. In introducing such an intervention one is hoping to accomplish two things at once: to protect Robert without defining him as vulnerable, and to help the group as a whole to shift from a restrictive solution.

(8) *Following the opening comment most persons talk but one member is persistently and conspicuously silent.* This may take the form of inconspicuous withdrawal, in which case it may take a little time for the leader and others to become aware of it, or it may take the form of a conspicuous, explicit indication (verbal or non-verbal) that the member *intends* to be silent. It is a reasonable guess that persons who behave in such ways at the very beginning are showing that they can feel safe in the group only if they can avoid overt participation. The best response is to do nothing, on the grounds that if the person is pressed into participation his

fears may escalate to the point where his only recourse is to flee from the group. His silence can be regarded as the only basis on which he can remain. He is regulating his exposure to group events, taking in and offering no more than he can tolerate at the time. As long as he remains in the group there are opportunities for his fears to subside through his passive observation of events. Spectator effects can begin to take place: as he notes that others take risks and are neither punished nor damaged in doing so his own worries may subside to the point where he begins, usually in a tentative way, to take the risk of participating.

A silent person sometimes becomes a problem for other persons in the group, who impose their own fantasies on his silence and assume that he is being critical or is the expert who could make things easier if only he would speak. Group members sometimes put pressure on a silent person in consequence of harbouring such fears or hopes. If a therapist or worker wishes to ease the pressure on the silent person he can adopt a strategy suggested earlier: declare the situation to be a problem for the group rather than for the silent person. One could ask: 'Why is it so important for Mary to talk?' Such a comment takes the heat off Mary without defining her as weak or in need of help. At the same time it places the problem where it belongs, with the group as a whole, and invites members to consider their own feelings and fantasies about the silent person. On several occasions I have had members tell me privately after a group session that I should do something about a silent member because he is being disrespectful to me as the conductor of the group. This seems particularly likely to happen if the silent person displays rejection of the group through some non-verbal behaviour likely to be seen as discourteous (e.g. reading a book) or by aggressively declaring his unwillingness to participate. When this happens I am inclined to say that I do not experience his behaviour as a sign of disrespect but that if it is troubling others they might wish to bring it up during a group session. What is happening here is that the members are instructing me as to how to feel and are avoiding confronting their own feelings about the silent person. My response is intended to place the responsibility for feelings inside the persons who are having them: i.e., they feel as *they* do; I feel as *I* do. In group focal conflict terms, I am avoiding colluding with a solution in which members project their own feelings on to the leader and expect the leader to deal with the situation as *his* problem.

(9) *The opening comment directs the members to engage in some activity or discuss some topic and the members refuse to join in.* For example, the worker or therapist asks for volunteers for role-playing and no one volunteers, or he asks a group of accident victims to tell about the circumstances surrounding their accident, and no one is prepared to do so. Such a beginning to a group can be very disconcerting and catch the therapist unawares since in planning for the group he has assumed that the structure that he has in mind is both suitable and possible for the group members. He is faced with having to handle his own feelings and make a very quick decision about what to do next.

As with other indications of resistance to structure, one wishes, before resorting to abandoning the structure, to try to get at the feelings which underlie the members' unwillingness to work to it. One can ask the reluctant role-players 'What is getting in the way of volunteering?' One can explain to the accident victims one's own thinking and ask for theirs: 'In planning for this group I was assuming that it could be helpful to talk about the circumstances of the accident and get it off one's chest. Does it seem different to you?' If resistance to the structure persists, one wishes to avoid getting into a futile debate with the members and, as in earlier examples, becoming their adversary. It is better to turn the situation into a shared problem which all can face together, by restating the purpose one had in mind for the group and asking for suggestions about alternative ways for getting at it. One could say, for example, 'Our real interest is in practising new ways of dealing with conflicts and quarrels. If we didn't use role-playing, how might we go about it?' Or, for the accident victims: 'Our real interest is in helping the persons in this group deal with any changes in their lives that this accident might require of them. We don't necessarily have to start by talking about the accident. I wonder how we *might* start?' These suggestions are consistent with the view that it is less important to hold to the planned structure than to find *some* structure which will serve the purposes of the group.

(10) *The opening comment is followed by a brief silence and then by members breaking down into sub-groups and speaking only to their neighbours.* Should this happen, one might decide not to interrupt for a short while on the grounds that the persons in the group are at least speaking to *someone*, even if they are

unable or unwilling to engage in general discussion. However, one does not want sub-grouping to go on for very long, because within such a pattern it is unlikely that events will occur which could pave the way for yielding it up. For this reason it seems appropriate to interrupt after some minutes, perhaps by calling the members together again and asking whether they can share with the whole group anything discussed in the sub-groups. Often, members will have gained some confidence through talking initially to only one or two others, and will be able to respond to this. Even if the responses are 'We were just talking about unimportant things' they provide one with the opportunity to say something like 'Well that's all right. We don't have to talk about important things all the time. We can start wherever we like.' Such a comment gives permission to the group to begin in some way which feels comfortable to them but which they may have thought was unacceptable to the therapist. Once a reasonable sense of safety is established in a group, breaking down into sub-groups is less likely to occur.

(11) *A member fails to turn up for the first session or comes the first time but then misses a session.* The issue for the therapist is whether to be in contact with the absent person, how soon and to what end. In a very new group especially, it seems appropriate to get into contact with the member soon after the session which he has failed to attend, on the grounds that one will otherwise have no idea of what accounts for his absence. Perhaps his car broke down or he was ill, and is now wondering uneasily whether he is still welcome. Perhaps as the time of the first session came nearer his fears about what might happen in the group escalated. Perhaps the events of the first session profoundly alarmed him and he is now fleeing in panic.

It was suggested in the previous chapter that dropping out can be a sensible self-protective measure, and then should be respected. But it can also occur almost accidentally, and then a little help or exploring can help the person to re-enter the group. If a person who has dropped out has already experienced some personal damage through being in the group, a further contact may help him or her to recover or to find some other form of help. A brief individual contact to find out what accounts for the absence and to provide appropriate support is indicated. Under some circumstances one might wish to adapt the kind of interview suggested in chapter 7, not with the intention of encouraging the person to return to the group if this seems against his best interests, but with the intention of helping him to understand his actions and get further support if he needs it. A person who flees in profound panic may need the reassurance of knowing that the therapist or worker does not hold it against him.

(12) *Within fifteen or twenty minutes after the opening comment, someone in the group announces that he does not intend to come back to the group.* Such a comment from a member deserves a quick question ('Can you say why?') on two grounds. First, because he has announced his intention to leave he probably *can* say more, and it is better both for him and for the group as a whole if his feelings and thoughts can be brought out into the open. It is better for him because it makes an opportunity for him to examine his feelings. It is better for the others because they will then have further information rather than merely an ambiguous comment on which to pin fantasies. Second, it is always possible that the feelings this person is experiencing are shared by others who are less able to express them. If the person who says he intends to leave is able to share his reservations, negative feelings or fears about the group, this constitutes permission for others to do the same. A therapist or worker can add his own permission by saying something like 'It would surprise me if David were the only person here to have any of these feelings. Is that so?' Permission reduces fear by declaring as understandable and acceptable feelings which members may have feared might elicit criticism or rejection from the therapist or worker.

It might be the case that the person who has announced his intention to leave the group is unable or unwilling to say anything further about it. Then one might say 'Well, I don't want to press you on it but I do wonder whether you are the only one here who might be thinking he might not come again or might be having reservations about how things are going.' One would then turn one's attention to the others. Such a comment is an invitation to others to share feelings about how the group is going, again on the assumption that one person might be functioning as a spokesman for others.

After exploring the situation in these ways one might find the person willing to stay in the group, after all (if he has found out that he is not alone in his fearful or angry feelings and thereby feels reassured) or one might find him just as determined to leave. The latter is less likely, since experience suggests that persons who are unambivalent about their wish to leave a group do so without raising the issue, for fear, perhaps, of being forced or persuaded to remain despite their strong feelings. Should a person hold to his intention to leave, one can help him to think out further plans and help the remaining members to examine the feelings which the departure of a member leaves them with.

(13) *After the opening comment or some time during the first session the members make it clear that they consider* any *group a second-best helping experience.* This is more likely to occur in therapeutic groups than, for example, groups directed towards skill-development or towards helping persons across transitions. It is not unusual for persons seeking psychotherapy to assume that *real* help can best be received in a one-to-one situation. If such complaints are made there is no point in getting into the position of defending group psychotherapy or seeking to persuade the members that they are wrong to hold such opinions. One needs instead to take such comments seriously and seek to understand them better. One could say: 'This makes me wonder: what *is* help, anyway . . .?' or one could ask what it is that group members expect in a one-to-one situation that they cannot get in a group. The answer provides information for all to see about expectations, assumptions, hopes and concerns, which can then be explored and discussed.

The principal error which can be made in the face of this situation is to get into an antagonistic position with regard to group members. That is, as they insist more and more strongly that the group cannot be of any use, the therapist insists more and more strongly that it can. This is fruitless and confirms the conductor and the group members as occupying opposing camps rather than being engaged in a mutual enterprise. Non-punitive exploring is on the other hand likely to make it possible to deal with obstacles to the members actually using the group as a medium for help.

Of the various situations just discussed which may arise in response to a worker's or therapist's opening comment, quite a few have to do with the members' either individually or collectively attempting to render the group a safe environment for themselves. During the formative phase of a group members can be expected to generate a sense of safety by establishing shared or collusive defences, or, in group focal conflict terms, restrictive solutions. While the conductor of a group wants the members to feel safe he also wants them to begin to take risks, usually by beginning to share experiences and express personal feelings, or by participating in planned activities and exercises. Restrictive solutions generate safety but limit risk-taking, and so tend to reduce the value of the group. It follows that one of the conductor's purposes and tasks is to monitor this aspect of group, to be aware of restrictive solutions when they emerge and to judge whether and how it might be useful to intervene.

Whether to intervene can be as important a decision as how to intervene. Examples have been provided of times when the best course of action is to say nothing at all, in order that members of the group through their own interaction may find ways of expressing and working through initial feelings. Sometimes one judges that one *should* intervene, either because one thinks the group could move more quickly or because one sees a particular member becoming excessively distressed in consequence of the way the group is operating. One guiding principle is to avoid contributing to the escalation of shared fears. This means not challenging a restrictive solution head-on but instead adopting the strategy of seeking to alleviate associated fears so that the restrictive solution becomes less necessary to the group. Useful interventions can be simple and brief, they can be directed to the members in general or to one person, and they can take various forms – comments, questions, read-outs, etc. Neither the form nor the target of the intervention is as important as how it bears on the dynamics of the group.

A distinction can be made between high-risk and low-risk interventions. While both kinds of interventions can be effective, different consequences follow if the members do not respond as one hopes. A high-risk intervention, if it does not elicit the intended response, can lead to the exacerbation of fears or mistrust of the conductor, place the conductor and the members in opposing camps as adversaries, and/or lead the members to resort to some still more intractable restrictive solution. In other words a high-risk intervention can set a group back if it does not work as intended. A low-risk intervention does not place the group in a worse position than before if the members do not respond as one hopes and intends. Examples of low-risk interventions are read-outs, invitations to share feelings, joining members within a meta-phor, extending permission to hold certain feelings, and some forms of placing meanings on events (e.g. turning a problem which everyone sees as belonging to one person into a problem which belongs to the group). Examples of high-risk interventions are interpretations which suggest deep meanings for observable events, likely to be regarded as implausible by members, and interpretations which impute unacceptable motivations. One can also imagine medium-risk interventions. I have suggested that a series of low-risk interventions, or a series which moves from low-risk to medium-risk can be more useful than a single 'grand' interpretation, which carries a higher risk, not least because the responses of the members to successive interventions provides the conductor with information as to how each intervention is being received and used and thus can offer guidance as to whether or not to press further. Arguing against 'grand' interpretations is not the same as arguing against a therapist or worker placing meanings on events different to those held by members. An intervention which redefines a situation as a problem for the group rather than for an individual does just that, and can be useful in the face of a member being pressed by others to assume a role within a restrictive solution which is generating distress for him, or in the face of pressures on a silent person to talk. An argument has been made against a therapist or worker actively colluding in a restrictive solution (e.g. co-operating in holding one person in the centre of attention when this is serving a defensive function). Another general point has to do with avoiding getting into an adversary position with members, but rather striving to get on the same side as the members in facing difficult situations. Avoiding adversary situations is not at all the same thing as acceding always to members' wishes and preferences, or avoiding confronting, as will be seen.

All of this adds up to a certain point of view as to how group-level phenomena may be understood and managed, which can be contrasted with other approaches which, for example, make more exclusive use of group-level interpretations, or of directives to members, or of direct challenges to shared defences.

Throughout the life of a group the worker or therapist is aiming to help the group to develop into and be maintained as a positive medium for help *and* to utilize situations which arise for the particular benefit of individuals. During the formative stage, when the viability of the group is still in doubt, the first of these is particularly important. It is for this reason that the fullest discussion of this issue has been presented in this chapter and in the preceding one. How situations which arise in groups can be utilized for the benefit of specific members is discussed in the course of the next two chapters, in the context of considering groups in their established phase.

Suggested exercises

If the opportunity is available it can be extremely useful to compare different openings and the responses which each elicits from the group. If a group of colleagues, all engaged in conducting groups, is prepared to tape the first fifteen minutes or so of a group which is meeting for the first time, all concerned can learn from listening to these. In particular, attention can be paid to the information conveyed by the opening comment, the emotional message conveyed by tone of voice, etc., and the nature of the demands which the opening makes upon the members. By listening with care to what happens next, one can see the impact of the opening and/or what the response confronts the conductor with. A tape-stopping technique is useful: either the group of colleagues accepts the convention that anyone can signal that he or she wants the tape stopped in order to comment or to query the person who actually conducted the group; or the conductor, who will know when he or she introduced an intervention, can stop the tape just before the intervention was offered, in order to elicit views as to what was going on in the group and how others would have dealt with the situation.

Chapter 11

The established phase of a group: character and purposes

In this series of chapters pertaining to the operation and conduct of the group I make the assumption that all groups, even if they are short-term and highly structured, can be seen to have a beginning or formative phase, a middle or established phase and a termination phase. The established phase may of course be longer or shorter depending on the overall duration of the group. During this phase the preoccupations of the formative phase are in the past and the preoccupations of the termination phase are yet to come. It is a period in which the viability of the group is usually not seriously in question, in which a variety of themes or tasks relevant to members can be expected to emerge or can be placed before the group, and in which such problems as arise can for the most part be managed and utilized positively for the benefit of the persons in the group.

What marks the shift from the formative phase to the established phase? When a group first starts much of what one sees can be understood in terms of the members grappling with establishing themselves as a group and, as individuals, finding a place in it. The planned structure is being tested, and members are struggling to find ways to establish the group as a 'safe enough' environment for themselves. All begin the task of getting to know one another, and of finding ways to use the group situation for personal benefit. During this early stage there is likely to be some degree of uncertainty, shared by all, as to whether or not the group will survive and thrive.

The established phase of a group can be said to begin when all concerned develop a sense that the group will 'work'. One way or another the group seems to have put its teething troubles behind it; its members show that they can work within the structure or else they have modified it or devised a new one; their initial worries about what they might be expected to do or say, or what might happen to them in the group are at least somewhat allayed. Such a group has become 'viable' in the literal sense of the term: the group will live and not die an early death. It will certainly have its problems from time to time. The sessions will not necessarily be easy or comfortable, and it remains to be seen just how useful the experience will be and how much of the time the group can work effectively. Nevertheless the group has left its formative stage behind, and can now be regarded as established.

The sense that the group will work occurs sometimes sooner, sometimes later in different groups. In a highly structured group which relies on activities, exercises or directed discussion, it may be apparent fifteen or twenty minutes into the first session whether or not the group will 'go'. In a longer-term group relying on open discussion it may be four, five, or six sessions before the members have worked through their initial concerns and one feels that the group has 'jelled'. Many therapists and group workers report that they can identify this moment of jelling through their own sharply experienced sense of relief that the group is a going concern and not an abortive effort.

In group focal conflict terms, one would say that the members have worked through their initial reactive fears, and have been able to shift from predominantly restrictive solutions as ways of dealing with them, to predominantly enabling solutions.

It is not the case that once a group moves past its formative phase that all can be expected to go smoothly from then on. In all kinds of groups – those which make substantial use of activities and exercises, those which rely on open discussion, those structured in terms of topics – one usually sees fluctuations between periods of active, productive, useful work and periods of fallowness, resistance, disorganization or apparent chaos. When the group is going well the worker or therapist is likely to feel pleased with the group, confident about its likely usefulness and confident about his/her own competence as conductor of the group. When the group is in the doldrums or in some state of disorganization the worker or therapist may experience disappointment, bewilderment and self-doubt. Anyone conducting a group is likely to manage both the group and his own feelings better if he can understand how it is that such fluctuations occur. I offer the following as an explanation.

During a period of active productive work the members of a group are engaged in working up to their current limits along some particular line or on some particular issue or task. During such periods members are likely to experience excitement and pleasure as well as bearable pain in the course of exploring issues important to them, discovering new things about themselves and others, and trying out new behaviours. As such work or activity continues, however, one or two persons, and then more, come to feel pressed beyond what is for them comfortable or manageable. As this happens, the sense of being 'safe enough' begins to deteriorate in the group as a whole. Persons reach their limit of tolerable anxiety. Someone is likely to say something or do something which constitutes a shift from the current theme or activity or mode of operating. If this person turns out to be the only one who needs to retrieve a sense of safety by moving away from what is happening, then no one will support or follow him. The group as a whole continues as before and the person who has reached the limits of his tolerance must find some other way of dealing with his feelings. He may withdraw, which has the consequence of making room for the rest of the group to proceed as before, or he may interfere actively with what is going on, in which case the group must stop and deal with the new situation which he has created. Quite often, though, the person who is the first to interrupt an ongoing exploration or activity is not the only one who has reached a point of substantial discomfort. Others besides him experience a worryingly reduced level of safety – an increased sense that the situation is becoming unbearably risky. If this is the case the initiator of the shift will gain support from others. The shift which then occurs is likely to be disorganized flight or else the establishment of some co-operatively maintained restrictive solution which closes off further work on the same theme or in the same mode. By such means the members regain a sense of being safe enough in the group.

To summarize this concisely, pushing at current limits leads to an exacerbation of fears which in turn necessitates flight from the situation, in the form of the erection of a shared restrictive solution or a breakdown in order. The group shifts from a period of working on some enabling solution to a period of no solution (which looks like chaos) or of searching for and then establishing some restrictive solution (which looks like regression and retreat). Often, members will resort to some restrictive solution which they have used in the past. The group, after all, has a history. The members have relied on a certain range of restrictive solutions earlier in their collective life. These are still accessible to them even though they are not always needed or used. When anxieties increase, group members are likely to fall back on one or another of the restrictive solutions which have been utilized earlier, although they may also establish new restrictive solutions.

Not infrequently, a period of fallowness or retreat starts at the beginning of a session which follows a particularly productive session. What may happen in this case is that the members were sustained in their risk-taking by the presence of others, all collaborating in maintaining an enabling solution which contained fears and allowed exploration. Between sessions, each member is deprived of the immediate experience of support and may be overtaken by a sense of having gone too far, of having taken too many risks. Each person then brings with him to the next session a readiness for or a need to retreat. This can happen in all kinds of groups. In an open-discussion group the members begin a session almost as if the previous one had not occurred – on a different, seemingly less relevant theme and/or in a different, usually flatter interactive mode. In a topic-oriented group the members begin by evading the topic or querulously complaining that it is not relevant to their concerns or will get them nowhere. When an activity or exercise has been planned, it doesn't get off the ground or it is 'spoiled' by the behaviour of the members. In the more structured groups this can occur through no fault at all in the planning, in that the exercise, activity or topic which has been planned is, in so far as anyone could possibly judge, entirely appropriate to the members' needs and capacities. But the members have in some way gone too far in the previous session and now need to retreat temporarily in order to re-establish an adequate sense of safety.

Such episodes can be both disappointing and puzzling to the worker or therapist. In an open-discussion group, a therapist or worker may be tempted to try to recapture the high note on which the previous session ended by re-introducing the same theme for further discussion. It is not often that this works, for reasons just put forward. In a group for which some topic or exercise has been planned and then resisted, the worker may be tempted to try to press or persuade them to carry out the plan. This also is unlikely to work. By the argument put forward above, the worker is standing in the way of a necessary retreat. In group focal conflict terms he is placing himself in a deviant position in the group with respect to a preferred solution, and thus becomes the group's antagonist rather than its helper.

Feelings of discouragement or frustration on the part of the therapist or worker are understandable when a group which has been working well shifts into a period of resistance, retreat or chaos. The explanation just offered suggests that a therapist or worker need not despair when this happens. Rather than being distressed by such periods, one can argue that a leader should worry if they do not occur. If they do not occur at all it is entirely possible that the group, perhaps without the therapist or worker being aware of it, has settled into some excessively comfortable and unchallenging way of operating, or some chronically maintained collusive defence which goes undetected because it bears a semblance to productive work.

In longer-term groups, especially, one can observe a form of development over time which is more than an alternation between periods of productive work and periods of recoupment. Rather than moving in a zig-zag, at the same time staying more or less on a level, the group moves in a deepening spiral. A sequence can be discerned in which some issue emerges, is developed by the members to a certain point, and then dropped. It is likely to be dropped, as I have already suggested, at a point where members have taken the issue as far as they can without experiencing an intolerable level of threat. At this point the members are likely to invoke some restrictive solution and move into a shorter or longer period of apparent retreat. As interaction continues, and members find ways to deal with their new or exacerbated shared fears, some other issue or theme is likely to emerge. This again is taken to a certain point before the members feel the need to shift, again because exploration of the theme has sooner or later led them into realms which they find too threatening to pursue. The group moves in this fluctuating and cyclical way, with earlier themes recurring repeatedly, each time taken as far as the group can manage. When issues recur, they are tackled in somewhat different ways, and taken each time a bit further than before. Groups do not deal and cannot be expected to deal with some theme thoroughly and completely and then never again need to return to it. (It is for this reason that groups structured by predesignated topics should be planned to allow members to return to earlier themes as and when they show the need to do so.) A therapist or worker need not worry if a group does not pursue an issue or theme as far as the therapist considers necessary or useful. If the issue remains salient, the members will return to it, providing always that they do not permanently get stuck in some restrictive solution which impedes further movement.

During the established phase, each session must and will begin in some way. As before, it is the worker's or therapist's responsibility to decide how to open each session, whether this be by doing or saying something himself, or by leaving it to the members to find a way to begin. How the worker or therapist opens the session depends, as before, on the structure being used and the kind of patient or client in the group. If the structure requires someone to function as a master-of-ceremonies (as for example in role-playing and many forms of exercises) then it is the leader's responsibility to do this or to see to it that someone else does. If the group needs to be reminded of the topic planned or agreed for the session then again it is the leader's responsibility to do this. If the leader judges that the members will not feel safe unless they hear his voice, then he should open the session even if this is not required on technical grounds. If the group is designed to rely on open discussion, then it is appropriate that the leader not be the first to speak (unless required to maintain adequate levels of safety), because he does not know what is important *now* to the members, and therefore must leave room for new themes to emerge or previous ones to be taken up.

During the established phase of a group the same instrumental purposes as those discussed in chapter 9 continue to guide a worker or therapist in managing the group and seeking to make maximum use of it for the benefit of its members. However, because the established phase is different in some respects from the formative phase, some of the instrumental purposes require less attention than before, while others become a more central concern for the conductor of the group. In what follows, I will discuss each instrumental purpose in turn, paying special attention to the flavour which each takes on during the established phase, and their relative importance during this phase.

Conducting the group so as to maintain a general sense of safety in the group at a level at which members feel safe enough to stay in the group and to take personal risks

Monitoring the level of sense of safety continues to be important during the established phase of the group. Yet it is also the case that under most circumstances neither the conductor of the group nor the members have to be quite so concerned about this issue as before, nor work so hard or consistently at it. The reason for this lies in the fact that by the time a group enters its established phase each individual member will have had successive experiences of finding, losing and refinding (etc.) a tolerable position in the group. Also, the group as a whole has established a repertory of solutions which can be drawn upon to regulate the level of sense of safety in the group. Although the members do not always feel safe in the group, confidence grows that a sense of safety temporarily lost can be re-established. For much of the time, the conductor of the group finds that the members have found ways of their own for managing the level of safety or threat in the group.

Even so, the conductor of the group may find that he needs to intervene actively with respect to this issue from time to time, particularly when something happens which leads fears to escalate to the point where they cannot be managed by anything in the group's already developed repertory of solutions. The something-which-happens could be a crisis which has occurred for one of the members, an external event of crisis proportions, or something emerging from within the group interaction. In groups with which I have worked the following events have occurred which sharply reduced the level of sense of safety in the group and for which the members had no readily available solution to hand: a member who was the victim of a rape; a suicide on the ward; the unexpected death by heart attack of a member of staff known to all the persons in the group; an unexpected and intensely bitter and hostile exchange between two members generated by one suddenly emerging as standing for the other's hated mother; unexpected bizarre behaviour on the part of one member who suddenly leapt from his chair and began to write his own epitaph on a blackboard; the assassination of President Kennedy. All of these events not only sharply reduced the level of sense of safety in the group but left the members immobilized or in agitated disarray.

It seems reasonable to assume that it is the unexpectedness of the event combined with its resonance with personal fears and apprehensions which catches persons and the group in general without adequate defensive or coping devices to bring to bear immediately. One can see that a repertory of collective defences or solutions which might include such devices as intellectualizing, allowing one person to dominate the discussion, engaging in trivial discussion, and the like, are simply inadequate for dealing with events of so catastrophic a character.

When such an event occurs, and depending on the members' immediate reaction to it, the therapist or worker needs to allow time for the shock to be absorbed and/or take some active part in helping the members to manage the situation. If immobilization or disarray persists and especially if he judges that one or more persons are reaching their limit of bearable pain, he will need to take on the task of managing the situation himself rather than wait for coping resources to emerge from the group. If the conductor of the group also feels immobilized, helpless or disordered, this is likely to intensify fears still more, because he is unable to be the person of last resort – the ultimate safety net – in the group. It is not of course always easy to maintain oneself in a helping role in the face of such events, since catastrophic events are as likely to touch the therapist or worker as anyone else. At the least, however, one can usually name one's own reaction ('I feel stunned' or 'John, when you leapt up like that I felt startled and frightened at first'). Naming an event and one's own feelings (providing one can do it without accompanying non-verbal or tonal indications of panic) is in itself a demonstration to the others that acknowledging feelings is possible and that persons are not alone in their reactions to the event.

Avoiding the irredeemable collapse of structure

For the most part, the structure of the group will have been tested during the early period of the group's life and has either been found to be usable or else has required modification and been replanned. Virtually by definition, a group cannot be regarded as established until it has found some structure within which members are able to work.

Nevertheless, the structure sometimes comes under threat in an established group. This is perhaps most likely to occur when there is some change in circumstances, for example when a new member is brought into the group who challenges or cannot operate within the structure, or when some outside event occurs which shifts the members' feelings or attitudes about the structure which they have been using.

Sometimes a group 'outgrows' its structure. It is as if the members have exhausted the possibilities inherent in the structure and become dissatisfied with the group. When this occurs it is appropriate for the conductor of the group to help the members to look at the source of their dissatisfaction and consider the best action to take in the face of it. It may be appropriate to disband the group, or to adopt a quite different structure. The members' frontier has shifted, and the old structure no longer fits the new frontier.

While threats to the structure can occur during the established phase of the group by some of the routes just referred to, on the whole if a structure survives the formative stage it is more rather than less likely to remain workable into and throughout the established phase. As with the issue of the level of safety in the group, it is important for the group worker or therapist to attend to this aspect of the group's functioning but it is less likely than before to require his active intervention.

Working toward the establishment and maintenance of norms which facilitate effective work: in group focal conflict terms, working toward the establishment and maintenance of enabling rather than restrictive solutions

When an established group shifts into operating on a restrictive solution, the therapist or group worker is faced, as before, with deciding whether or not and how to intervene. On the whole, the same considerations guide him during the established phase as during the formative phase. That is, under most circumstances it is sensible to avoid intervening for a time in order to see whether the processes of the group will lead to a shift away from a restrictive solution toward an enabling solution. Under other circumstances, particularly if the therapist or worker considers that a restrictive solution is harming some one member or if he thinks he can safely accelerate the process, he might choose to intervene. The same strategies are open to him as before.

With respect to this issue, the worker or therapist can rely for help from group members more than was the case during the formative phase. By the time a group moves into an established phase, the members of the group have had considerable experience with one another and with the conductor. The latter will have intervened from time to time in ways intended to help the group to shift away from operating on some restrictive solution. In doing so, he has provided a model for dealing with this aspect of the group's operation. For example, he may have provided read-outs, asked the members to say how they have been feeling, asked the members to consider how they might feel were they to shift their manner of operating, and the like. In consequence of this, members often learn to think in such ways themselves. They sharpen their own capacities to observe the operation of their group, and may offer comments which help the group as a whole to shift. Of course, no one will do this during the time when the restrictive solution is essential to the sense of safety of all the members of the group. However, the interaction which occurs during the time that a restrictive solution is in operation often begins to alleviate fears, at first perhaps for only one or two persons. As this occurs those one or two persons are released from the need to cling to the solution quite so firmly and may begin to participate in a different way. Someone may ask 'Why are we concentrating for so long on John?' or 'Why are we making such a joke of this?' Or, one person may express his or her own fears, thus making it easier for others to do the same.

The general point is that during the established phase the members of the group often become able to do this kind of work on behalf of the group themselves. It then becomes less necessary for the therapist or group worker to take as active a part. This does not mean that he relinquishes the task of monitoring the kinds of solutions on which the group is operating, nor that he abandons the responsibility for intervening should the members themselves prove unable to deal with a situation.

If the three instrumental purposes of maintaining safety, a workable structure and largely enabling rather than restrictive solutions are met, useful work will take place in and through the interactions of members. In open discussion groups, themes are likely to emerge which bear closely on individual problems and concerns. These are generated by the members in interaction with one another and are likely to have to do with closeness and intimacy, anger, conflict, wishes to be cared for and looked after, fears, guilt, power and weakness – in short, the basic themes of human experience. How and in what form these themes emerge depends of course on the specific composition of the group. Where members share some preoccupying concern the themes which emerge will be coloured by that concern. Where topics have been preplanned (providing they have been well selected and the conductor is prepared to allow some flexibility) members can be expected to explore topics in ways which are relevant to them or transform them into issues which more closely fit their concerns if this proves necessary. In groups structured in terms of exercises or activities, personal meanings emerge in and through the activities. In all groups it is the members who make something out of the structure, who create something unique and special out of their own interaction. As themes emerge, activities are engaged in and interactions occur, members comment, share, express opinions, give and receive feedback, compare their own reactions and opinions with those of others, support and challenge one another, and try things they have not tried before. By such means, considerable benefit can occur through members' interactions alone.

If this is so, need the therapist or worker do anything further to ensure benefit to individuals? Much of the time he need not, since the members of the group will do a great deal for themselves and for one another, given facilitating group conditions. However, there will be times when special opportunities for individual benefit arise which the members themselves do not or cannot exploit fully. It is at such times that interventions by the conductor of the group, made with specific persons in mind, can make the difference between an opportunity utilized and an opportunity missed.

Utilizing events occurring within the group for the specific benefit of individuals

In chapter 9 I argued that the conductor of a group should be cautious about focusing on one person because such focusing can support a structure which fails to make use of the *group* as a medium for help, and because one risks alienating some members by appearing to favour one or a few. One does not wish at any time to undermine the structure or to make it difficult for some persons to invest in the group, but these risks are less during the established phase than during the formative phase. During the formative stage the structure planned for the group is still being tested and is not firmly established. Fears on the part of the members that the therapist or worker may reject, devalue or abandon them may be present but not yet acknowledged or resolved. Under such circumstances specific attention to one or a few persons can intensify fears and generate feelings of discouragement, anger or apathy. The situation is different when a group has moved into its established phase. The structure has been tried and tested and is not likely to be threatened if one departs from it occasionally. The members have had enough experience of the group and of the leader to appreciate that if the conductor of the group focuses on one person briefly or even occasionally for longer periods this does not mean that he or she does not value the others. In other words, the conductor's behaviour is not so likely to carry the same meanings as before. One still needs to be careful that focusing on an individual occurs in the context of a theme, issue or activity which involves the group as a whole, or else that it is a response to a true personal crisis. If one breaks into a shared theme and takes up some entirely different issue with an individual then one *is* forming a special relationship with one person and leaving the other members behind.

Comments can be directed toward individuals as part of an associative flow or as a feature of a planned exercise, or in and among an activity. Interventions directed at individuals often can usefully consist of a single comment or query. Or, an intervention can be directed to the group as a whole, with its relevance to one or two persons particularly in mind. These brief comments have a conversational quality. They are a part of what is going on rather than an interruption of it. Extended focusing on one or a few persons is rarely required, but when it is, it is likely to be tolerated by others providing they see that it is in response to a special need or opportunity, and providing they feel basically assured that the therapist or worker is equally ready to invest time in them, should the need or opportunity arise.

One works with persons in groups because one thinks that they may benefit from the experience. It was suggested in chapter 3 that 'to benefit' can be defined as coping more satisfactorily with preoccupying concerns and/or moving beyond current frontiers, although it was also acknowledged that some of the persons with whom one may work in groups have little or no capacity for moving beyond current frontiers. Depending on the kind of patient or client with whom one is working, one's best hopes may be to maintain personal resources (but not expect much movement), to build new resources, or to unlock existing personal resources which the person is not using on his own behalf.

Special opportunities for helping persons to maintain, build or unlock personal resources are likely to arise when what is happening in the group in general bears on individual circumstances, experiences or feelings (a resonance exists between the dynamics of the group and the requirements or dynamics of the individual); when two or three persons get caught up in powerful interpersonal dynamics in which each carries some special meaning for the other(s); or when one person introduces a personal problem into the group as a matter of urgency, often following some event in his or her current life outside the group.

A worker or therapist is in the best position to recognize and utilize special opportunities if he knows each person in the group well enough to be aware of those issues and themes likely to be of special importance to him or her and if he is alert to the unfolding dynamics of the group as a whole. In other words, as a basis for intervening in order to benefit individuals, the leader needs to engage continually in the essential internal work of listening, observing and conceptualizing which was discussed in detail in chapter 8. With respect to increasing one's understanding of each individual in the group, clearly one has more and more opportunity to do this as a group moves into its established phase and one sees each person participating in more and more diverse contexts. One can organize one's increasing understanding of each individual person by thinking in terms of his or her unique and specific personal frontier and the particular character of his or her preoccupying concerns. I sometimes think of the day or the moment when a person moves beyond his or her personal frontier or makes some breakthrough with respect to a preoccupying concern as a 'red-letter' day. As one gets to know group members better, one often develops an understanding of just what, were it to occur, would constitute such a day for each of them. One might think 'it will be a red-letter day for Madge when she gets into town and back on the bus without getting panicky', or 'it will be a red-letter day for Mark when he sees that it is his own sarcastic behaviour which drives people away from him', or 'it will be a red-letter day for Sally when she acknowledges how profoundly angry she has been with her mother and is not overwhelmed by guilt about it.' If one has such ideas in mind one is more likely to be alert to group situations which could potentially form the context for special experiences, more likely to recognize such moments when they occur, and more likely to see opportunities for preparatory and follow-up work.

A whole range of interventions may be introduced into a group which bear on the experiences of individuals. They include sharing a personal view or opinion, naming a theme or referring to an activity and then extending a general invitation to participate to those who have not already done so, inviting one or several specific persons to participate, 'naming the unnameable' or 'saying what is', supporting persons in acknowledging feelings, under-lining feedback, summarizing, providing information, providing information and at the same time sharing one's own feelings, advising and instructing, teaching about what constitutes useful feedback or advice, suggesting ways of asking for feedback or advice most likely to get an individual what he wants, crediting a person for new accomplishments and understandings, underlining and emphasizing an important breakthrough, and placing altern-ative meanings on events (interpreting). Which interventions will be useful depends very much on how they are made and on their timing, that is, the individual and group circumstances under which they are introduced. The next pages constitute an expansion of this paragraph, with some briefly indicated illustrations.

Some feelings and issues are so much a part of the human experience that they are likely to be important to most or even all of the members of a group. When themes emerge which bear on these, comments addressed to the group in general may well have special meaning for a number of the persons present. For example, suppose that a number of members of a group are discussing problems with low self-esteem and that one suspects that this issue is important for virtually everyone. One might say something like: 'It is interesting how so many people go on feeling that they are no good even when there is plenty of evidence to the contrary.' The intention is to encourage all members to regard a poor opinion of oneself as a problem or an assumption rather than as an unquestionable fact, and to shift from thinking 'Isn't it too bad that I am so useless' to 'I wonder why I think so badly of myself'.

To take another example, suppose that a number of parents of physically handicapped children acknowledge that they sometimes resent the care they have to give to their children and even sometimes wish to be rid of them. Others are silent, yet one considers that the issue is just as important to them as it is to those who are participating actively. One might say something like: 'It is hard to admit to such feelings and yet they are very understandable, human feelings which most people with handicapped children do experience from time to time.'

The intention here is to convey to everyone, including those who have been silent, that negative feelings towards a child can be accepted by the therapist, can be acknowledged and examined like any other feelings, and are potentially acceptable by the self.

These interventions share a personal view or opinion. The therapist or worker is musing out loud in the group and by these musings hopes to offer permission and support with respect to acknowledging feelings, or to suggest a new perspective on an issue.

Another kind of intervention which may be directed to the members in general with a few particular members in mind consists in naming a theme or an activity and extending an invitation to participate to those who have not yet done so. For example, 'I think there are some people here who haven't participated in role-playing yet. Would any of those like to come into this one?' Or, 'We've been talking about how parents treat different children differently and sometimes favour some over others. What about those who haven't spoken? Has anyone else run into this?' Or, 'John and Christine have both said how much they resented it when I said I wouldn't be able to meet with the group for the next two weeks, but no one else has said anything about it. How about it? Is it only John and Christine? How do others feel?' By such comments one is trying to open a door, to make it possible for others to participate in an activity or exercise or to share feelings which one is fairly sure are there, but which have not yet been expressed.

Musing out loud and extending general invitations to participate are low-risk interventions. Musing out loud is entirely non-insistent and does not even require a response. A general question puts some pressure on members to respond but can fairly easily be evaded if members wish to do so. If members are able to respond to such interventions useful work is likely to follow. If they are not, the comment is simply not taken up and is unlikely to interrupt the conversation or the activity or to stir up unmanageable feelings.

Sometimes one or two persons are conspicuously silent and one particularly wishes them to participate. For example, Mary, one of seven members of a single parents group was usually quite active but subsided into silence when the conversation turned to feelings of impatience with young children when they absolutely refuse to go to bed at night. The worker knew Mary to be rather obsessively concerned with a wish to be a good mother to her two young and sometimes troublesome children, and judged that she was bound to feel impatient at times but might find it difficult to acknowledge this. As no one else noticed Mary's silence or urged her to talk, the worker said, 'How about you, Mary? Does this issue ever come up for you?' Again, this is a relatively low-risk intervention. One knows from previous experience that Mary is not usually reticent. The query is framed in a way which makes it easy for Mary to decline to respond if she so chooses, yet it offers a little encouragement and/or pressure.

Sometimes one wishes not only to invite silent persons to participate but to go much further in supporting and directing them. For example, Jason was present at one of the regular morning group meetings in a detoxification centre, intended to help those who had stayed at the centre overnight to plan their day. He was silent and appeared inattentive while others discussed what they might do that day. The worker asked him directly, 'Jason, what do you intend to do today?' When he said he didn't know, the worker, who knew that he needed to look for housing for himself, suggested this. Jason agreed that he should be doing this but still seemed reluctant, and the worker told him that she would arrange for someone to accompany him to the housing office later in the day.

Occasionally one knows from an earlier episode that an issue is important to someone, yet they are not taking advantage of a current opportunity to pursue it. In chapter 9 I described a young woman, Jane, who in the course of the first session of a therapeutic group turned to another woman in the group and said 'What are *you* doing here? You're beautiful!' I argued that it was inappropriate to pursue this issue with Jane at that time but that other opportunities for doing so were bound to arise. Let us suppose that later a theme develops about self-acceptance or personal hopes for oneself. Either of these might connect with Jane's feelings. In such a context Jane might well re-introduce her earlier point and explore it. If so, she is already seeing an opportunity and using it. Suppose, however, that she remains silent. The therapist might choose to say something like: 'Jane, do you remember in our first session saying something about Barbara being beautiful, and wondering why she was in the group? What does being beautiful mean to you?' Such a comment is directed to one person yet stays within the theme. One hopes that in response to the therapist's comment, Jane will recall her earlier remark and give thought to it in the light of what others are saying about self-acceptance and personal aspirations. Even if she remains silent she is likely to do useful internal work. If she participates actively others might well help her in her explorations and a further comment from the therapist or worker might not be necessary. Or, the therapist might see an opportunity a bit later on for a further single intervention, directed at Jane or with Jane in mind. The general point is that the conductor of the group does not have to engage with Jane at length in order for her to derive benefit.

Sometimes one judges that an individual is remaining silent at a time when it is utterly essential that he express himself – that is, when a failure to express himself will lead to further suffering on his part. For example, suppose that in the course of a team game one boy loses the game for his side by failing to catch a ball. In a post-game discussion there is some grumbling from the others about losing but this lad remains silent and no one talks directly to him. One might judge it important for all to get this issue out into the open, e.g. 'No one is mentioning Jim. Remember when Jim dropped the ball? What about that?' Such an intervention goes beyond merely inviting Jim and the others to speak. It also involves what can be called 'naming the unnameable' or 'saying what is'. It may seem unkind to draw Jim's failures to his attention or to open the way for the others to criticize him, but it is more damaging still to allow Jim to suffer in silence and the group to evade their feelings. In the discussion which follows, opportunities should arise for all to consider how they feel when they make a mistake, especially when it spoils something for others, whether they can forgive and accept themselves and whether others can forgive and accept them. If there was a tendency to heap criticism on Jim, one could offer a further intervention: 'Can anyone else think of mistakes they have made? How does that feel?' This further intervention invites a more shared discussion of the issue and, one hopes, creates a context in which Jim can acknowledge the event and at the same time see that he is not unique in making mistakes, can still be acceptable to others, etc.

There are times, and this might be one of them, when it is only the therapist or worker who is prepared to 'say what is' because although everyone is aware of the situation it seems too hazardous or awkward to get into. Situations experienced as too touchy to confront arise with some frequency in some kinds of groups. Sometimes an event is dramatic in character and highly noticeable yet everyone acts as if it hadn't happened. Sometimes it is evident that everyone is clearly aware of the event, but it is also evident that they are immobilized in the face of it. Here is another example.

In a group of young adults, one of the members, Violet, had obviously been putting on weight week by week and was looking definitely bloated. During one session, in a tone of anger and bitterness, Violet related an episode in which a friend of hers had said to her 'You are really getting fat.' Violet commented to the group, 'She really hurt my feelings. Don't you think that was a cruel thing to say?' There was a silence, during which members exchanged glances, then looked at nothing. As the silence continued, the therapist said to Violet, 'Well, maybe, Violet, but you *are* getting fat. We can all see it.' Violet began to cry and said 'You shouldn't have said that.' Nevertheless she began to talk about her horror at the way she had been stuffing herself with food lately. During these few minutes in the group, Violet's fat hung in the air (so to speak) as something visible, palpable and inescapable, and yet unnameable. It appeared that no one was going to name it if the therapist did not, so the therapist did. Probably Violet would never have mentioned her friend's comment if she were not ready for gain in weight to become a topic in the group. Yet the way in which she mentioned it conveyed a double message: 'Talk about my fatness; don't talk about my fatness because it will hurt me terribly if you do.' Perhaps it was the mixed character of the message which immobilized the others. It is unlikely that Violet could have talked about her weight gain in the face of silence from the group, despite her half-wish to do so. Although she protested at the therapist's naming of the unnameable and was clearly upset, she went on to discuss her overeating and the feelings connected with it. Had the therapist not confronted the situation and been prepared to 'say what is' he would have been supporting recourse to avoidance and confirming that the event was truly unfaceable. An opportunity for benefiting Violet would have been lost and the message to the group as a whole would have been 'There are some things which are too dangerous to get into in this group.'

Sometimes an event occurs which one judges to be especially important to some one person and one wishes to make sure that he or she really registers it. One can make a comment which *underlines* the event in order to make sure that it does not slide by unnoticed. Underlining can be a useful form of intervention in a number of circumstances. One such is when a person is receiving feedback from others in the group. The therapist or worker wishes to emphasize the feedback and lend his own weight to it. For example, in an out-patient group, Harry, a middle-aged school-teacher, frequently irritated the other members of the group by talking at length and repeating the same point many times. During one session the members tried to tell Harry how they felt in response to his behaviour but, perhaps because they were concerned that they might offend or hurt him, their comments were overly cautious and indirect. In an attempt to make sure that Harry didn't miss the point the therapist said, 'Are you hearing what everyone is telling you, Harry? People are saying that they are interested in what you have to say but when you repeat yourself so many times they get irritated and lose interest.' Harry was able to say that he recognized this as a problem but was always so worried that people wouldn't understand him that he kept trying to make sure. Others assured him that they *did* understand what he was trying to say the first time he said it, and Harry said he would make an effort to say things once only. He did so, and became much better regarded in the group.

This intervention, like many others, bears on both the individual and the group. It underlines a piece of feedback for Harry, and that is what the therapist had in mind at the time, but it also names what was happening in the group, and demonstrates that feedback can be provided in ways which are both direct and non-hurtful.

Sometimes feedback can be underlined for an individual by first addressing the group in general: 'Are you saying that you often hear a condescending tone in Matthew's comments that leads you to think he doesn't have much use for you?' If one receives confirmation from the members, one could turn to Matthew: 'How about this from your point of view, Matthew? Does it make sense to you that people could feel that way?' In one sense underlining adds nothing new. In another sense it adds something that could be of critical importance to the persons concerned: it emphasizes and confirms the importance of an event. It registers for a person something which might otherwise escape his attention.

It is not unusual in the course of an extended discussion on a particular theme to find a group member referring rather wordily to some related dilemma of his own. If his participation has been very lengthy and circumlocutious one can find an opportunity to state to that person the kernel of his situation and feelings, in the style of a Rogerian reflection: 'Alison, you seem to be asking yourself how you can satisfy your own need to care for this very handicapped child whose life you have saved over and over again and at the same time not neglect your other children.' Or, 'You're really wondering how you can face placing your (senile) father in a psychiatric hospital, which you know you have to do for the sake of the family, and still manage the guilt you expect to feel.' Or, 'I guess you're really saying to us: "How *can* I stay out of trouble with the police, when I'm so angry all the time that I just hit out in all directions before I even know what I'm doing."' Such interventions offer back to a person what he himself has already said in a more concise and pointed form. One hopes that this will help him to see the crux of his problem and/or the feelings involved.

A therapist or worker sometimes has information which the members do not, which bears in some way on the group's life. Most often, the information will have to do with some outside event which impinges on the members, or some policy or procedure which the therapist knows about and the members do not. It is often appropriate to share this information, so that the members can take it into account in their thinking or behaviour. For example, a patient on a psychiatric ward attempted suicide, and was prevented from jumping from a window at the last minute by a psychiatric nurse. When a group composed of persons from the same ward next met, rumours were flying. Members told one another about what they had heard about how badly the patient had been hurt, about how he had been locked up, etc. After twenty minutes or so the therapist said:

What actually happened was that Bill asked to go into the chapel and said he wanted to pray alone. Mr Johnson went with him and waited outside. Then Mr Johnson noticed a draught from under the door and went inside immediately. Bill had the window open and was ready to jump, and Mr Johnson got him down. Bill wasn't hurt. He isn't going to be transferred, as far as I know. You haven't seen him because he's been given some sedation and he's in that little room at the end of the hall.

The discussion turned to whether Mr Johnson had a right to interfere or not and whether Bill would be glad or sorry that his attempt had been interrupted. Later the members returned to the rumours and wondered why they had been so ready to believe that Bill would be punished.

By this intervention the therapist was providing information which made it possible for the members to discuss rumours against a background of known fact. The information, however, was offered after the members had had some time in which to discuss the event. An earlier intervention would have deprived members of the opportunity to discuss the rumours, which were vehicles for their own feelings. Had the information not been provided at all, they would have had no opportunity to sort rumour from fact and see how their own feelings connected in with the rumours.

Sometimes it is appropriate not only to provide information but to share feelings. In the course of another group, also conducted on a psychiatric ward, a psychiatrist in his thirties who was a member of staff unexpectedly died of a heart attack. He was well known to everyone in the group, although as it happened he had not been working directly with any of the patients. The group therapist attended the funeral, a fact which was known to the patients. When the group next met, the patients talked about their distress about Dr Frankland's death, how they had first heard of it, how odd it seemed not to see him around the ward, and so on. Someone said to the therapist, 'You went to the funeral, didn't you?' The therapist said, 'Yes, it was very sad and hard, because we had all worked together for some time, and he was so young, and a good man. His parents were very distressed.' In this comment the therapist both shared information and let the group know how he had felt. He was acknowledging a common sense of loss and showed that he was ready to share in the feelings which were being expressed. At the same time he did not depart from his therapist's stance. That is, he did not go on at length about his personal feelings but stated them briefly and made room for the members to say more about their own reactions to this death and then to go on to talk about other experiences of loss.

Group workers and therapists are often asked for advice in groups, see opportunities for giving advice or witness group members advising one another. Persons in a group often recount their problems or circumstances and then expect a therapist or worker to provide advice and offer solutions. The kind of advice being sought makes a big difference to how one can and should respond. If a person describes his son's insolent behaviour and then asks the conductor of the group 'What should I do to make him change?' he is asking for advice which the conductor cannot provide even if he wanted to. As a response is required, it must be along the lines of 'I don't think we can see yet what it might be best to do. We'd have to understand the situation a lot more fully first.' The conductor's use of the term 'we' is of course deliberate, as one of his intentions will be to declare the problem to be one which belongs to the person concerned, although he and others are prepared to help him to sort out his feelings about it. Such a request for advice expresses an understandable wish to find a solution quickly. The response affirms that short cuts and magical solutions don't exist. In contrast, advice can sometimes be provided easily if it refers to some practical matter which others have had experience with. Requests for practical advice addressed to the conductor can often be turned to other members. For example, if a group member says 'I am way behind in paying my electricity bill. What should I do?' the therapist or worker can ask the others if anyone knows about procedures for dealing with arrears. Advice can also often be provided by members to members about interpersonal situations which involve the care and management of others, for example when someone is responsible for an elderly senile relative or is trying to toilet-train a mentally handicapped child. In such instances, advice, suggestions and the sharing of personal experiences shade into one another. If someone in the group says 'I was faced with something like that and I tried . . .' he or she is sharing an experience and leaving it open to the other person to consider whether or not such a course of action would be likely to work in his/her own case. Advice about what to *do* seems best offered in the form of sharing experiences rather than in the form of a 'Why don't you . . .' recommendation. The latter is very likely to elicit a 'yes, but . . .' response, quite understandably since the advice-giving tends to be based on the unjustifiable assumption that persons and situations are so similar that what worked for one person will also work for another. The therapist's or worker's part during such a time might well be restricted to encouraging members to share experiences (if encouragement is necessary) or to caution or instruct members about the kinds of advice likely to be useful.

Suggestions or prescriptions about what might be tried outside the group between sessions (homework) can be built into the structures of certain kinds of short-term topic or task-oriented groups. For example, suppose that a group for persons with a recently acquired handicap has engaged in a role-playing exercise and discussion on 'how I might explain my handicap to friends when I return home'. A therapist or worker might suggest, 'Do you feel ready to try this with someone outside the group?' and agree a piece of homework with the group members. It seems important to place real power in the hands of members, with respect to whether or not they actually follow suggestions or carry out homework, so that if they are unable to do so, new worries do not arise about having failed to meet the conductor's expectations.

Everything said so far about advice pertains to what a person might do in the face of some practical or interpersonal problem. Advice in the form of 'you ought (or ought not) to *feel* that way' or 'you ought (or ought not) to *think* that way' is generally unusable. 'Don't let it bother you' is a common piece of advice which rarely if ever helps. Even advice about possible action is unusable unless it is concrete enough for the person to imagine how it would work in his own circumstances. Advice which urges people to 'be more patient with him' or 'next time, avoid a quarrel' refers to an imagined state but in no way helps a person see how to get to it.

Many circumstances arise in which advice is redundant, unusable, or even harmful. It is not unusual that a person who is facing a problem already knows what course of action makes most sense or what change in attitude or feeling would be to his advantage. His problem is not that he lacks advice, since he is already giving himself good advice, but that he is unable to follow it. Advice is worse than useless, and serves only to intensify his sense of helplessness and hopelessness. Some forms of advice in effect instruct a person to feel a failure by telling him that he could easily deal with his problems if only he did something which others find it easy to do.

In managing groups and trying to help persons to help one another in groups, it may be necessary at times to adopt a teaching stance and help members to see what kinds of advice can and cannot be useful, the circumstances under which it is and is not realistic to expect advice, and how requests for advice can most usefully be framed. Interventions which teach may also be necessary to help members to see which forms of feedback are likely to be useful and usable and which forms are not (see discussion of feedback in chapter 2). Teaching need not mean being 'teachy'.

Interventions offered by a therapist or worker to a group or to a particular member of a group often involve placing meanings on events other than those currently held by the members. Instances of this which have to do with maintaining the group as a positive medium for help have already been discussed in chapters 9 and 10, where it was suggested, for example, that when most members see a problem as belonging to only one person it is possible to introduce an intervention which turns the problem into one which is shared by most. New meanings can also be offered to individuals within the group. For example, in a group for persons looking after elderly relatives at home, the discussion turned to seeking relief from constant demands for offering care. One middle-aged woman virtuously said that she never left her elderly father alone except for necessary shopping. The therapist said, 'I wonder how it is that you don't allow yourself some of the ordinary simple pleasures of life?' By such a query the therapist is showing that he sees this woman's behaviour not as virtuous devotion but as questionable self-sacrifice. He is placing a different meaning on her behaviour than she herself has been placing on it.

In an adolescent group composed of young offenders one 16-year-old boasted of his misdemeanours. He said that his parents were constantly yelling at him but that he would go on doing as he wished and pay no attention to them. The worker said, 'It almost seems that you go on doing these things *because* you know they don't like it. That would mean that they still have a lot of influence over you.' In this intervention the worker is suggesting that behaviour which the boy sees as a sign of independence could instead be seen as reactions against his parents' wishes and therefore an indication that he is not thinking for himself.

A short-term therapy group was composed of university students who initially presented themselves as having study problems. In the context of a discussion about feelings of self-worth one young man presented as evidence for his being no good the fact that he had made a mistake in playing the classical guitar during a college concert. He clung to this view in the face of assurance from others that he was really skilful, that no one had noticed the error, etc. The therapist said, 'Is it really true that one mistake can prove that you are no good, either as a guitarist or as a person?' In part, this comment underlined what was already being said by members of the group. In part, it challenged a meaning which this young man was prone to place on his own behaviour, i.e. one error = being no good.

We are of course into the issue of offering interpretations to persons in the context of a helping group. Placing meaning on behaviours is something which everyone does all the time, and indeed must do if they are to get through the day (e.g. 'That driver is taking chances; better drop behind'; 'I think I hurt his feelings'). A therapist or worker will be placing meanings on the behaviours he observes in the group more or less continually. He will keep most of these to himself, but from time to time express them to the members. The question, of course, is if, when and how to do this.

It is often possible to build up to interpretations by other forms of interventions so that members get to the point of reconsidering the meanings which they place on events and constructing new meanings for themselves. If they do not and if one sees a new meaning which if adopted would work to their advantage, one might then offer such a meaning oneself. If the person has engaged in preparatory work he will be nearly at the point of perceiving a new meaning himself, and is likely to be ready to accept and use a meaning-imputing intervention from the therapist or worker.

Several kinds of interpretations are likely to work against the therapist's or worker's intentions for the group. One of these is what Foulkes refers to as the 'plunging' interpretation, that is, a version of events so highly improbable to the hearer that he cannot make use of it. At best he is baffled and at worst he loses all confidence in the therapist or worker as being a reasonable person.

Foulkes offered the following example of a plunging interpretation:

> Another example of what I consider an unwarranted type of interpretation is the following. The patient reported that when he was about sixteen, he had one day had an intuitive feeling that his house was being burgled and he telephoned home. When he got home, he found that the house had indeed been robbed, and he thought that his telephoning must have disturbed the burglars because they had been through his own and his sister's room and had been halfway through his parents' room when they broke off. The idea that he had interrupted the burglars made him feel omnipotent. After this he made his father put bars on all the windows and was so frightened that for two weeks he slept in the parents' bedroom. His therapist interpreted: 'The burglar whom you felt you must keep out is the bad father breaking in to have intercourse with mother. You feel that he will come and kill you for omnipotently and from a distance disturbing them in their room. Later you actually sleep in their room to make sure they don't have intercourse.' (Foulkes, 1968, pp. 442–3)

A plunging interpretation need not plunge quite so far as to be unusable by the person to whom it is directed. However stated, one is trying to avoid representations of reality likely to be seen as far-fetched, implausible or ludicrous to the person concerned or else likely to generate unmanageable anxiety and chaotic inner feelings. When plunging interpretations are offered they tend to place the therapist or worker and the group member into opposing camps. The person to whom the interpretation is directed fights against accepting the interpretation, and sometimes must do so for his own protection. Rather than accomplish what he hoped for, the therapist has failed to impress his version of events on to the person and has in addition placed himself in an antagonistic position, from which it is more difficult than before to offer help.

When a person to whom an interpretation is directed regards it as far-fetched, implausible or ludicrous such a response may be regarded by the therapist as a defence erected against an utterly correct interpretation. This may be the case. However it is also possible that the therapist was wrong. The response elicited by the interpretation cannot in itself reveal whether the interpretation was correct but premature or just plain wrong.

Another form of interpretation to be avoided could be called 'relentless pursuit through the use of interpretation'. The therapist or worker offers a series of interpretations in which almost everything that is said or done, however casual it might seem to the persons concerned, is assumed to have some profound meaning. If someone in the group comments that the room is stuffy and asks to open a window, the therapist suggests that the person wishes to escape from the group, etc. etc. Not only do members find this ludicrous but individually and collectively they learn to be guarded in what they say in order to avoid further such assaults on their own view of themselves and the world. Persons can be driven into complete silence by this form of relentless pursuit through interpretation.

One also sometimes sees what could be called a double-barrelled approach to interpretations. A therapist offers a plunging interpretation. When it is followed by signs of resistance he offers a second interpretation to the effect that 'my first interpretation must have been correct or you would not have to resist it so strongly'. This places the target of the interpretation in a 'no-win' position, increases guardedness, nourishes resentment, and places the therapist in a disadvantageous position for helping group members. Foulkes offers an example of such a pair of interpretations. He refers to a group which was exploring the theme of masturbation. In this context,

A patient had admitted with great shame that she masturbated. She appeared at a subsequent session wearing scarlet nail polish and spent the early part of the session tearing a piece of paper into small bits. This was accompanied by associations concerning her revulsion at having been breast-fed (there was reason to assume that this association was induced by the analyst's attitude). The therapist interpreted to her that she felt the breast was revolting because she felt she had torn it to bits with her nails which were stained with blood. She asked him not to say things like that as they terrified her, and the therapist interpreted that she felt terrified of this torn breast which she felt as an internal persecutor of which the therapist was the representative when he made these interpretations to her. (Foulkes, 1968, p. 442)

An aura of prestige seems to surround these deep, often 'plunging' interpretations for many therapists and workers. Perhaps it goes with the assumption that groups which are 'deep' and stir up powerful feelings are somehow intrinsically better than other groups, regarded as 'superficial'. This is a myth which may lead therapists or workers into utilizing interpretations inappropriately. If one is concerned with the consequences of one's behaviour, as one should be, then interventions which generate distrust, which create an unnecessary gulf between therapist and group, which drive members into greater guardedness than they would otherwise feel the need for, and which place the therapist in the position of the members' enemy, should surely be avoided.

For some persons 'moving beyond current frontier' involves and requires breaking away from some habitually maintained disadvantageous personal solution. For such persons one hopes that a corrective emotional experience, or several related ones, will occur. That is, one hopes that the person will find, through direct here-and-now experience, that some disadvantageous pattern of behaviour, unsatisfactory interpersonal relationship or unrewarding lifestyle which functions as a solution to some underlying conflict is no longer necessary and can be discarded. This will occur, the nuclear conflict/focal conflict model says, if the underlying fears can be confronted and faced, and found to be unfounded, exaggerated or bearable.

Persons are often aware of disadvantageous patterns of behaviour or of unsatisfactory interpersonal relationships or lifestyles and want to be rid of them, but do not appreciate what is holding them so firmly in place. A young woman does not wish to be obese (disadvantageous personal solution), yet without being aware of it *must* be obese lest she be abandoned by mother (reactive fear) for being sexually successful (disturbing impulse). A middle-aged man does not wish to continue his pattern of engaging in successive disastrous relationships with highly dependent and demanding women (disadvantageous personal solution) but at some level is convinced that only such women will need him enough to tolerate him. His underlying fear of rejection by women (reactive fear) is so great that his powerful wishes for a close, intimate relationship with a woman (disturbing motive) cannot be fulfilled, or rather can be fulfilled only partially within essentially unsatisfactory relationships. A young man sees for himself that his compulsive studying (disadvantageous solution) is getting in the way of his enjoyment of life but cannot will himself to change his behaviour. A nuclear/focal conflict model suggests that although this behaviour is unwanted and disadvantageous, it is nevertheless functional and is held in place by some underlying impulse and reactive fear which are in conflict with one another.

The crux of a corrective emotional experience lies in confronting unrecognized fears so that their manageability may be tested by *current* strengths and their base in reality be tested by *current* understandings. While a person cannot experience a salient under-lying conflict involving wishes and fears in its nuclear form (he cannot actually become a small child again) he can experience it in a derived, focal form which provides an arena for the necessary exploration and testing. In a group, this is most likely to occur when the group as a whole is operating on some enabling solution (because under those conditions the boundaries for exploration are wide), when the group focal conflict resonates in some way with the individual conflict (because then the individual is most likely to experience elements of the nuclear conflict in a derived form) and when group conditions do not support individually preferred solutions.

Experience suggests that corrective emotional experiences do not occur unless quite a lot of preparatory work is undertaken which places the person in a good position to confront rather than flee from such opportunities as arise. Nor can a corrective emotional experience in itself lead to a well-established personal change. The consequences of relinquishing a previously required solution need to be tested again and again in a range of circum-stances both inside and outside the group. These further test-outs constitute necessary follow-up work.

The question arises as to how a therapist or worker can facilitate preparatory work, the corrective emotional experience itself, and follow-up work. The point has already been made that meaningful explorations of all kinds are most likely to occur when enabling solutions are in operation in the group, so attention to this aspect of the group's functioning, as already described in chapters 9 and 10 can help to generate generally facilitating conditions. However, useful preparatory work can occur within a wide range of group conditions in the course of the ebb and flow of the group's life, as members develop successive themes and explore them within the limits set by one or another kind of shared solution. Therapist behaviours which encourage active participation in a theme, underline feedback, summarize wordy contributions, extend permission to acknowledge shameful feelings, name the unnameable, etc., can all function to pave the way for critical experiences.

One needs to understand individual members well enough to recognize opportunities when they arise. Some of the 'red-letter days' mentioned earlier relate to hoped-for corrective emotional experiences. For example, when one says 'it will be a red-letter day for Sally when she acknowledges how profoundly angry she has been with her mother and is not overwhelmed by guilt about it' one is really saying that one hopes Sally will some day confront her angry feelings (disturbing motive) without experiencing guilt (reactive motive). Not explicitly stated is the fact that one would like to see this happen *so that* Sally can give up the disadvantageous personal solution of (say) depreciating herself. When one says 'it will be a red-letter day for Mark when he sees that it is his own sarcastic behaviour which drives people away from him' one is really thinking of a bit of useful preparatory work for Mark: realizing that the dislike he experiences from others, which he is likely to see as a fact of life, is in fact an understandable response to his own heretofore unrecognized behaviour. In general, one can sometimes anticipate what will constitute a corrective emotional experience or a useful bit of preparatory work. If so, one is in a better position to see and use opportunities for helping this process along.

When one sees something happen for a person which one judges is critical or could lead to something critical, one can underline the event. One's intention is to help the person to 'nail' the experience, to offer him a cognitive handle so that he can register the experience and really see that it has happened. Such events require and deserve emphasis: 'Martin, I guess you are telling us that you see that you don't have to study so hard all the time to prove that you are a worthwhile person, because you *are* a worthwhile person.' Or, 'If you've always been afraid that your mother would practically throw you out of the house if you were as successful as she is with men, it's no wonder you have been keeping yourself fat all this time.' Or, 'John, you were very angry with Eric just now, and you told him so and didn't suffer in silence. That's new for you.' As these examples suggest, it does not seem necessary always to offer a formal statement which refers to all aspects of the nuclear/focal conflict plus solution. One underlines that which is most visible to the person at the time.

In the first example, Martin's newfound ability to discard the disadvantageous solution is emphasized, together with an indirect reference to the reactive fear of being worthless. In the second example all three elements – the wish, the fear, the disadvantageous solution – are mentioned, though clearly in an informal and colloquial way. In the third illustration the therapist calls attention to the relinquishment of a disadvantageous pattern and offers credit for it. One might over a period of time build up a fuller picture of the corrective emotional experience as more aspects of it become accessible. The examples given above stay with current experience, naming the corrective emotional experience or aspects of it as it has occurred in a derived form in the group, or as insights have surfaced in the group.

Sometimes an event which the therapist recognizes as a corrective emotional experience occurs outside the group and is reported in the group. Such experiences can be underlined and credited in the same way: 'You've told us before, Mary, that you always give in to your mother when she presses food on you, even though you know she criticizes you for being fat. Last weekend, it was different?' Or, 'You went to the movies on Saturday night instead of studying? Good for you! How did *that* feel?' Or, 'You told that waitress off when she didn't give you good service? That would have been hard for you to do a little while ago. What made it possible, do you think?' Some 'breakthroughs' are in the nature of preparatory work. These too can be underlined: 'I guess you are telling us that being better-looking wouldn't solve all your problems.' Or, '*You* got yourself into that mess, and now you can see what you could have done to avoid it. That ought to help you another time.'

Sometimes one sees a breakthrough occurring without understanding how or even whether it relates to internal dynamics. One can still underline and offer credit: 'Richard, I noticed that you joined in that game and didn't mess it up. You seemed really to enjoy yourself.' Or, 'This is the first time I've heard you say that you do sometimes resent your husband for becoming ill. Up to now, knowing that it wasn't his fault has stopped you from facing that.'

Sometimes one forms the opinion that it will be difficult for someone to move forward into a corrective emotional experience or register one which has occurred unless they see connections between it and other current or past experiences. For example, if

Jack does not see that he expects everyone to reject him just as he considers his mother always did, then he will continue to maintain distance between himself and others. If Rosemary does not see that her compulsive working, to the exclusion of all else in her life, is related to repeated vain attempts to please her parents by doing as well as her older brother, then she is unlikely to see that *now* is not *then*, and that behaviour which was necessary and understandable *then* is no longer necessary *now*.

In general, each group member has accessible to him experiences in the here-and-now of the group and in the there-and-now of current life outside the group, and he has the capacity to recollect and to some degree re-experience the there-and-then of his past life. Usually the person himself will show the worker or therapist whether or not making such connections is likely to be useful or necessary. For example, in a group for mothers of mentally handicapped children:

> Jane said 'Every time my mother comes to visit I can just *hear* her thinking "What a mess this house is. I could never get her to tidy up her room at home, either. Not a bit like her sister." ' May said, 'I don't suppose your sister has an 8-year-old hyperactive mentally retarded son, either.' Jane said 'No, but that would never occur to my mother.'

Not only is this situation rich with possibilities for Jane to link current outside experience with past experiences in her family but there are indications that she wishes to do so and may need to do so in order to free herself from still-powerful feelings of resentment towards her mother and forever frustrated wishes to be as valued as her sister. If the discussion continues in this vein (which is likely since the others seem prepared to stay with Jane and in any case she is probably not the only person to experience some such feelings) the opportunities will occur for exploration and comparison. Jane might well be able to make her own connections and distinctions or others might point them out. If the conductor of the group considers that the nub of the issue is not emerging in the course of group discussion he might himself invite Jane to make connections: 'It bothers you just as much now, when she criticizes, as it did then?' Or he might see a way to help Jane to distinguish now from then: 'Jane, I can see how devastating it must have been to you when you were younger, to have your mother making these criticisms of you, but I'm wondering if it still has to be so devastating, now that you are older and wiser, and can see for yourself what your circumstances are and what's possible and what isn't?' Note that such interventions do not tell Jane how she should be feeling, but either call her attention to a connection (the first intervention) or invite her to look to the differences between then and now (the second intervention). Jane might or might not be able to use these comments. They are nevertheless worth making, in case Jane can follow them up, or in case they facilitate some internal work whose fruits will show later.

When something which can be regarded as a corrective emotional experience has occurred, or when any breakthrough beyond a previous characteristic behaviour, attitude, acknowledgment of feeling (etc.) occurs, these typically cannot become firmly established unless further follow-up work occurs. Because the new behaviour, attitude, etc. typically works to the individual's advantage, motivation to maintain it tends to be present and the person usually finds his own opportunities to practise the new behaviour both inside and outside the group. Much follow-up work occurs outside the group and indeed must do so if the change is not to be restricted to the group setting itself. A change which is situation-bound is clearly of no use to a person in the longer run. Efforts to establish new behaviours and patterns in the world outside the group are often reported in the group and credited by other members, who appreciate the courage and effort required. For example, a middle-aged man who had found it virtually impossible to be assertive with others stood up to an aggressive fellow-member without bringing retribution upon himself. This was regarded as a corrective emotional experience. In later sessions he reported a succession of outside experiences: he had taken defective merchandise back to a shop; he had defended the rights of a stranger who was being ignored by the woman behind the counter of a magazine stand; etc. Others gave him credit for his newfound assertiveness, and the conductor of the group also found an opportunity to emphasize the fact that he was exercising assertiveness in many situations outside the group just as he had done with his aggressive fellow-member.

Sometimes an opportunity arises for benefiting an individual when that person becomes a central figure in a solutional conflict. That is, one individual is the only person present who is unable to accept some norm or belief (shared solution) which everyone else is able to accept. The person is in a deviant position: he or she *cannot* go along with the emerging new solution, but typically doesn't know why. Much pressure is likely to be put on a person under such circumstances. In trying to assist the group to resolve a solutional conflict so that it can move forward and at the same time take pressure off the deviant member, one might state this as a problem for the group ('Why is it so important that Florence accepts the same view as everyone else?'). At the same time an opportunity exists to say directly to Florence, 'We can all see that you just cannot go along with the views being expressed by others. Can you say more about it?' This is a direct invitation to Florence to explore her own feelings about the issue.

Sometimes opportunities for specifically benefiting individuals arise because two persons engage with one another in a pair relationship which is important to both. The resonance occurs, not between group-level and individual dynamics but between or among the personal dynamics of two or sometimes three persons. For example, Fred makes a comment to Sally which Arthur regards as hostile. Arthur chastises Fred who defends himself by saying it was a friendly remark. Fred and Arthur enter into a special pair relationship over this issue for a period in the group. It becomes possible to pursue this episode for its potential importance to Fred and Arthur, not losing sight of the fact that the issue of what constitutes hostility could well be important for others. To take another example: in an activity group one adolescent boy accuses another of stealing from him. These two are now in a special pair relationship although the episode has importance for all members of the group. There is scope here for looking at what the episode means for the two persons concerned, how each is feeling about it and handling it and how it may relate to other life experiences. Pursuing this opportunity can benefit others besides those who are most directly involved since the issues which might be explored during such an episode (getting blamed, defending oneself, asserting oneself) are likely to be important not only to the central persons but also to others.

Some of these special pair relationships involve mutual transference. Each person stands for a significant other person in past or sometimes in current life. Exploring the feelings involved, sorting out 'which is me and which is him', trying to see where distortions and unwarranted assumptions are being brought in, reliving the painful past through representations in the bearable present, finding new strengths, are all possibilities when such critical pair relationships surface. A therapist or worker can help both of the persons involved to gain from such affect-laden episodes. He stands figuratively with an arm around each person, trying to help both to exploit the situation as fully as possible.

During the established phase of a group a person may become the focus of a group's attention in consequence of having suffered some especially trying experience during the interval since the previous session. The experience is described with a good deal of affect and the individual shows that he *must* have the time and attention of the group. When this occurs, interventions by the worker or therapist may not be required, or may be required only now and then to lend weight to what is being said. Occasionally, however, the problem is so laden with powerful feelings that the other members are immobilized in the face of it. At such times the therapist or worker becomes the person of last resort and must be the one to engage with the person over the issue.

During periods when the focus is on one or two persons, others are placed in a more passive and less central position. They may gain some advantage from being in a spectator or helping role, but the nature of the situation is such that their own concerns are not explicitly in the forefront. Therefore, one has to have a very good reason for focusing at any length on individual members: an especially acute crisis, or a special opportunity for offering help. If one pre-empts the time of others, one should pre-empt for a good reason. Many statements about personal experiences do not require an intervention from the group conductor: 'I had a really bad night last night. Couldn't sleep, and had a terrible headache.' Or, 'I realized after the last session that I was really angry at Ralph but I couldn't bring myself to say anything at the time.' Or, 'I am getting more and more upset about my son. Yesterday he . . . .'

These are all instances of initiatives taken by individuals which are far better left to members of the group to respond to. If a worker or therapist moves in quickly in response to such comments he deprives other members of opportunities to share and help, and he interrupts the associational process and therefore prevents others from bringing in further issues or of developing the first one in ways which encompass the interests of more of those present.

Another point to hold in mind is that the therapist or worker is not the only helper present, and his specific participation is by no means always necessary to help an individual to explore, to try out, to understand. As most group therapists and group workers will testify, persons in groups can display extraordinary insight, care and sensitivity. It is to everyone's advantage to allow them to do so. It is when the members cannot, or when the therapist judges it useful to emphasize, underline, introduce alternative meanings or lend the extra weight of his authority, that it is useful for him to intervene.

Avoiding doing harm

In chapter 9 on the formative phase of the group, the possibility of harm occurring through persons being exposed to experiences which overwhelm defences was emphasized. In groups which rely on open discussion this seems less likely to occur during the established phase because the members, both individually and collectively, have learnt ways of regulating participation which offer protection to members whilst at the same time pushing the boundaries of the group outward. In groups organized in terms of pre-designated topics or exercises the risk is greater because an introduced topic or exercise has a good deal of power behind it and if it has a potential for harm-doing that power may override such self-regulatory mechanisms as have developed. Thus, a particular topic could confront members with more than they can easily manage although they have managed earlier topics with no difficulty. Particular exercises may by their nature carry substantial threat. Some workers and therapists deliberately introduce certain devices (for example placing persons in the 'hot seat') *in order to* heighten threat, although it will be clear from earlier discussion that I would not myself make use of such high-risk devices, nor see the need to do so. In a way, one could say that in more highly structured groups one is faced with decisions throughout the life of the group as to whether or not the structure suits the members and is manageable and usable by them, since one is introducing new 'mini-structures' session by session. Each time, one needs to consider anew the likely consequences for the members of introducing the topic or the device. Highly structured groups which include face-saving escape hatches are less likely to do harm by this route. It is more difficult to avoid doing harm in highly structured groups which make much use of peer or worker/therapist pressure to ensure participation.

Harm may also be done to a person by allowing him to remain a central person in a restrictive solution in which he is the object of attack, either through being maintained as a scapegoat or as a displaced target for attack. The reason that this is potentially harmful is not because it is so dreadful to be attacked but because the attack has more to do with the attackers than the attacked. That is, being attacked is not a direct consequence of own behaviour, and is in that sense not rational. A less obvious form of harm, but harm nevertheless, is done to a person who is maintained in the special role of expert within a restrictive solution. While he may enjoy this role it is likely to restrict opportunites for personal benefit.

Another not-so-obvious form of harm has to do with a person becoming encapsulated within the group in a position in which he tends to be ignored or somewhat contemptuously dismissed by others. This can occur because the person has violated some standard important to the others or has displayed behaviours which other members experience as too hot to handle and which have remained unconfronted.

Harm can be done through overinterpreting or through offering premature interpretations, if an individual is exposed to more than he can handle or is driven into defensive postures.

If a therapist or worker misses opportunities to benefit persons no active harm is being done, but in another sense the person is being harmed because the group is not being fully exploited on his behalf.

Now and then one sees harm being done to the therapist or worker in consequence of dynamics arising in the group. This can occur if the therapist or worker allows himself to be persistently attacked as a figure standing for some hated person or class of persons outside the group. To be in this position temporarily is not unusual: one would say in group focal conflict terms that the members have established the restrictive solution 'avoid facing feelings about mother (or father or persons in authority) by attacking the therapist or worker'. Such a restrictive solution yields or can be helped to yield and when it is replaced by a more enabling solution members can explore their feelings in more direct terms. However, if such a restrictive solution persists, then the therapist or worker experiences an abiding sense of internal injury and hurt (and the members remain deprived of an opportunity to explore).

Sometimes a group functions in a way which harms the environment – either literally, by destructive attacks on the walls, corridors, etc., or by doing psychological harm to fellow-patients or residents (by members' regarding themselves as elitist, for example), or by behaving in ways which harm the reputation of the agency or institution within which the group is operating.

Some forms of harm-doing are outside the control of the therapist or worker when they first emerge, but none of them needs to be allowed to continue over a period of time.

Discerning and retrieving errors

The task of being alert to errors and of seeking to retrieve them continues to be important throughout the life of the group. During the established phase certain errors are not so likely to occur as before. For example the structure is not usually under threat and therefore there are fewer opportunities for errors of hanging on to a structure for too long or impatiently pushing members to operate within an inappropriate structure. However, other errors are perhaps more likely to occur. For example, there is the continuing possibility that the conductor of the group could get so intrigued with the circumstances or problems of one particular member that he could pursue this to the point of leaving the rest of the group behind. There is the possibility that he could feel disappointed when a well-functioning group resorts to a restrictive solution and moves into a period of retreat or low productivity and in consequence presses the group prematurely to resume more 'therapeutic' work. There is still the possibility of a worker getting locked into the disadvantageous and futile position of adversary of the group. This is particulary likely to occur if someone in the group violates a personally held norm or a norm which the conductor considers essential to the continuing usefulness of the group. For example, in groups composed of young offenders it occasionally happens that a theft occurs. A worker can establish himself in an antagonist position by insisting that the thief acknowledge his deed and restore the money. A group member who has stolen money is unlikely to confess it under such circumstances and the group as a whole is likely to operate on a code which forbids tale-bearing. By insisting that everything must come to a standstill until a confession is made, the worker places himself in a powerless antagonist's position in the group. The group is likely to be immobilized as long as the worker retains this position. In the end he is almost certain to have to give in because his power does not extend to forcing a confession or forcing the members to break their own code.

An error to watch out for during the established phase is colluding in some restrictive solution. I have suggested earlier that one should expect periods when a group resorts to a restrictive solution during its established phase in order to maintain the necessary level of sense of safety in the group. If the therapist is caught up in the same fears as the members he may collude with them in maintaining the solution. Sometimes a therapist or worker colludes with a restrictive solution for self-protective reasons. For example, the members of a group might adopt the restrictive solution of displacing anger which belongs to the conductor on to one of their members. The conductor may experience relief that he or she is not the target of attack and may, without realizing it, collude with the members in maintaining the solution. This is not so likely to happen if the attack is blatant and obvious, but attacks can be disguised, sometimes in the form of pseudo-help, and if this is the case errors of collusion are more likely to occur.

The errors referred to so far are errors of commission. That is, the conductor of the group actually says something or does something which works against the best interests of one or more members or of the group. In many such instances, feedback is immediately available. One sees what follows an intervention and can form a judgment about the consequences of the intervention and so decide whether it was an error or not. Providing that one actually sees and uses the feedback which is available, one can usually find ways of retrieving errors. (See the discussion about the retrieval of errors toward the end of chapter 9.)

Some errors are errors of omission. The therapist or worker misses an opportunity to make special use of some situation or fails to intervene when his active participation is essential to maintain safety or to avoid doing harm to some one person.

One is bound to miss some of the opportunities for benefiting individuals which are cast up by group events. The group moves too quickly, the import of events cannot always be registered instantly, the therapist may at times be influenced by his own worries, disconcerted by unexpected events or caught up in the dynamics of the group in a way which leads him to lose, momentarily, his conductor's stance. Both his intuition and his cognitive skills are bound to fail him from time to time. Occasional errors of omission are not so serious in a group. If an issue is important it will re-enter the group as a theme in the same or in a somewhat different form. In other words, one error of omission will not prevent further opportunities from arising. If one makes good use of post-session discussions and reviews, one has a good chance of identifying such errors of omission, and then will be alert to the next similar opportunity when it arises. Even if one does not register an error of omission the next opportunity may arise in a somewhat different guise which makes one more likely to note it as an opportunity.

Sometimes failing to intervene can do active harm, either to the group as a positive medium for help, or to individual members. For example, suppose that a catastrophic event occurs to one of the members during the interval between sessions and is reported in the group. Suppose that this is met with a silence which lengthens and lengthens, with non-verbal indications of increasing distress. One may reasonably take the view that the members are substantially affected by the event but immobilized in the face of it, and that anxiety may be escalating toward an unmanageable level. At such a time it is part of the conductor's responsibility to intervene in order to prevent the sense of safety from dropping to some level which could make it impossible for members to stay, and in order to help members to make use of the event rather than to flee from it. Sometimes an event concerning one person *must* be acknowledged by the therapist or worker to forestall it remaining in the realm of 'too dreadful to mention' or 'too hot to handle'. Under such circumstances failing to intervene is equivalent to declaring a person or an issue to be beyond the pale – beyond what is acceptable, manageable or faceable in the group.

Sometimes one sees the same errors, either of commission or of omission, repeated over and over again in a group. A run of repeated, consistent errors can have serious consequences for a group. If a therapist or worker consistently fails to grasp the same kind of opportunity, repeatedly offered, or consistently diverts the group when it approaches some theme, then the consequence is likely to be that some potentially important issue remains undeveloped and unexplored. This of course limits the usefulness of the group, perhaps in general, perhaps for particular persons. Such errors can be very difficult to detect because they may occur as an expression of the worker's or therapist's need to maintain a personal sense of safety in the face of particular situations arising in the group, and/or because feedback is typically not immediately available. Usually one can perceive such errors only by looking at a series of sessions, either on one's own or even better with the help of a colleague or consultant. Then one might notice that certain issues remain untouched which one would ordinarily expect to emerge: angry feelings towards persons in authority, for example, or sympathy towards one beleaguered person in the group. If such is the case, then one can ask oneself whether one's own behaviour is influencing the situation. Is one doing something or failing to do something which is preventing the members from facing certain issues or exploring certain themes? Once perceived, opportunities for retrieving such errors can be found: it is the difficulty in perceiving them which tends to be the problem.

Deciding on what action to take if the operation of the group generates unforeseen problems with colleagues or with one's agency or institution

Back in chapter 1 the point was made that although one does one's best during the planning stage to anticipate the impact of the group on the work environment and vice versa, new informa-tion about mutual impact sometimes becomes available only after the group is well under way. As far as anyone could possibly judge at the planning stage, the group and the environment fit together well, yet as time goes on unanticipated problems emerge. If this happens then it is both appropriate and necessary for the therapist or worker to reassess the situation (see chapter 4 for a discussion of how Lewin's force field analysis may be utilized for this purpose). Such a reassessment is likely to suggest specific action: further discussions with colleagues on matters of policy, new forms of regular communication about the group, agreements about forms of reporting to colleagues after the group closes, etc.

During the established phase of the group one is, as always, striving to maintain the group as a viable, positive medium for help while at the same time utilizing such opportunities as arise for benefiting individuals. These are not incompatible purposes. Sometimes one has to defer attention to the group in order to pursue a situation important to an individual. Sometimes one temporarily defers attention to an individual in order to maintain the viability of the group. In either case one can find ways to catch up with either the group or the individual as events follow upon events. More often than not, one can find ways to intervene in successive situations arising in the group which simultaneously maintain the group and benefit particular individuals. Often, situations which strike one initially as problems or as difficult tasks constitute opportunities for benefiting individuals directly or by benefiting them indirectly by maintaining the group as a rich, varied and supportive experience-generating environment. Some examples of situations likely to arise during the established phase are described and discussed in the next chapter.

Chapter 12

Problems, opportunities, comings and goings during the established phase

During the established phase of a group situations arise from time to time which the conductor of a group may experience as problems. Someone monopolizes, someone seems particularly vulnerable, the group as a whole seems to be in the doldrums or in retreat, someone is being left out, etc. In some groups one or more persons may leave and new persons may join the group, thus facing the conductor with the task of helping those who leave and those who enter to manage and make good use of these transitions and the group as a whole to accommodate to changes in membership. Although one would wish to avoid it if possible, now and then there must be a change in therapist or worker. Sometimes the conductor of a group becomes worried because he feels confused about what is going on, or because although he considers that he understands what is happening he does not see how to intervene usefully.

Some problems are problems only for the conductor of the group. That is, although he is worried, the situation he is worried about is not a problem for anyone else or is likely to come right and meanwhile is harming no one. Some situations which the conductor of the group experiences as problems really do threaten the survival of the group or are rendering it less useful that it could be, limiting opportunities for gain for particular persons, or even harming someone. Situations may arise which a therapist or worker ought to recognize as a problem but does not.

A problem clearly lies in the eye of the beholder. So also does an opportunity. Many of the situations which the conductor of a group recognizes as a problem are also opportunities. That is, in the course of working on or through some problem situation or some special task, benefits can accrue for particular persons or the group can be helped to become a more useful medium for help than before.

This chapter discusses a number of situations which might arise during the established phase of a group. They include: uncontrolled behaviour and unmanageable affect; behaviour on the part of the members which is intolerable to persons outside the group and which threatens the continued existence of the group; monopolizing behaviour on the part of one member; a particularly vulnerable member; scapegoating and other forms of attack on members; attacks on the conductor of the group or the conductor's colleagues; a persistently silent person; frequent absences; a silent group; crises which occur for a particular member or someone in the group's environment; members who are stereotyped by others or encapsulated in the group; collusively maintained defences; bizarre behaviour on the part of one or two members; shifts in membership (members leaving or entering the group); a change in conductors; a group regarded by the conductor as having lost its usefulness.

Uncontrolled behaviour and unmanageable affect

A period of wild and uncontrolled behaviour can occur in a group through processes of contagion. When this occurs the conductor of a group is faced with a decision as to whether to interrupt it and if so, how. In many situations the best course of action may be to allow the episode to run its course, providing that no one is being hurt or overwhelmed. Here is an example.

As part of an activity programme some young teenage boys were playing a team game outdoors in a playing field. For no reason which the worker could detect, the boys abandoned their game and began to leap and run about, shout, and throw crab apples at one another. Since there was no indication that anyone was actually leaving the field, and every indication that their aim was poor, the worker walked to the edge of the field and sat down. Eventually a couple of the boys approached him and asked why he was just sitting there. He replied amiably that he was waiting until everyone calmed down so that the game could be resumed. The boys rejoined their friends, but within a few minutes the behaviour began to drop away. The worker then rejoined the group and the game restarted.

Sometimes one does not have the option of letting the episode run its course because someone or something is being hurt. Then one has to try to interrupt the behaviour. Onc has little chance of success in such an effort when the behaviour is first building up. At that point the affect is running high and the members are likely to be very effective at feeding and refeeding the contagion. Quite soon, however, there may be some indication of a crack in the behaviour – some one person not joining in quite so enthusiastically as the others, or a slight slowing of the pace. When this happens it can be taken as an indication that if the conductor tries to break into the pattern someone from the group may offer co-operation. A useful tactic is to intervene in a mode which stands in marked contrast to the mode being used by the group. This breaks into the episode behaviourally as well as in terms of content, and has some chance of being noted by the members.

> In a group of psychotic and near-psychotic patients one of them began to talk in a headlong and intense way about his fears of the army. One or two joined in, expressing similar anger and fears, and the interaction became more and more disjointed and intense. One patient who had been silent got up and began to move towards the door, and several others looked as if they might follow. The therapist then said in a clear, loud voice, 'Stop!' He turned first to those who had been active and said, 'I want you now to stop talking' and then turned to those who had been about to leave and said, 'Just stop for a moment.' He then said to the whole group, 'We have been talking about things which are important, but we must find a different way to talk about it.'

This comment broke into the panicky atmosphere which had been developing and members were able to discuss their feelings in a more measured way.

As a guide to deciding whether or not to intervene during an episode of contaged affect one needs to take into account the current impact and likely consequences of the period of high affect. If it is pre-empting or substituting for useful work, then one might want to intervene. If it shows signs of escalating to the point where the general sense of safety is so reduced that persons begin to flee, then one will certainly wish to intervene. If the members are excited but not overwhelmed and if no one and nothing is being hurt, it may be unnecessary to intervene.

When a group has calmed down after such an episode the therapist or worker can encourage a period of reflection about it, in order that feelings experienced while the episode was going on can be recalled and commented upon. Much learning can take place during such periods. Sometimes an episode of contagion can bring a person to the point of a corrective emotional experience, by drawing him into experiencing feelings which he ordinarily avoids.

Behaviour on the part of members which is intolerable to persons outside the group and which threatens the continued existence of the group

Sometimes the behaviour of members of a group is destructive of or a nuisance to the environment. The environment strikes back, so to speak, and the continued existence of the group is thereby threatened.

> A group set up for patients in the long-stay wards of a psychiatric hospital with the purpose of improving practical skills got to the point where patients were encouraged to go to the nearby town on public transportation to do their own shopping. On one such occasion the police were phoned by a frightened woman who complained that someone was loitering in the alleyway behind her house. A patient from the group proved to be involved, and the police returned him to the hospital. The hospital administration, concerned at possible damage to the reputation of the hospital, insisted that the therapist cease his efforts with this group of patients.

An understandable reaction on the part of the therapist or worker to such an event is to feel angry at the hospital administration for failing to display an understanding attitude, or failing to recognize that when trying to build up such skills with hospitalized patients some risks must be taken. However, an angry reaction is unlikely to serve the worker's main interest, which is to keep the group viable. A possible course of action would be to revise one's plan for the group in such a way as to ensure against further episodes of the sort – perhaps by prolonging the period during which patients are accompanied, or making definite distinctions between those who are permitted and those who are not permitted to go out on their own. This requires a recognition that although the management and the therapist are both concerned to maintain the reputation of the hospital and to improve the functioning of the patients, the management is not as prepared to risk the former for the sake of the latter as is the therapist. It is also salutary to remember who has the power – in this case it is the management.

In the next example, the outside persons who were concerned were not members of the leader's own organization.

Two group workers were interested in organizing a group for adolescents who had offended and were considered to be at risk of re-offending. A civic society agreed to allow them the use of their premises on two afternoons a week, after school hours. The room being used by the group was on an upper floor and to get to it members had to pass offices in use. There was a certain amount of rowdyism and noise, about which there were grumbling complaints. Matters came to a head when some members of the group defaced the walls of the meeting room. The privilege of using the room was denied to the group.

In this case, the behaviour of the members of a group had real consequences in that they were deprived of their meeting place. There was no use in expecting the members of the civil society to 'understand' (which means condone) the behaviour of the adolescents. Rather, in such a situation it is essential to confront the group members with what is happening: their behaviour, and its consequences in the real world. It is dysfunctional to do this in a punitive way. It can best be presented to the members as a shared problem: Do we want the group to break up? If not, what can we do, both in reparation and to convince the persons concerned that the group should be allowed to continue to use the premises? If we cannot use these premises, what alternatives are open to us? A possible error here is to seek to defend the group, that is, to stand between the members and the consequences of their own behaviour. Presumably, one is interested in helping members to see that behaviour *does* have consequences. Looked at in this way the episode is a golden opportunity to explore just this. If the group is important to the members, they will come up with a suitable course of action. One might come to the view that these adolescents, like the psychiatric patients in the previous example, are incapable of controlling their behaviour. If this were so, a restructuring of the group might be in order, for example, relying more on outside activities, where the same opportunities for destructive or nuisance behaviour do not exist.

Monopolizing behaviour on the part of one person

Can one person 'monopolize' the group? This term imputes a certain motivation to persons who talk a great deal in a group, i.e. they wish to be in control of others or they are trying to gain everyone's attention. Really, the heading of this section should be 'people who talk a lot', because this describes the actual behaviour. The dynamics which are involved can be quite different under different circumstances.

In chapter 10, which included examples of how members may respond to a therapist's or worker's opening comment, I suggested that when a person talks a great deal in the very beginning of a group it may be regarded as a restrictive solution which is being supported by other members: 'If Bernard talks and exposes himself to risk, then no one else will have to.' Another restrictive solution which can involve one person talking a great deal is 'Get advice from James since the therapist is not prepared to offer it (get James to be the substitute therapist in the group).' Both these restrictive solutions could lead to one person appearing to dominate or monopolize the group. They are not unusual at the beginning. During the established phase solutions such as these tend to be less necessary to members and one is less likely to see monopolizing behaviour fulfilling these functions. In an established group the members are less likely to *need* one person to dominate in these ways, and are therefore less likely to allow any one person to hold so central a position for these reasons.

Nevertheless, persons do sometimes dominate or monopolize a group during the established phase. Sometimes such behaviour is displayed by a new member, who may need to get into a central position to feel safe or who may get out of control in consequence of the anxieties he experiences in the new situation. The following is an example.

> Stephen was attending a group for in-patients on a psychiatric ward for the first time. He was silent for the first ten minutes, but then began to speak in a rapid manner, explaining to the others that he was in the hospital only because the government had to keep the numbers up in psychiatric hospitals and had therefore required every factory in the country to supply a certain number of patients. He himself had been picked because his boss didn't like him, had always had it in for him, and so on. As Stephen went on and on, his talk became more and more disjointed and hard to follow. Others became more and more restive but no one seemed to know what to say. The therapist asked, 'What is Stephen *really* saying?'

In this case the other members of the group were confronted with delusional behaviour which no one seemed to be able to respond to. The therapist's intervention led the members to speculate that perhaps Stephen was worried about coming into a group in which he didn't know anyone and was trying to prove that there was nothing really wrong about him. Stephen himself seemed somewhat relieved to hear this explanation and the members were able to tell him that they too had felt worried when they first came, that being in the group didn't mean that a person was crazy, etc. In this case Stephen's behaviour was not based in an active wish to dominate the situation but was an expression of near-uncontrollable anxiety. The therapist's comment encouraged the members to try to penetrate the meaning of the psychotic material, which they were able to do. The members were able to find some common ground with Stephen and Stephen's anxiety abated.

Sometimes the members of a group allow one person to monopolize because they are frightened of him.

> Ralph launched into an angry monologue. No one on the ward ever paid any attention to him. The food was terrible, the beds too hard, the nurses careless and ugly, and 'you lot are the worst of all.' His voice rose and he glared at each member in turn, most of whom averted their eyes. After five minutes or so the therapist said to Ralph, 'Calm down now, Ralph,

and tell us what you are really angry about.' He was unable to do so at first but the therapist insisted, 'It must be something. You don't always shoot off in all directions like this.' Ralph finally said that he had been asked to change beds and rooms, didn't like his new room and felt really pushed around.

In this example, Ralph's outpourings proved to be an expression of acute hurt feelings, but no one knew this at the time. The therapist judged that members were understandably frightened that if anyone said anything, Ralph would turn on them (which he very likely would). This is an instance in which the therapist must take the person on since no one else is able to. Once Ralph told his story he *did* calm down and he as well as others were able to use the episode as the basis for a fruitful discussion on the theme of how it feels to be disregarded so that the interests of others can be met, and what one might do about it.

'Yes, but . . .' persons can often remain in the centre of attention for long periods and in that sense dominate the group. In this pattern of interaction one person presents a problem and the others all attempt to act as helpers. They offer advice, only to be met by 'I tried that and it didn't work' or 'Yes, but if I try that he (or she) will only ignore me (hate me more, give up on me altogether)' or 'Yes, but I forgot to tell you . . .' The central person stays central by rejecting all help whilst continuing to present himself or herself as a sufferer in need of help. The other members remain caught in the help-offering mode by their reluctance to see the person continue to suffer or to see themselves as unable to help. The episode is thoroughly unproductive. Sometimes such episodes collapse of their own weight, when members weary of being ineffectual. Sometimes the therapist might wish to intervene, for example by offering a read-out. He might say, 'Since this session started, for about half an hour, Sally has been telling us about her problem with her mother and many others have been offering suggestions, none of which seem to help. How is everyone feeling about this?' This may well be enough to break the pattern and get the patients to explore the feelings stirred up by such an episode, and the function it is serving for Sally and for the group.

A group with a particularly vulnerable member

Now and then a group includes one member who is seen as so vulnerable by the others that either no one dares to interact with the person for fear of doing damage, or other members get caught up in guilty feelings about having already done damage. Some persons who are regarded as vulnerable really are vulnerable. Some persons so regarded are not as vulnerable as other members think but are defined as vulnerable partly because of how they present themselves but largely because others maintain fantasies about their own destructive powers. Sorting out reality from fantasy is both difficult and necessary. To complicate the picture further, some persons present themselves as highly vulnerable essentially in order to cue others to respond to them in particular ways. It can be hard for others to judge just how close to the brink of disaster such a person really is. In the following example a member declared herself to be vulnerable and behaved in a way which stirred up much guilt in others. Considerable sorting out was required to make good use of the situation.

In the course of the twelfth session of an out-patient group, several members told Wendy, one of the members, that they found her constant complaints difficult to listen to, and in the end lost patience with her even though they were sympathetic at first. Wendy seemed to accept this, but just as everyone was about to leave she told the group that several years earlier she had attempted to commit suicide and felt exactly the same way now as she had then.

Wendy did not appear for the next session. Fears were expressed that perhaps she had actually committed suicide. Members were terrified that their comments had done some awful damage. The therapist encouraged discussion along the lines of 'who is responsible for what?' Much useful work was done on the issue of appropriate and inappropriate guilt, but the worries about Wendy persisted.

Wendy returned to the group for the next session and was met by a mixture of relief and anger. In the course of the discussion Wendy was able to tell the others how angry she had been at their criticism, and others told her about the discussion the previous time about guilt. In this context Wendy told the group about her earlier suicide attempt, and she and others could see the large component of vengeful anger in it.

This situation was ripe with opportunities for benefit for virtually everyone in the group. Certainly the issue of appropriate versus inappropriate guilt touched everyone, and most had personal stories to tell. When Wendy returned to the group she and others could see how a declaration of personal weakness can constitute a threat and turn the 'weak' person into a very powerful person in terms of their influence on others. Wendy herself could use the episode to gain a better understanding of her earlier suicide attempt. The therapist acknowledged afterwards to his colleagues that he too had been frightened that Wendy might actually have committed suicide, although he kept this to himself during the session. This was an instance in which the therapist's own feelings helped him to understand the powerful responses which Wendy's behaviour stirred up in others. However, he retained his therapist's stance and did not compound the members' problems by adding his anxieties to theirs.

This episode could have gone another way. If, in the second session in the series, the members had ignored Wendy's absence, the therapist would have wanted to find an opportunity to wonder out loud how it was that no one had mentioned Wendy not being there. This would be an instance of the therapist 'saying what is' in the face of evidence that no one else was prepared to do so.

In another out-patient group a person regarded as vulnerable by others was allowed to dominate the group for long periods. In the course of almost every session Ruth got into telling some story at inordinate length and with many repetitions. Although members showed signs of not liking it, no one interrupted. During the ninth session of this group:

Ruth talked non-stop for nearly ten minutes and seemed to get more frantic as time went on. The others exchanged resigned glances but said nothing. Ruth finally threw up her hands and said, 'I know I'm boring you', and subsided. The discussion then proceeded with Ruth virtually silent.

After this session three group members came to the therapist privately and appealed to him to do something about Ruth, who, they said, was spoiling the group. The therapist said that it was the kind of situation which no one person could control but that if the members were concerned they could undoubtedly find some way to deal with Ruth during the sessions themselves. All three members protested that they couldn't say anything to Ruth because she would fall to pieces. The therapist said that he was confident that they would find a way, and the members left, dissatisfied.

About ten minutes into the next session Ruth again began to talk in her non-stop way. One of the members said, 'Ruth, listen, we all want to listen to you but you go on for so long that it gets harder and harder. It's a real problem for us.' Ruth was visibly relieved and said that she knew she went on for too long but did not know how to stop herself. The therapist asked Ruth, 'How can we help you?' and Ruth said, 'Just say to me, "Stop!"' The other members found it hard to believe that such an abrupt response could be acceptable but Ruth insisted. The next time that Ruth got out of control, which was later in the same session, someone did as she requested and said, 'Stop.' Ruth said, 'Thank you' and subsided.

In this example, Ruth certainly was vulnerable in certain ways but members exaggerated her vulnerability through their own fantasies. Had the therapist co-operated with them and tried to control Ruth himself, these fantasies would have continued untested. In this group the therapist was content with the members finding a way to help Ruth to control her behaviour and did not exploit the situation further. In failing to do this, he missed an opportunity. The situation could have been explored further, by looking at how it was that members had been afraid to tell Ruth how they felt, and how it was that Ruth was unable to control her behaviour herself.

Certain general points emerge from a consideration of these situations. They include the importance of facing a situation rather than pretending that it doesn't exist, of sorting out which feelings belong to whom, and of having and displaying confidence in the ability of group members to deal with difficult situations and persons. In addition, the example concerning Ruth shows the importance of the conductor of the group not accepting responsibility for problems which properly belong to the group as a whole and which he cannot in any case deal with single-handedly.

Scapegoating and other forms of attack on one person

'Scapegoating' is a term which is often applied loosely and imprecisely to situations in which one person is attacked by others. In fact, this term refers to a dynamic and not to a form of behaviour. That is, it is an explanation, not a description. What can actually be observed is that one person is being attacked, criticized or blamed by most or all of the others. The underlying dynamic may involve scapegoating, but it may also involve displacement, or an effort to deal with a deviant member.

With respect to scapegoating, Ken Heap, in his article 'The scapegoat role in youth groups', defines the concept precisely. He goes back to the Old Testament for the origin of the term (*Leviticus*, chapter 16, verses 10 and 22) and shows that the dynamic described there can be expressed in contemporary terms: 'The group possesses feelings and wishes which it cannot bear to acknowledge within itself, and deals with the resultant conflict by ascribing these same feelings or wishes to a selected individual who is then isolated and scorned for possessing them.' (Heap, 1965, p. 215).

In group focal conflict terms, scapegoating is a restrictive solution. It protects everyone apart from the scapegoat from having to acknowledge behaviour regarded as unacceptable. Scapegoating obviously involves role-differentiation. It cannot occur unless one person accepts the position of wrongdoer and others join in on an attack. The question of whether persons select themselves into a scapegoat role or at least show a readiness to be pressed into such a role has been the subject of much discussion. This certainly can happen, as when one sees one person virtually offer himself as scapegoat, but at other times the person who comes to occupy this position is simply a little more conspicuous than others in possessing a trait or displaying a behaviour. He may even fall into the role of scapegoat by accident.

> In an adolescent group one of the boys was seen by others masturbating in the toilets. When the group assembled, the tale was told and he was the object of much ridicule and scorn. The worker asked, 'How is it that everyone is acting as if Douglas were the only person ever to masturbate?'

An intervention of this form will almost always break up an

episode of scapegoating. A therapist or worker will always wish to interfere with such an episode because the person being scapegoated can be harmed by destructive attack. Further, from the group's point of view, as long as scapegoating persists others are allowed a free 'out' from acknowledging the same feeling or behaviour in themselves. The issue cannot be discussed in terms relevant to others. It may be tempting to intervene by some direct attempt to protect the scapegoat, since he is so obviously the victim, but this tends to define him as weak and is unsatisfactory on that account. Another inadvisable intervention is to keep the scapegoat in the centre of attention by making him the target of 'help'. Under these group circumstances 'helping' simply continues the pattern of scapegoating in a disguised and devious form.

Sometimes the underlying dynamic involved when one person is being criticized or blamed involves displacement. Anger which really belongs to one person is displaced on to another, usually because the attackers then feel safer from retaliation, abandonment, or other negative consequences. In group focal conflict terms a displaced attack is a restrictive solution. Often, the real object of the anger may well be the therapist or worker. Members may feel angry at the conductor of the group for one or another reason but be unable even to acknowledge their feelings because of the high risk which they feel attaches to displaying criticism or anger. Members may fear that their hopes for personal help will be dashed by the therapist retaliating through criticism or abandonment or by his forming an unmodifiable negative opinion of them. Such fears may be more or less profound, more or less primitive. They are not unusual. It is not surprising, therefore, that there are times when the first indication that group members are angry with the conductor is an attack on someone else. The person chosen for the attack and the form it takes tends to offer a clue as to whether or not such displacement is occurring. If the person attacked displays some characteristic or behaviour similar to that of the therapist and if the overall context suggests that the members *could* be experiencing some anger towards the therapist, then it becomes plausible to assume, as an hypothesis, that displacement is occurring.

A therapist announced to a group with which he had been working for some time that he expected to go on vacation in two weeks' time and would be away for a month. No one commented on this. The next contribution was from Madge, who said that she had phoned her mother the night before and asked her to be with her when she had to go in for minor surgery the next week. Her mother had refused, saying that she was busy, that Madge did not really need her, etc. Madge had been really angry and upset. Phoebe said that *her* mother hadn't even been to visit her new baby, saying that she lived too far away, but Phoebe knew she had been into town to shop. The therapist took up each of these topics in turn with the women concerned. After a pause, several members turned to Rhoda, who had frequently been absent, saying that she would never get anywhere if she did not attend regularly. Members sought to help Rhoda but their 'help' consisted of relentless pursuit and reproach. The therapist joined in on this. After some ten minutes or so of being at the receiving end of this 'help', Rhoda began to cry. One of the members abruptly shifted his tone and asked, 'Why are we all picking on Rhoda?' The therapist followed this by saying, 'After all, I am the one who is going to be away,' and the discussion turned to how the members felt about the therapist's impending absence.

In this episode the therapist made two errors near the beginning, but then with the help of a group member retrieved the situation. The first error was failing to recognize that the complaints about mothers, although real enough, were also indirect expressions of feelings towards the therapist, who had just announced his intention to be away. The second error was to join in with helping (= attacking) Rhoda, failing to see that this *was* an attack and failing to perceive it as an instance of displaced anger. It was when one of the members named the interaction as an attack that the therapist saw what was going on and could help the group to examine their feelings towards him.

Sometimes the attack may be displaced on to someone or something not actually present, and takes on the character of metaphor:

A therapist told her group that in three weeks' time she would be leaving to take another job, and that Dr Samuels would then be working with the group. The patients asked for some details about the new job and congratulated her on being offered it. They then spent the next half-hour complaining rather bitterly about a local college which, they said, would accept almost anyone even if their marks had been very low, but then failed a large proportion of students after the first year. This was unfair, they said, because it amounted to the college administrators making promises which they had no intention of keeping. The therapist asked how they felt when people let them down. The discussion turned to various personal experiences of having been disappointed, having had promises broken, etc. After some fifteen or twenty minutes of this, the therapist said, 'In this case, I am the one letting you down; I am the one not to keep promises.' The group then discussed their feelings of anger and disappointment towards the therapist.

In this episode the therapist's first intervention sought to shift the discussion from the symbolic content of complaining about the college without immediately tying it to the here-and-now situation in the group. The second intervention brought the issue to the feelings stirred up in the patients by the therapist's announcement that she was leaving.

In both these examples one can assume that feelings of anger towards the therapist were present from the start, but that at some unrecognized level direct expression of them was felt to be dangerous. Finding another target for the anger was a convenient defence, since some of the strong feeling could be expressed without fear of consequences. In both cases, had the restrictive solution of displacing anger on to someone or something else continued, the members would have missed the benefits which could follow from direct exploration of their feelings. An added factor in the first example was that the person on to whom anger was displaced was experiencing unnecessary and increasing distress.

The members of groups typically put pressure on a person who is unwilling to support an emerging group norm (in group focal conflict terms, a shared solution). If most members are prepared to accept that everyone present has problems and one person takes an opposing view, if most agree that envy is a universal trait and that no one therefore need feel ashamed of it and one person argues against this, if most members are prepared to acknowledge resentful feelings toward a handicapped child and one person resists and is shocked by the idea, then the person who cannot accept the general view occupies a deviant position in the group. In group focal conflict terms the group is in a state of solutional conflict, where most persons are prepared to accept an emerging solution but it is prevented from becoming fully established by the stance of one person who occupies the position of deviant. Solutional conflicts can also arise when a new person enters a group and proves unable to accept some already established group solution which forms the frame for the members' interaction together.

An early study (Stock, Whitman and Lieberman, 1958), confirmed by later observations, suggests that the first response on the part of members to a person who places himself in a deviant position is to put pressure on him to conform. When the deviant fails to respond to such pressures, as is usually the case, members may shift to trying to understand how it is that he maintains his position. In the end, the deviant person often forces a shift in the group solution and thereby influences the character and development of the group.

Pressures to conform do not necessarily take the form of an attack, but can do so at times. This seems most likely to occur when the deviant behaviour violates an emerging group solution which is also a commonly held norm outside the group. When this is the case the other members and sometimes also the therapist or worker may feel that the person *deserves* to be attacked. Group members who behave destructively or insensitively towards others, or who break confidences, may be in this position. Strictly speaking, such a person is in the same position as anyone else who cannot accept a group solution, but he is less likely to be tolerated by others than is, say, a person who for personal reasons is unable to accept an emerging group solution that everyone has faults.

A group member can also become the target of attack from others in consequence of the therapist or worker showing favouritism. This is of course an error. It seems more likely to occur during the formative phase of a group than in its established phase.

Attacks on the conductor of the group or the conductor's colleagues

Sometimes the conductor of the group comes under attack from the members. Persons in groups are often clever at finding a weak spot in the therapist or group worker, and if angry, may accuse him of inexperience, lack of involvement, being too affluent and comfortable to understand the members, etc. If the point has some truth in it (e.g. the therapist or worker *is* inexperienced), the conductor may feel disconcerted and find it difficult to deal with the situation. When one is the object of attack it is useful to ask oneself such questions as 'Why?', 'Why now?', 'Besides my being inexperienced, what else is this attack about?' The members may be angry because the leader is not behaving in the way the members expect and wish him to behave (e.g. he is not offering advice), or because he is behaving in some way that they do not wish him to behave (e.g. he brought in a new member who is proving difficult to deal with). An attack can be an expression of fear. Members are afraid that things will happen in the group which are overwhelming or unmanageable and that neither they nor the conductor will be able to handle them. Their accusations that the conductor is too inexperienced or too young are in fact expressions of that fear. Members also may be afraid that the conductor of the group may reject and criticize them through not being able really to understand their circumstances or feelings. Attacks on the therapist or worker for being too old, too young, too affluent, never married or never the parent of a handicapped child (etc.) and therefore not able to understand, can both mask and be an expression of such fears. If the conductor of a group can avoid becoming defensive he may be able to think enough about the situation to form some idea about what may lie behind the attack. He can enlist the members' help in this, for example, by first offering a factual response, if one seems called for, and then enquiring as to what lies behind the question or comment. The following are examples of such attacks.

In the fifth session of a group of hospitalized patients, a patient said to the therapist, 'You look young. How many groups have you conducted?' No one had challenged the conductor on these grounds before, and as he was not a great deal older than when the group first started he naturally wondered to himself why the issue came up just then. The therapist answered factually, 'I haven't had vast experience. This is my third group. Why is this important?' The ensuing discussion made it clear that a number of the patients were at the point of making a serious commitment to the group. Their concern had to do with worries that the therapist would not be able to manage the powerful feelings which might emerge. A bit later in the discussion the therapist found an opportunity to say, 'We don't know yet what might come out or how hard it will be for us. I will do my best to see what is happening and help us to face it. It will help if we all try.'

In an established group the following occurred:

The therapist brought in a new patient, Rose. Rose was so distressed during her first session with the group that she spent a lot of time weeping and reiterating her problems, which she found hopeless. Others tried to help her, but all offers of help were rejected as unlikely to make any difference. At the next session, Rose was absent. In the course of discussing her, the patients agreed that Rose was not ready to come into a group. Someone asked the therapist on what grounds he had thought to include her, and obliquely criticized him for showing poor judgment. The therapist said, 'I can see that you are cross with me about this. Can you say more about it?'

In the first example the conductor's firm and honest reply could well have a fear-alleviating effect (at least he hopes so). In the second example the conductor *named* the anger (which was being expressed only obliquely) and then used the situation to help the members to explore their feelings, both about the new member and about him for bringing her into the group.

In a group with two workers or therapists, a situation may arise in which one comes under attack, or one is defined as good and the other as bad. As with attacks on members, different events and dynamics can account for such episodes.

One possibility is that the two conductors behave differently and present themselves differently, and thus draw different responses from the members. Perhaps one of the conductors displays cold, unsympathetic or denigrating behaviour, or shows himself or herself as less able to handle situations arising in the group. The members' behaviours and attitudes could be understandable responses to what they see and hear in the group.

Another possibility has to do with here-and-now dynamics in the group. Perhaps the two conductors are in a state of covert conflict with one another. The members become aware of this through minimal cues. If this state of affairs remains covert and unacknowledged it can influence members' behaviour in that they begin to express some of the conductors' feelings for them.

Beyond these possibilities, there are times when the actual behaviour of the conductors or the here-and-now dynamics of the group do not seem fully to account for the behaviour of the members towards the therapists or workers or their attitudes towards them. If this is the case one looks to other explanations having to do with what members bring to the group from other experiences – the assumptions they make about persons in positions of authority or of nurturance and the feelings which may be placed and projected on to them. One possibility is that members feel angry towards *both* conductors for not helping or supporting them as much or in the ways in which members consider that they can and should, but at the same time have a continuing need to rely on the therapists/workers as sources of emotional supplies. Seeing one therapist as good and the other as bad functions as a restrictive solution. By seeing one therapist as good the members maintain their hopes of nurturance. By seeing one therapist as bad they find a way to express their anger. The device of 'splitting' makes it possible for the members to avoid facing their ambivalent feelings.

Another possible explanation is that an underlying wish is present to form a special relationship with one or both therapists. This can be better managed if a special relationship does not exist between the two therapists. Without realizing it, members may be seeking to create a division between the therapists by designating one as good and the other as bad.

Sometimes one can form a judgment as to which of these explanations is the most plausible by reviewing the evidence already available in the group and in one's own feelings. Taking the least elaborated explanation first, co-therapists or co-workers who find themselves in this position should certainly review their own behaviour in the group and their own feelings about one another, to check whether either of the first two explanations might account for events. Sometimes one can form an opinion based on the content and the timing of adverse comments. There are times, however, when one cannot form an opinion about the events or dynamics which might account for such behaviour until more evidence emerges from the group. An intervention which can help to open up such a situation is a query, something like: 'How does it happen today that everyone seems to be liking me but Tom can hardly say anything without being criticized?' *Naming* a situation is a useful and sometimes sufficient first step in initiating a more direct exploration of the feelings and of the resonant experiences which may be involved. Whatever proves plausibly to account for such attacks, taking the situation as an opportunity can help members to sort out their feelings about the therapists and through this their feelings about others, usually parents. Perhaps both parents are seen as potentially nurturing but withholding, or one parent is seen as preventing the establishment of a desired relationship with the other.

It is often far easier for two co-conductors to understand a situation in which one is seen as good and the other as bad as deriving from the fantasies and needs of members than to see such perceptions as accurate reflections of differences in behaviour between the two. Acknowledging the latter might require facing unpalatable truths about how the two conductors are actually behaving in the group. This is a situation in which the therapists' or workers' needs to avoid open conflict could lead them to inappropriately locate the dynamics primarily in the members.

The members of a group sometimes criticize a colleague who is not participating in the group. Here, as in other situations, the first question to ask oneself is 'What might lie behind this criticism?' One possibility is that the members are really angry at the therapist, that is, at oneself, but do not feel it safe to make a direct attack. It is easier and safer to attack someone else, not present, who is in a similar position in the agency or institution. A possible way to respond to this is to enquire first as to the reasons for the attack, criticism or dislike. It is then possible to express what one hears in general terms, abstracting it from the original target, and after this invite the members to re-attach the feelings to where they belong. For example:

A well-established out-patient group fell to discussing their first contact with the clinic. Each had been seen initially by a member of the staff who was not the group therapist. They built up a picture of a person who was insensitive to their needs and who utterly failed to see how much they were suffering and how much they needed help. The therapist said, 'You are saying that you don't get an understanding hearing from the very person you most need help from. When else has this happened to you?' Various stories emerged. Later the therapist said, 'What about here? In what ways do *I* not hear you?' The patients were able to respond to this, and a discussion followed as to what it is and is not reasonable to expect of others.

The therapist understood from the start that the attack on his colleague stood for an attack on himself. However, he chose to allow this to remain inexplicit, and took a route other than direct interpretation to facilitate the members' discussing their feelings about him.

When an attack is made on oneself or on a colleague one might be inclined to make one of several possible errors. One might defend oneself or one's colleague, or reproach the members for unfair attack, or become so disconcerted as to become immobilized. If one considers the attack a justified one (e.g. one thinks oneself that one's colleague is insensitive) it will be harder than otherwise to use the episode constructively, but it certainly is possible. One can still say: 'From what you say, you didn't get what you had every reason to expect, from someone who is officially there as a helper. How do you feel then? What do you do?' One is interested as always to use the situation for the benefit of the members and it will not help them if one becomes defensive or reproachful or gleefully joins the attack. These various possible errors are better guarded against if one expects attack from time to time and is not surprised by it when it happens.

A persistently silent person

In a group in which one member is persistently silent, it is virtually always the case that someone else in the group will invite them to talk, enquire as to why they are silent, what they are thinking of, and the like. Pressures on a silent person to talk may occur for several reasons: sheer friendliness; a wish to reach the person and make the group situation useful to them; a fear that the person is silently passing judgments on the others; or a fantasy that the silent person really knows the answers and could help but is not doing so. When members press a silent person to talk, his or her response will reveal whether or not he or she is able to begin to participate. If the person *is* able to respond, then the problem is dealt with. If not, I believe that the pressure should be lifted. A therapist may worry that a person who remains silent is gaining nothing from the group, but this is not necessarily the case.

> A woman of about 35 was a member of a mixed-sex out-patient group. She habitually said nothing, and sat with her hands in her lap, relaxed, turned upward, staring at them or at the floor. From time to time someone in the group asked, 'How do you feel about that, Loraine?' or 'What are you thinking?' or 'What are you doing at Christmas?' To all such questions Loraine replied with a sidelong look, a shake of the head or a muttered 'nothing' or 'nothing much'. This went on for four or five months, when one day Loraine asked if the meeting time of the group could be changed, as she could no longer come on Thursdays. When asked why the time was no longer convenient she said that she had taken a job as a check-out girl in a supermarket and would have to be at work. The members agreed on a different time. Loraine subsequently told the group that for four years she had hardly left the house, keeping house and cooking for her father and brother. Her brother always brought her to group sessions and waited for her. She suddenly felt dissatisfied with this life and so sought a job. When asked how it had become possible for her to seek and hold down a job she tried to find an explanation but could not.

It remained a mystery as to just what had happened which allowed Loraine to take this new, positive step. Presumably spectator effects were at work, as nothing other than the group was any different in her life.

It is not so very unusual during the formative stage of a group for one or more members to be silent during the first session or two. This usually means that they can feel safe enough to stay in the group only if they are allowed to be spectators rather than

participants. Much more often than not, observing others participate without eliciting criticism, ridicule, etc. or without coming to
harm through overexposing themselves is sufficiently reassuring
to make it possible for such persons to begin to participate. In
groups which include rather damaged and/or withdrawn psychiatric patients, certain persons may maintain their silence for very
long periods, even throughout the life of the group. Yet they
continue to come, and sometimes one sees from their behaviour
in other contexts that they are deriving some benefit. In out-
patient groups persistent silence is less likely but it does occur
from time to time and when it does it may be linked to unusual
life circumstances. Loraine, just described, had been living for a
long time as a virtual recluse with her father and brother. In
another group, conducted as a 'get acquainted with your neighbours' group in a day centre, the following happened.

> Priscilla, who had been persistently silent for eighteen months,
> attending regularly throughout, finally revealed that for two
> years she had been ill (with a complaint which she never
> revealed) and had been looked after by her mother at home.
> The household consisted only of the two of them, and during
> all that time she saw few other persons. For some reason
> which she could not explain, she decided to try to meet others
> and had joined this group. She explained that for a long time
> she could barely manage to come to meetings and certainly
> could not bring herself to talk.

For both Loraine and Priscilla their great achievement was in
coming to the group in the first place, which clearly required great
courage. Pressing either of these women to participate actively
before they were ready to do so could, in my view, easily have
driven them away. As it was, both stayed and both gained from
the experience.
The 'problem' of the silent person is a good illustration of the
point that it is usually productive to ask oneself 'to whom is this
behaviour a problem?' Often it is not a problem to the person
concerned, who is usually doing what he can and what he needs
to do to preserve a sense of safety for himself. It might be a
problem for the therapist, who may dislike mysteries, but if it is
he can discipline himself to contain his feelings. It might be a

problem for others in the group, which if named as such can then be explored.

Frequent absences

Some groups seem unable to maintain anything like a consistent attendance. Although one expects absences from time to time in any group, continuity can be maintained if these are not too frequent. However, there are groups in which one never can predict from one session to the next who will come and indeed whether a reasonable number of persons will turn up in order for useful work to go on. The group devolves either into a fragmented group or a group with a tiny core and a fringe membership. If one is attempting to conduct the kind of group which requires continuity this is an extremely frustrating situation for the group's conductor. There are probably two principal explanations for poor attendance: either the members are personally disorganized and unable to remember agreements and hold to them or else some members of the group find the situation so threatening that they regulate their exposure to it through frequent absences. It is only by close observation of the group that a worker or therapist can judge which explanation is the more plausible. Suppose that he has good reason to suspect that it is the first explanation which accounts for absences. Disorganized persons are easily diverted or distracted from intentions or commitments by trivial events or lack of pre-planning. A minor indisposition is taken as a reason for not attending; or they have not thought ahead of time enough to have done their shopping in time, ironed a shirt, etc. Perhaps the individual simply 'forgets'. If a group is composed largely of such persons then it is unrealistic to expect consistent attendance. Group workers sometimes deal with this problem by picking people up by car and bringing them to the group. Even this is no guarantee of attendance since the individual may simply not be at home when the worker arrives. Rather than continue to expect consistent attendance, it might be better to restructure the group in such a way that continuity from one session to the next is not essential. That is, the group could be redesigned so that each session stands on its own and constitutes a unit in and of itself. If the second explanation seems the more plausible it means that individuals are utilizing absence as a personal solution. Absence is a device for diluting an otherwise too intense experience. In group focal conflict terms, frequent absences, especially where generally accepted, may function as a restrictive solution. If the therapist suspects that this is the case, then he or she might try to help the members to get at what is worrying them about the group. If the fears and dreads which require the absence can be aired and tested they may lose some of their potency and absences can be expected to become less frequent. However, another possibility is that members who are absent frequently are accurately assessing their capacity to tolerate the group. If exploration of the issue seems to confirm that this is the case, then again it might be best to restructure the group in such a way that regular attendance is not essential to the usefulness of the group.

A silent group

How long does a general silence have to go on before it is regarded as a problem? Groups establish norms about silences just as they do about other matters. What is an acceptable silence in one group is inordinately long in another, so one has to judge this matter group by group. Certainly not all silences are problems, since a general silence can have so many meanings. There are thoughtful silences, uneasy silences, defensive silences, silences which are a communion of feelings in the face of some shared disaster, tense silences, and so on. It is just as much an error to interrupt a thoughtful silence in which much good individual work may be going on as it is to allow a tense silence to build up to the point of panic. If a silence goes on for a long time and the therapist begins to wonder what kind of a silence it is, he can always ask: 'I'm not sure what kind of a silence this is. What do you think? Tense, thoughtful, comfortable, uncomfortable?' As likely as not, someone will tell him. If the silence is serving a useful function, it can be allowed to go on. If it is not, the members can be helped to explore it and move beyond it.

A group can be pushed into a defensive or a vengeful silence by the behaviour of the therapist, through overinterpretation (as discussed in the previous chapter) or by pointedly failing to respond as members wish. If a therapist or worker recognizes that he has been overinterpreting and has driven a group into silence, he can usually find a way to undo this error. One possibility is to speculate out loud to the group: 'I have been reflecting that it may be hard for you to talk because I have been making more of some of your comments than makes sense to you. Is this right?' And then, whether or not he receives a response to this comment, 'I am going to try not to do this. If you notice me doing this, please say so.' Such a comment might be enough to bring someone to break the silence. The hard part is recognizing that one has overinterpreted. Conductors who offer 'plunging' interpretations which seem implausible to members are often quite pleased with themselves and so do not find it easy to regard such an interpretation as an error.

A conductor can also drive the members into an angry, vengeful silence by unnecessary behaviour.

A number of the members of an out-patient group were discussing their respective religious backgrounds. Someone asked the therapist what his religion was. The therapist, who did not want to share this information, simply was silent. There followed a long silence in the group, then the patients resumed talking on a different topic. No mention was made of the incident. Over the next twenty or thirty minutes it became evident to the therapist that he was being treated as if he were not there.

In an in-patient group set up as a transition group for patients nearly ready for discharges, a suicide had occurred on the ward (not a member of the group). The following occurred at the next session.

The patients discussed where they had been when the suicide occurred, how they had first heard of it, etc., and freely shared their feelings, which were of considerable distress and fear, and anger at the staff for not having prevented it. Someone asked the therapist, 'How about you? How did you feel?' The therapist said, 'Well, that's not relevant to our discussion, is it?' One of the patients said, angrily, 'One rule for us and another for you.' The group then subsided into an angry silence which lasted for the remaining twenty-five minutes of the session.

In both these episodes, I consider the therapist's behaviour to have been an error. By refusing to share any information or feelings (which could have been done with judicious regard for what it is and is not appropriate to share) the therapist in the first episode shows himself to be unresponsive and perhaps uncaring. In the second episode he is likely to have violated a norm which pre-dated the group, which perhaps never emerged explicitly but which nevertheless was operative, something like: 'When disaster befalls, we are all in it together.' In effect, he was declining to share in the patients' pain, and declining to be a human person with them. It is possible (although one cannot say for certain) that he presented a picture of the cold clinician who does not really care, a posture which could stir up both anger and fear.

Crises which occur for a particular member or for someone in the group's environment

Events happen to people in their lives outside the group, and when these events are of crisis proportions they are likely to be brought into the group and make special demands on the conductor of the group and the other members, who feel great pressure to offer some form of help. For example:

> In a group of prisoners' wives, Sheila entered the group in a dejected and angry mood. She said that her husband had been denied his expected parole. She had been counting on his return, hoping that he might get a job, and feeling that she could just about manage her loneliness until then. Now all her hopes were shattered and she did not see how she could cope. All of her statements were directed toward the group worker. It was as if the others were not there.

In the face of this crisis, Sheila needed time and space to ventilate her feelings and to find a way to gather resources for dealing with her disappointed hopes. The worker was faced with wishing to respond to this need and at the same time bear in mind the six other persons sitting in the room. In this case the worker and all the members heard Sheila out. The worker, to whom Sheila's comments were specifically directed, found opportunities to acknowledge the depth of the feelings involved, but soon began to make efforts to bring others in, through non-verbal signals (facing others besides Sheila, visually scanning the group). As the force of Sheila's comments began to subside and she showed signs of relaxing, others came into the conversation, at first by offering advice. Sheila could not accept the advice, and there was some discussion as to why this was so. Attention shifted towards several others, who shared experiences in which hopes had been dashed. Towards the end of the session members asked Sheila when her husband would next be considered for parole. Sheila and others began to spell out exactly what now faced Sheila, how much longer she would have to manage without her husband, etc.

Sometimes a crisis which has occurred to one person resonates instantaneously with others, such that the group is temporarily immobilized in the face of it.

In an out-patient group one of the members reported that Brigitte would not be coming because she had just had word that her father had sustained serious injuries in a car crash and might not survive. She had gone home to be with her mother and sister. There was a silence, then a long discussion ensued about how pointless it was to read newspapers and watch the news on television, since one heard nothing but bad news. There was much agreement on this, and hardly time for the therapist to intervene. After half an hour or so, the therapist asked, 'Has anyone been thinking of Brigitte?' One of the group said, 'No!' in an emphatic tone, 'Have you?' The therapist said that he had, and when asked what he had been thinking, said that he had been wondering how Brigitte might be feeling. The others then began to discuss illness in parents. Carl told the group for the first time that his father was suffering from a brain tumour likely to be fatal, and Christine told of her mother's very serious illness a few years ago. The patients shared their fears about these events or impending events.

In this episode the news about Brigitte evidently stirred up fears which the patients were unable for a time to tolerate. They retreated to a restrictive solution which took the form of a shared belief that ignorance protects people from pain. The therapist's intervention, which seemed spontaneous to him at the time, was in fact triggered (as the tape later revealed) by a patient saying that if one never reads newspapers or magazines one also misses out on a great deal.

The person who is stereotyped by others or encapsulated in the group

One person is sometimes placed or held in a position within the group which renders the group virtually useless for him. One way in which this can happen is through stereotyping – that is, some feature of the person is accepted as a statement about the whole person, such that the wholeness and complexity of the person is lost to view and remains hidden from others and inaccessible for exploration.

> In an in-patient group one man, Don, was both older than any of the others and had more status, having been a lawyer in outside life. During a period early in the group when the members were expecting but not getting certain forms of guidance from the two therapists, they did not challenge the therapists but turned to Don for advice. He was very ready to provide it. Even when the group moved on from this stage, Don continued to occupy this 'expert' role. He spoke little, but was very ready to come in when the group asked for his advice. Apart from his readiness to be an expert, Don remained unknown in this group.

This example is an instance of an error of omission on the part of the therapist. As long as the group *needed* Don to fulfil this expert role there is some argument for not interfering. In group focal conflict terms one would say that Don co-operated in a restrictive solution which was maintained by the group as a whole. However, Don persisted with this behaviour and the others allowed him to do so. For Don, no doubt being the expert was rewarding. For the others, having Don available as expert when needed remained a restrictive-solution-in-reserve. By not inter- fering with this, the therapist allowed Don to remain insulated from the group, and there was little opportunity for him to gain from the experience. The therapist could have found an opportu- nity, most probably at a point when Don's expertness was being invoked, to invite the members to consider how it was that Don was so regarded, what the group gained from it, what Don gained from it, what they all felt about it, etc. Later, there would certainly have been opportunities to observe to the group that there must be more to Don than his expertness – how is it that we recognize only that part of Don? By failure to break into this stereotyping, Don, and most probably others as well, lost opportunities for useful work.

The likelihood of stereotyping occurring in a group can be greatly reduced if one avoids including within the group composition only *one* person who is conspicuously different from the others – in this case a noticeably older person who also had had a high-status job outside the hospital.

The encapsulation of one person can also occur in a group. By this term I mean a process whereby a group places one individual outside their concern, attention or regard. He remains physically a member of the group but is not taken seriously, not heard, not considered. He thus also remains unknown or known only partially, and insulated from experiences which fuller membership could generate from him.

> In an in-patient group, Max continually complained that he never received enough from anyone – his parents, his teachers, his employers. It emerged in conversation that he had in fact, received substantial gifts from his parents. His parents also tolerated his not seeking a job and being financially dependent on them until into his thirties. The others considered Max a spoiled brat, and said so. Max in his turn told the others that the group meant nothing to him and could not help him.

In this case, as in the preceding one, an error of omission occurred on the part of the therapist. As long as Max remained outside the group in this way (even though he continued to attend) the group could be of little use to him. There must have been opportunities in the course of this group to invite explorations of how both Max and the others felt. One can speculate that the others felt envious as well as disdainful, or that Max was able to express forms of greed which others experienced but could not acknowledge. Since Max remained encapsulated within the group the opportunity never arose for other members to confront feelings of envy or greed or for Max to face how it was that nothing which he actually received ever felt like enough.

It is possible that the therapist was unable to help the group to break up this encapsulation because he too shared the members' feeling that Max did not deserve the group's attention. This would be an instance of the therapist colluding inappropriately with the members in maintaining a restrictive solution. As long as Max was regarded as a non-person (restrictive solution) no one need face their own envy or greed.

Bizarre behaviour on the part of one or two members

Several examples have already been provided of psychotic behaviour or delusional material breaking out in the group. This must occur through some combination of internal pressure and pressures deriving from group forces. The fact that verbal and other behaviour can be brought into interpersonal situations 'inappropriately' (that is, without reference to what is actually happening between or among persons) is well understood. Sometimes one can see that a prevailing group theme is the context and trigger for such behaviour. For example, delusional material about the police, the army, etc. can surface under group conditions in which there is a shared fear of being influenced and controlled or, conversely, of losing control. When this is the case, the other members are in a good position to understand the import of delusional material because, although they do not share in the delusion themselves, they share in the underlying affect which has triggered the emergence of the delusion at that particular time. Thus, an intervention such as 'What is Tom really trying to say?' or 'Bill, let's you and everybody try to understand what you are feeling when you talk about the army in this way' suggests to members that there is sense in the delusional material and encourages them to try to find it. Members of groups often display remarkable sensitivity under such circumstances. If they succeed in perceiving the import of the delusional material they accomplish something both for themselves and for the person who produces the bizarre content: they reseal the group in the face of a threat to its integrity by finding ways to relate 'crazy' talk to here-and-now dynamics, they communicate to the person concerned that he can be understood and they help him to get to the feelings which are being expressed through the delusion. Members cannot always manage this, and it is clearly more difficult when the material doesn't link to the group or links so tenuously or indirectly that connections are hard to see.

Not all internal pressures and preoccupations emerge in a visible form. For example, a patient who had been atypically silent for most of a session came up to the therapist after a session and asked, 'Do you think that they know my secret?' The therapist did not know that the patient *had* a secret and did not think it realistic to assume that the secret had already been penetrated by others, but it was clear that fears of exposure so preoccupied this man that he was immobilized within the group. It could well be that shared fears about self-exposure exacerbated his own fears and triggered this reaction.

What counts as 'bizarre' behaviour is a matter of opinion. It can only be defined in terms of norms about what is ordinary, 'normal' behaviour and what is not, either in general or in the context of a given group. The following episode occurred in a time-limited group intended to help professionals to perceive their own behaviour and its impact on others. Earlier in this group one of the members, Phil, had told the others about his powerful reluctance to be assertive with colleagues and others, but the point had not been developed. Well into the established phase of this group,

> Sam suddenly got up from his chair, knocking it over as he did so. He approached Phil and asked him to stand up. Phil somewhat uncertainly did so. Sam silently engaged Phil in a wrestling match. It seemed to start as a game, but it soon became evident that each was struggling as hard as he could and that Phil seemed to be getting more and more angry although Sam seemed to remain cool. After some five minutes of this, during which no one interrupted, Sam suddenly broke off and the two men returned to their chairs.

Following this episode, which certainly struck everyone as bizarre at the time, the feelings of all concerned were thoroughly discussed. Sam could not explain why he behaved as he did: he said he just suddenly felt like it. Those who were spectators, including the conductor of the group, felt frightened and immobilized. Phil said that he took it as a joke at first, but then became more and more angry and really wanted to hurt Sam. He added that although he knew he wanted to hurt Sam he also knew that he would not: 'I found out that no matter how angry I get I still will not lose control.' Phil then told the group about a terrible experience he had had when he was 18 years old. He got into a fight with an acquaintance and knocked him over. In falling, this lad hit his head on a sharp edge of concrete and died almost instantly. Phil still experienced almost unbearable guilt and pain over this. He never again dared to fight with anyone, or even quarrel, for fear of damaging someone again. He described almost suicidal excursions on his motorcycle, often in the middle of the night on deserted roads. The conductor of the group understood this behaviour to be a device for releasing powerful feelings and perhaps inviting disaster and punishment. The episode in the group constituted a corrective emotional experience for Phil. If one assumes an internal conflict something like 'angry feelings versus fear of own destructive power', with a long-standing personal solution of avoiding all situations involving assertiveness, then the challenge from Sam and the ensuing events and experiences constituted a demonstration to Phil that however angry he became, he would not lose control and would not actually harm anyone. As often happens, after this episode Phil found many opportunities both inside and outside the group to follow through on this experience. For example, outside the group he joined informal play with a frisbee (popular at the time) and took pride in both his aggressiveness and his capacity for control. He also, for the first time, engaged in rough-and-tumble play with his young son.

In the aftermath of this episode the issue of assertiveness, anger and self-control became a theme for the group as a whole. For a time, the group became an arena for exploring these feelings, which were, as one would expect, important for others besides Phil, although no one else had so dramatic or tragic a story to tell.

An interesting side issue is how it is that Sam initiated wrestling in the group and in particular how he came to choose Phil. Physical challenges were far outside the norms of this group. The conductor of the group saw Sam as a rather brittle personality and was somewhat concerned as to whether he could hold together under the pressures of the group. Sam had displayed bizarre behaviour before, both inside the group and as members were dispersing after a session. It seemed almost uncanny that he had chosen Phil as the person to engage with, although there had been the earlier clue (hardly registered by most) about Phil's inability to be assertive. Sam himself could not explain his behaviour. It appeared to be a case of 'the unconscious talking to the unconscious'.

Persons displaying bizarre behaviour in a group sometimes frighten themselves. At the least they feel they have behaved atypically or at a more profound level are deeply disturbed by what has emerged and by a sense of being out of control. At the same time other members may react with fear and immobilization. The conductor's task is a multiple one: to preserve the group; help the members to contain, make sense of and accept the person displaying the behaviour, if he can; and help the person displaying the behaviour to resolve his fears and to connect in with and maintain a place in the group. Episodes involving bizarre behaviour, although usually difficult for all, can often be utilized positively in the end.

Shifts in membership: comings and goings of group members

In the course of the established phase of a group, particularly if it is long-term and open-ended, changes in membership are likely to occur from time to time. One or more of the original members leave and new persons are brought in. In short-term groups persons may also leave, although in such groups new persons may or may not join.

Members leave groups because they have gained enough from the experience to operate without it (i.e. they are ready to leave) or because their personal circumstances have changed (e.g. they move away or are discharged from the hospital or institution) or because leaving the group is the only way they can find to face unmanageable threat (i.e. they are afraid to stay) or because the group has failed to connect with their own understanding of what they need or want (i.e. they see no point in it). If a person leaves a group for this last reason, it is likely to be early in the life of the group. Dropping-out as a self-protective measure is also more likely to occur earlier if it is to occur at all, although persons do sometimes drop out of established groups under exceptional circumstances. For the most part, a member who leaves during the established phase is probably doing so for one or the other of the first two reasons.

If someone declares an intention to leave, the therapist or worker should ensure that an opportunity is made for him to say more about it. If he can share his feelings and thinking then this and the responses he receives from others should help him as well as other members to understand better what is involved in his wish to leave. If he is ready to leave, this will become clearer. If his impulse to leave results from fear or in an expression of anger then an exploration of his feelings could well help him to face his fears or acknowledge his anger and make it possible for him to remain in the group.

When it becomes clear that a person is going to leave, it is a good idea to fix a departure date two or three sessions at least into the future, if the planned-for duration of the group allows for this. The reasons, which are twofold, can be stated explicitly in the group. First, it is usually useful for the person who is leaving to have enough time to think through what leaving actually means to him and to use the remaining time to bring out any issues which are important to him but have not yet emerged. Second, it is helpful to those who remain to think out what the loss of the departing person means to them. Such an explanation usually makes sense to the members of a group.

Sometimes it is not possible to arrange a period of time for discussion and reflection, for example if a person leaves without announcing his intentions or if he refuses to set his actual departure date a little in the future. The group members who remain are left with feelings, assumptions and fantasies associated with the abrupt loss of one of their members. Feelings can be particularly acute if the person leaves in anger or despair or with complaints that the group has not helped him or that members don't care about him. It is then the conductor's task to make sure that the remaining members of the group have an opportunity to express and explore their reactions. This is important both for the survival of the group and also because the loss of a group member can have special meanings for certain persons in the group and resonate with other life experiences.

If several persons leave a group at about the same time the question may arise as to whether this is an opportune time for the group as a whole to terminate or whether new members should be brought in. For some groups the therapist or worker should reserve this decision for himself but in others it is an issue which can be discussed with the group as a whole. If an agreement is made to close the group a termination date should be set for some little time in the future, to take advantage of opportunities arising during the termination phase (see chapter 13). If a decision is made to add new members and continue, a further decision needs to be made as to who shall decide which particular persons should be invited into the group. In some circumstances the conductor will wish to make this decision himself, and in that case will announce his intention to the group, leaving plenty of time for the members to express their feelings and opinions about having one or several new persons join the group. In other circumstances the conductor may decide to share the decision-making with the group, and therefore will open up the issue for discussion. The outcome might be that all agree that the decision should be left to the conductor, or that the members reach a general agreement about the numbers and kinds of persons to be brought in but place specific decisions in the hands of the conductor, or that the members decide to invite certain specified persons to join the group. Any of these routes towards bringing in new persons could be appropriate, depending on such factors as who in the group (the conductor only or the conductor plus all members) has information about a pool of potential new members, the conductor's judgment about the members' capacity to make such judgments, and so on.

However the decision is made, the group will soon be confronted with having to take in and accommodate a new member (or several) and the new member will soon be faced with having to find a place in a new environment which has a history in which he has played no part. The entry of a new member is unlikely to disturb a group in which little cohesiveness has developed and boundaries have been permeable all along. In some instances the group will have been structured so that each session stands on its own. Continuity is not a feature of the group and each session has had a somewhat different membership. Members of such groups hardly notice comings and goings. In other groups, however, more cohesive and with a steadier membership, the departure of a member and the entry of someone new is a significant event for all.

In a relatively cohesive group members will have established certain norms and expectations which guide their activities and form a context for their work. In group focal conflict terms the group has lived through a history which has included a sequence of restrictive and enabling solutions, erected in response to shared concerns arising from within the membership or in the environment. All will recall certain past critical events and may understand current experiences in terms of them. Members know what they can and cannot expect of the conductor of the group. A new person entering a group knows nothing of this, and typically there is no way of telling him because norms and expectations are so often implicit and the significance of some bit of past history may become evident only in the course of events. A colleague (Murray Horwitz) once likened joining a new group to entering a completely dark room where one knows that there are various bits of furniture, some with sharp corners, but one does not know where they are. One also knows that there is a light switch but doesn't know how to find it. The only way one finds one's way in this new setting is by stumbling against obstacles and quite possibly getting hurt in the process. The new person in the group is in this position. Like anyone else entering a new group he will seek to find a place in it that is comfortable for him. The attempts he makes may or may not fit in with the way of operating which the group has already established.

If, as could easily happen, the behaviour of a new member challenges existing norms, then he is in a deviant position and the others in the group are likely to try to get him to shift his behaviour or views. If such attempts fail, the behaviour of the new member may well force the group to rethink and revise their way of operating.

A new member of a group is an unknown quantity to the others. He can become a figure on to whom all sorts of fantasies are projected: 'Here is someone who will know all the answers', 'Here is someone who will dislike and despise us', etc. Sometimes, simply by virtue of his being a newcomer who has been brought in by the therapist or worker the entering member is cast by the others into the role of unasked-for sibling. Compounding this, on occasion, is the possibility that the new person actually displays traits and characteristics which make it easy if not inevitable that an existing member of the group establishes a significant pair relationship with him or her. In a long-term open-ended group of young adults, for example:

Martin, a new person brought into the group by the therapist, quickly displayed himself as a highly verbal, intelligent and intellectualizing person. He participated actively in the group. While everyone was faced with finding a place for Martin in the group, this task was particularly difficult for Jean, who (it later emerged) immediately experienced Martin as being like her younger brother, always regarded as the great success in the family. Jean, who had been quite active previously, subsided into an atypical silence which persisted over three or four sessions. She firmly failed to respond to invitations to speak during this period, and though she did not display visible signs of upset, was utterly clear that she had nothing whatever to say.

Jean responded with bland friendliness to all attempts to bring her back into active participation. The therapist could only wait and hope that internal work and spectator effects would eventually make it possible for her to share her feelings in the group. She did this in the fourth session following Martin's entry, when she expressed her intense dislike of some of Martin's behaviour and her resentment of the therapist for bringing Martin into the group and thus spoiling the experience for her. Once this emerged the feelings of all concerned could be examined. This event developed into a corrective emotional experience for Jean, who was able for the first time to experience and find that she could tolerate her intense feelings of anger and resentment towards her parents for bringing an unwanted sibling into the family in the first place, and then preferring him over her.

A change in conductors

It is sometimes the case that it is the therapist or group worker who must leave the group. This should be avoided if at all possible but sometimes a worker or therapist becomes ill, gets a new job, has to move to a different city, etc. To help members face such an event and gain maximally from it they need adequate notice. When it is the conductor of the group who leaves, intense feelings may be stirred up concerning abandonment, being let down, etc. Fear, anger, resentment, envy may all be involved, and for some members the loss of the therapist or worker may resonate with painful and still-unresolved life experiences. A period of notice provides an opportunity to acknowledge, face and explore such feelings and their possible special significance for particular persons.

A therapist or worker who takes over a group when a previous leader has left is faced with the same situation as is a new member. Further, because of the special position which he occupies in the group, he is likely to be the target of a whole range of hopes and fears. For example, the members may have unrealistic hopes of him, expecting that he will be able to accomplish what the previous therapist has not. Or, they may feel angry with him for not being the person they have lost. Or, fears may re-emerge similar to those they may have experienced at the beginning of the group with their original therapist or worker, of being abandoned or rejected or found in some way unacceptable or unlovable. They may test the worker in various ways in an attempt to reassure themselves that he is strong enough and competent enough to manage the difficult situations which could still arise. The members' sense of safety may be challenged or shaken, and work needs to be done to re-establish it. As is often the case during the formative stage of the group, concerns may emerge at first in indirect or symbolic terms. As advised earlier, the best course of action may be simply to allow the members time in which their own interaction can lead to confronting and resolving fears, or to work within such metaphors as the members may erect, or to find ways to alleviate underlying fears. (See chapter 9, section on working toward the establishment of enabling rather than restrictive solutions, and examples in chapter 10.)

A group which the therapist or worker considers has lost its usefulness

Now and then a worker or therapist comes to feel that a group with which he or she has been working has become stagnant and lost its point and usefulness. The view 'this group is no longer useful' is a kind of portmanteau: it contains within it a statement about the group and an expression of one's own feelings, all mixed together. To get a purchase on the situation one needs to sort out what is observable fact and what are feelings. A therapist or worker can do this by asking himself the following questions:

'What are my feelings?' 'How are the members actually behaving?' 'How do I think the members feel?' 'How am I behaving in this group?' Answering these questions for oneself sorts out feelings from behaviour and self from others. If the answer to the first question includes 'bored, disappointed' then the conductor is unlikely to be doing his best work on behalf of the members, and his first task is to acknowledge and attempt to deal with his own feelings.

I have known of therapists or workers in this position who continued to work with their groups in the face of such feelings, or else found a reason to transfer the group to someone else. Some such groups become interminable and are passed successively to four or five different workers, usually on the grounds that the group will provide a useful learning experience for a student or an inexperienced worker. Each new conductor then becomes bored or disheartened in his turn. If instead of passing the group along to someone else one confronts one's own feelings, one might find that one had unrealistic expectations of the group and is now disappointed because the group has not developed as one hoped, or has not been the exciting experience one had anticipated. Sometimes such self-acknowledgment can restore interest in the group, since one comes to a different understanding of the frontiers of the members and the kind of group experience which is suitable. Sometimes such an exercise reveals that the group has maintained itself on some plateau for a longish period, which has led to a sense of boredom in the therapist. If the plateau can be conceptualized as the operation of some restrictive solution, then new possibilities for intervening might suggest themselves.

Sometimes internal reflections on the basis of available evidence are not enough. Further information is required which only the members can provide. It is open to the worker or therapist to initiate a review of the group, whether or not this has been built into the structure. One can easily say, 'I have been thinking that it could be useful for us to tell one another how we think the group has been going and how we feel about it.' The discussion which follows should provide new information for all. If the members challenge the conductor to express his own opinions he can find ways to do so non-punitively, for example by saying something like: 'I have been thinking lately that we do spend a lot of time going over the same ground' or 'I have been concerned lately that we have fallen into a routine and wonder if others have been feeling the same.' (Of course a worker or therapist will not be able to make such comments non-punitively if he is still harbouring unacknowledged feelings of resentment or disappointment, hence the importance of acknowledging own feelings first and trying to establish a sympathetic internal stance toward the group.)

Invitations to share feelings about the group can lead to new information being made available to all. For example one might find that the members too are bored and dissatisfied but continue to come out of a sense of duty to one another and to the worker. Or, the members may have sensed the worker's feelings and are now relieved (although also possibly angry, resentful, etc.) to have an opportunity to talk about them. Or, through hearing the members say what they value about the group the conductor might see the contributions which it is making to members and find it possible to recommit himself to the group. Sometimes such discussions lead all concerned to see the appropriateness of restructuring the group, or closing it. If after such explorations the members still wish to continue and the conductor continues to find his involvement with the group essentially unrewarding to the point that he cannot expect to function well on the members' behalf, then he must find a way to stop working with the group. This may well involve turning the group over to someone else, which was his impulse in the first place, but one hopes that through the explorations which have taken place he can do this in a non-injurious way and not simply as an expression of unacknowledged personal flight.

Many of the situations described in this chapter, which the conductor may experience at first as problems or as special tasks, constitute opportunities for individuals to engage in useful work. I have argued that special opportunities for personal gain are likely to occur under conditions of 'resonance', that is, when group-level or interpersonal events connect with and bring into focus important personal issues, feelings and concerns for particular persons. Group-level and interpersonal events can connect with personal feelings and concerns in a variety of ways. One such is when a theme important to an individual emerges as a theme for the group as a whole, under an enabling solution which allows for wide exploration. This can form a general context for significant personal experiences in that group forces and phenomena support personal explorations and confrontations.

Another form of resonance can occur when a group is in a state of solutional conflict and the person occupying the deviant position is encouraged to examine how it is that he cannot accept an emerging group solution. This often leads to an examination of the function which a preferred personal solution fulfils for a person, and/or its origin in that person's family history. Sometimes group conditions are such that an individual is not allowed to maintain a personal solution (as when a person habitually contains feelings of depression by maintaining himself as an expert and the group dynamics do not allow him to do this). Then, a necessary personal solution cannot operate in the group and underlying impulses and fears are likely to emerge. This is somewhat risky for the person concerned, since he may be compelled to confront feelings before he is ready to do so. However if the group has developed a base of enabling solutions which offer support and lend courage, this will help a person to confront difficult feelings even if feelings of threat increase. Another route towards significant personal experiences is the emergence of significant pair relationships in the group, where one person stands for a significant other or a significant class of others. Resonances are sometimes triggered by unpredictable events which are outside the control of anyone in the group (see previous examples: the accident to Brigitte's father; the fact that Martin, a new member, happened to be rather like Jean's brother; a near-suicide on the ward; Sam's unexpected behaviour in challenging Phil).

The conductor of a group, by his or her behaviour, can increase or reduce the likelihood of such resonances occurring, and can recognize and exploit or fail to recognize and exploit them when they occur.

I have tried to emphasize, in the examples provided in this chapter and in the more general discussion in the previous chapter, that a therapist or worker can often capitalize on what is happening in the group for the benefit of individuals by straightforward and brief comments or queries which are part of the conversational or associative flow. Such comments and questions sometimes although not always offer alternative meanings for events, but they rarely need to involve elaborate interpretations. Under many group conditions the members themselves can and will do much of the work of helping one another, and at such times the participation of the worker or therapist may add little. However, the worker or therapist is the person of last resort in the group, the back-up person, the person whose courage does not fail, and this means that there will be times when it is the conductor of the group who must confront, take on a difficult situation, or be the one to 'say what is' in the group. Circumstances are likely to arise from time to time which require the conductor to engage with one person or with several persons for more extended periods of time.

Going back a bit further in this series of chapters (to chapters 9 and 10) it will be seen that the conductor's task is not only to take advantage of special opportunities for benefiting persons but also to work towards establishing group conditions under which especially rich opportunities are likely to occur. Going back still further (to chapter 8) I have emphasized the importance of the conductor trying to keep in touch with and maintain an ongoing understanding of events in the group, as a basis for offering interventions (or deciding to remain silent). Maintaining a dialogue with oneself as the group goes along is an essential prerequisite and accompaniment to making useful rather than pointless, redundant or ill-timed interventions in groups.

Suggested exercises

Problem clinics: very good learning can be achieved through discussions held by a small group of colleagues, all of whom are engaged in working with groups, which focus on a succession of problem situations or special tasks faced by one of them. Starting from the problem as the therapist or worker is first inclined to state it, such a working group can help the person concerned to factor out who feels what and who does what in the situation. Problems are typically stated at first in ways which mix up who is feeling and doing what. This exercise helps to clarify a situation by asking and getting answers to four key questions: 'How do I (the conductor) feel?' 'What do I do?' 'What do they (he, she) do?' and 'What do I think that they (he, she) feel(s)?' From such a factoring out one can usually come to see more clearly the nature of the problem, for whom it is a problem, and possible courses of action in the face of it. This exercise cannot be done through simulation, but has to be based on real situations in all their complexity. As an exercise it will only work if the members of the colleague group can form themselves into an effective working group in which members feel safe, and above all if they can avoid falling into 'Why don't you . . .' 'Yes, but' forms of interaction. The object of the exercise is to help a person who is facing a situation which feels to him or her to be a problem to understand it more clearly and fully so that he/she can arrive at some course of action which seems right. This exercise can be undertaken on one's own but one loses the benefit of differing perspectives on a situation.

Tape listening: as before, listening to tapes, especially in a group of colleagues, is bound to be a good learning opportunity. A tape can be stopped at intervals to allow for discussions about what is going on and to give each person time first to formulate a possible intervention and then to compare ideas about what if anything the conductor might say or do in the circumstances displayed by the tape.

Chapter 13

Terminating a group and the termination phase: special opportunities

The termination phase of a group is that period towards the end of its life when the therapist or worker and all the members know that the group will cease meeting in the near future on a specified date.

In a group which has been planned in the first place as a time-limited group, the termination date is known right from the start, and the termination phase can be said to begin when the conductor of the group (or someone else) reminds the group that only a certain amount of time remains before the group is due to close. In a group which has been planned to go on indefinitely, with new members brought in as persons leave, there may be no termination phase at all because the group is characterized by a slow shift in membership. On the other hand such groups do sometimes terminate, usually because a number of persons are ready to leave at about the same time, and a mutual agreement is then made that the time has come for the whole group to disband. Some groups which come to end cannot be said to have a termination phase in a psychological sense. Although a forthcoming closing date has been announced the members have not (and sometimes cannot be expected to have) invested in the group in such ways that the group's forthcoming end touches them personally.

When a group has been planned from the start to be time-limited, everyone 'knows' from the beginning that the group will have a life of, say, twelve sessions, or two years, or five sessions, or whatever. In longer-term groups, especially, this information tends to be lost to sight during the period of the members' struggle to establish themselves as a group and during much of the group's established phase. Members need to be reminded toward the end of the series that the group is soon to end so that the anticipation of termination can become an active force influencing the manner in which members participate in and make use of the group during this final period of its life. At what point such a reminder might be introduced depends on the planned duration of the group. If a group has been planned to meet for only four or five times it is sufficient to remind the group about termination at the next to the last session. If a group has been planned to meet for twenty sessions or so then one would wish to remind the group that it is about to terminate three or four sessions before the end. If a group has been planned to be a much longer-term group, for example, two years, then one would wish to remind the group that the group will soon end several months ahead of time.

When no specific end-point has been set or agreed at the start, the possibility of terminating usually comes up when three or four persons declare a wish or intention to leave the group at about the same time. Terminating is of course only one of several possibilities. If several persons declare themselves ready to leave it does not necessarily follow that it is in their best interests to leave nor if they do that the group must necessarily close. However, terminating the group is one of several options which may be considered (see chapter 12). Let us suppose that after careful explorations the members and the conductor of the group agree that not only are certain persons ready to leave but that it is appropriate to close the group for everyone. Once such a decision is made it is best to avoid too abrupt an ending, but to agree on a finishing date which is some little time in the future. As this route towards termination is likely to occur in longer-term groups, one would probably wish to aim for a half-dozen or so further sessions before actually terminating or a greater number of further sessions in really long-term groups.

Whatever the route toward termination, a definite termination period is indicated in order to provide time for members to make constructive use of the special opportunities attached to the termination phase, if they can. Special features of the termination phase include a 'time is running out' phenomenon, experiences of separation and mourning, and opportunities for self-assessment, stock-taking, and planning for the future.

'Time is running out'

It is not unusual for persons in a group to delay certain forms of risk-taking out of a sense that there will be time later to go into certain matters and therefore no particular need to explore a potentially painful or difficult issue just yet. Such postponements can go on for quite a long time, delaying the point at which a person engages in certain kinds of useful explorations or activities or allows himself to confront certain feelings. When persons know that the group will end in the relatively near future they become acutely aware that a limited and finite period of time is still available to them actually to make use of the group situation. If they are to examine certain issues they must do so soon. Under these situational pressures the wish to make use of the group for personal help whilst the group is still available can begin to outweigh the fears or worries that may be attached to confronting painful feelings or issues. On the other hand, some persons may experience such acute anticipatory fear that without realizing it they do their best to 'wait it out' and to resist pressures arising from a sense of time running out. In either case it is part of the conductor's task to facilitate use of this final phase to help members, in so far as possible, to deal with unfinished business. A worker or therapist who has come to know group members well over a period of time can often make good guesses as to what unfinished business consists of, in individual cases. He is then in a good position to be alert to last-minute surfacings.

Experiences of separation and mourning

Terminating means finishing, stopping, separating, leaving. If the group and persons in it have become important, if there has been substantial personal investment in the experience, then individuals may be faced with acute feelings of separation and loss. All concerned need opportunity and time to experience the impending loss and to think through and talk through what the separation will mean to them. They need to anticipate the ways in which they will feel distressed and the ways in which they will feel pleased or relieved; the things they will miss most and the things they will not miss at all; how they think others will feel when they themselves are no longer available to them; etc.

For virtually every adult the experience of separating from the group will be the most recent of a number of separation experiences. Losing the group (or specific members) may stand for earlier separations and become a vehicle for re-experiencing them.

When feelings associated with earlier separations have not been confronted or resolved, the termination phase of the group offers special opportunities to recapture those feelings and work on them and through them. Thus for some persons in a group significant experiences, including some critical corrective emotional experiences, may occur only towards the end of the group's life because it is only then that really significant resonances occur.

Opportunities for self-assessment, stock-taking and planning for the future

Many persons in all kinds of groups recognize the period immediately before termination as a time for looking at what has been achieved, at where one now stands, who one now is, what one still needs to work on, how one might arrange one's day-to-day life to maintain gains, etc. For some, this assessment may include the recognition that further help is required before gains can be consolidated, or that ongoing support is needed. In engaging in stock-taking, persons may have to face disappointments in that the group has not achieved all that they had hoped. The termination phase brings its own reality-facings. Persons may look not only at what has and has not been achieved but at what it is realistic to have hoped to achieve.

Sometimes the members of a group which is about to terminate want to mark the event with some form of ritual: a night out, or a farewell drink. They may construct a ritual at the very end of the group in which semi-formal statements are made about what the group has meant to them. In some groups the members may give the therapist or worker a gift. Such rituals can perform a useful function by marking the transition from a patient or client status to an 'I am on my own' status. They can express feelings about the group or about the therapist or worker in concrete ways and thus contribute to a sense that it is appropriate and right that the group should end. On the other hand one can imagine a ritual being used to mask feelings. The ritual can constitute a collusive defence or restrictive solution which is introduced at the end of the group. Because ritual can serve the group positively or negatively the meaning of ritual has to be judged in each specific instance of it.

During the termination phase it is as important as ever that as therapist or worker, one continues the internal work of expanding and refining one's understanding of each person in the group, of keeping in touch with the dynamics of the group as a whole, and of monitoring one's own feelings and one's own behaviour and its consequences. With respect to own feelings, the therapist or worker is usually not immune to the pressures associated with the termination phase. As conductor of a group one often has an acute sense of time running out. One has had hopes for the group and for particular persons in it and may find as the group draws to a close that not all of these have been realized. One is bound to feel pressure to use the remaining time to achieve these purposes and probably needs to guard against impulses to press overly hard at this stage more than at any other time since the group's very beginnings. It seems necessary and salutary to recognize that any helping experience is an interlude in a person's life: a special experience which one hopes can place him or her in a better position to face his/her own future, but not an experience to solve all problems, present, past and future. If, through a group experience, a person has reached some turning point, such that he or she now has developed further skills and understandings, a freer choice, a sense of resolve, a sense of personal strength for facing the future, then one can feel well satisfied even if one can see that more work, sometimes much more work, still needs to be done. In facing his own feelings of time running out the therapist or worker is somehow striving to be realistic about what has been accomplished, claiming neither too much nor too little.

The therapist will also participate in experiences of separation and mourning. These could very well parallel in some respects the experiences being undergone by the patients or clients in the group. Should the separation experience touch the conductor of the group in personal ways he is faced with the same task as always of maintaining his helping stance in the face of personal involvement.

With respect to stock-taking, the therapist too may find himself thinking over how he has functioned as conductor of the group, the errors he has made, and the like. While such stock-taking certainly *should* take place towards the end of the group or immediately after its close, it is not necessarily the case that it is useful to members for the conductor to share all such feelings. As before, the decision about sharing should be made on the basis of whether or not such sharing is likely to further the interests of members of the group.

I shall now turn to those instrumental purposes first introduced towards the end of chapter 1 as pertaining to the operating phase of the group and discussed in chapter 9 for their relevance to the opening phase and in chapter 11 for their relevance to the established phase of the group. These instrumental purposes remain important as guides to action right to the very end of a group's life.

Seeking to conduct the group so as to maintain a general sense of safety at a level at which members feel safe enough to stay in the group and to take personal risks

As in earlier stages in a group's life the special opportunities attached to the termination phase can best be realized if members feel safe enough to take risks. A sense of threat can escalate during this final phase of a group's life, particularly if the prospect of separation resonates sharply with important but unresolved feelings and fears on the part of a number of the members. As before, the members of the group can be expected to regulate the level of sense of safety themselves although one may find them doing so by resorting to restrictive solutions utilized earlier in the life of the group. It is important that the therapist or worker monitor this aspect of the group's life, but as in the established phase he can often rely to a considerable extent on the members themselves to regulate the level of safety in the group.

Avoiding the irredeemable collapse of structure

By this time in a group's life one can assume that the structure is appropriate to the members' requirements. A *possible* threat to structure at this stage is a collective rush towards premature termination. However, if this happens it seems more correct to view it not as a collapse of structure as such but as an active effort on the part of members to make use of collective flight as a shared defence, or in group focal conflict terms, a restrictive solution. By this argument, during the termination phase avoiding the irredeemable collapse of structure is an aspect of the next instrumental purpose.

Working towards the establishment and maintenance of norms in the group which support it as a positive medium for help: in group focal conflict terms, working towards the maintenance of primarily enabling solutions rather than primarily restrictive solutions

If when the issue of termination comes up the members insist that the group should end immediately it is a reasonable hypothesis that they are resorting to flight as a defence against whatever feelings they sense might be aroused by facing the group's end. In group focal conflict terms one would say that they are attempting to establish a restrictive solution involving flight or avoidance. If such a solution is acted upon the members of course will not have the opportunity to exploit the special opportunities attached to the termination phase. The task facing the therapist therefore is to forestall resorting to this particular restrictive solution. If members show signs of agreeing that 'since we are going to finish soon we might as well finish now', the therapist or worker should, I think, set himself against this. It is open to him simply to say *why* he thinks an actual termination date should be set a little in the future, e.g. that although no one can predict exactly, the period leading up to the group's termination is often used very profitably by members. If the members do not accept this immediately, one might follow it up by asking what everyone thinks might happen if the group went on for a bit longer. The response might be that the group will be boring, has lost its point, etc. If so, the conductor can urge them to put up with that possibility and to stay with the group in order to see what might emerge. It is worth being quite firm about this. By this stage in a group's life the members ought to be able, by virtue of their previous experience together, to tolerate direct urgings to remain in the group and to consider just what they fear might happen were the group to go on. Direct challenges and urgings to continue do not seem to carry substantial risk of intensifying reactive fears at this stage because of the extensive experience which the members have had with one another and with the conductor of the group.

One sometimes sees members wishing to prolong the group beyond an agreed termination date. Providing that the termination period has been reasonably generous this wish for prolongation can probably be best understood as another form of evasiveness or avoidance. By delaying termination the members avoid the pressures of feeling that time is running out and can avoid confronting remaining outstanding issues for a further period. Wishing to prolong the group beyond an agreed termination date can also constitute a test of the worker's or therapist's investment in the members. If this is a shared concern it is an error to allow it to be acted out in this manner. Members will gain more if they can confront their feelings about the conductor's investment in them directly. On the whole it seems best not to accede to demands that the group be further prolonged once a termination date has been agreed. This can be hard for a therapist or worker to do in the face of a consensus from members that more time is required. However, I believe that if one regards a request for more sessions as a restrictive solution, then one can see that this can be handled in the same way as other restrictive solutions. That is, members can be encouraged to consider what they hope to gain from more sessions, how they think they would feel if the conductor were unwilling to go along with this request, and the like. Such queries are intended to get out into the open the wishes and fears extant in the group so that they can be confronted. In making these suggestions that a therapist or worker stick to the agreed termination date I am assuming that it was realistically established in the first place and that the therapist or worker judges that what still needs to be accomplished can be accomplished within the remaining time. If he comes to the view that the agreed date has been an error then he can say so, say why, and renegotiate a termination date.

Utilizing events occurring in the group for the specific benefit of members

The special opportunities which attach to the termination phase – the sense of time running out, experiences of separation and mourning, and opportunities for self-assessment – render the termination phase potentially rich with opportunities for personal gain.

Thinking now in group focal conflict terms, such shared conflicts may emerge as a wish to remain close to the therapist versus fears of abandonment; feelings of unbearable loss versus fears of being overwhelmed by such feelings; anger at the therapist for acceding to a termination date versus fear of retribution or abandonment; and the like. The particular shared wishes and fears which emerge for the group are likely to resonate with personal conflicts and concerns experienced by some individuals. Where this is the case (and providing that enabling rather than restrictive solutions prevail in the group) special opportunities arise for a corrective emotional experience. A therapist or worker who is alert to such possibilities can make use of the situation on behalf of the individuals concerned in the ways already suggested in chapter 11. As an example of what may occur, the following event took place in the thirty-first session of a time-limited thirty-six session group.

In the context of discussing their feelings about the forthcoming end of the group, some of the members recalled earlier separation experiences, some going back to childhood. Janice told of having been sent to hospital at the age of 3 in an ambulance. She was sure that neither parent accompanied her, although she did not remember why. Her parents visited her once she was there, but at one point she was transferred to a different bed in a different ward. She was convinced that her parents would never be able to find her again, and was terrified. She bitterly resented her parents for causing her this distress, and thought that her emigration to another country as a young adult could be linked to this experience. Lydia, an older woman in the group, said that Janice's parents' behaviour was understandable. She herself had had to have her son hospitalized when he was 5. It was necessary for his health, etc. Janice turned on Lydia and in a voice full of scorn and reproach, said 'You! You did that to your son!' In the exchange which followed Janice poured out her resentment on to Lydia. Both women were upset and in tears.

What was happening here was that under pressure of the approaching termination, the theme of separation and loss emerged in the group. Janice was one of a number of persons for whom the here-and-now experience of impending separation resonated with important earlier experiences. When Lydia responded to Janice as she did, both women were immediately locked into an intense pair relationship in which Lydia stood for Janice's mother and Janice stood for Lydia's son. When these two women became so intensely involved the other members withdrew, with some indication that they found the sheer intensity of affect difficult to cope with. For some fifteen minutes or so the therapist was the only person to engage with Lydia and Janice. As the ventilation of powerful feelings gave way to more reflective work, others began to come back into the discussion. Janice was able to recognize that an abiding inability to trust others, which plagued her current relationships, had its roots in this earlier experience. With Lydia's help, she was able to acknowledge her parents' probable feelings at that time and to begin to understand their behaviour. The conductor of the group encouraged her to consider whether, as an adult, she still needed to carry feelings of mistrust and expectations of abandonment into every new relationship. Although the situation was less centrally significant for Lydia, she made use of it, after her first shock, as an opportunity to examine feelings of guilt concerning her son.

In more highly structured groups it is often useful to invite members to construct agendas for the remaining sessions of the group. One can ask members 'What do you particularly hope will happen between now and the time that the group ends?' or 'There might be certain things that you would really like us to do or to talk about between now and the time that the group ends, and would be disappointed if we do not. If we can all say what these are we can make sure of opportunities to get them in.' This explicitly reminds members that time is running out and encourages them to construct experiences especially likely to be useful to them. In some highly structured groups, a review period might be built into the final session of the group, and this can help persons to evaluate the meaning of the experience for them and what has been gained. In virtually all kinds of groups one can expect certain forms of evaluation to occur towards the end of the group's life. In less structured groups this is likely to occur in and among open discussion on themes around benefits, unrealized hopes, and the like. In more highly structured groups evaluation might take more structured forms. For example, persons might be asked to declare or even to write down on paper what they feel to have gained, what they hoped for but have not gained, events which stand out in their memory as having been particularly important to them, and the like. Such evaluation sessions create opportunities for members to review their group experience. They also provide the therapist or worker with information which might not otherwise be available to him for later use in evaluating the group experience.

Avoiding doing harm

Many of the points made in chapters 9 and 11 are also relevant to the termination phase. To these one can add the losses which can accrue to members if the group is allowed to utilize flight as a defence at this stage in its life.

Discerning and retrieving errors

A therapist or worker is vulnerable to making the same kinds of errors during the termination phase as during earlier phases of the group. In particular, he could be vulnerable to colluding in restrictive solutions which involve avoidance, especially if he himself finds separation difficult. A therapist or worker who is very eager to regard the group as a success might find it difficult to tolerate criticisms and expressions of disappointment which can be a feature of this phase. A conductor who is vulnerable in this way might need to guard against punitive responses or inappropriate defensiveness. The conductor of the group might also feel personally disappointed that more has not been achieved. I believe that one can arm oneself internally against feelings of disappointment or of anger towards members for not having accomplished more by trying to take a realistic view of what any helping experience can and cannot be expected to accomplish, and acknowledging that small changes can often lead to more substantial gains as time goes on.

Much of the discussion in this chapter could be summarized by suggesting that when faced with the ending of a group the important thing to do is to make room for and facilitate opportunities for all concerned to share in how they feel about the impending event. This requires time and a certain courage. If adequate time is provided and if restrictive solutions can be prevented from taking hold then the special opportunities inherent in the termination phase can be exploited and realized.

Chapter 14

The conductor of the group: power, responsibility, stance and style

In the preceding five chapters, which have been concerned with the conduct of the group while it is in session, references have been made from time to time to such issues as limitations on the therapist's or worker's power to influence events, getting caught up oneself in the dynamics of the group and so being less able to be useful to members, conditions under which it is and is not appropriate to share one's own feelings and experiences with members, and the like. These are issues which transcend developmental stage. Essentially, they have to do with the conductor's *position* in the group: the nature and extent of his power, his responsibilities to, in and for the group, his stance towards the group and its members, and his style.

Power, control and influence

The power of a group therapist or worker derives from his real powers over members in the form of fate-control, from his capacity to influence situations within the group, and from members' assumptions about the conductor's power and the ways in which he is likely to use it. The conductor of a group holds attitudes about his own power and may think that he has more power than he in fact has, or prefer not to exercise the power he has, or wish to give some of his power away.

Sometimes the conductor of a group is in a position to exercise 'fate-control' over the members of a group. That is, by virtue of the official records he keeps or his contributions to reviews he influences such decisions as date of discharge, weekend leave, and the like. These are real powers, and his decisions concerning them have to do with how to exercise powers and whether or not to inform members about his powers. I have argued earlier that members need to know about such powers and to have some idea of how the therapist or worker intends to use them, in order to regulate their own participation on the basis of fact rather than fantasy.

A therapist or worker is usually able to remove a patient or client from a group if he chooses to do so. This is another form of fate control. The conductor of a group should be very careful about exercising this power, because however sympathetically the expulsion is handled for the person who is asked to leave, the conductor's behaviour is likely to be received by others as an indication of his readiness to put into action an ultimate form of rejection. Removing someone from the group carries the substantial risk of introducing fears of expulsion into a group which are not mere fantasies but which are based on real and observable events.

A worker or therapist usually retains the power to make decisions about structure and to introduce new members into the group. This seems right: since the conductor of the group has assumed responsibility for the group this should be matched by the power to make such changes as he considers are in the group's and the members' best interests. He may decide to share such power or even to give it away, but the decision remains his as to whether or not to do so.

A mismatch between power and responsibility can mean that the conductor has assumed responsibility for a group but does not have the power to carry out these responsibilities in ways which seem best to him. Extreme instances of mismatches between responsibility and power do occur from time to time, as when a group member is actually transferred out of an institution by an administrator, and perforce out of a group, without the conductor being informed or consulted. Because the consequences of such mismatches can be so deleterious, it is important for a leader to try to establish agreements about his power with relevant persons in his organization before a group begins. If mismatches occur later, this is a serious issue which requires discussion and negotiation rather than passive acceptance.

Sometimes a therapist or worker decides to give certain of his powers away. Most likely, he will choose to place power in the hands of group members, rather than in the hands of persons with no direct connection with the group. For example, under some circumstances the conductor of a group might place the power for deciding on the structure of the group in the hands of the members, by utilizing the first session or two to plan collaboratively the tasks the group will undertake and the manner of its operation. If a group loses members some therapists or workers place the power for adding or not adding new members in the hands of the members, or might go further by allowing members to vet potential group members and decide whether or not to invite specific persons to join the group.

I believe that one should be careful about giving power away because once given, power is hard to take back without adverse consequences for the group. If one places the power to select new members in the hands of members and then comes to the view that the members have made an inappropriate decision, one cannot take the power back without generating unwanted consequences. Taking power back is likely to convey some such message as 'I thought I could trust you to make sensible decisions but I see I cannot' or 'I was tricking you' or 'I cannot be trusted to keep my promises.' It is clearly not in the group's interest to convey such messages. It is far better for the therapist or worker not to give power away in the first place if he is not absolutely sure he can accept whatever decisions the group then makes. One should not give power away if one thinks one has relevant information not available to group members. For example a leader is usually in a better position than members to be in touch with dynamics pertaining to the group as a whole. He may perceive, for example, where members cannot, that resistance to taking in a new member stems from the members' collective but unrecognized wish to keep the group cosy and overly safe, or from the members' worries about dealing with new, unknown 'siblings'. In group focal conflict terms, the members' reluctance to admit a new person constitutes a restrictive solution. By placing the power to decide in the hands of the members, the therapist or worker is colluding or risking colluding in a restrictive solution.

An argument is developing here that the power to make a decision properly belongs in the hands of those who have access to information relevant to the decision. It follows that it may be appropriate to place power in the hands of members if one judges that they have more relevant information than one has oneself. Thus, the members may know better than anyone else what structure is likely to suit them, so, providing one judges that adequate decision-making skills exist within the group (of sharing opinions, testing consensus and the like) then it is appropriate to place power in their hands. Or, if members have access to information about a pool of prospective group members and the therapist or worker does not, then he might consider giving this decision-making power over to members. At the same time I would wish to argue that just as the conductor retains ultimate responsibility for the group he should retain the ultimate power to decide in whose hands decision-making should be placed.

Persons in groups not infrequently assume that a leader has more or different powers than he actually has, and develop fantasies about the destructive or magically helpful ways in which he might or could use his power. Members might assume that because the conductor of a group actually has the power to expel members that he will in fact do so. Or they might assume that once a therapist or group worker knows the 'facts' about them he will be able to give advice which will 'cure' them or make them feel better. This fantasy may well be based on expectations transferred inappropriately from experiences with doctors and teachers, or from more primitive fantasies about the mother who is or ought to be forever-available and nurturing.

When fantasies emerge about the conductor's power they can have the effect of augmenting it. If members believe that the conductor may expel them, for example, they will regulate their behaviour accordingly. If they believe that the conductor can provide magnificent advice as soon as he has heard about their troubles they may simply sit back and wait for help once they have told their story rather than initiate further explorations. In effect, the conductor has influenced the members in ways which he prefers not to, by virtue of their fantasies about his powers.

While the conductor of a group has real powers, they are clearly limited. For example, he cannot make persons get better, he cannot force persons to use the group constructively, and he cannot force persons to behave inconsistently with powerfully held personal norms. He can declare rules, for example about confidentiality or regular attendance or what shall or shall not be discussed, but he cannot make these rules stick merely because he has asserted them. He cannot make people feel safe in the group if they do not; he cannot make people participate if they are disinclined to do so; he cannot make persons in the group take a sympathetic view towards one another; he cannot make a group shift from operating on a restrictive solution to operating on an enabling one; and so on. In short, the therapist or worker cannot legislate or directly control the feelings or behaviours of others.

On the other hand certain things lie within the conductor's powers. He can, for example, decide to go along with or decline to go along with the roles and behaviours which the persons in the group try to press him into. In group focal conflict terms he can co-operate actively or decline to co-operate actively in some restrictive group solution. He can decide when to disclose personal material and when not. He can decide when to intervene and when to be silent. He can give advice or refrain from giving advice, probe with questions or avoid asking questions, offer inter-pretations or keep his views to himself. He can press against defences or decide not to. He can express his angry feelings or seek to hold them privately. In short, the leader has power over his own behaviour inside the group. This is the limit of his *direct* power.

I find that the point I am trying to make here is frequently misunderstood. I am saying that the only power the leader has while a group is in session is over his own behaviour. He does not have direct power over other persons' behaviour or feelings. Of course, his behaviour has consequences for the group as a whole and for particular persons. Certain of his behaviours are highly likely to elicit certain responses from others or stir up certain feelings. Thus, a punitive intervention is likely to increase fears and reduce the level of sense of safety in the group. Calling attention to some event which the therapist judges may have special importance for a particular person in the group can increase the likelihood that that person will register that point. Focusing on one person for a prolonged period of time may have the consequence of stirring up feelings of envy and jealousy in others. And so on. The fact that particular behaviours on the part of the conductor of the group are likely to have certain consequences rather than others means that the conductor has potential influence over the course of a group and in the longer run over outcome. If the conductor's behaviour did not have consequences there would hardly be any point in his being in the group. But it is nevertheless true that when it comes right down to it the only thing which a therapist or worker can control directly is his own behaviour. He can influence probabilities but he cannot exercise direct control over events and outcomes.

While on the subject of the therapist's or worker's actual power in the group it is useful to make a distinction between the therapist's control over his feelings and his control over his behaviour. Events occurring in a group are bound to stir up diverse feelings in the therapist or worker from time to time. Rather than attempt to 'control' these, which must mean suppress or distort, he will be in a better position to help members if he acknowledges them to himself. However, acknowledging feelings to oneself does not necessarily mean expressing them in behaviour. Sometimes allowing feelings to be expressed in behaviour works to the advantage of a group; sometimes it does not. Like anyone else, the conductor of a group cannot expect always to be in touch with his own feelings or always able to hold to that separation of feeling and action which allows him to make split-second decisions as to whether or not to express a feeling in behaviour. Sometimes this does not matter. There are times when a leader is so well in tune with group events that entirely spontaneous behaviours which are the direct expression of feelings may well be both apt and effective. However it must be acknowledged that the spontaneous expression of a feeling through behaviour may just as well constitute an error which could lead to adverse consequences for the group or for some person(s) in it. On the whole, the conductor of a group is in a better position to be helpful to a group if he develops his capacity to be in touch with his own feelings and seeks to exercise control over their expression in behaviour.

Just as group members may have fantasies about the leader's power and assume that he can do things which he cannot do, a leader may also make erroneous assumptions about his own power. A leader who thinks that he can control confidentiality, or contacts amongst members outside the group, or lateness or absences, imagines himself to have more power than he in fact has. I have emphasized earlier that a leader can state a rule but whether or not it becomes established as a norm for the group is an entirely different matter, influenced by many factors other than the leader's mere assertion that a rule exists. Operating on erroneous assumptions about own power can have negative consequences both for oneself and for the group. For example, a therapist or worker who has assumed that he has the power to influence certain group events and has tried to do so and failed, may then experience disappointment, frustration or anger. What has happened is that he has been wrong in the first place about the character and extent of his power.

It seems not uncommon for a worker or therapist to wish that he had less power than he in fact has. This may have to do with prevailing notions about democracy and equality. It feels more 'democratic' for the conductor to assume that his powers are the same as that of any other person in the group. This is simply not so. A worker or therapist often has power which derives from his position in the organization and from the fact that he is the one who has made decisions about structure and membership. He also has power which derives from his stance *vis-à-vis* the group, which is different from that of the members. Because of this stance he has a different perspective on the group than do the members and operates on a different information and knowledge base. He is not necessarily *more* powerful than certain of the members but his power is different in kind. Far from wishing to get rid of his powers it seems to me part of a conductor's responsibility to acknowledge and use his powers to further his purposes in undertaking work with the group.

Few adults are altogether unconfused about their own power and that of others. It follows that concerns and confusions about power are likely to emerge in virtually all groups. When they do it is clearly in the members' best interests to confront and explore them. Often these emerge in terms of the here-and-now of the group: the conductor's power, how he will use it, fantasies about power, wishes and resentments about power, etc. Here-and-now experiences about power become a hook on which to hang explorations of feelings concerning power. A group conductor who has thought out his own power position is in a better position to make use of such opportunities when they arise than one who has not.

The conductor's responsibilities to, in and for the group and its members

The term 'responsibility' takes on a somewhat different meaning depending on the preposition which follows it. The conductor's responsibility *to* the group and its members can be stated in general terms as an obligation or duty to do everything he can, to the best of his ability, to work towards his overall purpose of utilizing the group for the benefit of the members. His responsibility *in* the group, that is, while actually conducting it, is to be clear about instrumental purposes, attentive to events as they unfold, and ready to anticipate and note the consequences of his behaviour and to regulate his behaviour according to how it bears on instrumental purposes.

What is the conductor of the group responsible for? For example, is he responsible for outcome; for whether or not persons actually gain from a group experience; for what actually happens in sessions? The answer to these questions must be 'yes and no'. The character of the conductor's power is a relevant factor. If one asks if the conductor has the power to control or determine outcome, the answer is no. If one asks whether he has a powerful influence on outcome, the answer is yes. If one asks if by his own behaviour he can render a positive outcome impossible for certain members then the answer is again yes. It *is* possible to spoil a group by the way one behaves in it as conductor. It *is* possible to render the group unhelpful or even damaging to individual members by one's own behaviour. At the same time the conductor's behaviour in the group is only one of a number of factors which influences outcome, and it is not necessarily the most important one. He cannot realistically be said to be solely responsible for outcome, but he has a degree of responsibility for outcome through his power to conduct himself in ways likely to tilt probabilities towards or away from preferred outcomes. Is the conductor responsible for what happens during sessions? Again, he cannot be entirely or exclusively responsible because too much else besides his own behaviour influences group events. On the other hand there is no question but that his own behaviour has consequences in the group and influences events at least some of the time, sometimes critically.

The conductor of a group may feel guilty if things do not go well. Sometimes this is appropriate, if he has made avoidable errors. Sometimes it is inappropriate, if unwished-for outcomes have occurred which are outside his control. What it is appropriate to feel responsible for (and guilty about), one can argue, depends a great deal on power, limitations on power, and how one uses power.

Stance

'Stance' refers to the position which the conductor assumes in the group with respect to the members, and includes such variables as perspective on the group, distance and closeness, extent and kind of self-disclosure, and level of participation. The issue of stance is worth thinking through with some care since the stance adopted can place a therapist or worker in a good or a poor position to use his powers to meet his responsibilities.

Everyone, of course, has a perspective on the group. While a group is in session everyone present has an opportunity to see and hear that which is open to public view, that is, that which is being said and done in the group. Each person registers some but not all of this, since each perceives selectively. Moreover, each person places some meaning on the events which pass through his or her personal filter. The meaning which different persons place on 'the same' events varies markedly from person to person, as is well known both from ordinary experience and from social psychological research. In a group, every person places his own meaning on events. Sometimes these have quite a lot in common, but sometimes meanings vary so much that one almost wonders whether everyone can be referring to the same episode. Where does a leader stand amidst all this?

I believe that the conductor of a group is in a better position than others to hold to a perspective which encompasses group-level events and their possible import for the experience of individuals. This is not because he is more expert or skilful at this than others, although of course he may be, but because his reasons for being in the group are different from that of others. Unlike the other persons present, the therapist or worker is not concerned to use the group for personal benefit. While the group is in session he tries to put his own needs and preoccupations to one side. His energy and attention, being freed from such preoccupations, can range across the group, registering how individuals are entering into, contributing to and responding to ongoing group-level events. Were the conductor to be a member of a therapeutic group he would be in a different position: he would properly be attending to his own preoccupations, and his own feelings and experiences would be more in the forefront of his attention, with less energy available to look to group-level and interpersonal events except as they pertain to him.

Maintaining an observing and listening stance does *not* mean that the therapist or worker places himself outside the group, participates little, or takes a cold and distant perspective on the group. A listening and observing stance is entirely compatible with warmth, sympathy and a conversational style of participating.

One sometimes hears the argument made that a leader should in time become another member of the group. Stated in this way, the issue is made overly simple. Experience suggests that as a group goes on over a period of time the members become both more able and more likely to introduce some of the behaviours which at the beginning tended to be introduced by the conductor. For example at the beginning of a topic-oriented discussion group the worker may need to call to the members' attention the fact that they are straying from the topic. As time goes on the members, partly through taking the worker as a model, become more able to monitor their own interaction and to make such interventions themselves. As members become more able to introduce such interventions there is less need for the worker to do so. In a therapeutic group at the very beginning the therapist will be in the habit of looking for collusive defences or restrictive solutions and the members will not. The whole idea that members of a group can seek to protect themselves through unrecognized collaborative efforts is likely to be a foreign one. In the course of their experience together the therapist will have worked through a number of such episodes with the patients or clients. Although he will not have used technical language the group members will have become familiar with the idea that persons in groups can sometimes work against their own best interests by getting together without realizing that they are doing so in order to protect themselves from unrecognized fears. As this understanding grows the members themselves develop skills in recognizing such episodes and begin to do some of the therapist's work for him. The conductor of the group and the members come to resemble one another more in how they participate in the group. This does not occur through the therapist becoming a member of the group, but through the members taking on some of the functions which initially were performed by the conductor.

Another phenomenon which may render the behaviour of the therapist or worker and the members more similar is the likelihood that all concerned will feel safer more of the time as the group moves along. A therapist who brings into the group his own defences (for example who protects himself from feared attack by maintaining a substantial distance between himself and the group) may feel less need to invoke personal defences as time goes on. He will then become more flexible in his style and pattern of participation, and his behaviour could well come to resemble that of the members more than before.

By such routes as these the therapist or worker may become more like the members of the group. However, this does not mean that he loses his identity as conductor. He must retain this identity because of the responsibilities which he has assumed, the tasks associated with those responsibilities, and the self-discipline which such tasks impose on him. To mention some obvious examples: other persons may allow themselves to miss sessions or to come late, but for the conductor to be absent or late is an abrogation of responsibility. Group members may lapse into inattention or self-preoccupation but the conductor maintains attentiveness despite possible personal preoccupations. Group members may make demands on the group's time to explore some urgent personal problem but it is not appropriate for the therapist or worker to use the group's time in this way.

There is, I believe, an overriding factor which supports the general point that the therapist should remain in a special position throughout the life of the group. Persons in groups are supported in feeling safe enough to take risks if they can hold on to the sense that there is one person in the group who retains sufficient understanding, strength, courage and disinterest to handle acutely difficult situations and emergencies should they arise. Even though such situations may arise rarely, the members need to know that when they do, the worker or therapist can be relied on to carry out his special responsibilities from his special position.

Another aspect of stance has to do with the character and extent of self-disclosure. When does it serve a conductor's purposes to share his or her own feelings and experiences in the group and when does it not?

It has become almost fashionable among some group therapists and workers to assume that self-disclosure and openness is in itself desirable. In my view, the particular responsibilities which the therapist/worker has assumed require him to be careful about the forms and timing of personal disclosures. Apart from other considerations, a therapist who engages in extensive self-disclosure pre-empts the time of the group. Even brief self-disclosures may be pre-empting through their power to distract. The guiding principle as to whether or not self-disclosure is appropriate is its likely contribution to overall and instrumental purposes. In itself, self-disclosure cannot be defended as either desirable or undesirable.

Certain forms of self-disclosure should be ruled out on grounds that they are unlikely to have desirable consequences for the group. One such goes something like: 'I used to have this problem and I got over it by . . .' Such a comment is unlikely to be helpful not only because one person's solution is not another's but because it naively assumes that a solution need only be mentioned to be put into operation. The comment also communicates without saying so in so many words 'You are making much out of something that can easily be dealt with.' Such a message depreciates the person who is presenting the problem and can convey to him that the therapist is not taking his situation seriously.

Another form of disclosure involves informing the group about notions or hypotheses which the therapist or worker is developing in his own mind about particular persons in the group or about certain group-level processes. Does he divulge such ideas, opinions or hypotheses? Again, sometimes it will be helpful to do so, sometimes not. The conductor of a group may develop a notion about an individual in the course of a discussion in which something quite else is in the forefront of the group's attention. If he revealed his views at this time it would interrupt and distract the group from a currently more salient issue. He need not of course let go of his ideas altogether but it could be the better choice to tuck them away ready for use when the context is more favourable. Sharing a view about the group is inadvisable if it is likely to be seen by members as wildly improbable.

Sharing one's own feelings and reactions in the group can be a valuable thing to do when all of the persons in the group, members and therapist alike, have been exposed to the same distressing event. Sharing in an experience which touches everyone is both a human thing to do and a therapeutic thing to do. It can facilitate the members' sense of the communality of human experience, it can model for the group a willingness to confront difficult or distressing feelings, and it can demonstrate a willingness to depart from a professional stance when circumstances seem to warrant it. Sharing is also indicated when failing to share is likely to be seen by members as unnecessary withholding. In general, whether or not to share experiences and feelings should be a decision made in the light of circumstances rather than a hard-and-fast rule (always; never). Like other decisions, it needs to be made in the light of the likely consequences for the group and for particular members.

Still another aspect of stance is one's feeling of like and dislike for persons in the group. In general, a worker or therapist is in a better position to be useful to the members of a group if he likes them and has a generally sympathetic attitude towards them than if he dislikes them. Many persons who become members of groups do not present themselves as particularly likeable persons. They may behave in deprecating, insensitive, disregarding or dominating ways, or be so unresponsive as to offer few rewards to those who seek to interact with them. Nevertheless it is usually possible to penetrate beyond surface behaviours and reach the likeable core of initially offputting or unrewarding persons. If one can do this, then one can avoid forming an abiding dislike of individual members and place oneself in a better position to understand them more fully, attend to them, and perceive opportunities for offering specific help within the group.

An underlying, abiding feeling of liking and respect for a person is not at all incompatible with transient feelings of liking or disliking, which can arise in response to particular events, nor with disapproval of specific behaviours. Transient feelings can be utilized to develop one's understanding of a person or an event. Abiding feelings of either liking or disliking can lead one to miss opportunities for generating benefit.

With respect to activity level it is possible for a group worker or therapist to be too active or too passive in general, or too active or passive for a particular population or group structure. A conductor who talks a great deal of the time or who directs discussion or activities virtually moment by moment restricts opportunities for the members to make active, self-directed use of the group situation. A therapist or worker who says hardly anything is likely to become a figure of mystery on to whom much is projected, or may be seen as cold and uncaring. He is likely to generate pervasively high levels of anxiety in the group since few persons can tolerate long periods of no feedback from one whom they are likely to see as being in a powerful position.

Beyond these general points, just what constitutes an appropriate level of activity depends very much on the characteristics and requirements of the members and the structure adopted for the group. If the structure involves activities, exercises, or topic-oriented discussion, then the conductor will necessarily have to be more active than if the structure involves open, essentially undirected discussion. How active or how passive it is appropriate to be also depends somewhat on the level of vulnerability of the membership. Persons who are highly vulnerable seem able to maintain an adequate level of sense of safety only if they hear the therapist's voice relatively frequently. It is as if they need to be reminded that the therapist is present and available to them. Persons not so vulnerable can tolerate longer periods of non-participation.

In earlier chapters I have referred from time to time to the inadvisability of the conductor placing himself in an antagonist's position with respect to the group, either through pressing on them interpretations of events which they cannot accept or through trying to force the abandonment of still-needed shared defences (restrictive solutions). In positive terms this means trying to establish and maintain what is sometimes called a 'working alliance' or a 'therapeutic alliance'. The conductor of the group and the members stand together and together face the task of finding ways to tackle issues and/or engage in activities likely to lead to benefit. This does not mean that the conductor and the members never come into conflict or that the conductor does not confront and name situations which members sometimes prefer to avoid. Nor does it mean that members consistently maintain a positive opinion of the conductor or never attack or criticize him. However, if both conductor and members can come to see that they are basically on the same side, trying to use the situation as fully as possible for the benefit of members, then confrontations, dissatisfactions, and the like are contained within a sound working alliance. From such a base, much that is difficult can be faced.

This discussion raises the issue of what constitutes 'confrontation'. One sometimes sees this term used to refer to a challenging stance, in which the conductor fairly continuously presses the members to do and say more, and do and say it sooner than feels right or safe to them. I am using the term 'to confront' in another sense, that is, to acknowledge and say what is really happening in the group. There are a number of examples of this in earlier chapters: when no one could mention Violet's fatness, the conductor did so; when no one could face the implications of the accident to Brigitte's father, the therapist found an opportune moment to refer to it; when no one referred to Jim's error in dropping the ball and losing the game for his team, the worker did so. This use of the term is consistent with dictionary definitions. The *Shorter Oxford Dictionary* defines 'to confront' as 'to stand or meet facing', while 'to challenge' is defined as 'to object to, to call in question, to summon to a contest of any kind'.

Style

Style can be regarded as the expression in behaviour of one's attitudes about one's own power and its proper use, one's ideas about responsibility, and the stance one tends to adopt, especially with reference to closeness and distance, self-disclosure, and level of activity. All of this in turn seems often to be linked with the conductor's personality, that is, to the relatively stable set of preferences, concerns, preferred modes of interaction, preferred defences and personal solutions which group workers and therapists, no less than clients and patients, bring with them to any group endeavour.

Thus, a therapist who is uneasy about anger and hostility may see self assertion as a form of hostility and adopt a relatively inactive, non-confronting style. A group worker with strong needs to be liked and appreciated might feel compelled to offer advice or might find it difficult to listen for very long before trying to help. Conductors of groups are not cast from one mould and can hardly be expected to be similar to one another in either personality or style. There is a good deal of room for varying styles in work with groups. However it is not the case, in my view, that any and every style can be regarded as acceptable because some styles work against the best interests of group members. Some very challenging styles are so challenging that they generate dysfunctionally high levels of anxiety. Some remote styles are so remote that group members experience the conductor as uncaring and in consequence become disheartened and uninvolved. A conductor who puts certain of his own personally preferred solutions into operation in a group may thereby close off certain areas of life experience which could otherwise be explored. One looks to the consequences of a style for the experience of members when judging acceptability.

While therapists and workers cannot be expected to transform their personalities at short notice, becoming aware of one's own preferences and vulnerabilities can help a great deal in controlling their unchecked and unnoticed expression in behaviour. Within certain limitations imposed by own personality and experience, most workers and therapists can and do vary their styles at least to some degree. A capacity to vary one's style is an asset since different populations and group structures do impose different style requirements on conductors.

Part IV

After the group ends

Chapter 15
Making decisions about future work in the light of experience

After a particular group or programme of groups has ended, the worker or therapist who planned and conducted it has a great deal more information than before, based on experience. He or she is then in a position to make use of that further information and experience in planning future work.

The information available to the worker or therapist is likely to be a conglomerate of informal notes made as the group went along, case notes, reports to colleagues, data emerging from informal or formal evaluation studies, and a wealth of impressions and recollections of the group. This information needs to be mined and ordered so that future planning is based on a consideration of all the information available, rather than on selected bits.

Pinning down one's experience while it still remains accessible and thinking through its implications need not be a lengthy nor laborious task. It can be guided by asking oneself and seeking to answer a series of straightforward questions.

(1) *Did the members of the group benefit from the experience in the ways in which I hoped?*

During the planning stage one will have identified certain benefits which one hoped would accrue to persons through participating in the group. When the group ends these same hoped-for benefits become criteria against which one can assess the relative success or failure of the group. As one came to know the members better one may have worked out in more specific detail the particular, unique benefits which one hoped that each could achieve. If so, these become further criteria, specific to each person, against which success can be judged.

One does not expect all members of a group to benefit to the

389

same extent. Experience suggests that some will have benefited substantially in exactly the ways hoped for; some will have benefited partially; and a few may have achieved no discernible benefit. Certain spin-off benefits may have occurred which one did not anticipate at all. One or a few persons may have dropped out along the way. In seeking to assess benefit one needs to look at *each* person in the group in turn, forming a view as to where he or she now is, compared with his/her position at the beginning.

(2) *Was the group effective and efficient as a medium of help for its members*?

It is unrealistic to expect consistent efficiency and effectiveness with no lapses whatsoever. One would have to imagine a really fortunate composition and an unimaginably ever-alert, perfectly skilled conductor for such super-efficiency to exist. Usually on looking back over a group one sees a certain number of missed opportunities and a certain amount of lost time. Perhaps certain factors which threatened the group's internal or external viability were not noted as soon as they might have been, or were not satisfactorily dealt with. In particular, on looking back one might see that there were some 'dead' periods which went on for longer than was perhaps necessary, that certain periods of high threat with subsequent immobilization or retreat could have been avoided or curtailed, that one or several issues likely to have been important never emerged, that a difficult member continued to be a problem, or that someone got lost in the group. Occasionally one sees a group which got stuck in some restrictive solution early in its history and failed to progress beyond the preoccupations of the formative stage (although if this were happening one would hope and expect to note and deal with it long before the group's official close). Such a failure in development could occur in consequence of a difficult composition, an unsuitable structure, or unrecognized collusion on the part of the conductor in maintaining some restrictive solution.

Giving thought to the factors which led to less-than-optimal development or the unsustained maintenance of a group as a viable medium for help can lead one to see which difficulties could have been forestalled or better managed and which were beyond one's capacity to influence.

(3) *What do the patients or clients think they have gained?*

The conductor of the group usually has some information about this, either through discussions held by members toward the end of the group or through more systematic or formal reviews held during the last session(s). Setting members' perceptions of gain and of what has been important or difficult for them during the course of a group's life against the conductor's views is an illuminating exercise. There is no reason to expect that members' and conductors' views will be the same, although each should be understandable in the light of the other. Sometimes members report gains which the conductor was not aware of, or refer to significant events which the conductor had not seen as such or might not even remember. Occasionally a member declares that he has received no benefit although there is clear evidence that he has. For example, in an in-patient group a young man declared that he was glad that the group had ended since, although he had enjoyed it at first, he was now bored by it, hadn't benefited and in any case was now too busy with other activities to come to the group. In fact, the therapists judged that it was through experiences within the group that this patient had become sufficiently unblocked to engage in these other activities and that a great release of energy and upsurge of hope had occurred in consequence of his group experience. At the same time it was understandable that he might deprecate the value of the group because it was so important to him to see himself as standing on his own two feet. This story is told not to encourage therapists or workers to delude themselves into believing that everyone benefits, including those who insist that they have not, but to emphasize the importance of accepting both the conductor's and the member's perspectives and seeking to understand and reconcile differences between them when they occur. Sometimes, of course, members' and conductors' perceptions and judgments coincide.

(4) *What were the further outcomes of conducting the group, and am I satisfied with them?*

One often hopes for certain further outcomes beyond hoped-for benefits for members. For example, one might hope that groups of the kind just conducted will be more favourably viewed by colleagues, or that junior colleagues associated with the effort will have learnt from the experience, or that one will have developed one's own skills further or learned from trying out an unfamiliar structure or style of conducting a group, or that persons in the environment will have developed a more positive opinion of some category of patient or client. When the group has ended one can review these further outcomes and judge whether one has achieved all that one hoped.

If through answering these first questions one is clear about the outcomes actually achieved one can go on to some further questions about factors associated with outcome, turning first to planning. Planning is clearly not everything, and the best of plans do not guarantee an effective and satisfying group, but sound planning can influence the likelihood of a group going well, and it is therefore a good idea to review the planning in detail after a group finishes. The very first planning task, which is a foundation for all further planning, has to do with assessing the population. Therefore one might first ask:

(5) *Did I anticipate correctly the frontier and/or preoccupying concern of the population I was working with? If not, in what ways would I now modify or amplify my understanding of that population? Would I modify design, structure or leadership approach?*

Just after one has completed work with a group one is likely to be vividly aware of the uniqueness of each person in it. To think in terms of 'population' requires shifting back to another logical level and trying to think in terms of what the members of the group did and did not have in common. This can help one to judge whether one was working with persons drawn from a single population for whom the structure of the group worked; with persons from a single population for whom the structure did not work; with persons drawn from several populations (or sub-populations), all of whom could benefit from the planned structure; or with persons drawn from several populations or sub-populations where the structure worked better for some than for others.

It can be a useful exercise to speculate about how the persons one has just finished working with would have responded to an entirely different structure from the one used. If one made use of a series of topic-oriented discussions, could one instead have used open discussion? Might one have reached some issues more quickly had one made use of certain exercises? If one relied on open discussion, was this easily manageable by the persons in the group? Would it be better another time to make use of activities and exercises, or exercises followed by discussion?

Sometimes one is generally satisfied with the structure which one has used but sees ways of improving it. For example, one may be satisfied with exercises as a general device but in retrospect see that some of them worked well while others baffled or over-faced the members.

(6) *Am I satisfied with the details of my planning?*

One might, for example, decide that another time, tea or coffee should be provided, or that each session should be somewhat longer, or that there should be more frequent sessions. One might decide that one should be careful, another time, to end sessions on time. All of the detailed planning decisions discussed in chapter 5 can be reviewed in the light of experience.

(7) *Did the composition work, or not? Was the combination of persons in the group such that the group jelled and the members were able to work together constructively most of the time?*

Sometimes one finds in retrospect that one or two persons never found a place in the group or felt to belong to it, or that one person was so much more vulnerable than anyone else that he adopted a highly defended position and never moved from it, or that two sub-groups with different and conflicting preferred defences or modes of operating remained mutually threatening or in conflict.

One should be a bit cautious here, since it is always possible that a therapist or worker could have found a way to help the group to deal with such issues and situations but simply failed to do so. In other words, the composition was difficult but not impossible, and the failings of the group might better be attributed to management rather than to composition.

(8) *Did I do enough groundwork and the most useful kind of groundwork with my colleagues, and with my agency or institution? What should I do next time which is different?*

A worker or therapist might realize only after the completion of some project involving groups that he did not anticipate correctly the full impact of his work on the wider environment and on persons in it, or that he made unwarranted assumptions about colleagues' attitudes about his plans and requirements. The close of a group is a good time to review the place of one's work within the wider setting, and to rethink how and with whom one needs to communicate at the planning stage, whose permission or co-operation needs to be sought, and what powers one should try to negotiate for oneself.

(9) *Am I satisfied with the kind of communication I maintained with my colleagues while the work was going on?*

Here, the therapist or worker is asking himself whether he communicated enough, too much, the right things or the wrong things during the life of the group. In retrospect, does he think he breached confidentiality or was unnecessarily secretive? What were the full consequences of the procedures adopted for communicating with others in the work setting? Should more or different persons have been brought into the communication network?

(10) *Would I, in future, like to work with a co-therapist or worker, or do I prefer to work alone? What do I look for in a co-conductor?*

Whether or not the work just completed involved working with someone else one probably has emerged from it with some sense of one's preferences in this matter. If one worked alone, one can ask oneself what one missed or found difficult and whether a co-therapist or worker might have helped. If one worked with a co-leader one can ask oneself whether one found the experience supporting or interfering, and why. One will have a much better sense of the kind of person one finds it easy or difficult to work with, and a better foundation for making such decisions in the future. If one intended that two or more conductors should take different stances in the group or assume different roles, one can ask whether this worked out as planned, and proved useful or not. If there were differences in status and responsibility was this satisfactory to the two leaders or not? Was it supportive or not of the group's work? Each experience of working with someone else should provide a fuller basis for deciding in the future the kind of person one can profitably work with. One also gets a clearer idea of how to go about finding out whether a potential co-leader is compatible or not before making a definite commitment.

(11) *If I were to conduct a group again with persons drawn from the same population as before, would I open the group in the same way or in a different way?*

If one has decided to make use of a different structure, then one might well have to open the group differently. However, even if one decides to make use of the same structure one might wish to consider some other way of opening, especially if the events which followed the opening drew a response which proved difficult to deal with.

(12) *How do I feel now about the devices I adopted for monitoring and evaluating the group?*

One may have tried a range of devices for monitoring the group. If so, in looking back one can judge which of these were most useful and might be more consistently utilized in the future, and which were less useful and might be discarded. One might have thought only afterwards about devices which could have been used but were not. With respect to evaluation one sometimes realizes afterwards that certain fairly simple devices for assessing the state of the members at the point at which they entered the group could have been employed which would have provided a more satisfactory base for later evaluation. Although too late for the group which one has just finished working with, the assessment of the next group can be better planned.

Having looked at planning in detail, one can turn one's attention to the actual events of the group and ask:

(13) *Did events occur which limited benefit for particular persons? Were these inside or outside my control? Did I make errors or miss opportunities for benefiting members?*

Quite a number of sub-questions can be asked. For example: Did any of the persons in the group get locked into a position which made it difficult for them to benefit? If so, what led to this? Possibilities include the members, collectively, maintaining some restrictive solution which required one of their members to occupy a defined and limited role in the group; the conductor developing an abiding like or dislike of someone which held them in the position of therapist's helper, spoilt child, etc.; or the members' dealing with a deviant by isolating him. A conductor can sometimes get a better idea, in retrospect, of the dynamics which might have been operating and of his own possible part in it.

By failing to underline and emphasize critical events or offering credit for achievements did I miss opportunities to help individuals register and build on gains?

Did I at any time fail to confront issues which could have been a rich opportunity for benefit for one or several persons in the group?

Looking particularly at persons who seemed to have gained little, what do I now think could have accounted for this? Did it have to do with the state of readiness and the personal resources which those persons brought with them to the group or did it have to do with forces generated within the group through the interaction of the members? Did I as conductor inadvertently support evasiveness, resistance or non-involvement in particular members?

In short, one can review the kinds of errors of commission and omission which can reduce benefit for individuals (see sections towards the end of chapters 9 and 11) and in the relative calm of the post-group period reflect as to whether any of these occurred undetected during the life of the group.

One can equally profitably look to the group's successes:

(14) *Who benefited most, and what can account for this*?

Whether or not one has conducted some form of systematic evaluation one usually has a good idea of who benefited substantially and who did not. There are likely to be a number of persons whom one sees as having made substantial gains. It is a useful piece of learning to look back and work out to one's satisfaction just what contributed to this. Sometimes one sees a happy accident in the composition of the group, such that a member found someone else who could stand for a significant person in his/her own life and become a vehicle for developing new understandings or trying out new ways of coping. Sometimes one can see that one's own behaviour was critical, through providing support at the right moment, through underlining, through offering credit, through confronting and helping persons to confront significant experiences and feelings, through helping persons make connections between here-and-now experiences and important experiences and relationships in current and past life. Sometimes one can see group forces resonating with individual concerns in ways which supported useful explorations and experiences. Sometimes one can see that a person was in such a state of readiness that they quite clearly created their own opportunities for help in the group.

Reviewing successes in this way constitutes a form of underlining for oneself, such that one is encouraged to do more of what one is already doing well.

Several further questions can be asked which take a somewhat longer view of oneself as the conductor of groups.

(15) *What have I learned about my own style of conducting a group? Am I satisfied with my style or do I wish to change it in some way?*

Any group experience, whether it is one's first, tenth, or fiftieth, can contribute to a better understanding of oneself and of oneself as a conductor of groups.

One can look to one's level of participation and note whether it was in general suited to the group's structure. One can look to the closeness and distance which one maintained, and to the level and kind of self-disclosure. On looking back one might detect a certain monotony of style: tending most of the time to ask questions, or to address the group as a whole to the exclusion of addressing individuals (or vice versa), or to restrict oneself largely to offering summaries. Perhaps one notes a tendency to use overly elaborate or technical language rather than plain speaking, or to make long interventions with so many points in them that members find them hard to follow.

In general one can ask whether the style one displayed suited the needs of the persons with whom one was working or whether, for example, it might have been experienced as cold, intrusive, overly demanding, too matey, etc.

Examining features of one's own style is done with the intention of modifying it so that it more consistently and directly serves one's purposes in conducting a group. One might also wish to try to expand one's style, deciding, for example, to try a different approach with the same population (supposing that one considers it equally suitable) or to work with a different population likely to require a different structure and style.

(16) *Should I continue to work with groups, or do I prefer some other helping mode?*

Some professionally trained helpers – psychiatrists, social workers, counsellors, clinical psychologists – who have developed substantial competence in, say, one-to-one psychotherapy or marital work or family work simply do not take to groups and do not easily develop competence in working with groups. There is no rule, of course, which says that all helpers must find all helping modes equally congenial. Sometimes persons do not take to groups because their previous training has so accustomed them to working with one person at a time that they find it difficult to shift gears into using a group as a medium for help. In particular it may be difficult to tolerate what may feel like constant interruptions in one's efforts to get to know individuals or to help them. One might feel unhappy about the forms of power and the limitations on power which characterize the conductor's position. One might feel overfaced by the complexity and the fast-moving character of most group situations.

Some persons who function effectively as group therapists or group workers nevertheless find that they pay a high personal price. They worry about the group or the members between sessions or experience substantial stress during sessions. On these grounds they may well decide not to engage in further work with groups.

It seems to me right to legitimize enjoyment and reward, or its absence, as reasons for choosing whether or not to make use of a particular helping mode. It is often difficult to specify just what contributes to a general sense of reward or of unease, but one usually knows whether one approaches a group with a sense of pleasure, excitement and positive anticipation or whether one approaches it with a sense of boredom or dread. If one can work out for oneself the sources of boredom and dread, then one is in a good position to do something about it and to continue working with groups. However if one cannot find ways actually to enjoy this kind of work (acknowledging all its difficulties and strains) then one might well wish to find other ways of deploying one's helping skills.

I would think it a pity if a person decided against working with groups on the basis of a single difficult or distressing experience. I have known persons who undertook as their first group experience extraordinarily difficult groups which would tax the skills and understandings of the most experienced of group workers and therapists. Not unsurprisingly, they emerge convinced that groups are useless or not worth the effort, or that they themselves lack and can never develop the necessary skills. If one's first experience has proven difficult for reasons of the character of the population, the group composition, an incompatible co-leader, etc., then it is worth trying at least one further group, seeking to plan one's work in a way which avoided these difficulties.

(17) *What kinds of persons do I prefer to work with in groups? Are there some populations I should avoid working with, because I get little or no reward from doing so, or because I don't seem to work well with that kind of person?*

One cannot really answer this question on the basis of one or a few experiences with groups. One needs to conduct a number of groups of varying types before one gets a sense of where one's special skills and interests lie. For example, some workers and therapists seem to have special skills and a definite preference for working with regressed or institutionalized psychiatric patients; others find this unrewarding. Some persons take special delight in working with adolescents while others find it difficult. And so on. It seems sensible to take these preferences and special skills and sympathies into account when planning one's work, providing one is basing one's decisions on reasonably diverse experiences.

(18) *The next time I work with a group, would it be a good idea to build work with the group into a wider programme? If so, what form might that wider programme take?*

Sometimes one can see that the pay-offs of one's work would have been greater if one had, at the same time as working with a particular group, supplemented that effort by some additional form of work with the same persons or with related others.

For example, if one has been working with a group of young offenders in a group which relied on open discussion, one might come to the view that while this should be continued, it could usefully be combined with a programme of activities, or a tracking scheme, or family therapy. If one has been working with persons recently admitted to a psychiatric hospital one might consider starting a group for relatives, to run in parallel with one's work with the patients.

(19) *When I next conduct a group, what kind of professional and personal support will I need and how will I find it?*

I take it for granted that anyone who conducts a group will need some form of support from others, at least at times. This might be afforded by a co-worker or co-therapist, by a colleague, or by a support group of persons undertaking similar work. If one is working in isolation and none of these forms of support is available, one might arrange to send tapes or notes to someone at a distance, indicating what one needs help with, and receiving a spoken or written response.

One does not necessarily learn from experience. Conducting more and more groups can simply mean doing more of the same rather than developing further skills and understandings as one goes. Something more than the mere accumulation of experience is required: careful and critical thought to successive experiences and bringing to bear varying perspectives on one's work. With respect to the latter I have been struck by the fact that the questions suggested in this chapter as guides to learning from experience all involve, in one way or another, juxtaposing two or more points of view. Either one is comparing one's retrospective understanding with one's understanding at the time, or one's own perspective with that of group members, or one's own perspective with that of colleagues. Many of the learning devices suggested earlier also had this character: comparing one's own point of view with that of a colleague to whom one relates an account of a session; comparing one's own point of view with that of colleagues as all listen to or watch a tape of a session; comparing one's own point of view when watching a tape of one's own work with how it seemed at the time. In every instance, noting similarities and divergences, seeking to understand them, and being ready to revise one's own understandings is the route toward gain. If one plans such learning activities for oneself, no experience is wasted and there is a high likelihood that one will gain in competence and confidence as one undertakes successive work with groups.

Selected references

Chapter 2

In an earlier article, Lieberman, Lakin and Whitaker listed and discussed
six *capacities* of groups: to develop cohesiveness; control, reward and
punish behaviour; define reality; induce and release powerful feelings;
distribute power and influence; and provide a context for social comparison and feedback (Lieberman, Lakin and Whitaker, 1968). The list
presented in the first part of this chapter evolved from that earlier effort.
Agazarian and Peters (1981) offer as *group dynamics constructs* in therapeutic groups: norms, goals, roles, cohesiveness, structure and communication, and define these from the perspectives of the individual (person
member) and of the group-as-a-whole (role, group). On a slightly
different tack, a number of authors have sought to identify *curative
factors*. Corsini and Rosenberg (1955), in a much reprinted article, examined the pre-1955 literature on group psychotherapy and identified by
means of factor analysis nine major categories: acceptance, universaliz-
ation, reality testing, altruism, transference, spectator therapy, interaction, intellectualization, and ventilation. Yalom (1970) placed curative
factors into ten primary categories which overlap to some extent with
those identified by Corsini and Rosenberg. He suggests: imparting of
information, instillation of hope, universality, altruism, the corrective
recapitulation of the primary family group, development of socialization
techniques, imitative behaviour, interpersonal learning, group cohesiveness, and catharsis. Corder, Whiteside and Haizlip (1981), Marcovitz
and Smith (1983) and Rohrbaugh and Bartels (1975) report on patients'
perceptions of curative factors. Lieberman, in a study of change mechanisms based on a categorization of participant-identified 'important events',
found that high-change persons referred to a very wide range of experiences, including expressivity of positive and negative feelings, self-disclosure, feedback, experiencing intense emotions, cognitive events (insight,
information, understanding), communion or similarity, altruism, specta-
torism, involvement, advice-getting, modelling, experimentation with
new forms of behaviour, the inculcation of hope, and the re-experiencing
of the group as a family (Lieberman, 1983). Taking still another approach
to identifying features of groups, Heap (1977) discusses group formation,

differentiation and integration, communication, interaction, group structure and group development, drawing on a wide range of literature including psychoanalysis, ego psychology and group dynamics.

Turning to specific features of groups, useful general discussions of group norms in task or problem-solving groups have been presented by Napier and Gershenfeld (1973, chapter 4) and by Sherif and Sherif (1973) among others. Lieberman and his colleagues, in a study of varying kinds of encounter groups, employed factor analysis to identify five dimensions or features of norms (Lieberman, Yalom and Miles, 1973). MacKenzie has discussed the importance of norms in group psychotherapy and means by which they may be measured (MacKenzie, 1979), and in another article links norms with group climate (MacKenzie, 1981). In a descriptive account of a T-group, Bond develops the view that members who deviate from group norms stimulate a group to engage in self-definition and to make explicit that which is and is not acceptable (Bond, 1972). In a recent publication, Bond presents a model of norm regulation which contains the phenomena of consensus, deviancy and risky behaviour (Bond, 1983).

Yalom has offered an extensive discussion of cohesiveness in his book *The Theory and Practice of Group Psychotherapy* (1970) and argues that behaviours which support the therapeutic effort are more likely to be found in cohesive groups, and less likely to be found in non-cohesive groups.

Fritz Redl has presented a psychoanalytic explanation for the phenomenon of contagion in groups (Redl, 1956) and for processes accounting for individuals occupying a central position in groups (Redl, 1942, 1966).

A number of models of group development are to be found in the literature. Bruce Tuckman, in a well-known review article published in 1965, reviewed the group psychotherapy literature up to that time and offered a summary of views in terms of 'forming', 'storming', 'norming' and 'performing'. Agazarian and Peters (1981) offer a model for group development which makes substantial use of Bion's thinking (Bion, 1961). Saravay presents a model of group development based on psychoanalytic models of psychosexual development (and includes a useful bibliography) (Saravay, 1978).

Based on a review of a large number of studies of different kinds of groups, Lacoursière identifies orientation, dissatisfaction, resolution, production and termination as successive stages in groups (Lacoursière, 1980). MacKenzie and Livesley (1983) identify five stages: engagement, differentiation, individuation, intimacy and mutuality, and add termination. In their view, by the time the fifth stage, mutuality, is achieved, the group has become a working system, so the first four stages can be seen as steps toward the development of mutuality. Beck and her colleagues have identified nine stages, moving from creating a 'contract' to evaluating the group and acknowledging members' significance to one another in a defined termination period (Beck et al., 1983). Whether differences in models of group development are apparent or real is an issue currently being considered by Beck in an article still in preparation at the time of this writing.

The positions which persons come to occupy in groups, or occupy from time to time, is considered in several of the articles already cited: the central person in therapy groups (Redl, 1942, 1966) and deviant members (see publications on norms, above). Livesley and MacKenzie (1983) identify four social roles in psychotherapy groups: the sociable role, the structural role, the cautionary role and the divergent role. They link social role to personality and also show how operating in terms of roles influences the development of the group. Beck and Peters identify four behaviour clusters which may be displayed by either the designated leader or by members of a group. These are described under the headings 'task leader', 'emotional leader', 'scapegoat leader' and 'defiant leader'. Like Livesley and MacKenzie, Beck and Peters link these ideas to the development of the group (Beck and Peters, 1981; Peters and Beck, 1982).

Comprehensive models and theories of psychotherapeutic groups which emphasize the generation of group-level phenomena through associative processes include most prominently Bion (1961), Ezriel (1950a, 1950b, 1956, 1973), and Foulkes (Foulkes and Anthony, 1957; Foulkes, 1964, 1975). Also see Pines on 'The contributions of S. H. Foulkes to Group Analytic Psychotherapy' (Pines, 1978). In referring to group-level phenomena Bion utilizes the concept 'basic-assumption culture', Ezriel speaks of the 'common group tension' and Foulkes talks in terms of the 'group matrix'.

Accounts of psychoanalytic group therapy have been presented by Mullan and Rosenbaum in a second edition (1978) of their earlier book (1962). Earlier accounts in this tradition include Locke (1961) and Wolf and Schwartz (1962). Yalom (1970) is more eclectic and makes considerable use of group dynamics concepts.

In recent years, several authors are finding systems theory a useful framework for containing phenomena belonging to the group as a whole and for conceptualizing links between individual and group phenomena. See Durkin (1981) and MacKenzie and Livesley (1983).

Agazarian and Peters (1981) and Kellerman (1979), in quite different ways, have attempted to integrate across a broad spectrum of parent theories. James (1982) has offered an integration of Foulkes's concept of the group matrix and Winnicott's ideas about transitional phenomena.

Shaffer and Galinsky (1974) have described and compared eleven models of group therapy and of sensitivity training.

Chapter 3

Aplin (1977) has advised that if a worker is to design an effective programme of group work he needs to take into account three elements: the agency perspective (value systems, functions, purposes); the client perspective (the consumer's view of needs, feelings about and views of the group experience); and the practice perspective (tasks falling to the worker). Willson (1978), in discussing the task of designing a group, suggests three dimensions (client characteristics, staff characteristics and skills, and client resources and needs) which, considered as the axes of a three-dimensional figure, produce a number of intersecting points each representing a kind of group. Some of these are non-viable, some represent potentially viable groups which could suit particular client populations. Schamess has offered a number of models for group work with latency age children, and suggested which models might be appropriate for children in different diagnostic categories (Schamess, 1976).

With respect to specific models, Maxmen (1978) describes an educative model for use with psychiatric in-patients; Levine and Poston (1980) describe a 'coffee lounge' approach for use with elderly narcissistic patients; Sharp (1982) describes a mixed activity/discussion/information-offering group designed to prepare old people for admission to a residential facility; Hersen and Luber (1977) describe a programme of group experiences undertaken in a partial hospitalization scheme and aimed at developing basic skills. Epstein and Altman (1972) describe converting activity groups into verbal group therapy. These are some of many semi-descriptive accounts which suggest designs for groups which are geared to particular patient or client populations. They are to be found in the various professional journals. A good source is the *International Journal of Group Psychotherapy*.

For discussions of co-therapy see Benjamin (1972); Dick, Lessler and Whiteside (1980); Levine and Dang (1979); Gans (1962); Heilfron (1969); McGee and Schuman (1970); and Mintz (1965).

Chapter 4

A view of how organization structures and policies may function defensively, based on constructs central to Melanie Klein's theory of personality development (M. Klein, 1959; Klein, Heimann and Money-Kyrle, 1955) has been put forward by Jacques (1955) and further elaborated by Menzies (1970). This line of thinking is well summarized by de Board (1978). Klagsbrun has illustrated from his own experience how the culture of an institution may influence the success or failure of a group (Klagsbrun, 1969).

D. Klein cautions us that those who resist change may do so for good reasons (D. Klein, 1966).

It is difficult to find a concise statement of force-field analysis, even in Lewin's own writings. The best account produced by Lewin himself can be found in *Field Theory in Social Science*, edited by D. Cartwright (1951). Other relevant references are Lewin, 1948; 1972. Coch and French offer an illustration of the use of this model in a study on overcoming resistance to new production processes in a manufacturing plant (1948). G. Whitaker has described the character and impact of pathogenic leaders in organizations and suggested ways of dealing with the problems generated by their behaviour (G. Whitaker, 1982).

Chapter 5

By far the largest literature on any of the detailed planning decisions discussed in this chapter has to do with games, exercises and activities. A number of Games Handbooks and guides to exercises have been published, among them the series of handbooks produced by Pfeiffer and Jones (1972 and following), Pfeiffer and Heslin (1973), and Brands and Phillips (1978). Lennox has described a large number of games and exercises for use with children, based on transactional analysis and on behavioural approaches (Lennox, 1982).

Writers who have analysed the nature of games or activities, predicted their impact, or provided guidelines for choosing among them include Briscoe (1978), Gump and Sutton-Smith (1955a, 1955b), Davies (1975, chapter 6), Heap (1979, chapter 5), Vintner (1974) and Whittaker (1974).

Fulkerson, Hawkins and Alden have discussed group size (1981) and van der Kleij has considered physical setting (1983).

Chapter 6

A number of articles which summarize and evaluate research on group psychotherapy have appeared in the course of the years. These include articles by Rickard (1962), Gundlach (1967), Pattison (1966), Psathas (1967), Grunebaum (1975), Parloff and Dies (1977), and Dies (1979). In 1951 Jerome Frank published an article, 'Some Problems of research in group psychotherapy' (Frank, 1951), and twenty-five years later (Frank, 1975) concluded that progress in conducting research had been disappointing, citing as bright spots the work of R. Liberman (1971) and of Lieberman, Yalom and Miles (1973).

Weigel and Corazzini have discussed design problems encountered in conducting research on small groups (1978). Bednar (1970), Lieberman and Bond (1978) and Parloff and Dies (1978) have turned their attention to problems in and ways of identifying suitable outcome variables. Coché (1983) has described a number of instruments which may be used for assessing outcome. Gundlach (1961) has considered how a therapist's clinical judgment can be turned into an hypothesis testable through research. Bennis (1961) takes the reader through the kind of dialogue-with-oneself which may occur when trying to think out how an interest might be developed into a research design.

Lieberman, Yalom and Miles's book, *Encounter Groups: First Facts* (1973) may be taken as a useful model for bringing both hard and soft data to bear on complex issues in groups.

Fitz-Gibbon and Morris have produced a useful guide for those who wish to undertake formal evaluation research (Fitz-Gibbon and Morris, 1978).

Chapter 7

There is a considerable literature on the selection and preparation of persons for group psychotherapy and on group composition.

In considering indications and contra-indications for including certain kinds of persons in therapeutic groups, authors emphasize reachability, the likelihood of regression or decompensation and potential disruptiveness. See Freedman and Sweet (1954); Slavson (1955); Neighbor *et al.*(1958); and Yalom (1970, chapter 7).

Another approach looks at persons who drop out of groups relatively early in the group's life and seeks to identify factors, either in the individual himself or in the group composition or process which could account for this. See Yalom (1966); Grotjahn (1972) and Koran and Costell (1973). Kotkov discusses favourable indications for group attendance (Kotkov, 1958).

Bond and Lieberman, in a comprehensive review of research on selection, matching and early drop-outs, conclude that little has emerged of direct practical use to the practitioner, and that part of the reason lies in difficulties in appraising and predicting the impact of the group-as-environment (Bond and Lieberman, 1978).

With respect to group composition, J. Melnick and M. Woods prepared a comprehensive review article which is directed to both research and to theory (Melnick and Woods, 1976). Also see Yalom (1970, chapter 8).

Wolf and Schwartz (1962) describe the utilization of individual interviews to prepare patients for group analysis. Research by Yalom *et al.* (1967) supports the use of individual preparation. A number of authors support the idea of a relatively brief group experience as preparation for group psychotherapy: Arriaga, Espinoza and Guthrie (1978); Dibner *et al.* (1963); McGee and Larsen (1967); and Stone, Parloff and Frank (1954). In an article, 'Preparing patients for group psychotherapy', Rabin (1970) describes the use of factual material, recorded material, lectures or explanatory interviews, a group experience, and individualized preparation. Agazarian and Peters (1981) suggest that preparatory interviews can help a person to find a place for the group in his own life space, allay initial anxieties and begin to shape useful group norms.

Chapter 8

Fritz Redl, in a short article called 'What is there to "see" about a group?', suggests being alert to the emergence of group roles and role distribution, group codes and deviation tolerance, group tastes and aversions, sub-group formation and contagion clusters, group manageability, and one's own feelings while with a group. In another short article, 'Just what am I supposed to observe?', Redl, thinking of children in residential settings, suggests that one might keep a log on each child, noting attitudes towards adults, towards other children, towards the total group, towards routine and discipline, interests and aversions, special strong points, problem trends, health and body attitudes, and thoughts, fantasies and fears. Although written with children in mind, Redl's points are also relevant to groups of adults (Redl, 1966, pp. 333–48).

M. Williams has discussed the fears and fantasies of inexperienced group psychotherapists (Williams, 1966).

In the course of discussing alternative interpretations which may be offered to a therapeutic group Yalom considers the import of successive events in a group and how an understanding of them can help one to choose among alternative possible interpretations (Yalom, 1970, chapter 6).

Chapter 9

For now-classical discussions of how group-level phenomena may be commented upon and interpreted in groups, see Bion (1961), Ezriel (1950a, 1950b, 1956, 1959 and 1973), Foulkes and Anthony (1957) and Foulkes (1964, 1975).

Horwitz has more recently suggested that interventions can most usefully first be introduced with reference to individual contributions and then be generalized into comments relevant to 'groupwide' phenomena (Horwitz, 1971, 1977).

'Restrictive solutions', as discussed here, describe a particular form of resistance where a number of members collaborate to maintain some defence against the group experience. The term 'resistance', as usually used, also includes individual resistances. See discussions by Wolf and Schwartz (1962), Yalom (1970) and Grotjahn (1977, chapter 2).

Katz (1983) has argued that under some circumstances metaphoric discussions of here-and-now events and feelings should not be interpreted but can be utilized positively if the therapist operates within and in terms of the metaphor.

Accounts of the formative phase of psychotherapy groups in group focal conflict terms have appeared in several earlier publications (Stock, 1962; Whitaker and Lieberman, 1964; D. S. Whitaker, 1976).

Rosensweig and Folman (1974) discuss premature termination in group psychotherapy. A number of articles on selection deal with the issue of drop-outs (see Yalom, 1966; Grotjahn, 1972; Koran and Costell, 1973; and Bond and Lieberman, 1978).

Chapter 10

H. M. Rabin and M. Rosenbaum (1976) have edited a book *How to Begin a Psychotherapy Group: Six Approaches* which includes four chapters which describe the beginnings of varying kinds of groups: J. M. Sacks on 'The psychodrama group'; S. B. Hadden on 'The homosexual group'; E. M. Scott on 'The alcoholic group'; and I. Z. Youcha on a 'Short-term in-patient group'.

Yalom (1970, pp. 231–5) and Agazarian and Peters (1981, chapter 5) have addressed themselves to the character and management of the group during its formative stage.

Chapter 11

For discussions of how group and individual dynamics may link see articles by Lieberman (1967) and by Arsenian and Semrad (1967). Earlier discussions of such linkages in group focal conflict and nuclear conflict terms can be found in Whitman, Lieberman and Stock (1960), Whitaker and Lieberman (1964) and D. S. Whitaker (1982). Kellerman discusses group psychotherapy and individual personality as 'intersecting structures' (Kellerman, 1979). Foulkes uses the term 'resonance' to refer to the fact that 'each individual picks out of the common pool what is relevant to him' and accounts for that which is selected by 'the specific level of regression, fixation or developmental arrest on which his main disturbances and conflicts operate'. (Foulkes, 1977, pp. 52–3).

In an earlier article by this author fairly detailed accounts are provided of two persons who benefited from a therapy group through undergoing corrective emotional experiences, and preparatory and follow-up work and the part played by insight are illustrated (D. S. Whitaker, 1965).

Turning to how the conductor of a group may function within sessions, Foulkes, in his article 'On interpretation in group analysis', discusses interpretation as an internal process and as a form of intervention (Foulkes, 1968). In general, group conductors working within a psychoanalytic or a Kleinian tradition tend to emphasize interpretation, but the relative emphasis on individuals or the group-as-a-whole varies. See the references to Bion, Ezriel and Foulkes cited at the end of chapter 9. For interpretations which tend to emphasize the individual see Wolf and Schwartz (1962) and Grotjahn (1977).

For a discussion of diverse ways of utilizing paradoxical interventions see Goldberg (1980). Kinseth (1982) has discussed spontaneous nonverbal interventions in group therapy, and Jacobs (1974) suggests a range of feedback devices.

Grotjahn (1979) discusses mistakes in analytic group psychotherapy. The literature on counter-transference is relevant to certain forms of therapist/worker error. See Grotjahn (1977) and Mullan and Rosenbaum (1978).

Chapter 12

For discussions of persons occupying various special roles in groups see Bogdanoff and Elbaum (1978) on monopolizers, mistrusters, isolates and 'helpful Hannahs'; Berger and Rosenbaum (1967) and Peters and Grunebaum (1977) on help-rejecting complainers; Heap (1965) and Scheidlinger (1982) on scapegoats and scapegoating; and Stock, Whitman and Lieberman (1958) on deviant members.

Redl, in a now classic article, discusses the individual and group dynamics which may thrust a particular person into a central position for a time in a group (Redl, 1942). Discussions of social role (Livesley and MacKenzie, 1983) and of forms of distributed leadership (Beck and Peters, 1981, Peters and Beck, 1982) are also relevant.

With respect to comings and goings, Kaplan and Roman (1961) have discussed responses to the introduction of new members. McGee (1974) has considered situations in which a therapist must leave an ongoing therapy group.

Chapter 13

For accounts of the termination process and the termination phase see articles by Johnson (1974), Kauff (1977), McGee, Schuman and Racusen (1972) and Weiner (1973).

Chapter 14

I have not been able to find references to a number of the issues discussed in this chapter.

Dies has presented an extensive review of theory and research concerning group therapist transparency (Dies, 1977). The *content* of therapist self-disclosure is taken into account in an article by Dies and Cohen (1976).

Discussions of the working alliance between the conductor of a group and members have been provided by Dickes (1975), Glatzer (1978) and Kanzer (1975).

Bibliography

Agazarian, Y. and Peters, R. (1981), *The Visible and Invisible Group: Two Perspectives on Group Psychotherapy and Group Process*, London, Routledge & Kegan Paul

Aplin, G. (1977), 'Some thoughts on teaching the design and evaluation of group work practice', in N. McCaughan and K. McDougall (Eds), *Group Work: a Guide for Researchers and Practitioners*, London, National Institute for Social Work, NISW Papers, no. 7.

Arriaga, K., Espinoza, E. and Guthrie, M. B. (1978), 'Group therapy evaluation for psychiatric inpatients', *International Journal of Group Psychotherapy*, vol. 28, pp. 359–64.

Arsenian, J. and Semrad, E. V. (1967), 'Individual and group manifestations', *International Journal of Group Psychotherapy*, vol. 17, pp. 82–98.

Beck, A. P. and Peters, L. N. (1981), 'The research evidence for distributed leadership in therapy groups', *International Journal of Group Psychotherapy*, vol. 31, pp. 43–71

Beck, A. P., Dugo, J. M., Eng, A. M., Lewis, C. M. and Peters, L. N. (1983), 'The participation of leaders in the structural development of therapy groups', in R. R. Dies and K. R. MacKenzie (eds), *Advances in Group Psychotherapy*, pp. 137–58.

Bednar, R. L. (1970), 'Group psychotherapy research variables', *International Journal of Group Psychotherapy*, vol. 20, pp. 146–52.

Benjamin, S. E. (1972), 'Co-therapy: A growth experience for therapists', *International Journal of Group Psychotherapy*, vol. 22, pp. 199–209.

Bennis, W. G. (1961), 'A case study in research formulation', *International Journal of Group Psychotherapy*, vol. 11, pp. 272–83.

Berger, M. M. and Rosenbaum, M. (1967), 'Notes on help-rejecting complainers', *International Journal of Group Psychotherapy*, vol. 17, pp. 357–70.

Bion, W. R. (1961), *Experiences in Groups and Other Papers*, New York, Basic Books.

de Board, R. (1978), *The Psychoanalysis of Organizations: a Psychoanalytic Approach to Behaviour in Groups and Organizations*, London, Tavistock.

410

Bogdanoff, M. and Elbaum, P. L. (1978), 'Role lock: dealing with monopolizers, mistrusters, isolates, helpful Hannahs, and other assorted characters in group psychotherapy', *International Journal of Group Psychotherapy*, vol. 28, pp. 247–62.

Bond, G. R. (1972), 'Deviants and their effects on group norms', unpublished paper.

Bond, G. R. (1983), 'Norm regulation in therapy groups', in R. R. Dies and K. R. MacKenzie (eds), *Advances in Group Psychotherapy*, Monograph I, American Group Psychotherapy Monograph Series, New York, International Universities Press, pp. 171–89.

Bond, G. R. and Lieberman, M. A. (1978), 'Selection criteria for group therapy', in J. P. Brady and H. K. Brodie (eds), *Controversy in Psychiatry*, Philadelphia, W. B. Saunders.

Brands, D. and Phillips, H. (1978), *The Gamesters' Handbook*, London, Hutchinson.

Briscoe, C. (1978), 'Programme activities in social group work', chapter 14 in N. McCaughan (ed.), *Group Work: Learning and Practice*, National Institute Social Services Library, no. 33, London, George Allen & Unwin.

Coch, L. and French, J. R. P. (1948), 'Overcoming resistance to change', *Human Relations*, vol. 1, pp. 512–32. Reprinted in D. Cartwright and A. Zander, (eds.), *Group Dynamics: Research and Theory*, Evanston, Illinois, Row, Peterson & Co, 1953. 2nd edn 1960.

Coché, E. (1983), 'Change measures and clinical practice in group psychotherapy', in R. R. Dies and K. R. MacKenzie (eds), *Advances in Group Psychotherapy*, Monograph I, American Group Psychotherapy Monograph Series, New York, International Universities Press, pp. 79–99.

Cohn, R. C. (1971), 'Living-learning encounters: the theme-centered interactional method', in G. Gottsegen, M. Gottsegen and L. Blank (eds), *Confrontation: Encounters in Self and Personal Awareness*, New York, Macmillan.

Corder, B. F., Whiteside, L. and Haizlip, T. M. (1981), 'A study of curative factors in group psychotherapy with adolescents', *International Journal of Group Psychotherapy*, vol. 31, pp. 345–54.

Corsini, R. and Rosenberg, B. (1955), 'Mechanisms of group psychotherapy: processes and dynamics', *Journal of Abnormal and Social Psychology*, vol. 51, pp. 406–11.

Davies, Bernard (1975), *The Use of Groups in Social Work Practice*, London, Routledge & Kegan Paul.

Dibner, A. S., Palmer, R. D., Cohen, B. and Gofstein, A. G. (1963), 'The use of an open-ended group in the intake procedure of a mental hygiene unit', *Journal of Consulting Psychotherapy*, New York, Hoeber.

Dick, B., Lessler, K., and Whiteside, J. (1980), 'A developmental framework for cotherapy', *International Journal of Group Psychotherapy*, vol. 30, pp. 273–85.

Dickes, R. (1975), 'Considerations of therapeutic and working alliances', *International Journal of Psychoanalysis and Psychotherapy*, vol. 4, pp. 1–24.

Dies, R. R. (1977), 'Group therapist transparency: A critique of theory and research', *International Journal of Group Psychotherapy*, vol. 27, pp. 177–200.

Dies, R. R. (1979), 'Group psychotherapy: reflections on three decades of research', *Journal of Applied Behavioral Science*, vol. 15, pp. 361–74.

Dies, R. R. and Cohen, L. (1976), 'Content considerations in group therapist self-disclosure', *International Journal of Group Psychotherapy*, vol. 26, pp. 71–88.

Dies, R. R. and MacKenzie, K. R. (eds) (1983), *Advances in Group Psychotherapy*, Monograph I, American Group Psychotherapy Monograph Series, New York, International Universities Press.

Durkin, J. E. (ed.) (1981), *Living Groups: Group Psychotherapy and General Systems Theory*, New York, Brunner/Mazel.

Epstein, N. and Altman, S. (1972), 'Experiences in converting an activity group into verbal group therapy', *International Journal of Group Psychotherapy*, vol. 22, pp. 93–100.

Ezriel, H. (1950a), 'A psychoanalytic approach to the treatment of patients in groups', *Journal of Mental Science*, vol. 96, pp. 774–9.

Ezriel, H. (1950b), 'A psychoanalytic approach to group treatment', *British Journal of Medical Psychology*, vol. 23, pp. 59–74.

Ezriel, H. (1956), 'Experimentation within the psychoanalytic session', *The British Journal for the Philosophy of Science*, vol. 7, pp. 29–48.

Ezriel, H. (1959), 'The role of transference in psycho-analytic and other approaches to group treatment', *Acta Psychotherapeutica*, vol. 7, pp. 101–16.

Ezriel, H. (1973), 'Psychoanalytic group therapy', in L. R. Wolberg and E. K. Schwartz (eds), *Group Therapy: 1973, An Overview*, New York, Stratton Intercontinental Medical Book Corp., pp. 183–210.

Fitz-Gibbon, C. T. and Morris, L. L. (1978), *How to Design a Program Evaluation*, Beverley Hills, Sage Publications.

Foulkes, S. H. (1964), *Therapeutic Group Analysis*, New York, International Universities Press.

Foulkes, S. H. (1968), 'On interpretation in group analysis', *International Journal of Group Psychotherapy*, vol. 18, pp. 432–44.

Foulkes, S. H. (1975), *Group Analytic Psychotherapy: Method and Principles*, London, Gordon & Breach.

Foulkes, S. H. (1977), 'Notes on the concept of resonance', in L. R. Wolberg and M. L. Aronson (eds), *Group Therapy 1977, An Overview*, New York, Stratton Intercontinental Medical Book Corp., pp. 52–8.

Foulkes, S. H. and Anthony, E. J. (1957), *Group Psychotherapy: The Psychoanalytic Approach*, London, Penguin.

Frank, J. D. (1951, 1975), 'Some problems of research in group psychotherapy', *International Journal of Group Psychotherapy*, vol. 1, no. 1. Reprinted in the same journal, vol. 25, pp. 141–5.

Frank, J. D. (1975), 'Group psychotherapy research 25 years later', *International Journal of Group Psychotherapy*, vol. 25, pp. 159–62.

Freedman, M. and Sweet, B. (1954), 'Some specific features of group psychotherapy and their implication for the selection of patients', *International Journal of Group Psychotherapy*, vol. 4, pp. 359.

French, T. (1952), *The Integration of Behaviour: Basic Postulates*, University of Chicago Press.

French, T. (1954), *The Integration of Behaviour: The Integrative Process in Dreams*, University of Chicago Press.

Fulkerson, C. C. F., Hawkins, D. M. and Alden, A. R. (1981), 'Psychotherapy groups of insufficient size', *International Journal of Group Psychotherapy*, vol. 31, pp. 73–81.

Gans, R. (1962), 'Group cotherapists and the therapeutic situation: a critical evaluation', *International Journal of Group Psychotherapy*, vol. 12, pp. 82–8.

Glatzer, H. T. (1978), 'The working alliance in analytic group psychotherapy', *International Journal of Group Psychotherapy*, vol. 28, pp. 147–61.

Golan, Naomi (1981), *Passing Through Transitions: A Guide for Practitioners*, New York, Free Press.

Goldberg, C. (1980), 'The utilization and limitations of paradoxical intervention in group psychotherapy', *International Journal of Group Psychotherapy*, vol. 30, pp. 287–97.

Grotjahn, M. (1972), 'Learning from drop-out patients', *International Journal of Group Psychotherapy*, vol. 22, pp. 306–18.

Grotjahn, M. (1977), *The Art and Technique of Analytic Group Therapy*, New York, Jason Aronson.

Grotjahn, M. (1979), 'Mistakes in analytic group psychotherapy', *International Journal of Group Psychotherapy*, vol. 29, pp. 317–23.

Grunebaum, H. (1975), 'A soft-hearted review of hard-nosed research on groups', *International Journal of Group Psychotherapy*, vol. 25, pp. 185–97.

Gump, P. V. and Sutton-Smith, B. (1955a), 'Activity-setting and social interaction: a field study', *American Journal of Orthopsychiatry*, vol. 25.

Gump, P. V. and Sutton-Smith, B. (1955b), 'The "it" role in children's games', *The Group*, vol. 17.

Gundlach, R. H. (1961), 'Problem: to convert a clinical judgment into a research design', *International Journal of Group Psychotherapy*, vol. 11, pp. 265–71.

Gundlach, R. H. (1967), 'Overview of outcome studies in group psychotherapy', *International Journal of Group Psychotherapy*, vol. 27, pp. 196–210.

Hadden, S. B. (1976), 'The homosexual group: formation and beginnings', in H. M. Rabin and M. Rosenbaum (eds), *How to Begin a Psychotherapy Group: Six Approaches*, London, Gordon & Breach.

Heap, K. (1965), 'The scapegoat role in youth groups', *Case Conference*, vol. 12, pp. 215–21.

Heap, K. (1977), *Group Theory for Social Workers*, Oxford, Pergamon Press.

Heap, K. (1979), *Process and Action in Work with Groups*, Oxford, Pergamon Press.

Heilfron, M. (1969), 'Cotherapy: the relationship between therapists', *International Journal of Group Psychotherapy*, vol. 19, pp. 366–81.

Hersen, M. and Luber, R. F. (1977), 'Use of group psychotherapy in a partial hospitalization service: the remediation of basic skill deficits', *International Journal of Group Psychotherapy*, vol. 27, pp. 361–76.

Horwitz, L. (1971), 'Group centered interventions in therapy groups', *Comprehensive Group Studies*, vol. 2, pp. 311–31.

Horwitz, L. (1977), 'A group-centered approach to group psychotherapy', *International Journal of Group Psychotherapy*, vol. 27, pp. 423–39.

Jacobs, A. (1974), 'The use of feedback in groups', in A. Jacobs and W. Spradlin (eds), *The Group as an Agent of Change*, New York, Behavioral Publications, pp. 408–48.

Jacques, E. (1955), 'Social systems as a defence against persecutory and depressive anxiety', in M. Klein, P. Heimann and R. Money-Kyrle (eds), *New Directions in Psychoanalysis*, London, Heinemann.

James, C. (1982), 'Transitional phenomena and the matrix in group psychotherapy', in M. Pines and L. Rafaelsen (eds), *The Individual and the Group: Boundaries and Interrelations. Vol. I: Theory*, New York, Plenum Press.

Janis, Irving L. (1958), *Psychological Stress*, New York, John Wiley.

Janis, Irving L. (1969), *Stress and Frustration*, New York, Harcourt Brace Jovanich.

Johnson, C. (1974), 'Planning for termination of the group', chapter 15 in P. Glasser, R. Sarri and R. Vinter (eds), *Individual Change through Groups*, New York, Free Press.

Kanzer, M. (1975), 'The therapeutic and working alliances', *International Journal of Psychoanalysis and Psychotherapy*, vol. 4, pp. 48–68.

Kaplan, S. R. and Roman, M. (1961), 'Characteristic responses in adult therapy groups to the introduction of new members: a reflection on processes', *International Journal of Group Psychotherapy*, vol. 11, pp. 373–81.

Katz, G. A. (1983), 'The noninterpretation of metaphors in psychiatric hospital groups', *International Journal of Group Psychotherapy*, vol. 33, pp. 53–67.

Kauff, P. F. (1977), 'The termination process: its relationship to the separation-individuation phase of development', *International Journal of Group Psychotherapy*, vol. 27, pp. 3–18.

Kellerman, Henry (1979), *Group Psychotherapy and Personality: Intersecting Structures*, New York, Grune & Stratton.

Kinseth, L. (1982), 'Spontaneous nonverbal intervention in group therapy', *International Journal of Group Psychotherapy*, vol. 32, pp. 327–38.

Klagsbrun, S. C. (1969), 'An analysis of groups that never were', *International Journal of Group Psychotherapy*, vol. 19, pp. 142–9.
van der Kleij, G. (1983), 'The setting of the group', *Group Analysis*, vol. 16, pp. 75–80.
Klein, D. (1966), 'Some notes on the dynamics of resistance to change: the defender role', in G. Watson (ed.), *Concepts for Social Change*, Cooperative Project for Educational Development Series, vol. 1, National Training Laboratories, Washington, DC.
Klein, M. (1959), 'Our adult world and its roots in infancy', *Human Relations*, vol. 12, pp. 291–303. (Also published as Tavistock Pamphlet, no. 2, London, Tavistock.)
Klein, M., Heimann, P. and Money-Kyrle, R. (eds) (1955), *New Directions in Psycho-analysis*, London, Tavistock.
Koran, L. M. and Costell, R. M. (1973), 'Early termination from group psychotherapy', *International Journal of Group Psychotherapy*, vol. 23, pp. 346–59.
Kotkov, B. (1958), 'Favorable clinical indications for group attendance', *International Journal of Group Psychotherapy*, vol. 8, pp. 419–23.
Lacoursière, R. (1980), *The Life Cycle of Groups: Group Developmental Stage Theory*, New York, Human Sciences Press.
Lennox, D. (1982), *Residential Group Therapy for Children*, London, Tavistock.
Levine, B. E. and Poston, M. (1980), 'A modified group treatment for elderly narcissistic patients', *International Journal of Group Psychotherapy*, vol. 30, pp. 153–67.
Levine, C. O. and Dang, J. C. (1979), 'The group within the group: the dilemma of cotherapy', *International Journal of Group Psychotherapy*, vol. 29, pp. 175–84.
Lewin, K. (1948), *Resolving Social Conflict*, edited by G. W. Lewin, New York, Harper.
Lewin, K. (1951), *Field Theory in Social Science*, edited by D. Cartwright, New York, Harper.
Lewin, K. (1972), 'Need, force and valence in psychological fields', in E. P. Hollander and R. G. Hunt (eds), *Classic Contributions to Social Psychology*, London, Oxford University Press.
Liberman, R. (1971), 'Behavioural group therapy: a controlled study', *British Journal of Psychiatry*, vol. 119, pp. 535–44.
Lieberman, M. A. (1967), 'The implications of total group phenomena analysis for patients and therapists', *International Journal of Group Psychotherapy*, vol. 17, pp. 71–81.
Lieberman, M. A. (1983), 'Comparative analyses of change mechanisms in groups', in H. H. Blumberg, A. P. Hare, V. Kent, and M. Davies (eds), *Small Groups and Social Interaction*, vol. 2, New York, John Wiley.
Lieberman, M. A. and Bond, G. R. (1978), 'Self-help groups: problems of measuring outcome', *Small Group Behaviour*, vol. 9, pp. 221–41.
Lieberman, M. A., Lakin, M. and Whitaker, D. S. (1968), 'The group as a unique context for therapy', *Psychotherapy: Theory, Research and Practice*, vol. 5, pp. 29–36.

Lieberman, M. A., Yalom, I. D. and Miles, M. B. (1973), *Encounter Groups: First Facts*, New York, Basic Books.

Livesley, W. J. and MacKenzie, K. R. (1983), 'Social roles in psychotherapy groups', in R. R. Dies and K. R. MacKenzie (eds), *Advances in Group Psychotherapy*, Monograph I, American Group Psychotherapy Monograph Series, New York, International Universities Press.

Locke, N. (1961), *Group Psychoanalysis: Theory and Technique*, New York, New York University Press.

McGee, T. F. (1974), 'Therapist termination in group psychotherapy', *International Journal of Group Psychotherapy*, vol. 24, pp. 3–12.

McGee, T. F. and Larsen, V. B. (1967), 'An approach to waiting list therapy groups', *American Journal of Orthopsychiatry*, vol. 37, pp. 594–7.

McGee, T. F. and Schuman, B. N. (1970), 'The nature of the co-therapy relationship', *International Journal of Group Psychotherapy*, vol. 20, pp. 25–36.

McGee, T. F., Schuman, B. N. and Racusen, F. R. (1972), 'Termination in group psychotherapy', *American Journal of Psychotherapy*, vol. 26, pp. 521–32.

MacKenzie, K. R. (1979), 'Group norms: importance and measurement', *International Journal of Group Psychotherapy*, vol. 29, pp. 471–80.

MacKenzie, K. R. (1981), 'Measurement of group climate', *International Journal of Group Psychotherapy*, vol. 31, pp. 287–95.

MacKenzie, K. R. and Livesley, W. J. (1983), 'A developmental model for brief group therapy', in R. R. Dies and K. R. MacKenzie (eds), *Advances in Group Psychotherapy*, Monograph I, American Group Psychotherapy Monograph Series, New York, International Universities Press.

Marcovitz, R. J. and Smith, J. E. (1983), 'Patients' perceptions of curative factors in short-term group psychotherapy', *International Journal of Group Psychotherapy*, vol. 33, pp. 21–39.

Maris, Peter (1974), *Loss and Change*, London, Routledge & Kegan Paul.

Maxmen, J. S. (1978), 'An educative model for in-patient group therapy', *International Journal of Group Psychotherapy*, vol. 28, pp. 321–38.

Melnick, J. and Woods, M. (1976), 'Analysis of group composition research and theory for psychotherapeutic and growth-oriented groups', *Journal of Applied Behavioral Science*, vol. 12, pp. 493–512.

Menzies, I. E. P. (1970), *The Functioning of Social Systems as a Defence against Anxiety*, Centre for Applied Social Research, London, Tavistock Institute of Human Relations.

Mintz, E. E. (1965), 'Male-female co-therapists: some values and some problems', *American Journal of Psychotherapy*, vol. 19, pp. 244–55.

Mullan, H. and Rosenbaum, M. (1978), *Group Psychotherapy: Theory and Practice*, (2nd edn), New York, Free Press.

Napier, R. W. and Gershenfeld, M. K. (1973), *Groups: Theory and Experience*, Boston, Houghton Mifflin.

Neighbor, J. E., Beach, M., Brown, D. T., Kevin, D. and Visher, J. S. (1958), 'An approach to the selection of patients for group psychotherapy', *Mental Hygiene*, vol. 42, pp. 243–54.

Parkes, Colin Murray (1972), *Bereavement: Studies of Grief in Adult Life*, New York, International Universities Press.

Parloff, M. B. and Dies, R. R. (1977), 'Group psychotherapy outcome research 1966–1975', *International Journal of Group Psychotherapy*, vol. 27, pp. 281–320.

Parloff, M. B. and Dies, R. R. (1978), 'Group therapy outcome instrument: guidelines for conducting research', *Small Group Behavior*, vol. 9. pp. 243–85.

Pattison, E. M. (1966), 'Evaluation of group psychotherapy', *Current Psychiatric Therapies*, vol. 6, pp. 211–17.

Peters, C. B. and Grunebaum, H. (1977), 'It could be worse: effective group psychotherapy with the help-rejecting complainer', *International Journal of Group Psychotherapy*, vol. 27, pp. 471–80.

Peters, L. N. and Beck, A. P. (1982), 'Identifying emergent leaders in psychotherapy groups', *Group*, vol. 6, pp. 35–40.

Pfeiffer, J. W. and Heslin, R. (1973), *Instrumentation in Human Relations Training*, Iowa City, University Associates.

Pfeiffer, J. W. and Jones, J. E. (1972), *The 1972 Annual Handbook for Group Facilities* (and subsequent annual handbooks), Iowa City, University Associates.

Pines, M. (1978), 'The contribution of S. H. Foulkes to group analytic psychotherapy', in L. R. Wolberg, M. L. Aronson, and A. R. Wolbnerg, *Group Therapy 1975, An Overview*, New York, Stratton Intercontinental Medical Book Corp.

Psathas, G. (1967), 'Overview of process studies in group psychotherapy', *International Journal of Group Psychotherapy*, vol. 17, pp. 225–35.

Rabin, H. M. (1970), 'Preparing patients for group psychotherapy', *International Journal of Group Psychotherapy*, vol. 20, pp. 135–45.

Rabin, H. M. and Rosenbaum, M. (eds) (1976), *How to Begin a Psychotherapy Group: Six Approaches*, London, Gordon & Breach.

Redl, F. (1942), 'Group emotion and leadership', *Psychiatry*, vol. 5, pp. 573–96. Reprinted in an expanded form in F. Redl, *When We Deal with Children: Selected Writings*, New York, Free Press, 1966.

Redl, F. (1956), 'The phenomenon of contagion and "shock effect"', in K. Eissler (ed.), *Searchlights on Delinquency*, New York, International Universities Press. Reprinted in a revised version in F. Redl, *When We Deal with Children: Selected Writings*, New York, Free Press, 1966.

Redl, F. (1966), 'Just what am I supposed to observe?', in F. Redl, *When We Deal with Children: Selected Writings*, New York, Free Press. pp. 333–37.

Redl, F. (1966), 'What is there to "see" about a group?', in F. Redl,

When We Deal with Children: Selected Writings, pp. 338–45, New York, Free Press.

Rickard, H. C. (1962), 'Selected group psychotherapy evaluation studies', *Journal of General Psychology*, vol. 67, pp. 35–50.

Rohrbaugh, M. and Bartels, B. (1975), 'Participants' perception of curative factors in therapy and growth groups', *Small Group Behavior*, vol. 4, pp. 430–56.

Rosensweig, S. P. and Folman, R. (1974), 'Patient and therapist variables affecting premature termination in group psychotherapy', *Psychotherapy*, vol. 11, pp. 76–80.

Sacks, J. M. (1976), 'The psychodrama group', in H. M. Rabin and M. Rosenbaum (eds), *How to Begin a Psychotherapy Group: Six Approaches*, London, Gordon & Breach.

Saravay, S. M. (1978), 'A psychoanalytic theory of group development', *International Journal of Group Psychotherapy*, vol. 28, pp. 481–507.

Schamess, G. (1976), 'Group treatment modalities for latency-age children', *International Journal of Group Psychotherapy*, vol. 26, pp. 455–76.

Scheidlinger, S. (1982), 'Presidential address: on scapegoating in group psychotherapy', *International Journal of Group Psychotherapy*, vol. 32, pp. 131–43.

Scott, E. M. (1976), 'The alcoholic group: formation and beginnings', in H. M. Rabin and M. Rosenbaum (eds), *How to Begin a Psychotherapy Group: Six Approaches*, London, Gordon & Breach.

Shaffer, J. B. P. and Galinsky, M. D. (eds) (1974), *Models of Group Therapy and Sensitivity Training*, Englewood Cliffs, New Jersey, Prentice-Hall.

Sharp, M. (1982), 'Getting ready for Part III', *Community Care*, 3 June 1982, pp. 14–15.

Sherif, M. and Sherif, C. W. (1973), 'Acceptable and unacceptable behaviour defined by group norms', chapter 16 in M. Argyle (ed.), *Social Encounters*, Penguin.

Slavson, S. R. (1955), 'Criteria for selection and rejection of patients for various kinds of group therapy', *International Journal of Group Psychotherapy*, vol. 5, pp. 3–30.

Stock, D. (1962), 'Interpersonal concerns during the early sessions of therapy groups', *International Journal of Group Psychotherapy*, vol. 12, pp. 14–26.

Stock, D., Whitman, R. M. and Lieberman, M. A. (1958), 'The deviant member in therapy groups', *Human Relations*, vol. 11, pp. 341–72.

Stone, A. R., Parloff, M. B. and Frank, T. B. (1954), 'The use of "diagnostic" groups in a group therapy program', *International Journal of Group Psychotherapy*, vol. 4, pp. 274–84.

Tuckman, B. W. (1965), 'Developmental sequence in small groups', *Psychological Bulletin*, vol. 63, pp. 384–99.

Vintner, R. D. (1974), 'Program activities: an analysis of their effects on participant behavior', chapter 13 in P. Glasser, R. Sarri and R. Vintner, (eds), *Individual Change through Small Groups*, New York, Free Press and London, Collier Macmillan.

Weigel, R. G. and Corazzini, J. G. (1978), 'Small group research: suggestions for solving common methodological and design problems', *Small Group Behavior*, vol. 9, pp. 193–220.

Weiner, M. F. (1973), 'Termination of group psychotherapy', *Group Process*, vol. 5, pp. 85–96.

Whitaker, D. S. (1965), 'The processes by which change occurs and the role of insight', *Acta Psychotherapeutica*, vol. 13, pp. 126–41.

Whitaker, D. S. (1976), 'A group centred approach', in H. M. Rabin and M. Rosenbaum (eds), *How to Begin a Psychotherapy Group: Six Approaches*, London, Gordon & Breach.

Whitaker, D. S. (1982), 'A nuclear and group focal conflict model for integrating individual and group level phenomena in psychotherapy groups', in M. Pines and L. Rafaelsen (eds), *The Individual and the Group: Boundaries and Interrelations, Vol. 1: Theory*, London, Plenum Press, pp. 321–38.

Whitaker, D. S. and Lieberman, M. A. (1964), *Psychotherapy through the Group Process*, New York, Atherton Press and London, Tavistock.

Whitaker, G. (1982), 'Pathogenic leadership in organisations', in M. Pines and L. Rafaelsen (eds), *The Individual and the Group: Boundaries and Interrelations, Vol. 1: Theory*, New York, Plenum Press, pp. 405–29.

Whitman, R. M. and Stock, D. (1958), 'The group focal conflict', *Psychiatry: Journal for the Study of Interpersonal Processes*, vol. 21, pp. 269–76.

Whitman, R. M., Lieberman, M. A. and Stock, D. (1960), 'The relation between individual and group conflicts in psychotherapy', *International Journal of Group Psychotherapy*, vol. 10, pp. 259–86.

Whittaker, J. K. (1974), 'Program activities: their selection and use in a therapeutic milieu', chapter 14 in P. Glasser, R. Sarri and R. Vintner (eds), *Individual Change through Small Groups*, New York, Free Press and London, Collier Macmillan.

Williams, M. (1966), 'Limitations, fantasies, and security operations of beginning group psychotherapists', *International Journal of Group Psychotherapy*, vol. 16, pp. 150–62.

Willson, M. (1978), 'The pragmatics of groupwork in social work', *Social Work Today* vol. 10, pp. 12–15.

Wolf, A. and Schwartz, E. K. (1962), *Psychoanalysis in Groups*, New York, Grune & Stratton.

Yalom, I. D. (1966), 'A study of group therapy dropouts', *Archives of General Psychiatry*, vol. 14, pp. 393–414.

Yalom, I. D. (1970), *The Theory and Practice of Group Psychotherapy*, New York, Basic Books.

Yalom, I. D., Houts, P. S., Newell, G. and Rand, K. H. (1967), 'Preparation of patients for group therapy: a controlled study', *Archives of General Psychiatry*, vol. 17, pp. 416–27.

Youcha, I. Z. (1976), 'Short-term in-patient group: formation and beginnings', in H. M. Rabin and M. Rosenbaum (eds), *How to Begin a Psychotherapy Group: Six Approaches*, London, Gordon & Breach.

Index